Pottery in the Archaeological Record: Greece and Beyond

Acts of the International Colloquium held at the Danish and Canadian Institutes in Athens, June 20-22, 2008

Edited by Mark L. Lawall & John Lund

Aarhus University Press | 𝄞

POTTERY IN THE ARCHAEOLOGICAL RECORD: GREECE AND BEYOND
© Aarhus University Press and the authors 2011.

GÖSTA ENBOM MONOGRAPHS

General editor:
Bodil Bundgaard Rasmussen.

Editorial board:
Mark Lawall, John Lund, Dyfri Williams.

Gösta Enbom Monographs is a peer reviewed series.

Published with support from The Foundation of Consul General Gösta Enbom.

Graphic design:
Nina Grut, MDD.

Printed at Narayana Press.

Typeset with Stone Serif and Stone Sans.

ISBN 978-87-7934-587-4
ISSN 1904-6219

Aarhus University Press
Langelandsgade 177
DK-8200 Aarhus N

White Cross Mills
Lancaster LA1 4XS
England

Box 511
Oakville, CT 06779
USA

www.unipress.dk

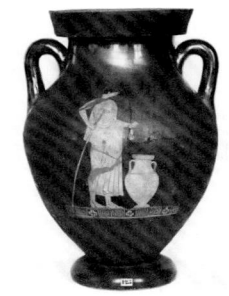

Amphora attributed to the painter Syriskos, Athens 500-470 BC, Collection of Classical and Near Eastern Antiquities, The National Museum of Denmark, inv.no. Chr. VIII 320.

Front cover:
Tondo of black-figured kylix. London, British Museum B 432, Courtesy the British Museum.

Back cover:
Repaired Ionian cup from the Pabuç Burnu shipwreck, early 6th century BC, photo Mark Lawall (AJA 112, 2008 698 fig. 24); jetty constructed from amphorae at Mons Claudianus.

Table of Contents

5 Per Kristian Madsen
Preface

7 Mark L. Lawall & John Lund
Introduction

11 Eleni Hasaki
Crafting Spaces: Archaeological, Ethnographic, and Ethnoarchaeological Studies of Spatial Organization in Pottery Workshops in Greece and Tunisia

29 Elizabeth Murphy & Jeroen Poblome
Producing Pottery vs. Producing Models: Interpreting Workshop Organization at the Potters' Quarter of Sagalassos

37 Mark L. Lawall
Greek Amphorae in the Archaeological Record

51 John Lund
Iconographic Evidence for the Handling and Use of Transport Amphorae in the Roman Period

61 Søren Handberg
Amphora Fragments Re-used as Potter's Tools in the Rural Landscape of Panskoye

67 Kathleen Lynch
Depositional Patterns and Behavior in the Athenian Agora: When Disaster Strikes

75 Benjamin Costello IV
The Waste Stream of a Late Roman House: Case Study of the Commissary Block in the Earthquake House at Kourion

85 Archer Martin
Olympia: Roman Pottery in the Archaeological Record

95 Kathleen Warner Slane
Repair and Recycling in Corinth and the Archaeological Record

107 Roberta Tomber
Reusing Pottery in the Eastern Desert of Egypt

117 Susan I. Rotroff
Mended in Antiquity: Repairs to Ceramics at the Athenian Agora

135 J. Theodore Peña
Roman Pottery in the Archaeological Record: Some Follow-Up Comments

139 **Bibliography**

167 **List of authors**

Preface

BY PER KRISTIAN MADSEN
DIRECTOR GENERAL
THE NATIONAL MUSEUM OF DENMARK

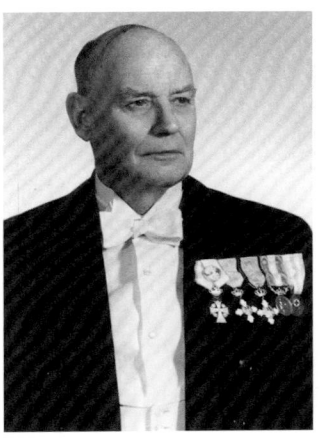

*Consul General Gösta Enbom
(1895-1986).*

The study of classical antiquity and languages may seem a luxury when considering the more practical needs and issues of present day societies. However, knowledge of the foundations of our common European past is necessary in order to understand present day history and to secure the preservation of the remains of earlier times for the future.

This is why the Danish National Museum has from its establishment more than 200 years ago consistently aimed at being an "international" National Museum. The present volume is an embodiment of this ambition. It is the first in a new series intended to publish the results of "Pots, Potters & Society in Ancient Greece", a research programme launched by the National Museum in 2008 thanks to a generous grant from The Foundation of Consul General Gösta Enbom.

The initiative focuses on two central themes within this potentially huge subject: 1) the societal and economic aspect: the production of – and trade in – pottery as a source for understanding the ancient economy, and 2) the ideological/iconographical aspect: vase paintings and other iconographical evidence as a source for understanding the life and thoughts of the ancients.

"Pots, Potters & Society in Ancient Greece" seeks to further our knowledge of both themes and if possible to develop new theoretical approaches by combining existing expertise with fresh ideas. To realize this objective, eminent scholars are invited to do research in the National Museum, and in 2008 a PhD scholarship was established in collaboration with Aarhus University – hopefully the first of more such ventures. Furthermore, international thematic colloquia are held at regular intervals as venues for discussions of relevant issues.

"Pottery in the Archaeological Record: Greece and Beyond" comprises the proceedings of the first colloquium, which was hosted by the Danish and Canadian Institutes in Athens in June 2008. The contributors all aimed at making sense of the pottery appearing – mostly as innumerable sherds – from excavations throughout the Mediterranean,

seeking to further our understanding of the "life cycle" of ancient pottery and in particular of its re-use. Many such instances were discussed, and more might be added, for example that of coin hoards hidden or kept in pottery vessels which were often buried, rapidly it seems, in times of war. This pottery is normally in rather good condition and may seem fairly well dated by the coins. Still, this class of evidence raises questions, not least why some treasure owners, who actually survived, seem to have let their capital rest in the ground without using it or telling about it to their heirs? Did they really prefer to end their life without divulging the whereabouts of their hidden money? Like the issues highlighted in these proceedings, this is a question which has a relevancy that reaches well beyond classical antiquity in space as well as time.

The new series is appropriately named after the remarkable man who made it all possible: Gösta Enbom, a Swede who served for many years as Danish Consul General in Greece, making his fortune there as agent of the leading Danish diesel engine producer Burmeister & Wain. Enbom supported the Swedish excavations at Asine in the 1970s, and later set up his foundation in Denmark to enable the National Museum to carry out research in the world of ancient Greece.

I wish to extend my sincere thanks to those who made all of this possible, not least to the Danish and Canadian Institutes in Athens which hosted the colloquium, to Mark Lawall, who kindly consented to co-organize it and co-edit the proceedings, and to the contributors to this volume.

Introduction

BY MARK L. LAWALL AND JOHN LUND

Archaeologists in general and ceramics specialists in particular often hope for a close relationship between the periods of production, use and discard of pottery. The latest date indicated by the pottery in a given context is generally assumed to approximate the closing date of the deposit. In the quintessential closed context, the shipwrecked cargo, there is the further assumption that all (or most) of the pottery will be of approximately the same date of manufacture (and that all or most pieces were in some state of use when the ship sank). There are, of course, various generally recognized aspects of the presence of ceramics in the archaeological record that complicate this relationship. Old sherds may continue to appear in much more recent contexts as 'residual' pottery. Old pots may be repaired and remain in use for many decades; old amphorae may be refilled and reused for various purposes. But by and large there has been a tendency to minimize the impact of these complications in interpreting the ceramic record.

Over the past decade or so in Classical Archaeology, attention to the processes creating archaeological deposits has increased dramatically. A conference in Padova in 1995 was devoted to the study of drainage facilities created by amphorae (and hence creating some of our best preserved large assemblages of amphorae).[1] In 1996 a conference in Rome addressed the problem of residual pottery in independently datable contexts.[2] More recently, the papers from a conference held in Poitiers in 2002 significantly integrated analyses of faunal and botanical deposits with study of ceramic discard.[3] And in 2007, a supplement to the *Corpus Vasorum Antiquorum* was dedicated to the problem of both ancient and modern repairs of Greek fine ware pottery.[4] This volume began to draw attention to the details of how even thin-walled ceramic vessels might stay in use for many years or decades.

In his 2007 monograph, *Roman Pottery in the Archaeological Record*,[5] J. Theodore Peña brought many of these threads together by offering the first extended consideration of how ceramic vessels were made, used and stayed in use serving various secondary purposes, before finally entering the archaeological record. He highlighted the importance of both the physical characteristics of the vessels and their socio-economic circumstances in shaping the observable patterns in ceramic use, re-use, and ultimate discard.

In describing these paths from production to discard and how the archaeological record will be affected, Peña was clearly influenced by work on site formation processes in other fields of archaeology, especially the work of Michael Schiffer and others working outside the realm of Classical Archaeology.[6] Their goal was to arrive at rules to describe the transformation of artifacts from their state of use in the past to their appearance in the archaeological record. Such rules were intended to replace the simplistic view that the archaeological record was simply past life frozen in time with artifacts simply dropped near where they were used. This research identified many different natural and cultural factors or processes that created the archaeological record we study today.[7] Even in the area of the ceramic record (much of this research is not limited to ceramic artifacts), the range of potentially significant factors is quite wide including variables such as artifact size, shape, hardness, and quantities originally in use. A wide range of culturally-based behaviors will have also affected the use-lives of vessels, the treatment at the point of discard, and the many different possible motivations for discard.[8] Use-life has become a complex concept including production, intended use, later re-uses and recyclings, initial discard, possible recovery and further use,[9] and subsequent re-deposition episodes. Such studies of artifact lives, including many aspects of production, but also wear-patterns from

1 Pesavento Mattioli (ed.) 1998.
2 Guidobaldi *et al.* 1998.
3 Ballet *et al.* (eds.) 2003.
4 Bentz & Kästner (eds.) 2007.
5 Peña 2007.
6 Schiffer 1972; 1983; 1996; Shott 1996 and 1998; Sullivan 2008.
7 While much of the interest has been on cultural forces creating the archaeological record, natural processes may also be significant, see Wood & Johnson 1978 and Hilton 2003.
8 For a case comparing artifact distributions with expectations raised by various hypotheses concerning their reason for discard, see Sullivan 1989. On the impacts of cultural beliefs (as opposed to purely practical matters of efficiency), see Gumerman 1997; Hutson & Stanton 2007.
9 For an example of the recovery and reuse of sherds at Jerash, see Kehrberg 1992.

the period of use, longevity of vessel use, discard practices, and site-abandonment practices, have depended heavily on ethnoarchaeological research.[10] And yet, this use of analogy has come under criticism on many different levels. Without rejecting the role of ethnography entirely, other studies have pursued such questions of artifact use-life and discard patterns through comparisons between actual accumulation patterns and the expectations raised by hypothetical models.[11] The fact that Peña grounds his considerations entirely within the familiar realm of Mediterranean archaeology, however, has the effect of bringing theories, models, and the very discussion of site formation processes comfortably into the Mediterranean mainstream.

Peña's book is an absorbing and challenging read which chips away at many of the comforting assumptions commonly held by classical archaeologists, yet also provides a way out, a methodological salvation of sorts. By focusing our attention on new aspects of the finds, new ways of looking at old patterns, and new ways of structuring our thoughts, he succeeds in pointing out problems with existing paradigms without sinking into a pessimistic quagmire rendering future progress impossible.

Two significant challenges arise from Peña's treatment of Roman pottery: 1) the need to consider what cultural forces may have had similar impacts on pottery in periods and regions not treated in his research; and 2) the need to continue the process, started by the introductory and concluding sections of Peña's book, of building and developing explicit interpretive models of ceramic life-histories in Mediterranean archaeology.

With a view to beginning to address these challenges, the editors of this volume invited a group of specialists in the pottery of Greece to a workshop at the Danish Institute in Athens from the 20th to the 22nd of June 2008 entitled "Pottery in the Archaeological Record: A View from the Greek World". We asked each contributor to reconsider aspects of her or his own work that inform the life cycles of Greek pottery and to present papers with reference both to the general models and approaches and to the specific circumstances or examples presented by Peña. We encouraged a focus on transport amphorae, because much of his detailed study of the life histories of pottery dealt with this category of vessels, but we were also interested in the contributions from other classes of pottery.

The papers are ordered here largely following the structure of Peña's book: we begin with issues of production, then use and re-use, and finally questions of discard. Eleni Hasaki uses a combination of ethnographic and archaeological evidence to examine the consistencies of workshop size, numbers of kilns, limited storage area and size of workforce that may assist in the socio-economic interpretation of partially excavated workshop-sites. Elizabeth Murphy and Jeroen Poblome draw attention to the many dimensions of the archaeology of ceramic production and how such studies can contribute to studies of ancient economics and society far beyond the mere technical details of production.

The next three papers focus on transport amphorae and their particular life-histories. Mark Lawall takes up the Greek evidence for use, distribution and discard of transport amphorae. Potentially significant contrasts with the Roman record as proposed by Peña raise possibilities for how Greek and Roman economies differed and how such differences are manifest in the archaeological record. John Lund provides a supplement to Peña's coverage of the representational evidence in art in terms of the use of amphorae in the Roman period (though for the most part from the Eastern Mediterranean). He notes the preponderance of imagery of amphorae in rural settings and wonders whether these behaviors might go far to explain 'off site' scatters of amphora sherds so commonly encountered in field surveys. Indeed, just such finds are the focus of Søren Handberg's paper, but in this case the amphora sherds from rural surveys in Crimea show signs of having been modified for further use as tools – no longer serving the amphora's primary function as a container. Such tertiary uses of amphora fragments would never be depicted in the sorts of artistic representations collected by Lund, but they do appear to have brought amphora sherds into the fields.

Two papers follow that deal with the problem of reconstructing behaviors creating specific archaeological deposits: the Persian sack deposits at the Athenian Agora (Kathleen Lynch) and the 'Earthquake House' at Kourion (Benjamin Costello). In the cases presented by Lynch, we are seeing Athenians' responses to a man-made disaster in a situation where some sort of large-scale refurbishment of the city center was clearly needed. Of considerable importance here is the potential degree to which emotions or other non-material factors (the thrill of victory, the concurrent grief at loss, possible religious ideas of pollution, etc.) may have influenced the specific actions creating the archaeological record. In the case of Kourion, Costello is faced with a disaster that ended use of the house, so that the resulting artifact scatters can be used to track the 'waste stream' or discard practices within the building just before the earthquake.

The three subsequent papers apply Peña's overall approach to Roman period pottery in three different areas of the Eastern Mediterranean that were not particular points of focus in Peña's study: Olympia (Archer Martin), Corinth (Kathleen Slane) and sites in the Eastern Desert of Egypt (Roberta Tomber). Martin's contribution moves through the same stages of ceramic use-life, from production to discard, as used by Peña, and along the way highlights a number of important elements of Olympia's ceramic record that will bear further investigation (e.g., deliberate location of owners' graffiti on exterior parts of vessels and the presence of repairs only on selected imported vessel types). Slane focuses her attention on repairs and reuse, and in doing so highlights the wider range of instances of such activity in the Roman period at Corinth as compared with other periods. Tomber's contribution highlights the importance of the nature and circumstances of the site in question (sites of difficult access as opposed to more easily accessible urban centers). Access to new material has a direct impact on choices to reuse, recycle, or reclaim from discard. Slane ultimately raises the question of the extent to which such reuse and recycling actually influences our interpretation of the ceramic record. Tomber addresses the same question noting that, in an aggregate view, such practices might not have much impact on our interpretations, but at a more microscale level they do influence our understanding of the 'cultural biography of things'.

While both Slane's and Tomber's papers note examples of repairs and hence ongoing re-use of ceramics, the problem of vessel repairs is addressed most comprehensively by Susan Rotroff in her survey of repaired vessels from roughly 3000 years of activity in the area of the Athenian Agora. Certain periods are under-represented in terms of repairs; details of repair methods may be quite revealing as to the ethnicities of the peoples involved. Such close attention to the traces of ancient behavior adds many further layers to our understanding of the people behind the pottery – even behind the broken pottery. The volume closes with further thoughts from Peña.

The organisers want to express our sincere thanks to the speakers who kindly accepted the invitation to take part in our venture, in particular J. Theodore Peña, who came the furthest, and whose vision was at the core of the papers and discussions of the workshop. We wish to thank also all other participants and contributors to this publication, no less than all who supported the initiative and publication financially or in other ways. We are grateful to the "Generalkonsul Gösta Enbom's Foundation" for making everything possible, and also to the Canadian Institute in Greece, notably its Director David Rupp and Assistant Director Jonathan Tomlinson, and the Danish Institute at Athens, in particular its Director from 2004 to 2010, Erik Hallager, and its staff. The conference closed with a very fruitful visit to Corinth, where Guy Sanders and Kathleen Slane hosted a tour of the excavations' storerooms. We are most grateful to the Corinth excavations for their hospitality.

---

10 For ethnoarchaeological research on various aspects of ceramic production, see Costin 2000. For studies of wear patterns in ceramic vessels, see for example Arthur 2003. For research identifying the many variables that might affect the use-life of a given vessel, see Shott 1996; Tani & Longacre 1999; Hildebrand & Hagstrum 1999; Shott & Sillitoe 2001. For studies of discard practices, see Beck & Hill 2004 and Beck 2006; on discard and episodes of disaster, see Dawdy 2006. For examples of studies evaluating the archaeological data against patterns encountered in the ethnographic record, see Kent 1999 and Frankel and Webb 2001. On abandonment processes from a mixture of ethnographic and archaeological evidence, see Deal 2008. Shott & Sillitoe 2004 compare ethnographic evidence with mathematical models of accumulation, and then consider the implications for archaeological data.

11 For examples, see Varien & Ortman 2005; Varien & Potter 1997; Pauketat 1989.

Crafting Spaces:
Archaeological, Ethnographic, and Ethnoarchaeological Studies of Spatial Organization in Pottery Workshops in Greece and Tunisia

BY ELENI HASAKI

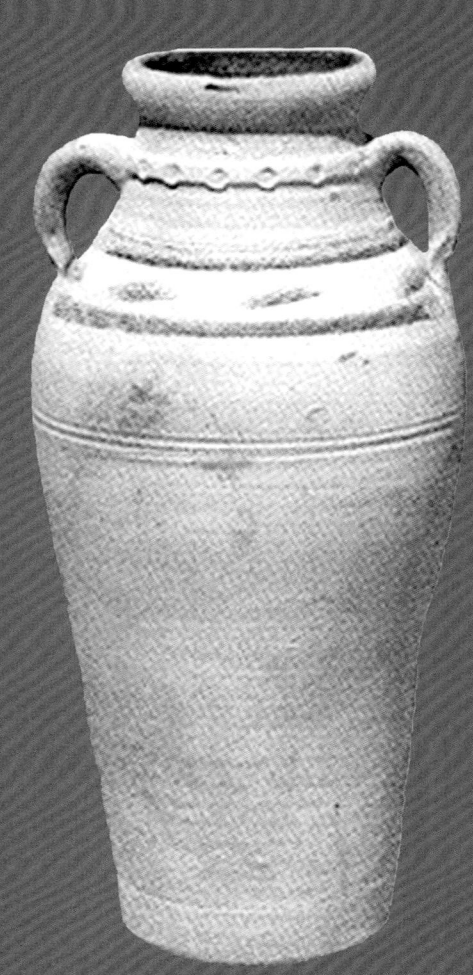

Crafting Spaces:
Archaeological, Ethnographic, and Ethnoarchaeological Studies of Spatial Organization in Pottery Workshops in Greece and Tunisia

BY ELENI HASAKI

Potters' workshops have always been a welcoming place for anthropologists and archaeologists alike: the former usually visit and study contemporary potters' communities and the latter excavate the material remains of the ceramic products and workshop installations. Both groups aim to study and reconstruct the organization of a workshop, its production mode, and its technology. Ethnoarchaeological studies have offered the median place where both anthropologists and archaeologists can combine their methodological arsenals and develop projects conducted in contemporary contexts but aimed to answer archaeological inquiries.

The present study integrates archaeological evidence from ancient Greece with ethnoarchaeological and ethnographic evidence from the modern Mediterranean, especially from the potters' quarter in Moknine, Tunisia. The data gathered on sizes and layouts of potters' workshops in a Mediterranean context can then be examined against the archaeological evidence from ancient Greece. Although the Tunisian test case is geographically remote from Greece, the similarities in climate conditions of the Mediterranean basin, in the techniques and organization of pottery manufacture, in the size of workforce, as well as the lack of electric machinery make the two geographical areas comparable.

This interest in the spatial layout of pottery workshops stems from a desire to move away from the individual technological fixtures that anchor a pottery workshop (e.g., the kilns) and feature most often in the archaeological record, and to move towards larger questions of spatial requirements.[1] Ultimately, a combination of kiln-focused archaeological studies with attention to patterning in the spatial layouts of ancient and modern Mediterranean workshops can allow the size and number of kilns

excavated to stand as a reliable proxy both of the total space that a workshop once occupied and of its scale of production.

The aims of the study are threefold. First, to assess both quantitatively and qualitatively the space occupied by the traditional workshops in Tunisia. Second, to develop a dataset for spatial analysis that can assist archaeologists to refine their survey/excavation techniques. And third, to set realistic expectations about the "visibility" and "legibility" of the archaeological record about the manufacturing processes taking place inside a workshop.

The picture emerging from our investigation is that there is a positive and consistent relationship between the intensity of craft production and various spatial or scalar variables: the extent of the workshop, the size of its equipment (namely kilns), the size of its workforce, the space (or better the lack thereof) allotted to long-term storage, and ultimately the size of the available means of land or sea transportation. If one of these variables changes all others tend to adjust accordingly. Furthermore, a firm understanding of the spatial limitations of a workshop permits a more accurate estimation of the size of workforce that could operate in such spaces. Such estimates challenge older pictures of ancient Greek pottery production, which postulated a master potter employing a large number of apprentices and assistants on the model of Renaissance workshops. In addition, the available space has further implications for the lifecycle of a pot. If, for example, pottery workshops dedicated little space to short-term storage, then pots must have left the initial production context very quickly to enter subsequent use contexts.

STUDIES OF SPATIAL ANALYSIS

Workshop space may not have received much scholarly attention in the area of ancient pottery production, yet studies of other types of space have proliferated and provide useful theoretical and methodological frameworks. For much earlier periods of human history, spatial analysis and activity-area analysis has been instrumental in inferring the range of activities performed at open-air sites for hunter-gatherers.[2] In Classical Archaeology, Roman archaeologists have been pioneers in using spatial analysis to address issues of domestic layout, such as the distinction between private and public spheres as well as between male and female spheres of activities in Roman houses.[3] Others have examined the spatial configuration in larger settlements, such as Pompeii.[4] Studies of ceramic workshop space have recently begun at Pompeii and at Albinia, considering total space occupied as well as sequence of tasks and projected cycles of production based on daily tasks.[5] In the Greek world, spatial analysis has already been successfully applied to the study of the layouts of sanctuaries as well as to domestic space, especially at Olynthus and Halieis.[6]

Whether studying contemporary or ancient workshops, researchers have the tendency to study the workshop as a "point" to which raw materials arrive and from which finished goods are distributed through simple or more complex trade systems. Strategies for procurement of raw materials (e.g., clay, temper, and fuel) and the distance of these sources from the workshop have already been researched extensively.[7] Other studies focus on the potter's control of clay composition and enhancement, equipment (e.g., the wheel or the kiln), and interaction with the workforce.[8] Additional venues of research include the potters' apprenticeship methods, connoisseurship, archaeometric studies, the potters' daily output, and standardization of vessel size and shape.[9] Even ancient philosophers dealt with workshop spaces, but only so far as to allocate a specific sector of their ideal city to the establishment of artisanal quarters (e.g. Plato, *Laws*, 846-849; Aristotle, *Politics* 1331a-b).[10] Sometimes the use of the term "workshop" does not even correspond to a specific location/point but is used to describe the artistic style shared by many different (usually unnamed) artists.

Despite attention to so many different issues, the physical space of the workshop itself and the interaction of the workforce with it have managed to escape archaeological attention. Basic issues remain ignored such as the average space required for an ancient workshop and the size of the workforce that can be accommodated.

Ethnographic studies of traditional workshops and archaeological reports of ancient workshops in the Mediterranean have been rather numerous and successful, but their respective results have not been integrated into a larger attempt to extrapolate the spatial requirements and configurations for ancient workshops. The fundamental question remains: can ethnography and ethnoarchaeology help us reconstruct the activities that took place within the archaeological remains of an ancient workshop?

USE OF SPACE IN ANCIENT GREEK POTTERY WORKSHOPS – ARCHAEOLOGICAL EVIDENCE

Workshop space in ancient Greece is difficult to address due to the scarcity of both excavated remains and ancient textual or iconographic references. Iconographic evidence is limited to a handful of ancient representations on Archaic terracotta plaques from Penteskouphia, near ancient Corinth, and few a Athenian black-figured and red-figured vessels. These images indicate interior space or separation of covered/semi-covered as opposed to open-air space by including such elements as a shelf or a column (Fig. 1).[11]

No ancient documents, whether literary, epigraphical, or papyrological, record any dimensions of ancient workshops. The lease of a workshop by a potter in return for a specific amount of vessels (P.Oxy. 50.3595, dated to

---

1 See Hasaki 2002 and 2006 with earlier bibliography. This study includes ca. 500 kilns dating from the Bronze Age to the Byzantine period.
2 Binford 1983, 144-192; Kent 1984; Kroll & Price (eds.) 1991; a recent overview of studies of spatial analysis can be found in David & Kramer 2001, 255-283.
3 Wallace-Hadrill 1988; Grahame 1997. For the social meaning of space in general, see Samson (ed.) 1990; Pearson & Richards 1994; Allison (ed.) 1999.
4 Laurence 1995.
5 Pallecchi 2007; 2008 (Albinia); Peña & McCallum 2009 (Pompeii).
6 For space in sanctuaries, see Bergquist 1967. For domestic space, Cahill 2002; Ault 2005; Lang 2002; Ault & Nevett 2005.
7 Arnold 2005.
8 For the potter's wheel, see Roux & Corbetta 1989. For kilns in Greece, see Hasaki 2002; 2006 with earlier bibliography.
9 For children's apprenticeship in Southwest ceramics, see Crown 2001. See Boardman 2001 and Cuomo di Caprio 2007 with further bibliography on several aspects of Greek decorated pottery.
10 For a critical discussion of literary testimonia and archaeological inquiries on urban artisanal quarters, see Sanidas n.d. I thank Dr. Sanidas for providing me with a copy of his paper in advance of its publication.
11 For depictions of shelves, see also the Penteskouphia plaques, Berlin Antikensammlung F 640+fr and 641 (the former is published by Zimmer 1982b, fig. 20.2). Athenian depictions of potters' workshops space also include: a black-figured hydria (Munich Glyptothek 1717; Leagros Group; *c.* 520 BC); a red-figured crater (Caltagirone Museo Regionale della Ceramica, inv. 961; *c.* 440 BC); and a red-figured bell-crater (Oxford 526; Komaris Painter; *c.* 430 BC). Generally on Corinthian and Athenian scenes of potters at work, see Cuomo Di Caprio 1984; Sparkes 1991; Boardman 2001; Vidale 2002; Papadopoulos 2003; Χατζηδημητρίου 2005; Hasaki forthcoming.

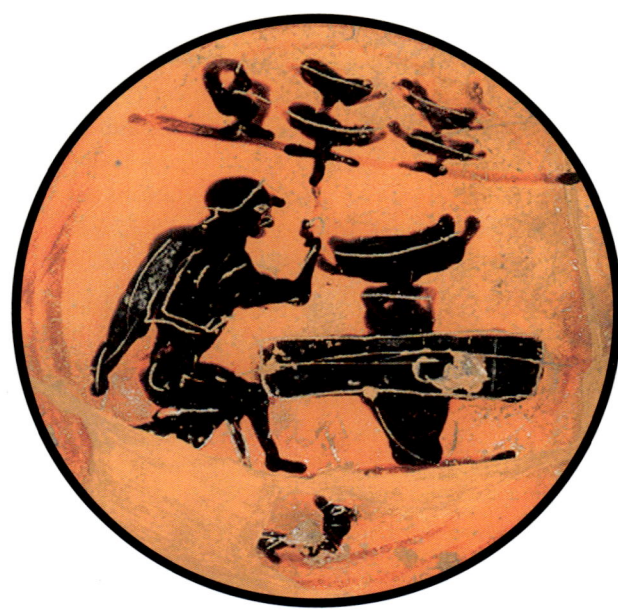

Fig. 1 Tondo of black-figured kylix. London, British Museum inv. B 432, Unattributed; ca. 500 BC.

AD 260) vaguely refers to the workshop space as "…in the large farmstead of your estate around Senepta together with its storerooms, kiln, potter's wheel and the other equipment." Later in the lease, the potter agrees to "… hand over the aforesaid jars on the drying floors of the said pottery from the winter manufacture…".[12] We are told of the various areas in the workshop, such as storerooms and drying floors, but no information is conveyed on the total size of the workshop or the spatial relationship of the areas mentioned to each other.

Very few ancient Greek workshops have been excavated in their entirety. Various criteria, either individually or in combination, have been used to locate or propose the location of a pottery workshop (Table 1).[13] Sites are identified through excavation of kilns, settling basins, large dumps, or wasters. The first two permanent features are safe indicators of original site of the workshop, but the dumps and wasters, which can easily be moved through various depositional processes, can only approximate the location of a workshop. But in all these archaeological attempts to detect workshops, the focus remained on identifying or approximating the "location" of a workshop, rather than analyzing "the space" of a workshop itself.

More than 450 ancient Greek kilns are known, belonging to ca. 250 excavated sites.[14] Even in those excavated examples, only part of the workshop has been recovered. Most kilns came to light during salvage excavations strictly limited to specific building lots.[15] Only a dozen or so pottery workshops in ancient Greece have been excavated more extensively (Table 2).[16] A noteworthy exception of a workshop excavated to its entirety is a Late Classical-Early Hellenistic workshop recently excavated in Pella. It is a rectangular plot measuring 20 x 20 m. Its rather

---

12 Cockle 1981. Based on the description of the capacity of the vessels produced (jars of four choes), this workshop must have required the same space as the medium-sized workshops discussed below. See also a more recent discussion of all pottery workshop leases (total of 39) in Mees 2002. Other references to parts of a workshop include: P. Lond. 3.0128 (AD 517), P. Cair. Masp 1.67110 (AD 565). Even when tax payment on a workshop is mentioned, the size of the workshop is not recorded, only its location and owner (e.g., BGU 06.1282). Interestingly, even workshop leases from the 19th century AD are written in a similar manner (e.g., a lease signed by a group of itinerant pithoi makers at Thrapsano, Crete, who leased a countryside lot that already contained a kiln; Ψαροπούλου & Σημαντηράκης 2007, 29).

13 A number of scholars working on Bronze Age Greece have presented similar lists of archaeological criteria for identifying craft workshops. Tournavitou 1988 listed architecture, pottery, facilities, tools, material worked (e.g., raw material, half-worked pieces, waste, finished objects), connection with central administration (e.g., Linear B tablets); Evely 1988 also recommends a mental checklist: physical appearance and position, relatively immobile furniture, the raw substances; objects in the course of manufacture and debris resulting from the forming; Platon (1993) has suggested a similar list of criteria for studying over twenty Minoan palatial workshops: unworked, raw material, unfinished objects, wasters, tools, equipment, and finished products. Michaelides (1993), in his study of eight sites with Minoan pottery workshops, listed as criteria: clay disks, clay jars, basin, and architectural elements such as benches and occasionally the kiln. P. J. Arnold (1991, 87-91), in his study of household production in Mexico, identifies production areas based on three categories of criteria: production implement, production residues, production results. Tools can easily be moved to other contexts and cannot be a secure indicator on their own.

14 Hasaki 2002. A kiln is undoubtedly the strongest criterion for the location of a ceramic workshop, as it is most resilient to post-abandonment processes.

15 The same situation holds true for many pottery production sites excavated elsewhere in the Mediterranean. Cuomo Di Caprio 1971/1972 (for Italy); Nijboer 1998 (for Early Italic and Etruscan sites); Swan 1984 (for kiln sites in Great Britain); Le Ny 1988 (for tile works sites in France).

16 In other areas, such as Italy, the dataset of sizes of pottery workshops is equally slim (see Table 3: section I,2).

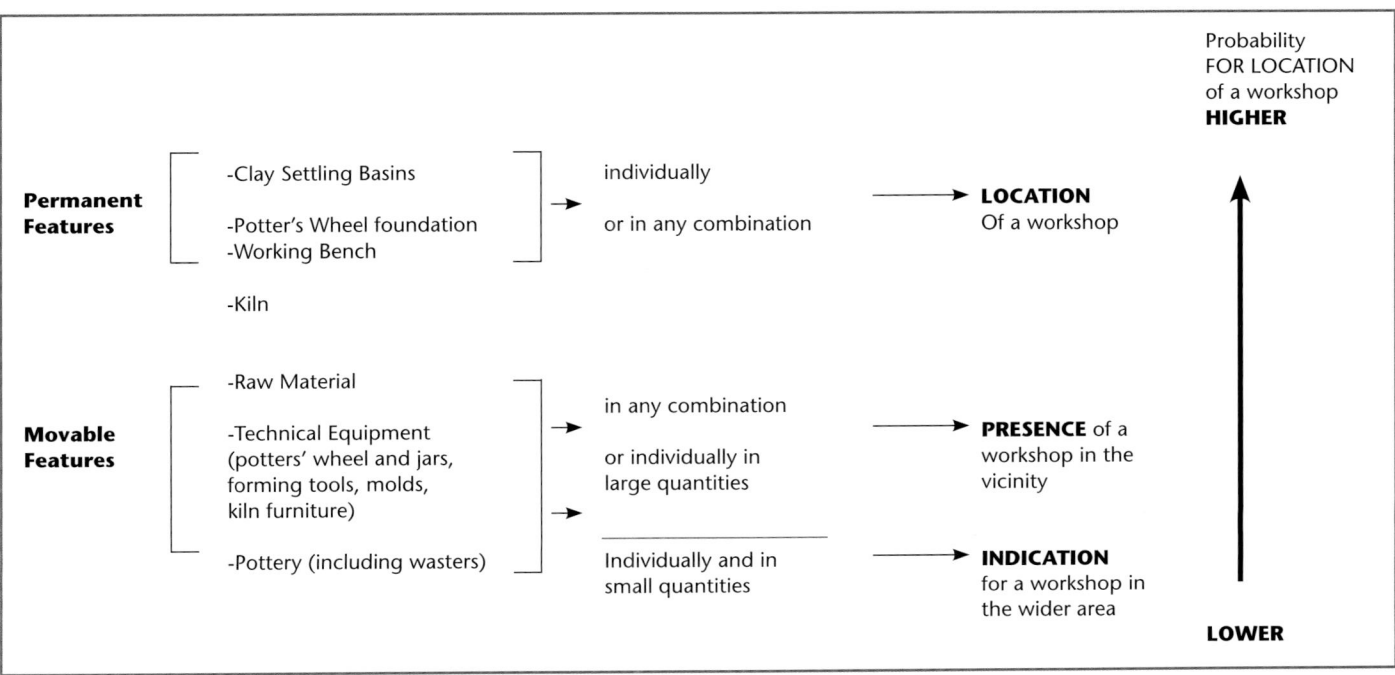

Table 1 Archaeological criteria for identifying and locating spatially a ceramic workshop. After Hasaki 2002, 262 Table VI.2.

Date	Site*	Dim.	Area excavated	
			≤ 2 kilns	> 2 kilns
Bronze Age	Kirrha, Delphi	10x10	>100 m²	
	Gouves Area C, Crete	30x25		>750 m²
Archaic	Prinias, Crete	20x15		>300 m²
	Phari, Thasos	31x13	>403 m²	
Classical	Tile Works, Corinth	26x16	>416 m²	
	Athens, Lenormant Ave.	10x3	>30 m²	
	Sindos, Macedonia	9x4	>36 m²	
Hellenistic	Atalante, Phokida	18x9	>162 m²	
	Krannon, Phokida	12x12	>144 m²	
	Pella, Tsagarli Plot	19x23		>437 m²
	Pella, Town Workshop**	20x20	400 m²	
	Pherai, Stamouli-Bolia Plot	6.50x6.50	42 m²	
	Corfu, Figaretto	11x16		>176 m²
Roman	Paros, Paroikia Tholakia	10x12		>120 m²
	Patra, 212 Karaiskaki and Kalamodgarti Sts	8x12	96 m²	

* Note: each entry may reflect more than one workshop active at that site; **fully excavated.

Table 2 Excavated areas of ancient Greek pottery workshops and tile-works. Data expanded from Hasaki 2002, 274 Table VI.5.

SITES	"HOUSEHOLD INDUSTRY" Workshop and residence	"WORKSHOP INDUSTRY"			"MANU-FACTORY"	NUCLEATED WORKSHOPS	REFERENCE
		Small	Medium	Large			
1. ARCHAEOLOGY							
1.1. ANCIENT GREECE							
See Table 2 above Kotzia Square						>2,120m²	Ζαχαριάδου and Κυριακού 1988
Corinth Potters' Quarter						>6,000m²	Stillwell 1948
1.2. ANCIENT ITALY							
Marzabotto, Etruscan				>540m²			Nijboer 1998, 179, fig. 42
Morgantina A (Late Hellenistic)		>114m²					Cuomo di Caprio 1993
Morgantina B (Late Hellenistic)		>152m²					Cuomo di Caprio 1993
Morgantina C (Late Hellenistic)				>486m²			Cuomo di Caprio 1993
Morgantina D (Late Hellenistic)				>726m²			Cuomo di Caprio 1993
Pompeii, Via Di Nocera	100m²						
Pompeii, Via Superior	120m²						
Scoppieto						>1,050m²	
1.3. ANCIENT TUNISIA							
Leptiminus		>300m²					Stirling et al. (eds.) 2001
2. ETHNOGRAPHY-ETHNOARCHAEOLOGY							
2.1. GREECE							
Orei, Euboea			ca. 175m²				Hampe and Winter 1965
Istiaea, Euboea			ca. 324m²				Hampe and Winter 1965
Tsikalario, Kentri, Crete A: household items			ca. 300m²				Blitzer 1984
Trikalario, Kentri, Crete B: household items			ca. 180m²				Blitzer 1984
Korone, Messene A: large pithoi and water jugs				ca. 600m²			Blitzer 1990
Korone, Messene B: water jugs			ca. 140m²				Blitzer 1990
Marousi, Athens A: coarsewares				ca. 625m²			Valavanis 1990
Marousi, Athens B: finewares	ca. 80m²						Schreiber 1999, 32.
Ermioni, Argolis				ca. 240m²			Kardulias 2000
Molos, Thasos			340m²				Παπαδόπουλος 1999
Loggos Thasos			2,500m²				Παπαδόπουλος 1999
Platanaki, Thasos			832m²				Παπαδόπουλος 1999
2.2. ITALY							
General locations		100-150 m²	300-400 m²	500-1,000m²			Cuomo di Caprio 2007
2.3. TUNISIA							
Moknine Quarter		120 m²	350 m²	750 m²			Hasaki 2005
2.4. INDIA							
Rajasthan (Jodhpur and Udaipur)	30-100 m²						Kramer 1997

Table 3 Areas of pottery workshops, ancient and modern. All dimensions (except for Moknine, Tunisia) were calculated from the published plans. Not all publications mention the types of pots produced. For irregular layouts of workshops I calculated the smallest rectangle within which all features are included.

standardized size and shape must have been conditioned to some extent by the size and shape of blocks in the Pella grid plan.[17]

USE OF SPACE IN CONTEMPORARY GREEK POTTERY WORKSHOPS – ETHNOGRAPHIC EVIDENCE

When we turn to the ethnographic record in contemporary Greece and Cyprus, this scarcity of the evidence does not change drastically. Most attention is paid to distinct activities (e.g., clay collection, forming, firing, decorating), design and function of wheels and kilns, types and nomenclature of vessels, genealogies of potters; but not on the space itself. Roland Hampe and Adam Winter visited numerous pottery and tile workshops in the Mediterranean, from Cyprus to Sicily during the 1950s and 1960s, yet one finds only two workshop plans annotated according to uses of space in their otherwise richly illustrated ethnographic accounts.[18] Frederick Matson provided an interesting ecological and technological account of the Messenian potters in the late 1960s, again without providing any workshop plan.[19] In the 1970s and 1980s, Mary Voyatzoglou meticulously studied the itinerant pithoi-makers at Thrapsano, Crete.[20] Plans of entire workshops are absent even from the very extensive accounts of the Aegean potters by Betty Psaropoulou, which are otherwise very helpful about potters' genealogies, nomenclature of shapes and technical equipment.[21] The extensive and seminal ethnographic and ethnoarchaeological literature on Cypriot potters still rarely includes workshop plans.[22]

There are various noteworthy exceptions. Harriet Blitzer included plans of workshops and detailed description of the use of space in her studies of the potters' communities on Crete and in Messenia.[23] Stratis Papadopoulos, in his study of traditional workshops on Thasos, included several workshop plans along with indication of use, and attempted a first analysis of spatial and temporal sequence of tasks within the workshops.[24] A rich corpus of detailed plans of traditional pottery workshops is found in Wagner's study of Siphnos.[25] Though focused on matters of architecture for the most part (e.g., floor plans, construction materials used), Wagner does provide a detailed typology of the main working room in the workshops and the kilns. Alongside these exceptions, a few other studies on ancient or traditional pottery production include single plans of

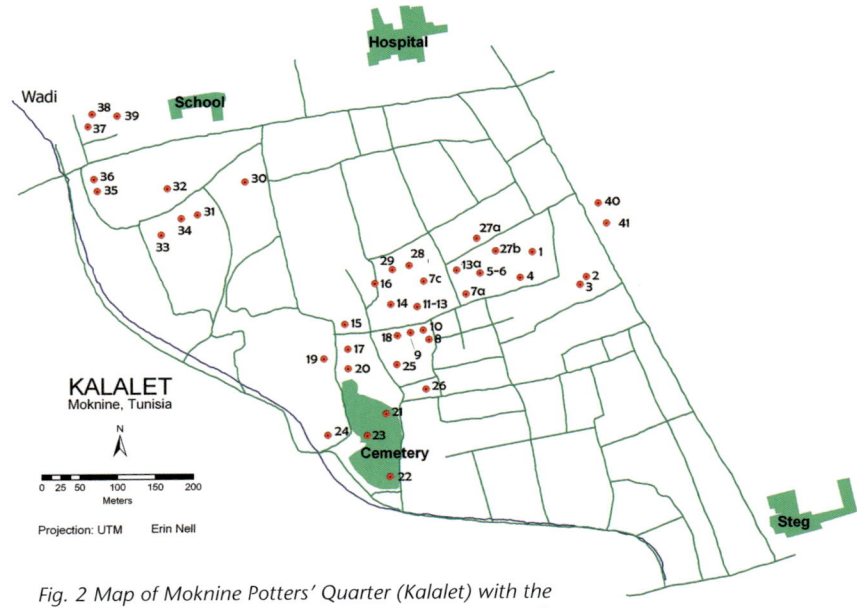

Fig. 2 Map of Moknine Potters' Quarter (Kalalet) with the location of the 41 workshops indicated. Map by Erin Nell.

17 Λιλιμβάκη & Ακαμάτης [2008] forthcoming. My sincere thanks to Dr. Lilimbaki Akamati and to Mr. N. Akamatis for information on the Pella workshop.

18 Hampe & Winter 1962; 1965. The plans are of two Euboean workshops: at Istiea firing 500 unspecified pots per firing and at Orei for making jars and amphorae (Hampe & Winter 1965, 135-136 figs. 124, 126). Both plans are reprinted in Peacock 1982, 30 fig. 11; 45 fig. 15). A partial plan of a workshop at Camerata in Italy is also included (Hampe & Winter 1965, 4-5, figs. 2-3). Some of their panoramic shots of workshops could receive further attention to stress the importance of exterior space in most pottery workshops.

19 Matson 1972.

20 Voyatzoglou 1972, 1973, 1974, 1984.

21 Psaropoulou 1986, Ψαροπούλου 1990; 2005; Ψαροπούλου & Σημαντηράκης 2007. In 1987, Psaropoulou founded the Center of the Study of Traditional Pottery in Athens, which has had a major impact in the promotion of the study and preservation of traditional potters in Greece. See also the interesting monograph on the shape repertoire of Greek traditional ceramics by Κυριαζόπουλος (1984).

22 London at al. 1990, Ionas 2000; London 2000.

23 Blitzer 1984, 1990.

24 Papadopoulos 1995; Παπαδόπουλος 1999.

25 See Wagner 2001, where 18 potters' settlements numbering over 100 workshops on Siphnos are documented in detail. The abandoned Siphnian workshops represent a hybrid state of preservation, where the shell of the workshop is still standing, as well as the permanent architectural features, but the remaining areas are void of any artifacts, simulating thus the archaeological record.

contemporary traditional workshops.[26] Even when the workshops plans are included, their total area is never explicitly stated but can be estimated by the scale provided on the plans (Table 3).

USE OF SPACE IN TUNISIAN POTTERY WORKSHOPS: THE ETHNOARCHAEOLOGICAL EVIDENCE

The Moknine Ethnoarchaeological Project: Setting and Goals

The Moknine Ethnoarchaeological Project, a research project intending to address (among other goals) the problem of spatial arrangements of potters' workshops, was started in 2000 with a focus on traditional workshops for coarse wares in the potters' quarter of Moknine, Tunisia. Moknine, an industrial city of 50,000 inhabitants located ca. 180 km south of Tunis, [27] is one of the three major centers of ceramic production in Tunisia together with Nabeul (for glazed pottery) to the north and the island of Djerba (for coil-built large jars) to the southeast.[28] The city emblem, consisting of a pot, a brooch, and a piece of tapestry, eloquently celebrates its strong artisanal legacy in ceramics, jewelry, and textiles.

The potters' quarter of Moknine, locally known as the Kalalet, lies to the east of the city center and covers an area of 0.14 km² (=140.000 m²) (Fig. 2). The Kalalet houses 41 workshops, where over 120 workmen specialize in the production of wheel-made, unglazed, coarseware pottery ranging from small bowls to water jars, to larger coiled-made and wheel-finished *zirs* (Fig. 3). Moknine ceramics owe their distinctiveness to a characteristic self-slip, which fires white-yellowish due to the salt added to the clay paste.[29] Some shapes are used in the local households, but most are exported to other Tunisian cities and to Europe as decorative items. The workshops operate all year round, and, besides the one or two potters per workshop, they have an additional workforce of 2-3 persons giving a total of 4-5 persons per workshop.[30] In addition to workshops, the Kalalet is also a residential area, where mostly potters have their homes.

The Kalalet was chosen as the focus of research for three reasons: first, there was a certain urgency to record rapidly-vanishing vernacular architecture;[31] second, the workshops specialize in a wider range of forms and heights, rendering the observations on spatial requirements more widely applicable for potters producing a wide range of

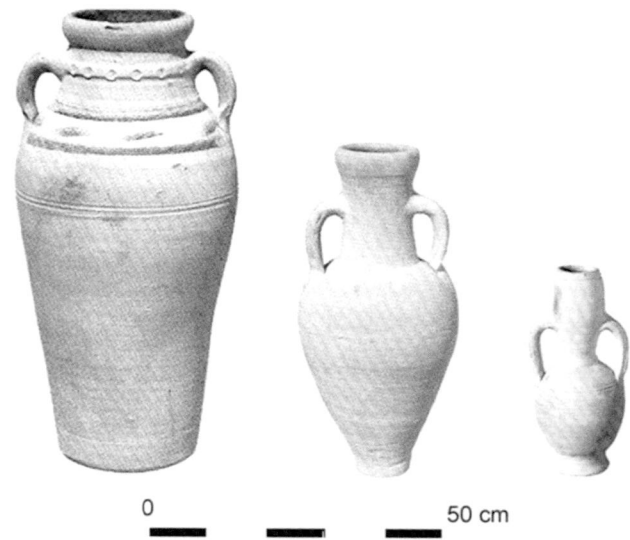

Fig. 3 Representative large, medium and small vessels produced at Moknine's Kalalet.

shapes; finally, with the relocation of the potters to the new site and the construction of new spaces, there is the unique opportunity to conduct a long-term comparison of old vs. new strategies of use of space. Therefore, this project addresses questions both of "salvage" and "long term" ethnoarchaeology.[32]

During three field-seasons (2000, 2002, 2005), the project made a detailed study of all 41 workshops in the area using a standardized questionnaire with sections on biographical data, history of the workshop, workforce size, specialization of production, as well as data on equipment such as wheels, electric clay-mixing machines, and kilns.[33] A separate section of the questionnaire addressed specifically the workshops' architectural layout.

The Moknine Ethnoarchaeological Project: Methodology

The 41 workshops in the Kalalet belong to two categories in terms of physical appearance: a) those, older in age, that are independently standing and b) the newer workshops, which partially occupy a modern residence. Such division of contexts is a direct result of the relocation and, hence, transformation that the potters' quarter is undergoing. The older workshops are built in a traditional manner either with vaulted ceilings or carved in the soft rock of the area. Some of these original workshops are still active; others

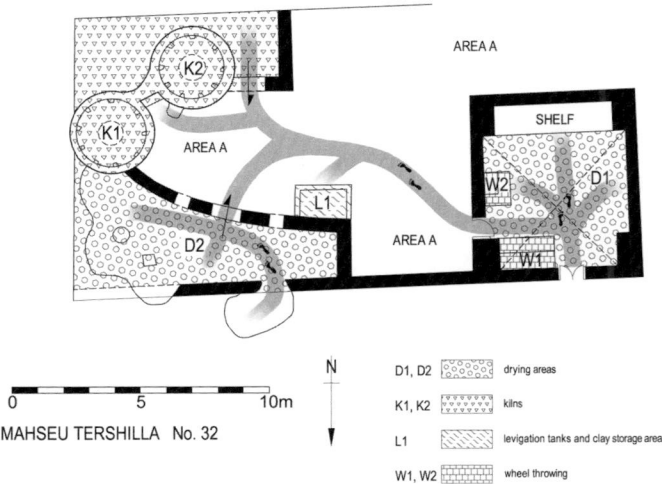

AREA A

SHELF

K2

K1

AREA A

AREA A

L1

D2

W2 D1

W1

0   5   10m

MAHSEU TERSHILLA No. 32

N

D1, D2   drying areas

K1, K2   kilns

L1   levigation tanks and clay storage areas

W1, W2   wheel throwing

Fig. 4 Detailed plan and functional analysis of a traditional workshop (Fig. 2, no. 31), producing small vessels at Moknine. Drawing by N. Bayrem; digitization by D. Welle and R. Lyng.

are abandoned awaiting demolition. The second category, the newer workshops in the Kalalet, is comprised of an increasing number of workshops functioning on a limited scale, housed in the ground floor of the newly-built house of a potter who has already established his main workshop in the new, relocated potters' quarter away from the Kalalet. I recorded the architectural plans of the 15 older workshops that retained most of their original layout (Fig. 2: workshops 1, 2, 5-6, 11-13, 14, 16, 20, 21,27a, 28, 29).[34] These 15 workshops provide valuable evidence of spatial patterning of the potter's activities.

Analysis of the plans focused on the total space of workshop, the spatial requirements for different stages of manufacture, and the extent of roofed and open-air space.[35] First, I calculated the total space of each workshop based on its periphery to determine the overall space available to potters. Vertically-expanded space and outdoor space used by the workshop was added to the total area of the workshop. I then calculated the percentages of roofed, semi-roofed and open space in the workshop. Next, I studied the internal arrangement of the workshop and calculated how much space each pottery manufacturing stage requires, from preparing the clay to storing the fired pots, (e.g., clay basins, potters' wheels, benches to knead the clay, drying space and, of course, kilns and fuel supply areas).[36] In

26 Sparkes (1991) reproduces a workshop plan by Blitzer (1984) in his survey of ancient Greek pottery; Schreiber (1999) includes the plan of an Athenian pottery workshop in her handbook for replicating ancient Greek pottery shapes; Kardulias (2000) provides a workshop plan in his ethnoarchaeological study of a potter's establishment at Ermione.

27 Hasaki & Nell 2004; Hasaki 2005. Previously the quarter had received little attention (Balfet 1958; Sethom 1964). Any quantitative results (number of workshops, number of potters, etc.) are as of 2003.

28 For Nabeul, see Lisse & Louis 1956. For Djerba, see Combès & Louis 1967, 43 and 47 figs. II.5-6.

29 Sheriff et al. 2002.

30 Excavations have also brought to light Roman workshops near the western limits of Moknine, testifying to the centuries-long potting tradition of the area, but these have not been published. For a Roman amphora workshop in the nearby town of Leptiminus, see Stirling & Ben Lazreg 2001 (the area of the partially excavated workshop is *c* 300 m²). Generally on Punic and Roman pottery production centers in Tunisia, see Peacock et al. 1989; Mackensen & Schneider 2002; Stirling 2006. For recent discussions of Roman pottery production in North Africa, including Tunisia, see Bonifay 2004 and Humphrey (ed.) 2009.

31 A long-planned process of relocating is now under way and the old quarter is rapidly losing its traditional appearance. This original Kalalet is now being relocated to a new designated industrial zone, one mile further to the east, away from residential areas. What was once a remote location for the installation of a Kalalet, gradually expanding around its original kernel, a Jewish cemetery, has now been enveloped within a rapidly developing residential quarter.

32 For salvage ethnoarchaeology, see David & Kramer 2001.

33 The questionnaire was published in its entirety in Hasaki 2005.

34 Use of Autocad allowed accurate measurement of the many irregular spaces in the plans.

35 For pottery making stages of manufacture, see Rye 1981; Rice 1987; Cuomo di Caprio 2007.

36 I used the following area designations: D: Drying areas: for long-term drying; G: General areas: often used for short-term storage, but mostly left empty; K: Kiln areas: kilns and the staircases to reach their underground stoking channels and fuel storage areas; L: Levigating clay areas: The clay basins and the area occupied by the electric clay-mixing machine. Many times, the two form an architecturally tight unit; W: Wheel-forming areas: rectangle including the wheel and the bench; Walls: total area covered by walls. Circulation paths: I assigned a 'mental' passageway 1 m. wide from one opening to the other, always choosing the most direct way. For open areas, I assigned major pathways that connect one room/structure to another as well as access paths for use of the kilns. I calculated only the minimum space used by potters for these access paths. It is possible that the potters would block permanently or temporarily the most direct access. My aim though was to be consistent and assume the minimum area required.

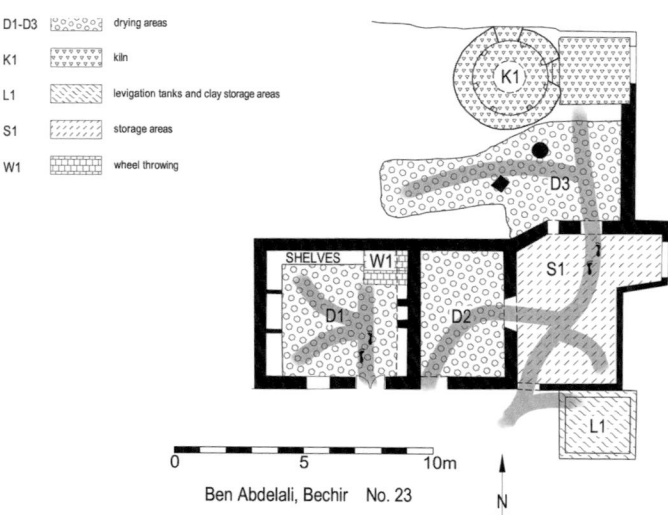

Fig. 5 Detailed plan and functional analysis of a traditional workshop (Fig. 2, no. 23), producing medium-sized vessels at Moknine. Drawing by N. Bayrem; digitization by D. Welle and R. Lyng.

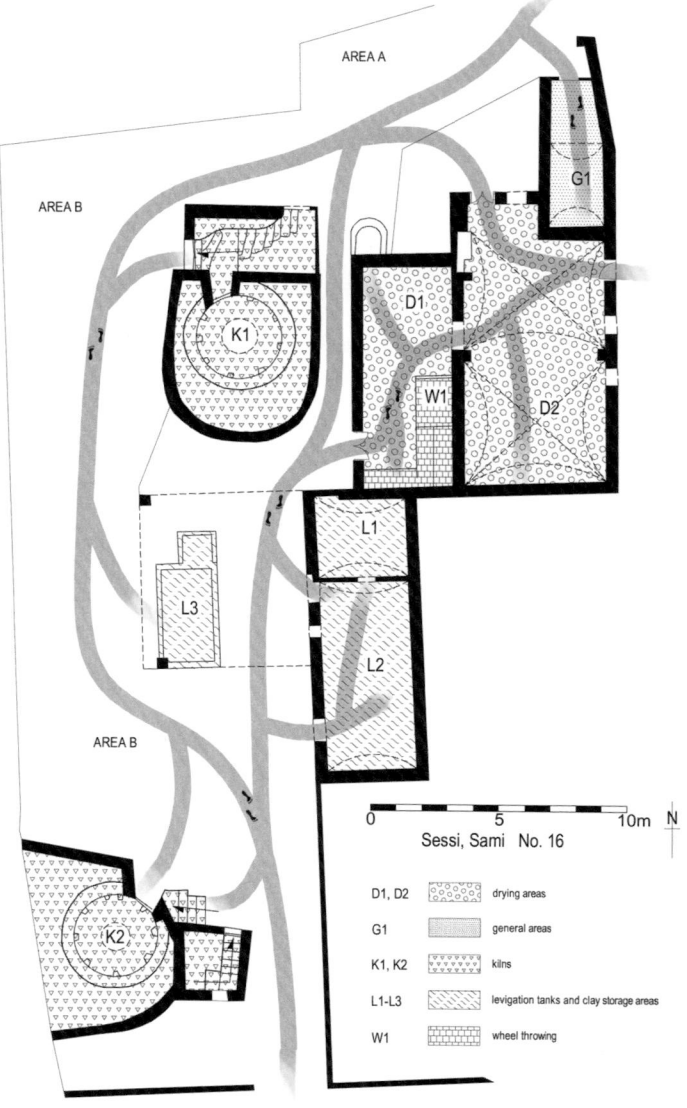

Fig. 6 Detailed plan and functional analysis of a traditional workshop (Fig. 2, no. 16), producing large vessels at Moknine. Drawing by N. Bayrem; digitization by D. Welle and R. Lyng.

addition to the stage-specific measurements, I also took into consideration the need for some basic circulation paths (even if those change from time to time), which have to remain relatively unobstructed in order for workers to move vessels and materials freely. When measuring the spatial requirements for each stage, I also examined whether use of space is rigidly reserved for a single function or flexibly adapts to the needs of the potters and fulfills more than one function.

Alongside such measurements, the workshops were also classified according to the size of the pot they produced: a. small (up to 0.15 m in height), b. medium (0.16-0.40 m in height), and c. large-size vessels (above 0.40 m in height) (Figs. 4-6). This criterion was based on a potter's comment, which particularly struck me during the interviews: "I do not throw any pot above 40 cm in height." Their emic system describing specialization focuses more on the total height of a pot rather than its exact form. The shape of the vessel, the feature that most often dominates the archaeologists' typological classifications of most ancient pottery, is clearly less important to the Moknine potters.

The potters at Moknine produce mostly unglazed and undecorated pottery. In the few observed cases where the pots were decorated, the potters used the same areas as they used for production of undecorated pieces, so the additional stages added more time to the production without requiring more space.

Once gathered in this way, the data was regrouped according to visibility and legibility in the archaeological record. Of the various measured spaces, what percentage of the space would leave enough material remains to allow its recovery, its identification as potters' space, and its assignment to a specific stage of pottery manufacture?

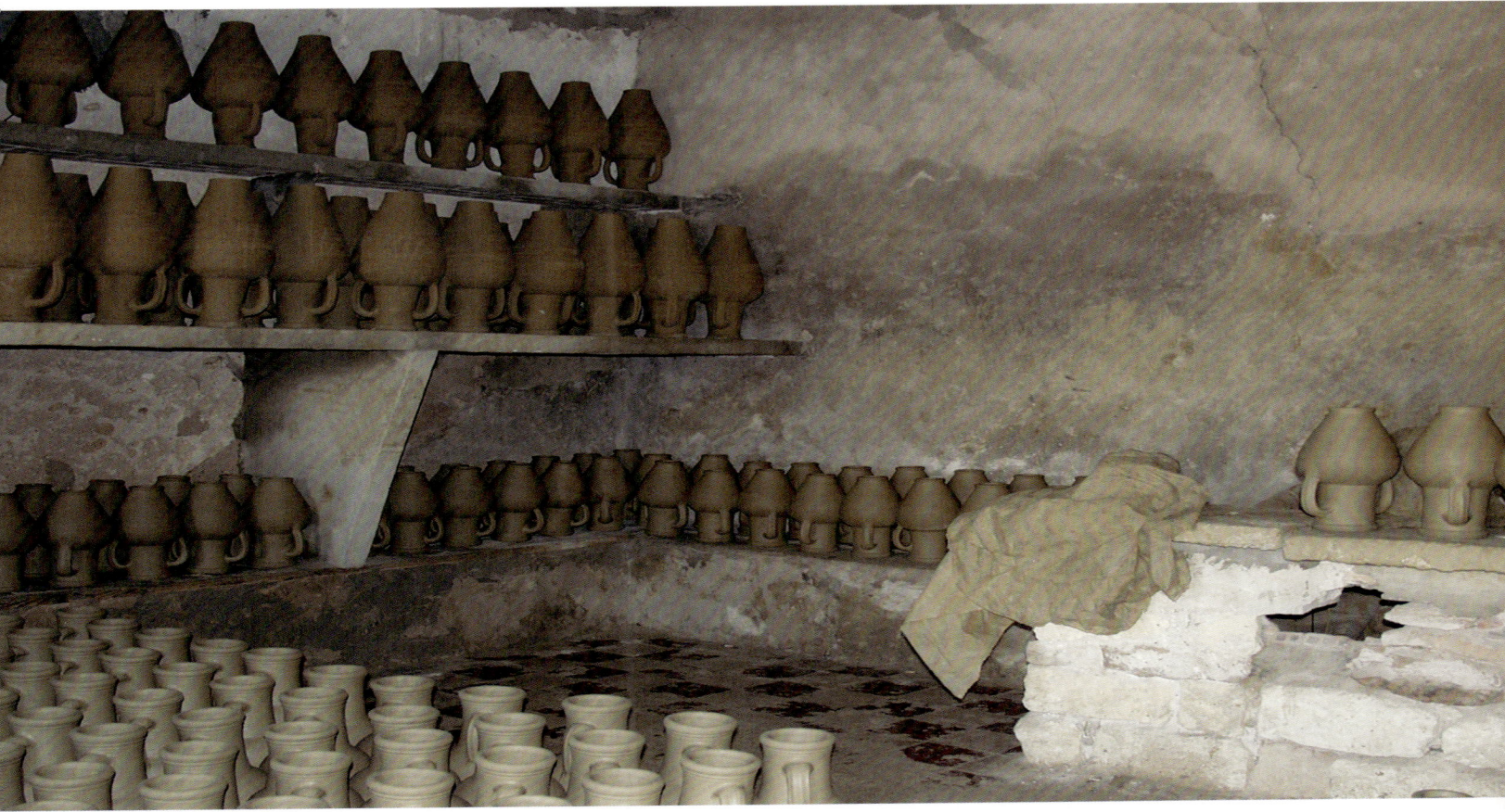

Fig. 7 Interior space of a Moknine workshop (Fig. 2, no. 23) with potter's wheel to the right and internal shelves shown. Photo by author.

The Moknine Ethnoarchaeological Project: Preliminary Observations

Detailed analysis of these fifteen workshops informs three main issues: a) the total area of a workshop and the enlargement of space by spreading horizontally or creating more vertical space with shelves and stacking; b) the space required by each stage of manufacture; and c) areas for storage and discard.

Horizontal and Vertical Spaces and Workshop Expandability

Workshops at Moknine producing small-size pots require an average space of 120 m² to function; those producing medium-size pots require 350 m² on average; and finally the workshops producing large-size pots require 750 m² – almost six times more space than the small pots workshops

(Figs. 4-6).[37] In addition to the overall space occupied by the workshop as visible on a two-dimensional plan, there is additional space available. Potters regularly use the external walls of their workshops to stack fired pottery for sale, raw materials, or fuel. An even larger area outside the walls is claimed by the potter during the initial drying period of the vessels. Therefore, a temporary spatial expansion of the workshop is observed. This expansion is not consistent and cannot be easily measured since it varies with the tasks required and even with the climatic conditions. For the

37 Only basic calculations will be provided here. A more detailed publication of all Moknine workshops with their numerical data is currently in progress (Hasaki forthcoming).

quantitative analysis of the workshop, I included a strip 1 m wide along the exterior walls. Inside the roofed or semi-covered areas of the workshop, potters of small and medium-sized vessels regularly use wooden or stone shelves for the long-term drying (Figs. 7-9).[38] Such vertical space, often seen in ancient representations and modern contexts, is vital to the unobstructed use of the limited space of the smaller workshops.

Accessibility

Overall the pottery workshops in Moknine are easily accessible places thanks to their ample courtyards.[39] Few spaces are more than two rooms deep. Most rooms do not communicate directly with others. The potter enters a space, performs a certain step of manufacture, and then must come out into the open space to enter another room. The courtyard is the main artery of traffic. There are rare instances where two rooms have both access to the courtyard and communicate internally to each other; also rare are the cases where one room leads to another one at the back.

Spatial Requirements for Individual Stages of Pottery Production

The average percentages of space allotted for each function – clay-levigation basins and storage of clay, wheel-throwing areas, and kilns – exhibit a certain consistency regardless of the size of the vessels produced. The clay-refining activities use 2% of the space, throwing requires 3%, drying 14%, and firing (kiln and fuel) occupies ca. 12% of the space. The areas for processing and preparing clay for forming vessels are noticeably reduced since most workshops buy pre-processed clay from a regional company. However, most workshops still use their old levigation basins to recycle clay shavings or defective unfired vases. By contrast, there is high variability in the amount of drying space: potters of large vessels require substantially more drying space, since these vessels usually need at least two-weeks in shady areas before firing. Approximate circulation paths cover an average of 13% of each workshop, and the walls a considerable 14% of the total space.

Storage Areas

The workshops at Moknine do not exhibit extensive storage spaces. The pots spend very little time in the production context.[40] Instead, they move quickly to their use-life

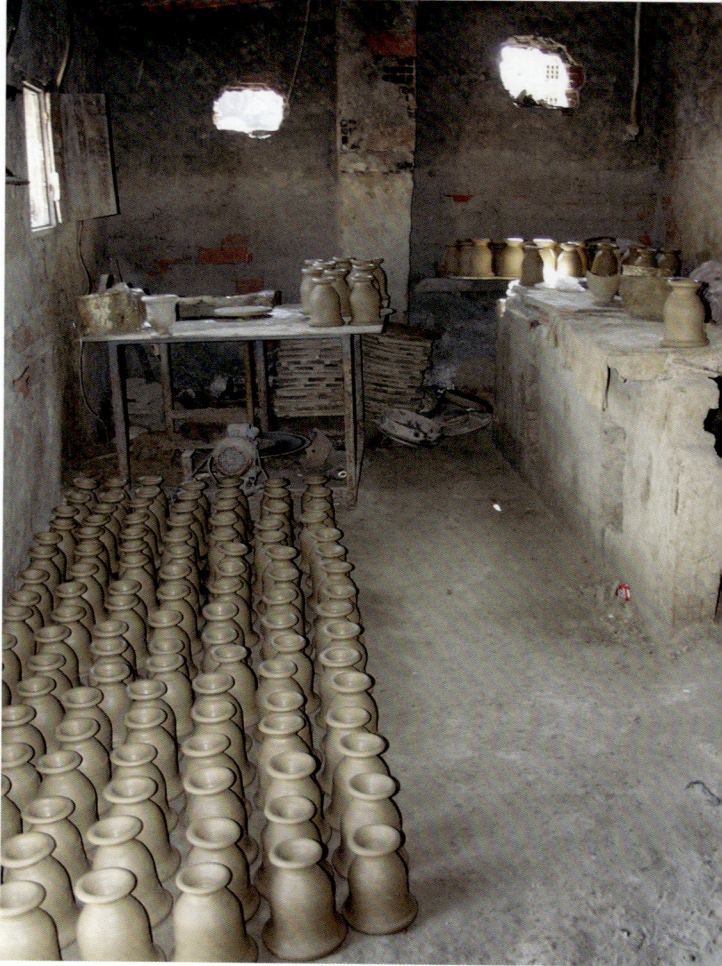

Fig. 8 Internal space of a workshop at Moknine showing potter's wheel to the right, wheel-heads in the center back and drying pots on the left. Photo by author.

context. In the most traditional workshops the potters stack their wares against the exterior walls of the workshop usually very close to its entrance. In the transitional workshops, where the main production takes place in the new potters' quarter and the modified residence (the former workshop) serves more as a depot than as a production area, the storage capacity is much larger.

Extent of Mechanization

Some Moknine workshops have already undergone semi-mechanization in a few stages of the manufacturing process (e.g., the use of pre-fabricated clay or in-house processing of clay with mixing machines). Some potters in large-size

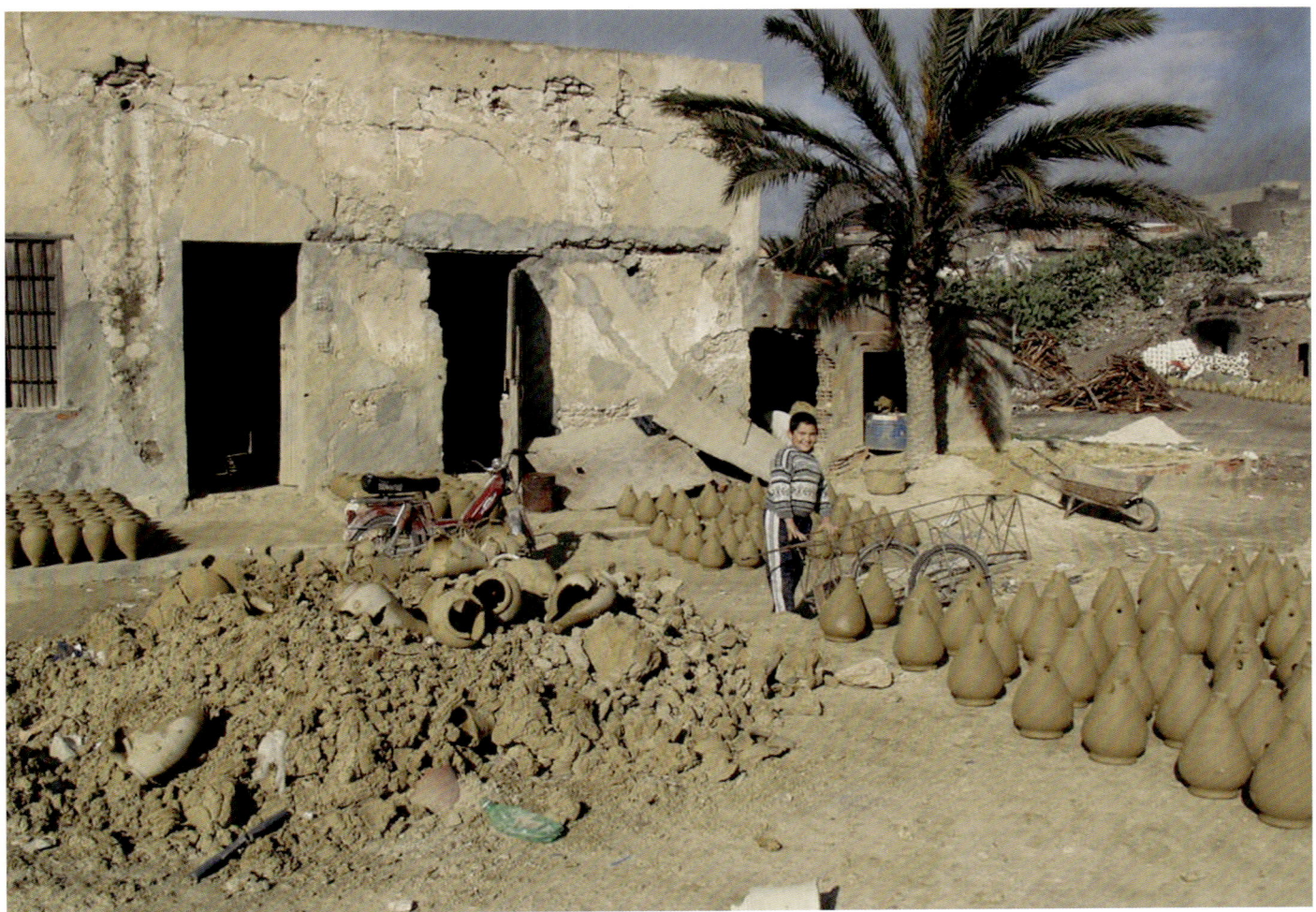

Fig. 9 External space of the same workshop as Figure 7. Photo by author.

workshops have also invested in a clay-fabricating machine, thereby reducing considerably the use of space originally required to levigate and tread the clay prior to the forming of the vessels. From an archaeological point of view, this mechanization of clay procurement has not altered the spatial arrangement especially for the workshops of small and medium-sized pots, since the old clay-settling basins are still in use, albeit for other purposes (as noted above). The pre-processed clay can easily be stored within the available space of the workshop, without making special accommodations. The picture is slightly different for workshops of large pots where the space for temporary storage of clay is quite substantial (3-6%).[41]

38 The potters of large vessels make little use of shelves due to the prohibitive weight of their pots, especially in the unfired stage. Annis (1988) emphasized both the horizontal and vertical dimension of a workshop by providing both plans and with vertical cross-sections the four-phase modification (within 40 years) of the internal arrangement of a pottery workshop in Sardinia. I thank Dr. Annis for informing me of the duration of each phase.
39 For access analysis conducted in ancient domestic architecture, see Grahame 1997 (for Roman houses) and Yiannouli & Mithen 1986 (for Greek traditional houses).
40 Peña 2007, fig. 1.1.
41 Likewise, in a Messenian workshop for the making of large storage jars, the area set aside for keeping the unprocessed clay amounts to ca, 16% (total size of the workshop: 600 m²); see Blitzer 1990.

Discard Areas

The workshops, comparatively speaking, are clean places without much broken or flawed pottery lying around. During the time I spent recording their activities there was a very low breakage rate, and no areas within the workshops or the quarter were specifically designated as dumps.[42] Pots and sherds could be reused to form a bedding inside the kiln in the lowest lever, to hold smaller pots during firing, to insulate the dome insulation of the kilns, or to block off the stoking channel.[43] The predetermined space allocated for each phase of manufacture as well as the need for unobstructed circulation paths militate against the accumulation of trash. This need for regular maintenance explains the low visibility of wasters and other types of trash within workshop areas both during use and in the post-abandonment period. Discard areas and refuse disposal are usually studied in domestic contexts or urban settings, and to differentiate between sedentary and migratory populations, but more rarely do scholars focus on production space.[44] Studies of production space often aim to differentiate location of use from location of manufacture for light crafts, such as like flint-knapping, which do not require an architecturally-distinct workshop and can be carried out even within a residence.[45]

Open vs. Covered Space

All workshops rely heavily on their open space; in most workshops open space accounts for 45% of the total footprint, leaving 55% for covered space. This emphasis on open space fits the warm Mediterranean climate, but the organization of covered vs. open-air space may exhibit a different pattern in colder climates.

Single Function vs. Multiple Functions

Philip Arnold, in his seminal study of Mexican household pottery production, divided the production stages between *spatially-flexible* activities, such as vessel-forming, and drying, and *spatially-inflexible* activities, such as firing.[46] The household setting and scale of pottery production described by Arnold allows for some spatial flexibility. Once production leaves the domestic sphere and enters the workshop, however, the space becomes more rigidly structured. Allocation of workspace, as practiced at Moknine, is largely inflexible. Use of space tends to follow closely the sequence of manufacturing stages: collecting clay, preparation of paste, forming, drying, decorating, firing.

In short, the *chaîne opératoire* is imprinted in the *espace opératoire* of the workshop.[47] Even so, a few areas can fulfill additional functions: e.g., part of the drying areas, when not it use, can sometimes be used for storage. Open spaces can be used more flexibly for temporary storage of fuel, clay, or pots to be sold. Overall, however, space is allocated to mostly one function, or to some few alternatives, but it is rare to find much flexibility in the use of space.

Long-term Ethnoarchaeology of Workshop Space

As mentioned above, the potters' quarter at Moknine is currently undergoing relocation to a new site. Therefore it offers the opportunity to compare the observations reported here with studies of the newly built workshops in the new area, and the impact of new variables can be explored.[48] For example, the new area has a very high water table, which forces the potters to introduce technological changes in the entirely above-ground construction of their kilns. It will be interesting to see if this technological change will have an impact in the spatial organization. One can also examine the social dimensions of the clustering of workshops. Will the old proximity pattern of workshops with owners who have close kinship ties be replicated in the new location?

Spatial analysis of the potters' quarter at Moknine can add a new analytical tool to the arsenal of methodological approaches to the study of pottery production in the ancient and modern Mediterranean. One should not overlook, however, the fact that detailed observations as to the function of each area were made during one field campaign of the summer 2002, and therefore are static in character. I did not examine repeatedly how a specific area was utilized over many years, and during different seasons. It is noteworthy, however that during my repeated visits to the Kalalet, I did not notice any major spatial rearrangement inside the workshops. But this dataset can easily be compared to the spatial arrangement in the new potters' quarter.

IMPLICATIONS FOR SPATIAL ANALYSIS IN ANCIENT AND MODERN MEDITERRANEAN POTTERY WORKSHOPS

Returning, now, to the archaeological context, can these observations allow us to estimate size and possible allocations of space in ancient ceramic workshops that have been partially excavated? Settling basins and kilns are the safest criteria for identifying the location of a pottery workshop, as mentioned above (Table 1). Yet such elements at Moknine account only for 15% of most workshops, regardless of the size of pot they produce. The space occupied by kilns alone at Moknine quite consistently amounts to 14% of the total footprint, and they are normally placed at the edges. This consistent ratio of kiln area to workshop area could assist excavation teams to project the approximate extent of a workshop. And yet, a discouragingly high percentage (70%) of the space does not leave a distinctive architectural sign in the archaeological record. Even so, various points of consistency in the assembled data have important implications for the interpretation of archaeological remains of ceramic workshops.

Overall Size

The Moknine project provided some, admittedly preliminary, numerical data for the total sizes of workshops. This systematically-collected data is echoed by spatial data from other workshop sites, whether ancient or contemporary (Table 3). Two pottery workshops have been excavated to their entirety at Pompeii.[49] They both produced small-size vessels, and their areas (100-120 m²) fit nicely within the common dimensions of Moknine workshops for production of small vessels. Cuomo di Caprio, in her long study of traditional Italian workshops, has also proposed three similar workshop space categories: a. 100-150 m²; b. 300-400 m²; and c. 500-1,000 m² (the highest range especially applicable for tile works).[50] A preliminary survey of traditional pottery workshops in Greece points to similar trends in total workshop space and allocation of space to specific stages. Small workshops tend to extend over 200 m². The larger workshops with two or more kilns cover a minimum area of 300-400 m².[51] Thus the Moknine data alongside these other examples indicates that a range of total space from 120 m² to 750 m² can be used tentatively as a viable size for a family-based workshop industry producing wheel-thrown pottery and operating full-time and for much of the year. It should be emphasized that this estimate applies only to pottery workshops, and not to tile works, which have much larger spatial requirements.

Economy of Spatial Layout

In the Moknine workshops it is evident that the work flows efficiently from room to room through the courtyard. Such an access system also guarantees the best ventilation for all rooms. Wagner reaches the same conclusions about the centrality of the courtyard in the pottery workshops on Siphnos.[52] Papadopoulos (1995), in his discussion of two traditional pottery workshops on Thasos, concluded that almost all routes connecting different areas of the workshop are efficiently direct and thus economizing in both time and energy.

Limited Storage Areas

The conspicuous absence of extensive storage space should not be overlooked. The Moknine potters do not stockpile large quantities of finished product awaiting distribution. Similarly they do not invest in large quantities of clay or fuel, either through intermediaries or by personal collection, for later use. Raw materials are only gathered

42 At the Kerameikos at Metapontum, in an area of ca 1,100 m², the excavators dug four kilns and over 20 dumps. The dumps were clustered in two groups covering a total of only one quarter of the entire area (D'Andria 1975).

43 In Messenia, in the late 1960s entire vessels provided extra strength in the outer rings of the kilns; see Matson 1972, pl. 15.7. Scenes of kiln firings on the plaques of Penteskouphia also show how potters recycled the upper parts of Amphorae or other similarly-shaped vessels as chimneys for a better draft in their kilns. For example, the Penteskouphia plaques (Berlin, Antikensammlungen inv. nos. F 524+694; F 614; F 631; F 802). These plaques are illustrated and briefly discussed in Cuomo di Caprio 1984. For other ethnographic examples of recycling of pots inside the workshop, see the Cypriot pottery workshops (London 1990).

44 Arnold 1990 studied the correlation of clean maintenance of patios in Mexican houselots and the high degree of structured activities. Such studies provide a good example of how people, regardless of domestic or industrial context, tend to keep the surroundings where they conduct many activities relatively clean. Generally on the ethnoarchaeology of refuse disposal, see Staski & Sutro (eds.) 1991.

45 Murray 1980.

46 Arnold 1991.

47 Lemonnier (ed.) 1993.

48 Long-term ethnoarchaeological projects can better document continuity and change. See London 2000.

49 Peña & McCallum 2009. The two workshops are Via Di Nocera pottery facility producing mold-made lamps and wheel-made cups and Via Superior pottery facility. The extensive excavation of these sites has allowed the authors to assign or postulate a function to each area of the workshop.

50 Cuomo di Caprio (2007, 258, 261, fig. 77) provides only the average size, without mentioning specific workshop examples.

51 Papadopoulos (1995) believes that a minimum area of one stremma (1.000 m²) is required for the establishment of a pottery workshop; however, his study examines only a handful of workshops on Thasos.

52 Wagner 2001, 138-145.

for the immediate production needs, and finished products quickly enter the distribution system. The resulting revenues then permit the purchase of raw material for the next batches. The Moknine potters, with their short cycle of production and sale and their tight budgets, use similar financial strategies to many other fellow potters in the Mediterranean.[53] If a similar lack of storage space is encountered in archaeological settings, then interpretations should consider the possibility of similar economic constraints and practices.

A similar conclusion for the short cycle of production can be drawn from the size and number of kilns in ancient Greek workshops. The average diameter of known ancient Greek kilns is 1.10-1.50 m regardless of period or region, and most workshops function with one or at most two kilns.[54] Such kilns have a capacity that will have been filled by one to two weeks of full-time potting.[55] Even the loss of an entire batch during the firing process will not strike a terrible financial blow to the workshop, whereas large kilns with large capacities also mean large-scale risks for the potter.

If nothing else, the evidence from Moknine and elsewhere raises the possibility that we should disassociate large storage areas from manufacturing/industrial sites. The stockpiling of fired ceramics in large quantities perhaps for a short period of time and perhaps from different producers could also fall under the activities of middlemen, i.e., part of the distribution process rather than production. To minimize even further the need for stockpiling empty vessels, especially those which would contain agricultural products, the ancient potters often established their workshops near farms, as seen in the close proximity of some amphora workshops and wine presses in Hellenistic Egypt.[56] The presence, therefore, of many stored jars at a site raises the possibility that the area was a depot, or retail area, rather than a place of primary manufacture.

Space and Scales of Production

Since the size of workforce remains the same in small, medium, and large size workshops, we should not equate large space with large workforce. Instead, in workshops of large vessels, potters need ample space to place the clay, to dry the pots, and to store them temporarily. The workshop space also behaves like an organism. Since specific circulation patterns are prescribed from the sequence of pottery manufacturing phases, no change in the spatial layout can take place without the rearrangement of the entire area. As a result, the workshop space enjoys a relative stability.

A contrast to the pottery workshops described here is found in potters who produce hand-made pots in a domestic setting. In C. Kramer's work on potters in Rajastan, India, there are extensive and very informative plans of several workshops. The average total size of the residence and workshop of a potter producing small hand-made pots is ca. 30-34 m², those producing medium size pots, 70 m², and those producing large size pots, ca. 90-100 m².[57] At the other end of the spectrum, in a manufactory of the 1st century BC at Scoppieto in Italy (where many potters literally worked under one roof, as evidenced by the remains of their wheels), the partially excavated area, mostly covered, measures over 1,050 m².[58] Even those sizes of workshops falling into the largest of the three categories defined here are still far outstripped by the more complex industrial establishments like that of Scoppieto and those found in later times, such as the Medieval Nantgarw Pottery in South Wales (over ca. 1,125 m²).[59]

Scales of Production and Transportation

This spatial dataset can be further used to estimate the original size of partially excavated workshops. The total space required of potters producing specific sizes of vessel might allow archaeologists to approximate the original size of a partially excavated workshop. The size and number of kilns in a workshop are reliable indicators of the size and level of production. As I have argued elsewhere, the majority of ancient Greek workshops had 1 or 2 kilns at most (the same pattern as in modern Moknine),[60] and their sizes, like those at Moknine, vary between 1.10-1.50 m in diameter.[61] From the clay storage facilities, to the number of workers employed, to the size of the kilns, and the overall size of the workshop, the emerging picture for most of the Mediterranean pottery workshops (of the workshop industry type) is a full-time, small size, most likely family-based workshop. The vessels produced in this type of workshop are then distributed by sea in small boats and by land on pack animals. Excavated shipwrecks and archival photographs from traditional potting communities showing small boats filled with wares reflect similar strategies for distribution of products across the centuries.[62] Both the archaeological and ethnoarchaeological data, therefore points to a similar organization of pottery production for ancient Greek and modern Greek and Tunisian workshops.

Space and Partially Excavated Workshops

The consistencies emerging over the ethnographic evidence and the admittedly partial archaeological remains can suggest uses of space in excavated workshops where the assemblages are of little help. For example, a pottery workshop (dated to the 1st century BC - 1st century AD) was partially excavated on Paros in the Cyclades.[63] Within the excavated area, six kilns and four areas came to light. Not all these kilns were used at once. No artifactual evidence for use of space was recovered. Based on the patterns in use of space presented here, it is possible to exclude some functions from some areas with a certain degree of confidence. For example, the rooms adjacent to the kilns were probably not reserved for forming vases, but for drying or for short-term storage.

Space and Occupancy

The consistently modest size of workforce in the pottery workshops studied here challenges former suggestions about the size of workforce for ancient Greek pottery workshops. For example, using attributions to different painters' hands, Scheibler suggested that 20-40 painters must have been employed at Nicosthenes' workshop in Late Archaic Athens.[64] Nothing in the architectural layout of ancient or recent workshops can support such intense human traffic, even if some of them were only employed part time. More recently, Tosto, taking into consideration a number of ethnographic and ethnoarchaeological studies of pottery production, decreased the Nikosthenes workshop to 3-8 people, a size that is more consonant with the patterns seen in our data.[65] Robin Osborne recently also challenged the large number of Athenian red-figure painters who have been presented as affiliated with masters. He, too, advocates for workshops with a smaller size crew.[66] Such limitations on space in workshops will also have constrained the number of apprentices that might be trained at any one time. Space and scheduling of the pottery manufacturing stages (from clay quarrying to firing) are mutually dependent.[67]

Space in Other Ceramic Industries

This model of analysis of the potters' space can be adapted to study use of space in other clay-using industries, such as tile works. Tile works have usually been detected through their large rectangular kilns, but they also require extensive drying sheds, which leave few archaeological traces. The Archaic workshop of architectural terracottas at Poggio

MODES OF PRODUCTION

Household Production; Household Industry; Individual Industry; Workshop Industry; Village Industry; Large Scale Industry

	VARIABLES
ECONOMY	-raw materials (clay, temper, water, fuel) -time involved; -persons involved; -gender; -hired hands; -time per pot; -organization; -labor division; -seasonality; -investments; -market; -status; -locality
TECHNOLOGY	-manufacturing techniques; -tools/facilities (sed.basin, wheel, drying shed, firing/kiln) -raw materials (clay, temper, water, fuel) -range of pottery -range of functions per pot
SPACE	-space requirements;-storage areas and stockpiling capacity

Table 4 Space added to the variables of different modes of ceramic product-ion organization (adapted from Leeuw 1977 and David & Kramer 2001).

Civitate (Murlo) in Etruria had a semi-covered structured, called the South-East Building, which could have functioned as a "drying-shed". It measured at least 48.50 m

53 See literature in the section above on "Use of Space in Contemporary Greek Pottery Workshops – Ethnographic Evidence".
54 Hasaki 2002; 2006.
55 A replica of an ancient Greek kiln in Tucson, with a diameter of *c*. 1.00 m, requires the work of a full-time potter to be filled (for the project, see http://aiatucson.arizona.edu); Hasaki 2004.
56 El-Ashmawi 1998.
57 Kramer 1997, 185, 188, 199, 200.
58 Bergamini (ed.) 2007.
59 Peacock 1982, 30, fig. 11; 45, fig. 15.
60 Another interesting, multi-kiln site is at Figareto on Corfu with a dozen kilns enclosed within the very small space of 172 m² (Preka-Alexandri 1992). It is unclear how many of these kilns were contemporary or even operated concurrently and whether we have one or more workshops represented.
61 Hasaki 2002; 2006.
62 Παπαθωμά 2001; Hasaki 2002, 275-276, 314-315.
63 Κουράγιος & Δετοράτου 2002; Hasaki 2010.
64 Scheibler 1986.
65 Tosto 1999, 195.
66 Osborne 2004a; 2004b.
67 Pallecchi 2008.

x 6.00 m, covering an area of 291 m².[68] The footprint of the partially excavated tile works at Corinth is more than 410 m².

Density of Potters' Quarters

The Moknine example can also inform future studies of the spatial patterning and density of organized potters' communities both in ancient and in traditional societies. A partially excavated kerameikos at ancient Corinth measures ca. 6,000 m² (= 0.006 km²) which is 23 times smaller than the Moknine quarter.[69] The excavators were disappointed that no kiln was found during what they believed to be the excavation of an extensive area. When compared though with the density at Moknine (41 workshops in 0.14 km² = 0.003 km² on average per workshop), then the area excavated at Corinth likely covered only 2-3 workshops; the associated kilns did not happen to fall within the excavated areas. By contrast, at Kotzia square in downtown Athens at least 40 kilns and several levigation basins have been excavated in an area of 2,134 m² (or 0.002 km²).[70] If we postulate that each workshop operated two kilns, then each workshop covers ca. 106 m² (i.e., in the range of a small-size workshop); and indeed, many of the Kotzia workshops did produce lamps.

In light of all these various topics that can be addressed by combining archaeological and ethnographic data, one should look not only at the increase of workforce, its part-time or full-time employment, the permanent character of the equipment, but also at the spatial needs for operation. Therefore the list of variables proposed by van der Leeuw in his seminal study on the Economics of Pottery Making should include the considerations of space (Table 4).[71]

CONCLUSIONS

The emphasis placed here on spatial data from pottery workshops aims to introduce space as a crucial factor in future discussions of production and distribution in ancient economies and the archaeological means of studying such behaviors. Workshop space is considered here in terms of its extent, its expandability (both vertically and horizontally), and its constant interaction with the workforce in question. Workshop space, by being at the beginning of the economic chain from manufacture to trade, is an important factor to consider in our attempts to reconstruct the scale of ancient pottery production. Estimates of a potter's productivity rate, a vase-painter's output, or a boat's loading

capacity, although useful to some extent, should all be constrained by the size, layout and productive capacity of the workshops in question. A set of interrelated calculations of many factors, such as space and storage limitations, size of personnel, size and number of kilns per workshop, and capacity of means of transportation, can be combined to produce a more accurate picture of scales of production than would be possible if any of these factors were treated alone.

The built environment has always been studied to address questions about economic, political, and social organization. If analysis of the domestic space can shed light on so many facets of social organization, it is only worthwhile studying the production space for its potential to address issues of economic, technological and social organization. Modern potters and their predecessors craft their spaces with the same attention that they extend to their products, and if we do not consider the *espace opératoire* of the *chaîne opératoire* we will be missing an important element in the strongly interrelated world of craft production.

---

68 Nielsen 1987.
69 Stillwell 1948; an industrial building within the Potters' Quarter, labeled the "Terracotta Factory", covers an area of 280 m².
70 Ζαχαριάδου & Κυριακού 1988; it would be interesting to study the density and expansion pattern of mainland versus coastal potters' quarters. For example at Platy Yalos on Sifnos, in a narrow strip ca. 40 m wide and ca. 800 m long (total area of ca. 32,000 m² or 0.03 km²), 14 workshops were active, Wagner 1974.
71 Leeuw 1977.

ACKNOWLEDGEMENTS

My sincere thanks to my fellow workshop participants, for their insightful comments. Dr. N. Ben Lazreg, from the Institut National du Patrimoine in Tunisia, facilitated my work immensely. Dr. L. Stirling and Dr. D. Stone (Leptiminus Excavation and Survey Project) encouraged me to undertake this ethnoarchaeological study. The project has received financial support from the University of Cincinnati (University Summer Research Grants) and from the University of Arizona (Faculty Small Research Grants). D. Weibel and R. Lyng, from the University of Arizona School of Architecture, developed the Autocad drawings of the workshops.

Producing Pottery vs. Producing Models:
Interpreting Workshop Organization at the Potters' Quarter of Sagalassos

BY ELIZABETH MURPHY AND JEROEN POBLOME

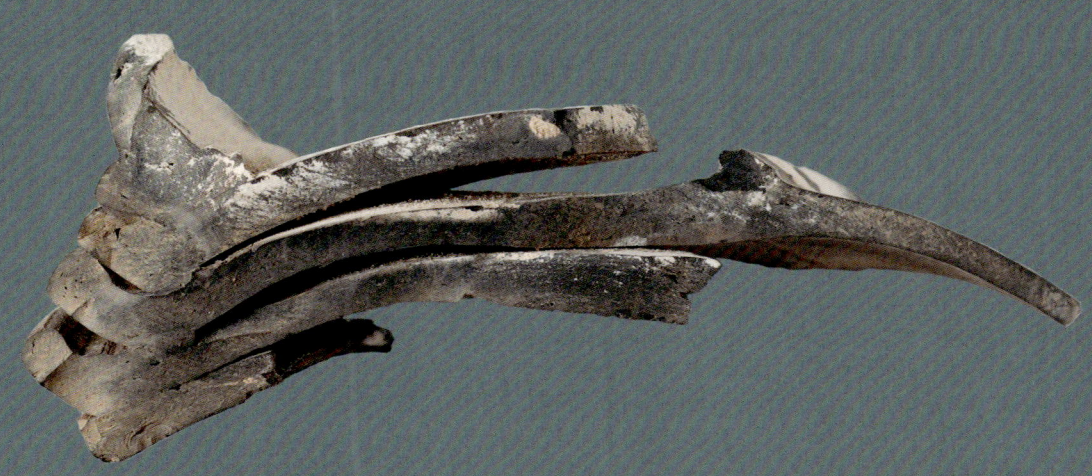

Producing Pottery vs. Producing Models: Interpreting Workshop Organization at the Potters' Quarter of Sagalassos

BY ELIZABETH MURPHY AND JEROEN POBLOME

Production studies hold significant and ever-developing potential for the field of ceramology, in ways that intimately tie into discussions of use-life. The role of production on the subsequent "life" of pottery can be considered in myriad aspects fundamentally related to the object, including its physical design and properties of its function. When considering manufacturing, Peña rightly remarks on the possibilities for detailed studies of production defects on pottery, noting the manner in which such material comprises part of the use-life of archaeological assemblages.[1] In addition, numerous social and economic dimensions are contingent on the character of production and the organization behind it, including the social position of artisans, cultural influences on the development of design, utilization of technologies, nature of distribution, and role of industry in contemporary economy. These themes are gradually being developed in the field, thereby providing greater relevance for ceramology and material culture studies to the broader archaeological discipline.[2]

In this paper we will argue that, in order to continue to develop upon these social themes and in order to more fully consider the role of production in the use-life of ceramic objects, it is first necessary to develop methodologies to begin to consider production settings and their associated material in multi-dimensional ways. No single line of study should be considered in isolation, but rather the workshop must be considered as a complex network of social, cultural, economic, and technological interactions that influence and recursively are influenced by each other, and which can be elucidated from the material record.[3] Integrated methodologies that attempt to provide a broader and multi-faceted dataset from pottery workshop settings are being developed and applied at the Potters' Quarter of Sagalassos, and some of the preliminary results and potential applications for the study of broader social issues will be discussed.

PREVIOUS SCHOLARSHIP

In the process of developing methodological approaches to consider issues related to production at the site of Sagalassos, the works of two scholars have proven foundational to the formation of a broad conceptual framework. First, discussions of Roman period production organization and scales of production have very much centered on the important work by David Peacock in *Pottery in the Roman World: an Ethnoarchaeological Approach*.[4] This text, fundamental in the promotion of ceramic production studies in Roman archaeology,[5] defines modes of production by classifying industries according to organizational complexity. Peacock, himself, warns against the potentially reductionist nature of this classification, which oversimplifies and blurs fundamental variability expressed in the archaeological record.[6] Likewise, although the present authors have drawn heavily on the conceptual framework and variables outlined by Peacock,[7] we posit that such classificatory schemes too narrowly define workshop settings and, as will be highlighted in the work being performed at Sagalassos, this classification system only begins to address the complexity of workshops present within even a single potters' quarter. Additionally, the work of Dean Arnold, *Ceramic Theory and Cultural Processes*,[8] has proven seminal to ancient ceramic production studies. This text impressively integrates a large corpus of ethnographic ceramic production data in an early attempt to theoretically blend systems thinking with cultural ecology.[9] Once again, although providing a very useful conceptual framework, which has been utilized by the present authors,[10] the generalizing theoretical nature of this text must be employed solicitously allowing for unique variability of each archaeological site.

In addition to the works by Peacock and Arnold, recent archaeological scholarship on crafts production in other regions has begun to proceed in different theoretical directions and to expand the application and interpretive potential of production studies. Aspects such as ritualized production, social value, *chaîne opératoire*, control over and transmission of knowledge, gender, and social standing of artisans, are beginning to take centre stage in the investigation of crafts industries in antiquity.[11] These avenues of study expand the implications of production studies and offer alternative means of integrating ceramology into broader archaeological inquiry. With these considerations, a diverse set of questions arises related to the ceramic industries of the Roman period. Indeed, Roman period industries, by encompassing a broad range of production expressions, hold particular potential for the pursuit of such objectives. Yet, in many respects, systematic and detailed analyses of these archaeological settings are still maturing. Lines of evidence must be identified and formulated for the study of social and economic dimensions of production. A multiplicity of methodological approaches for the material should be integrated in order to develop interpretations and models of workshop activity that appropriately express the complexity of the material record. These systematic methodologies should be expanded to permit comparative studies between production sites while addressing the uniqueness of each assemblage. Thus, having recognized these concerns and complications regarding the study of production settings, a first step in the integration of methodological approaches has begun to be implemented at the Potters' Quarter of Sagalassos.

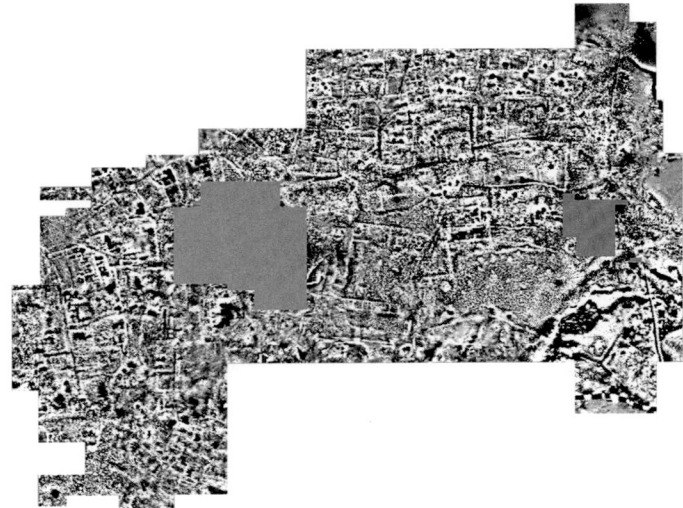

Fig. 1 Geophysical magnetometry across the area of the Potters' Quarter, Sagalassos. Dark lineaments appear to indicate the presence of walls and passageways. White dots appear to indicate the presence of kilns/furnaces.

DEVELOPMENT OF METHODOLOGIES:
THE POTTERS' QUARTER OF SAGALASSOS

Situated in the interior of southwestern Turkey, the ancient city of Sagalassos has been excavated since 1990 by the Sagalassos Archaeological Research Project under the direction of Mark Waelkens of the Katholieke Universiteit Leuven. Among the numerous discoveries unearthed at the urban site, a large, six-hectare potters' quarter has been identified in the eastern *suburbium* (Fig. 1).[12] At least from the 1st century BC to the 7th century AD, this industrial quarter witnessed the production of tableware with a primarily regional distribution: Sagalassos Red Slip Ware.[13] Study of ceramic production at the site has attempted to utilize and integrate numerous lines of evidence from the wealth of material thus far excavated from the Potters' Quarter. Particular emphasis has been placed on specific workshops concerning their infrastructure, abandonment material, and refuse found in associated production dumps. The workshop-specific material has subsequently been considered in comparison with significantly more extensive, contemporary production dumps from nearby areas of the Potters' Quarter.[14] Studies of such production refuse have successfully assessed the manner in which the workshop material is consistent with or divergent from material deriving from the large-scale production dumps of multiple workshops, which represent more comprehensive expressions of pottery production from the entire industrial area.

In addition, recent excavations in the Potters' Quarter are continuing to supply local workshop case studies for *comparanda*. By considering nuanced variability of production organization, comparative analyses between workshops are being performed regarding social and economic implications (i.e. potential production output, fiscal contribution to local industry and economy, social status of artisans, identity, roles, and ritual). These comparative considerations can then be used to assess variability across space (in terms of differentiation both within a production "centre" and between production "centres") in order to identify and track local and regional

1 Peña 2007, 33-35.
2 Poblome *et al.* 2006; Poblome *et al.* 2007.
3 Poblome 2004, 30.
4 Peacock 1982; Dark 1990, 7-8; Fülle 1997; Whittaker 2002, 18.
5 Peacock 1982, 8.
6 Peacock 1982, 8; Costin 2008, 144-5.
7 See for instance Poblome *et al.* 1998.
8 Arnold 1985.
9 Arnold 1985, 12-15.
10 See for instance Poblome 1996; Degryse & Poblome 2008.
11 Hruby & Flad 2008; Dobres 2000.
12 Mitchell & Waelkens 1987.
13 Poblome 2006a.
14 Poblome *et al.* 2002.

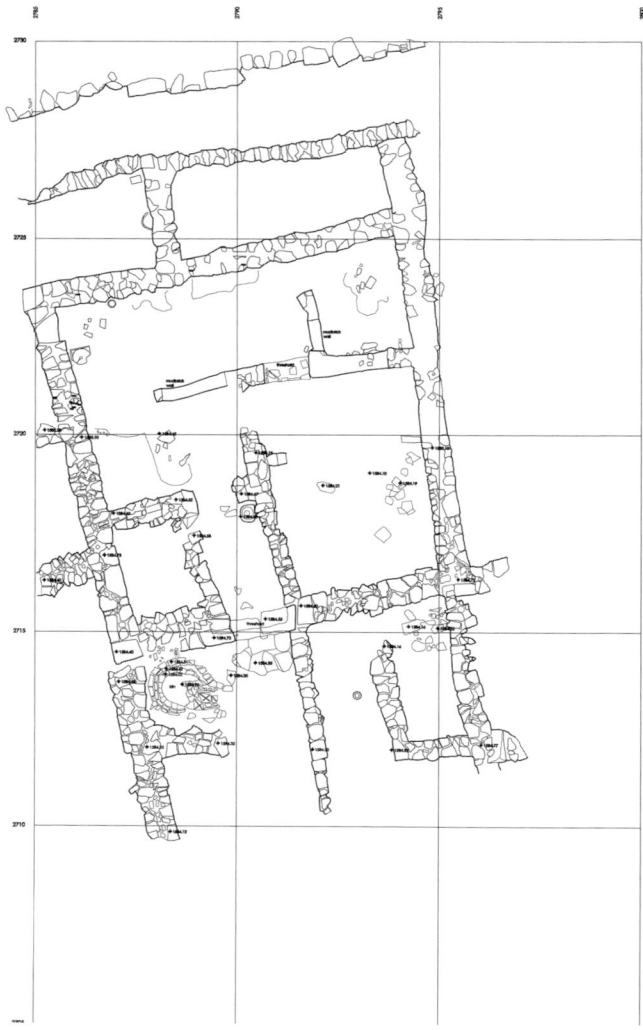

Fig. 2 Plan of a late Roman (4th - 6th centuries AD) coroplast workshop in the Potters' Quarter of Sagalassos.

LINES OF EVIDENCE

In developing methodologies for the study of workshop contexts, this project has emphasized (but is not limited to) four approaches. These lines of evidence include: workshop infrastructure analysis, material studies of production contexts, ethnographic considerations, and conceptual modelling exercises. Together, these areas of study present complementary considerations of the workshops, and although the full breadth of analyses cannot be explained in detail in this paper, as many such analyses are still on-going, some examples of the types of investigations being performed within each of these approaches will be described.

INFRASTRUCTURE

Recent investigations into the workshops of the Potters' Quarter at Sagalassos have resulted in a comparative study between two contemporaneous workshop contexts. The two late Roman (4th-6th centuries AD) Sagalassos Red Slip Ware workshops – a tableware production site,[16] and a coroplast workshop complex (Figs. 2-3) (producing *oinophoroi*, oil lamps, and figurines) – have been identified by remote sensing techniques as being situated on the same street within the Potters' Quarter, and are located circa 50m from each other. Both workshops are constructed using similar architectural styles – mudbrick walls on a rubble-rock foundation. In this spatial and chronological respect, the two workshops can be considered as components of the same production "centre".

Superficially the two workshop settings also present very similar pictures of production. Both workshops utilized the same clays and slips and most likely were integrated into the same distribution networks of raw materials, particularly those providing Çanaklı clay from a valley source eight kilometres down-slope from Sagalassos. Likewise, both workshops utilize similar technologies, including potters' wheels, and simple updraft kilns with combustion chamber diameters measuring less than 1.5 m. Moreover, many of the same tools (potters' ribs, fettling knives, stamps, hairpins and *styli*) appear among the remains of both workshops. However, on closer evaluation of the architectural and infrastructure remains, the workshops begin to demonstrate very different internal organizations that may not only be a function of the different wares being produced. In terms of their relative architectural infrastructure, the two workshops are very different in their contextual settings. While the tableware workshop is an architecturally independent building,

trends. In many respects, the types of observations being recorded may appear to be unexceptional and routine avenues of study; however, due to the monotonous and time-consuming nature of such analyses, these investigations have often been avoided or only partially pursued. The potential for such detailed analyses of production contexts and associated waste to provide important data for archaeological inquiry has been repeatedly invoked by ceramologists.[15] Nevertheless, this material still remains largely understudied, and projects like that at the Potters' Quarter of Sagalassos are still in their early stages.

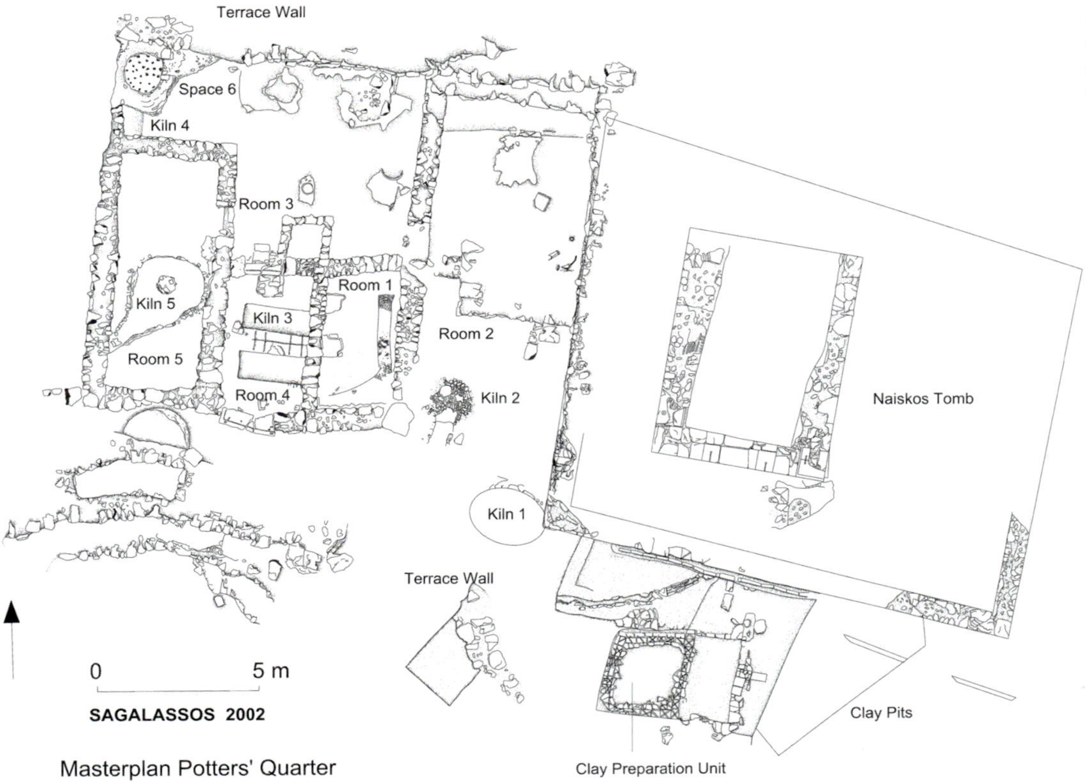

Fig. 3 Plan of a late Roman (4th -6th centuries AD) tableware workshop in the Potters' Quarter of Sagalassos.

the coroplast workshop is situated within a broader architectural "complex" comprising possibly four or five adjacent, yet discrete, workshops – each with exterior courtyards containing kiln(s). All of the workshops of this "complex" appear to be producing coroplast wares of similar types (namely *oinophoroi*, figurines, and oil lamps). In addition, stamp/mould matches have been identified in abandonment contexts between these workshops, suggesting some degree of exchange and interaction of tools and resources between the coroplast production units. In contrast to the independently situated tableware workshop, the coroplast workshop is organized according to a much more integrated production complex with separate, yet closely related neighbouring workshops. Thus, it is argued that even within a single potters' quarter, significant contemporaneous variation is expressed by the architectural plans and organization of the workshops.

MATERIAL STUDIES

In addition to the infrastructure analyses described above, material from abandonment contexts from individual

workshops within the Potters' Quarter has been analyzed. These abandonment contexts represent a variety of material types including Sagalassos Red Slip Ware, coarse wares, tools, kiln furniture, and wasters. The development of methodologies for the study of ceramic material from production contexts is in many respects divergent from traditional typo-chronological considerations of pottery assemblages. By identifying, documenting, and quantifying secondary traces of production techniques evidenced on ceramic sherds from various contexts, this study has developed numerous classifications of the material record from the Potters' Quarter. Drawing upon the typological framework of Sagalassos Red Slip Ware by one of the present authors,[17] quantifiable changes in the frequency and occurrence of these secondary production indicators are being tracked through time and between workshops in

---

15 Rye 1981, 110; Peña 2007, 35.
16 Poblome 2006b.
17 Poblome 1999.

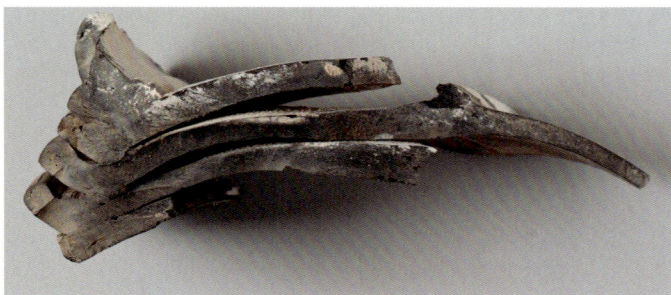

Fig. 4 Profile of a fused stack of SRSW vessels (type 1B230) from a late Roman (4th – 6th centuries AD) production refuse deposit.

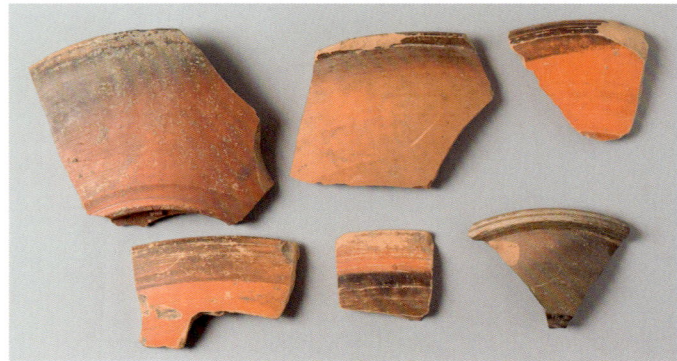

Fig. 5 Examples of SRSW sherds with reduced/oxidized rim discoloration zones (various vessel types) from a late Roman (4th – 6th centuries AD) workshop abandonment context.

the material record from the production site.

For instance, material derived from the late Roman table ware workshop and contemporary refuse deposits at Sagalassos has yielded much information, particularly regarding kiln stacking and firing techniques commonly being utilized between the 4th and 6th centuries at the site. By integrating several lines of evidence (fused stacks of over-fired vessels, oxidation/reduction patterns of surface coloration on vessels, and fragments of secondarily applied clay to support stacks of vessels in the kiln), detailed reconstructions of kiln loading procedures have been developed. For example, fused stacks of over-fired wasters demonstrate that vessels of the same type are typically nested together in the same stack (Fig. 6). The flow direction of partially melted vessels indicates that vessels are overwhelmingly stacked "right side up". Likewise, delineated reduction/oxidation zones (e.g. reduced rims with oxidized bodies), demarcate vessel parts that had been differentially exposed to firing environments within the kiln (Fig. 4). Such surface colour transitions can occur due to a variety of firing circumstances (tightness of stacking, points of contact between vessels in stacks, placement of stacks within larger vessels, etc.). Patterns in such surface oxidation/reduction zones are tracked according to specific vessel forms; these observations are then compared to patterns observed in fused wasters of the same vessel types, and consequently, some of the circumstances dictating these surface coloration patterns can be interpreted. Finally, the excavation of production refuse contexts has recovered numerous fired clay fragments, which appear to have been used to support stacks of vessels in the kiln during firing. The morphology of these fragments – often with distinctive rim impressions still extant – suggests strategic placement of

the clay pieces against stacked vessels just prior to firing. In some instances, examples of wasters have been observed to which the secondarily applied clay pieces are still attached. These sherds preserve evidence regarding the method by which such clay was applied in the stacking process and support kiln loading reconstructions based on fused stacks and reduction/oxidation patterns of wasters. The material from the Potters' Quarter offers a large corpus from which to extract typical measurements of distances (e.g. distance between vessel rims in a stack), which are recorded according to vessels and dimensions of vessel types (Fig. 5). These measurements are then used to spatially model kiln loads for use in production volume studies. The results from these analyses indicate that many form-specific techniques for loading the kilns were implemented in the Potters' Quarter during the 4th to 6th centuries AD, and the selection/adaptation of these techniques would have been related to the product repertoire of each workshop.

Furthermore, close analysis of "waster" vessels from these production dumps yields significant data concerning aspects of production "defects".[18] In fact, such bodies of material present a broad range of material that appears to have been purposely discarded in the production setting. Numerous examples of spalling, cracking, warping, over-firing, etc., have been observed and documented by the ceramic production study. These observations can then be used to compare Sagalassos Red Slip Ware types in order to identify forms that may have been more "prone" to specific defects. Utilizing the detailed chronology of Sagalassos Red Slip Ware typology, it is possible to temporally correlate

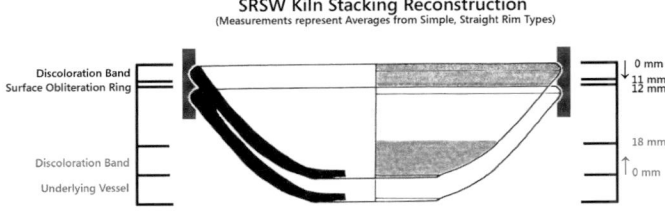

SRSW Kiln Stacking Reconstruction
(Measurements represent Averages from Simple, Straight Rim Types)

Fig. 6 Example of kiln stacking reconstruction of simple, straight rim vessel types and spacer strips.

Sagalassos Red Slip Ware from various contexts across the site of Sagalassos. Ceramics deriving from urban contexts can also be compared with the Potters' Quarter refuse dumps to consider thresholds of production defects – as related to local distribution and consumption patterns. Detailed observation from such large deposits of Sagalassos Red Slip Ware has already identified changing patterns in surface oxidation/reduction through the centuries of production in the Potters' Quarter. From the 4th century AD, Sagalassos Red Slip Ware from the Potters' Quarter begins to display a notably darker (more reduced) surface coloration than material from the preceding centuries. Such surface coloration changes, intentional or not, can be the result of numerous alterations in the firing process (differences in kiln type, stacking procedures, fuel type, duration and intensity of firing, etc.). Through detailed analyses of production settings (specifically related to kiln design and furniture, use of container forms to hold stacks of tableware, and archaeobotanical observations of changing fuel types from the city), several of these variables are being evaluated for applicability or rejection. Although the exact motivation for this change is still being investigated, this example demonstrates that significant changes in production techniques (and possibly technologies) occurred over time within the Potters' Quarter.

In addition to wasters and kiln furniture, production contexts have provided numerous tools. These instruments include potters' ribs, trimmers, *styli*, moulds, roulette wheels, stone palettes and hand mortars, axe heads, and turntable fragments. This corpus probably only represents a small fraction of the tools originally used in the production process. Nevertheless, the tools recovered demonstrate a range of morphologies utilized in the Sagalassos Potters' Quarter and suggest specific technological constraints on production. By comparing the tool morphologies represented in workshop contexts with the secondary production traces visible on ceramic products, moulds and stamps, it is possible to discern specific uses of tools for ceramic production. For example, it is clear that fettling knives found in high frequency in the coroplast workshop are typically used to cut excess clay protruding from the edges of moulds and to cut neck holes for oinophoroi. Multiple incising tools (i.e., combs, hairpins, and styli) are often used in combination for the production of a single decorated mould. In addition, personally inscribed objects, particularly potters' ribs and moulds, appear to demarcate possessions (and perhaps reflect roles) of craftspeople within the production environment. This may have significant implications for the way in which tasks were internally organized, as spaces for at least three potters' wheels were observed in a late Roman tableware workshop suggesting that throwers were working side-by-side in the production setting. In addition, what would often be classified as "non-pottery" related objects (i.e. hairpins and *styli*) have been found in high frequency in the workshop settings and may have implications for the way in which ancient potters related the broader contemporary material world to their craft. It is important to note – for the purpose of highlighting workshop variability – that inscribed objects are not consistently represented across all tool types. Rather, certain types (e.g. lamp moulds) appear to be more frequently inscribed with potters' marks than others (e.g. *oinophoroi* moulds). Such variation possibly hints at organizational variability in producing different object classes even within the same workshop settings.

ETHNOGRAPHIC CONSIDERATIONS
Use of ethnographic approaches for archaeological purposes has justifiably raised much criticism,[19] concerning both ethical concerns and analogy with archaeological remains. When used with care, however, ethnographic studies can demonstrate the potential variability and complexity of ceramic industry organizations, give insight into specific technologies for which few other sources exist, and offer a humanistic reflection on ancient industries that is often only represented by fragmentary archaeological remains.

18 As described by Peña 2007, 32-33.
19 Gould & Watson 1982; Bahn 1989; David & Kramer 2001.

For the purposes of this study, ethnographic analogies are referenced as a means of conceptualizing the complexity of ceramic production without dictating archaeological interpretations. For instance, efforts to estimate ancient workshop output at Sagalassos amply demonstrate the value of considering ethnographic evidence. Much previous archaeological literature regarding this topic for the Roman period has centred both on analyses of kiln loading accounts from sites, such as la Graufesenque,[20] Arezzo,[21] Pergamon,[22] and Pisa,[23] and comparisons of kiln size from workshops.[24] The evidence for kiln size is of particular interest for this project, as the updraft kilns thus far excavated in the Potters' Quarter can be considered to be of relatively "modest" dimensions (typically with firing chambers between 1 m. and 2.5 m. in diameter). However, workshops are often associated with small courtyard/outdoor areas containing two or more of these kilns, thus raising questions concerning the relation of firing frequency to production output. Ethnographic case studies offer some important insight. A workshop at Gujrat, Pakistan, described by Owen S. Rye and Clifford Evans, alternately fired two wood-fired updraft kilns (each with c. 2 m. firing chamber dimensions) – while one heated, the other cooled, and firings were performed every four to five days.[25] Such rapid firing rates described ethnographically have, consequently, influenced our perceptions of the relationship between kiln size, number of kilns, and production output potential. This example illustrates that simple associations between isolated aspects of infrastructure must be re-evaluated with reference to the organization of the entire workshop complex. We argue that such investigations can begin to be pursued by developing integrated multi-dimensional archaeological methodologies that conceptually consider ethnographic accounts.

CONCEPTUAL MODELS OF PRODUCTION

Initial observations and reconstructions deriving from the methodologies cursorily outlined above for the ceramic production study of the Potters' Quarter at Sagalassos suggest that many earlier models of ceramic production, which have been utilized in Roman ceramology, should begin to be revisited. The detailed nature of such investigations that support more complex reconstructions of workshops can be used to assess the applicability (or inapplicability) of such models and to formulate new conceptual frameworks based on greater diversity of

production expression and operation in the Roman world and even within the same production "centre". Such diversity is beginning to demonstrate patterns reflecting local/regional variability and/or temporal changes in production activities, which may have social, cultural, economic, and/or technological implications. Initial observations deriving from the ceramic production study at Sagalassos suggest variability in infrastructure within the production "centre" among contemporaneous workshops, variable production markings present on different types of moulds within a single workshop, and changes in firing techniques occurring throughout the Potters' Quarter beginning in the 4th century AD. Thus, the archaeological patterns being observed by employing the methodologies described in this paper suggest that many of the early models developed for ceramic production "centres"[26] do not adequately manage the variability being interpreted for the archaeological remains of the Sagalassos Potters' Quarter workshops. That is, the generalizing nature of the models is not able to adequately classify the broad range of behaviours and production organizations that are emerging in the archaeological record. Instead, new models of complexity utilizing the breadth of evidence derived from these approaches should be formulated for the assessment of Roman-period production.

The development of these methodologies represents a first step in the pursuit of more complex questions that are beginning to be revealed in the archaeologies of other regions. But by generating detailed reconstructions of production organization and models of complexity, this projectprovides necessary groundwork from which more social questions related to ancient industry can be conceived in dynamic ways both in comparison between production settings and within individual production "centres". The Roman period ceramic industries, already recognized as possessing a wide range of variability, in particular, offer tremendous potential for the application of such studies.

20 Marichal 1988.
21 Johnston 1985.
22 Poblome et al. 2001, 164-165.
23 Camodeca 2006.
24 Fülle 1997, 136.
25 Rye & Evans 1976, 87.
26 Leeuw 1976, Peacock 1982.

Greek Amphorae in
the Archaeological Record

BY MARK L. LAWALL

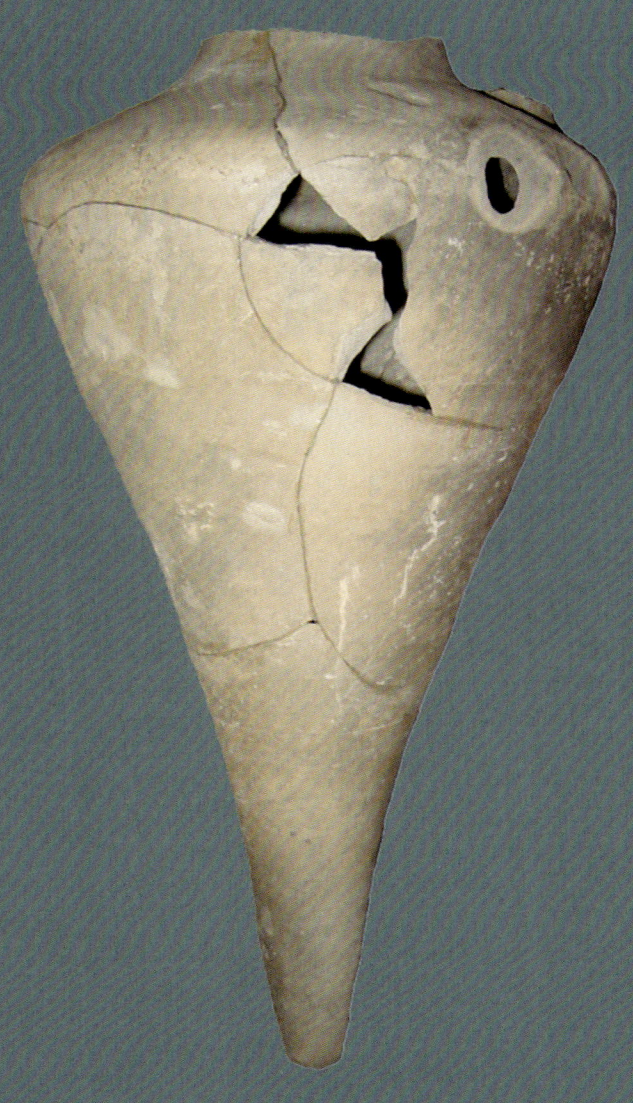

Greek Amphorae in the Archaeological Record

BY MARK L. LAWALL

Since much of *Roman Pottery in the Archaeological Record* considers ceramic life histories in terms of the use of amphorae in the Roman world, a natural follow-up topic is amphora use in the Greek world. While some studies have considered the practical aspects of amphora use, especially in terms of methods of sealing, packing, and moving, and while there are scattered references to the subsequent re-use of the jars, there has been no comprehensive view of the broader use life of amphorae that would parallel Peña's treatment of the Roman period.[1] As a starting point towards this broader goal, I propose here to move through a fairly wide range of issues and examples highlighting various implications of Peña's approach for the study of amphorae and amphora-related shipping in the pre-Roman Mediterranean. The result is not intended to be comprehensive, but the extent of the examples and references is intended to provide an initial view of the Greek amphora world in the terms set out by Peña. This process not only draws out a comparison between Greek (roughly pre 100 BC) and Roman (post 100 BC) amphora use and hence between Greek and Roman economies, but also highlights the importance of many of the methodological challenges raised by *Roman Pottery in the Archaeological Record*.

Peña's book opened and closed with a series of flow diagrams illustrating the life histories of various classes of Roman pottery. In order to compare the situations for Greek amphorae with those for Roman, this paper, too, is structured with a view towards building similar flow diagrams. Current research interests related to Greek amphorae and pre-Roman Mediterranean trade, including differing scales of production, the use of amphora stamps, and the intersection between the archaeological record on land with the maritime record, all encourage the introduction of some differences between Peña's diagrams and those offered here. While no more conclusive than their prototypes offered by Peña, these 'Greek' flow models are offered as heuristic devices drawing attention to new research targets.

This paper, thus, on a smaller scale than its model, moves through the life histories of Greek amphorae starting with the initial stages of production and filling. Once filled, the jars are either used locally or exported. The length of this primary use period can be approximated using the evidence provided by closely datable Greek amphora stamps. The final discard of the amphorae into the archaeological record might then be delayed by re-use, whether for re-filling and re-shipment, ongoing storage, or radically different re-uses as construction materials. To some extent the life histories of Greek amphorae appear similar to the situations Peña has documented for their Roman counterparts; however, certain significant differences also begin to emerge as one moves through the comparison.

PRODUCTION AND FILLING

Differences between Greek and Roman practice may be found at the earliest point in the life histories of Greek amphorae in the spatial relationship between amphora production sites and agricultural zones. While Peña can justifiably downplay the phase of movement between the amphora production site and the site where the jars were filled for Roman period activity,[2] movement between potter and agriculturalist in the Greek world may have been a more substantial phase in the use life of Greek amphorae.

The Location of Production

The location of the amphora production site, in relation both to the production sites of the goods destined for the jars and to the initial point in the jars' distribution (local market, port, etc.), shapes the initial stages of the life history of the amphorae. Were the jars stockpiled for later distribution, circulated to filling stations in small batches as they are fired, or gathered by middlemen for onward distribution to the filling stations? Once filled, were the jars shipped overland again to the distribution points (ports or access points to overland routes), or could they be simply exported from the production site? There is a tendency to assume that amphorae were produced near filling stations; and yet kilnsites are also noted to occur along the coast with proximity to maritime transport offered as the primary explanation. Proximity either to market centers, whether urban or rural, or to major port sites (as opposed to minor anchorages) will also have played a role in shaping activity involved in amphora production and initial distribution. Depending on the regional geography, these factors need not be incompatible, and yet determining the relative importance of such factors is often difficult due to the uneven knowledge of workshop locations. A brief summary of some better-studied regions illustrates the situation.

The scatter of workshop sites around Thasos must have resulted in proximity between farms and kilns even if another (or the) motivation for placement of the Thasian kilns was their proximity to accessible, high-quality clay beds.[3] The distribution of Thasian kilnsites, however, might be considered, too, in terms of access to the points of export. The highest density of known kilnsites is on the west coast of the island while the better anchorages and the major ancient settlement sites are on the south and east coasts between Thasos in the north and Demetrion (Limenaria) in the southwest.[4] In the case of Paros the Hellenistic kilnsites are situated around the Bay of Naoussa and the northeastern coast of the island in areas where the better agricultural land extends to the coast. For Naxos the two known sites are likewise bordering agriculturally viable land, though neither appears as well situated for shipping as is the case with the Parian sites clustered in the Bay of Naoussa. Empereur and Picon raised the possibility that underlying geology, this time shaping locations for successful viticulture, helped determine the location of kilnsites found on Paros and Naxos. On both islands the sites appear on the coast generally where the better agricultural lands continue towards the sea.[5] Empereur noted a similar coastal distribution of the widely scattered Rhodian workshops, though none of those reported in passing has been published.[6] In most cases the broader rural or urban context of kilnsites is poorly understood. For example, the many kilnsites in the vicinity of Knidos and the Rhodian Peraea seem to be rural establishments for the most part, but there is little or no information on nearby rural settlements or evidence for wine or oil production (e.g., press stones from rural survey).[7] The Reşadiye kilnsite is described as being in the middle of the plain that divides the two more mountainous sections of the Datça peninsula. With such a location, the site may be very near the main road linking Knidos to the mainland while at the same time being near many farms as well as access points along the coast. Amphora production sites on the islands of Peparethos and Ikos are well-situated for access to the sea, the urban centres and agricultural territory; though one on Peparethos (the Gkikas site) is situated more inland than the others.[8] Many workshop sites are better viewed as urban or suburban, and many of these show a mixture of amphora and plainware

production. The amphora kilns from early 6th century levels at Klazomenai,[9] the Classical kilnsites at Kos and Kerkyra[10] and the early Hellenistic kilnsites at Akanthos and Mende,[11] the Hellenistic and later kilns at Sinope,[12] and the very late Hellenistic/early Imperial site at Aigio are all within or very near the ancient urban centers.[13] For the most part, however, the spatial relationship between kilnsites and urban centers or rural farmsteads has not been a focal point for scholarship; there has been some greater interest in the relationship between the kilnsites and agriculturally advantageous land.

The likelihood that empty jars would have been transported some distance to be filled finds support in the Hellenistic papyri describing orders of empty jars by wineries for filling; in some cases these are new jars, in other cases re-used.[14] In either case, the movement of empties to the filling station was clearly an important and potentially difficult step in the chain of amphora-use. In one notable episode, 3000 jars of various types (including Chian, Parian, Paphian, and Kouriote) were shipped by mule and wagon from Syron Kome, at the eastern margin

---

1 For the methods of primary use of amphorae, see Koehler 1986; specific cases of re-use are cited below.

2 Peña 2007, 35 and 325.

3 Picon & Garlan 1986, 293-294 on the proximity to areas where geological fault zones might generate higher-quality clays; Ian Whitbread observes that the landscape and geology of Thasos makes placing a kiln distant from a geologic fault zone and water source rather difficult (1995, 182-184).

4 Garlan 2004-2005, 270 fig. 1; cf. Lazarides 1971, fig. 32.

5 Empereur & Picon 1986a, 496-498.

6 Empereur & Picon 1986b, 115; see also Lund in press.

7 Empereur 1988; Empereur & Tuma 1988; Empereur, Hesse & Tuna 1999; Empereur & Picon 1986; Tuna et al. 1991; Doğer 1994; Doğer & Şenol 1996; Cankardeş Şenol et al. 2004.

8 Doulgéri-Intessiloglou & Garlan 1990, 368-371.

9 Ersoy 2003; and Doğer 1986 (including later workshops).

10 Kos (Κάντζια 1994); Kerkyra (Preka-Alexandri 1992).

11 Akanthos (Τρακοσοπούλου–Σαλακίδου 2004[2006]a and Garlan 2004[2006]a; 2006), the kilnsite is between the area of the necropolis on the beach and the city center at the mouth of the Souilos river; Mende (Αναγνωστοπούλου–Χατζηπολυχρόνη 2004[2006]; Garlan 2004[2006]b), the site is on the coast, outside, but not far from, the urban center.

12 For the most comprehensive discussion, see Garlan 2004 for the Hellenistic period kilnsites; also Kassab Tezgör 1996 and Kassab Tezgör & Tatlıcan 1998 for later Roman period kilns.

13 Aigio kilnsite is largely unpublished, but see notice in ADelt 36 (1981) B1, 171.

14 The provision of jars to wineries is discussed by Dzierzbicka 2005, 37-41; Mayerson 2000a; and Kruit & Worp 2000, passim.

of the Fayoum, and from Kerke, about 25 km north of Syron Kome along the Nile, to Philadelphia (just over 10 km from Kerke and at least 25 km from Syron Kome) for re-coating, presumably for later refilling.[15] An even greater transportation distance of empty jars may be implied by the Ahiqar customs list of 475 BC (?)[16], in which the duty paid by Ionian ships includes both coated and uncoated empty jars. Thirty empty jars tend to be paid in duty for each 'large' ship, perhaps indicating a total empty cargo of 150 empty jars per large ship.[17] For perspective, the same ships tend to carry 107 wine jars and 47 oil jars.[18] These 'empty jars' may have been smaller, perhaps plain and fine-ware vessels, not amphorae at all.[19] Less impressive, but also perhaps more reflecting common practice, is the ostrakon (O. Bodl. I 346) referring to Kolophonian amphorae being re-used to package local wine; whether these jars were emptied and stockpiled at the winery or brought in empty from elsewhere is unknown.[20] Despite such attestations of the use of empty amphorae in Ptolemaic Egypt and likely earlier, the term κούφα does not appear denoting empty amphorae until the Augustan period.[21] Such a shift in vocabulary could reflect a more intensive or at least more formalized use of empties from the 1st century BC.

The Timing of Amphora Production

A further variable in this early stage in the amphora's life is the need for stockpiling jars ahead of their being filled. For the most part in the Greek world we do not know how constant or seasonal amphora production might have been; seasonality tends to be assumed. For example, Christoph Börker's discussion of the order of months in the Rhodian calendar is based on the assumption (informed by Hampe and Winter's studies of modern potters) that winter dampness will have slowed drying time and decreased production.[22] In his reconstruction of the sequence of Rhodian months, the rising and falling numbers of Rhodian stamps naming the different months corresponds well with the fluctuations of rainfall levels in the Aegean. The resulting order of the months, with Badromios in early Spring (February) and Karneios closing out the Fall (October) works with the few relevant inscriptions and gives a quite regular bell-curve of amphora production rising to a peak in Panamos (July) when rainfall is at a minimum, and declining smoothly into the Fall. Ju. S. Badal'yants, however, proposes a somewhat different order for the later summer and Fall months, precisely those least well-fixed by epigraphical evidence.[23] Following his reconstruction of the calendar there is a significant slow-down

in production around August (Karneios), followed by another period of high production in September (Dalios) and October (Thesmophorios), before the decline in mid winter (Diosthuos, Pedageitnuos and Badromios).

Production of the agricultural goods to go into the jars was obviously seasonal, with the vintage in late summer and olive pressing in the winter. At this point the disputed order of the later months becomes significant for the interpretation of the link between amphora production and the production of amphora contents. Using Börker's calendar, one might see either 1) a considerable effort expended to produce and stockpile jars ahead of the vintage, with bottling perhaps in the late Fall and exports in the following summer sailing season, or 2) amphora production for more immediate bottling of the previous Fall's vintage and shipping through the summer. In the former case, amphorae could be a year old at the time of initial export; in the latter case, the jars would be very new while the wine was older. Papyrological evidence for bottling at the winepress and allowing the wine to finish its fermentation in the amphorae would argue against the shorter span between bottling and shipping envisioned in this latter scenario; however, the precise sequence of fermentation and bottling remains a topic of debate.[24] Furthermore, the placement of so many kilnsites with seemingly more interest in access to agriculturalists as opposed to major port facilities also weakens the link between potters and shippers. Using Badal'yants' calendar, the intensive production during the summer could again be seen as preparatory for the Fall vintage, but the second spike in production later in the Fall might be seen as preparation for the oil pressing. Such a bimodal distribution of production is difficult to interpret in terms of bottling on demand for shipping in light of the general view that maritime trade slowed considerably in the winter months. The extent to which shipping entirely shut down in late Fall and Winter has perhaps been overstated, so the link between late Fall amphora production and shipping rhythms cannot be entirely ruled out.[25]

Without hoping to resolve these conflicting views of the Rhodian calendar here, I raise these possibilities simply to highlight the implications that might be drawn from such particularly detailed aspects of the Greek amphora record.

PRIME-USE TO DISCARD

While the Rhodian class is the only one to offer such details as the month of production, quite precise dates of production can be assigned to Greek amphorae of various other classes, too (e.g., Thasian, Sinopean, Chersonesan, and, to a lesser extent, Knidian[26]). Such closely datable amphorae in closed deposits allow consideration of the period from production to deposition. Many stamped Greek amphora assemblages can be studied in terms of their rate of accumulation before the point of their entry into the archaeological record. Such an exercise can be carried out on only a few Roman amphora assemblages, those involving jars marked with consular names.[27] In these terms anyhow, the Greek record can be studied with much more precision and breadth. And yet, Greek amphora assemblages have rarely been studied with this question in mind. More often, the graphs of stamp counts from specific deposits (when considered at all) are interpreted in terms of fluctuations of imports under the assumption that each year's (or period's) count reflects the amount imported compared with other years. The focus of Peña's work shifts the question to one of differential chances of entry into the discard context depending on a wide range of variables including the time lag between production date and the time of final discard.

In many cases for the Greek archaeological record, it is possible to compare three variables:

P – the relative scale of production, as indicated by, for example, counts of known eponym stamps from a wide range of sites around the Mediterranean;

I – the relative scale of imports, as indicated by the amounts per period at the site in general; and

D – the distribution of datable stamps in the given deposit itself.

If values for *P* correlate well with values for *I*, and values for *I* correlate well with values for *D*, then fluctuations in quantities at the site and at the deposit in question depend simply on levels of production. The amphorae must have been discarded soon after importation in order for particular deposits to retain the patterning of relative intensity of production (and importation) from one period to the next. On the other hand, if *P* and *I* are not correlated with one another, but *I* and *D* are correlated, then patterns of trade or local historical circumstances must have negated the impact of rates of production; but as before, discard must have occurred soon after arrival to retain the patterning of the imports in each specific deposit. Finally, if there is a lack of correlation between *I* and *D*, then practices of use and discard play a larger role than patterns of imports in shaping the composition of the given deposit.

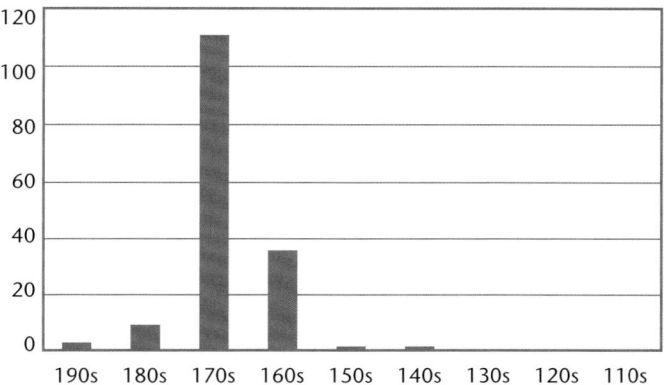

Fig. 1 Numbers of Rhodian eponyms datable within ten-year intervals from the Olbia Cistern (based on Леви 1964).

One example illustrates the process. The Rhodian amphora stamps from a cistern fill from the temenos area at Olbia Pontica (Fig. 1) may be compared against the

15 Kruit & Worp 2000, 86-87, citing PCair Zen IV 59741, including Kouriote, Paphian, Parian, along with Chian. Interestingly Syron Kome was home to a Jewish potter and his family in the 2nd century BC (BGU VI 1282).
16 The difficulties with the date are reviewed by Briant & Descat 1998, 61-62.
17 Yardeni 1994 suggesting a tax rate of 1/5 on Ionian ships' cargoes; cf. Briant & Descat 1998, 78-79 on the complexities of the tax rates used and hence the difficulties of reconstructing the sizes of the original cargoes in question.
18 Yardeni 1994.
19 Cited by Briant & Descat 1998, 71.
20 Kruit & Worp 2000, 82.
21 Mayerson 1997.
22 Börker 1978; cf. Hasaki this volume.
23 Бадальянц 1970.
24 On further fermentation in amphorae, see Mayerson 2000b, 164; Dzierzbicka 2005, 73-75; cf. Kruit 1992, especially 273-276. On bottling at wineries see Mayerson 2003. If, as Kruit argues, the wine was fermented in vats and not bottled until it was finished, the bottling would start in early summer perhaps using 'new' jars.
25 The Elephantine papyrus records no ships for the months of Thoth and Paophi (roughly January and February), see Yardeni 1994, 69; however Horden & Purcell 2000, 143 raise the likelihood of some continued sailing through the winter, particularly for those ships involved in fairly short distance circulation of goods (as seems to characterize amphora circulation for the Archaic and Classical periods, see Lawall 2006). The seasonality of Mediaeval sailing is detailed in McCormick 2001, 450-468.
26 For recent chronological studies of these classes, see Garlan 2004-2005; Garlan 2004; Stolba 2005b; for Knidian, see Grace 1985.
27 Peña 2007, 51-54.

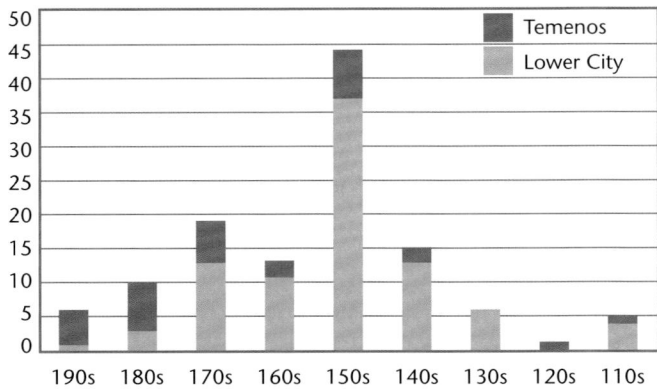

Fig. 2 Numbers of Rhodian eponyms datable within ten-year intervals from the Olbia temenos and the Lower City (based on Диатроптов 2006 and study by the author).

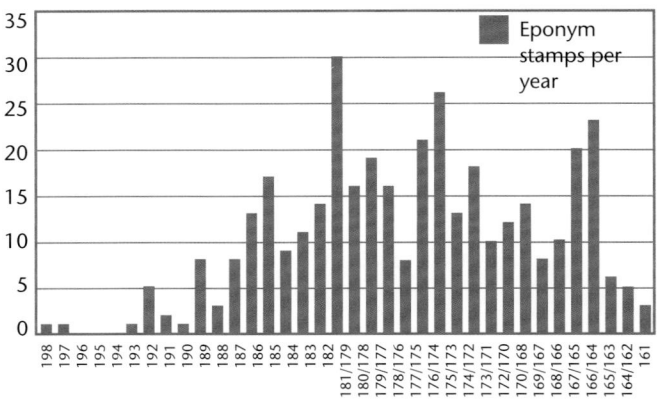

Fig. 3 Chronological distribution of Rhodian eponyms in the Pergamon deposit (Counts based on Börker, dates based on Finkielsztejn 2001).

aggregate pattern for imports (*I*) to the site as built up from recently published Rhodian stamps from the temenos (not including the cistern) and from the Lower City (1985-2000 excavations) (Fig. 2).[28] For a comparative view of Rhodian production (*P*), one can refer to the graph compiled by John Lund synthesizing data from various sites on Rhodes itself.[29] In that graph, Lund illustrates a peak in Rhodian production ca. 200 BC followed by a significant decline to a plateau lasting from the 170s through the end of the 2nd century. The pattern of fluctuation in Rhodian imports to Olbia, *I*, differs from *P* in the low counts for the 190s and 180s and the sharp rise in the 140s. Clearly, the general pattern of Rhodian imports to Olbia was not determined by fluctuations in Rhodian production; other political and/or economic factors in the link between Olbia and the southern Aegean must have played a role in shaping the record of imports to Olbia. The distribution of datable stamps in the Olbia cistern fill, *D*, differs further from both *I* and *P*. Both the *D* and *I* show an increase into the 170s followed by a decline to the 160s, though they differ in magnitude. The curve for *D*, however, bottoms out with only a few examples datable to the 150s and 140s. These differences indicate that not every year's Rhodian amphora imports are represented in the cistern fill as a representative portion of those that were imported in each year. Fragments that were more than twenty years old by the time the cistern fill ceased accumulation do follow the pattern for *I* fairly well. Jars of the past generation, therefore, were sufficiently broken up and sufficiently common in trash collections as to reflect the original patterns of imports.

Jars of more recent decades, however, had a much-reduced chance of having entered a discard context.

A similar pattern of noticeably declining accumulation well before the final closure of the deposit in question is found in many other pre-Roman sites. The Pergamon Deposit, excavated and first published in the late 19th century, provides a well-known example. The topography and architectural phasing of the area make it very likely that the Rhodian amphorae comprising the bulk of the deposit had been in storerooms upslope from the deposit terrace and that the deposit itself was created once those storerooms were destroyed to make room for Palace V.[30] Figure 3 graphs the numbers of eponym stamps pertaining to each year (following Gérald Finkielsztejn's chronology) as reported from the deposit.[31] Most of the accumulation occurred into the middle decade or so of the period represented by the deposit; the last five years include relatively little new accumulation.

While the local circumstances of trade, specific behaviors surrounding these deposits, and reliance simply on the datable amphora stamps are all potential problems, there is a striking consistency across these deposits in terms of the observed drop-off in numbers a decade or more before the close of the deposit. Both the degree to which such drop-off occurs and the degree to which such patterns correlate with overall patterns of imports at a site together inform our understanding of amphora discard practices as well as the accumulation of debris at each site and each specific context.

This initial, admittedly incomplete, glimpse differs

from the Roman archaeological record. At both the Castro Praetorio site and the Carthage amphora wall there are increasing numbers of jars closer to the end date of the deposit.[32] In the various Greek contexts just discussed, the peak of datable stamps occurs a decade or more earlier than the closing date. The entry pattern of amphorae' into the discard realm must have differed to achieve these two distributions of datable pieces.

TYPE A RE-USE

A significant factor creating such patterns of discard, indeed in delaying the entry of jars into the discard context, is Type A re-use: the refilling and reshipment of amphorae with either their principal or irregular contents.

Principal Contents Problem

A major impediment to estimating the extent of Type A re-use is the basic identification of amphorae as having contained principal or irregular contents. This very concept of primary and irregular contents is seemingly more problematic in Greek archaeology as compared with Roman.[33] Romanists tend to associate particular amphora types with particular contents. Hellenists more often argue that amphorae were simply containers intended for carrying a wide range of products.[34] This view is supported by the presence of pitch lining amphora shapes traditionally associated with oil. The multi-use view is also supported both by the rarity of multiple shapes from a single production area despite textual and other evidence for diverse crop production in that area,[35] and by descriptions of primary-use contents from Hellenistic papyri. Papyri describe Chian amphorae as containing wine, honey, hazel nuts, and olives; Thasian amphorae as containing wine, honey, and processed fish products; Rhodian amphorae as containing wine and honey (as well as beer, but this is considered to be an instance of local refilling).[36] Archaeological examples complement and supplement this impression of diverse amphora contents: olives in 'wine' amphorae,[37] cattle ribs in 'oil' amphorae,[38] pitch filling – not just lining – 'wine' amphorae,[39] some sort of mastic product in 'wine' amphorae,[40] almonds in 'oil' amphorae.[41] Granted, most – though not all – of these examples come from minor components of shipwreck cargoes and may represent Type A re-use, but at the very least they complicate any neat equation between amphora fragments and quantities of one imported product.

Shipwreck Evidence

Naturally, most of the evidence for contents comes from shipwrecks, and the concept of Type A re-use has a direct impact on interpreting shipwreck cargoes and amphora distribution patterns in general. A dominant view of ancient shipping sees mixed cargoes resulting from coastal trading over relatively short distances.[42] And yet, in many cases, the cargoes are either not mixed at all or there is a sharp quantitative distinction between the main (unmixed) cargo and the (very diverse but also very small) secondary assemblage, which might involve ship's supplies, leftovers from old cargoes, or actual small consignments. Put in terms of the use and re-use of amphorae, the main cargo is mostly comprised of amphorae in primary use while

---

28 The counts for the cistern are based on Леви 1964; for the temenos, Диатроптов 2006; for the lower city, counts and readings were compiled by Tatiyana Samoilova, Pavel Diatroptov and myself. Those stamps appearing in selected closed contexts are published in Lawall et al. 2010.

29 Lund 1999, 189-195; see also Lund in press.

30 Lawall 2002, 309-318.

31 For the Rhodian eponyms in the deposit, I follow Börker's updated publication (1998) of the material, replacing Schuchhardt 1895. For the chronology, see Finkielsztejn 2001. Chronological modifications suggested by Badoud forthcoming will change certain details of this graph but not the overall conclusions to be drawn.

32 Peña 2007, 51-54.

33 I address the issue in more length in a forthcoming publication of the papers from the second conference Production and Trade of Amphoras in the Black Sea (Lawall in press).

34 For recent and contrasting statements, see Opaiţ, 2007 and Garlan 2000, 67-91.

35 The cargo of the Siracusia is described as including 10,000 jars of pickled Sicilian fish along with grain, wool and other goods (Athenaeus V.206-209); Peparethos, whose epithet is 'euoinos' and whose wine is often praised (see Doulgèri-Intzessiloglou & Garlan 1990), was the source of salted fish in a broken keramion noted in the Zenon archive (Curtis 1991, 118). Doğer 1991 argues for Klazomenian production of both oil and garum, though only one amphora type is known for the city.

36 Kruit & Worp 2000.

37 Frey 1982, 5.

38 At Tektaş Burnu, see Carlson 2003, 589-590.

39 Also at Tektaş Burnu, Carlson 2003, 588-589.

40 From a wreck explored off the coast of Chios, see Hansson & Foley 2008.

41 From the Kyrenia shipwreck, see Katzev 2005.

42 Horden & Purcell 2000, 137-152 for a carefully nuanced discussion of cabotage and long-distance, directed shipping along standard routes, and 368-372 on "the normality of the mixed cargo"; and see McCormick 2001, 422.

the secondary assemblage involves amphorae at various stages of re-use. These re-used amphorae may be quite old. In this view of the maritime archaeological record, Type A re-use does not appear very common at least within the Aegean basin (and this point is well exemplified by the Serçe Limanı Hellenistic wreck, where any diversity in the cargo is represented by a single, perhaps older Thasian amphora, and in the main cargo only one eponym appears repeatedly[43]). Indeed, the more diverse cargoes with large numbers of Aegean amphorae come mostly from wrecks found in the western Mediterranean, e.g., the Porticello and El Sec wrecks.[44] Here the range and diversity of vessel types per cargo is much greater than within the Aegean. This contrast between the Aegean and Western Mediterranean maritime archaeological records leads to the perhaps expectable conclusion that Type A reuse is more likely to occur the farther one gets from the core production zone.

Not surprisingly, detailed examination complicates matters. The Kyrenia shipwreck would, at first glance, provide a good example of a main cargo of approximately 320 Rhodian amphorae of full size and approximately 25 fractional Rhodians all in primary use, and a scatter of other types most likely associated with thousands of almonds representing Type A re-use and perhaps even some Type B storage re-use for the ship's crew. The stamps on the Rhodian amphorae, however, introduce a complication. From the reasonable assumption that on these very early Rhodian amphorae one of the two abbreviations found on most of the stamped jars pertains to the eponym and the other to the fabricant (as will be the case in later Hellenistic Rhodians), there are at least four different years (eponyms) represented by the Rhodian jars.[45] If we assume that these are four consecutive years, then some of the jars were four years old when the ship sank. Yet, this assumption is not necessary. If these Rhodian amphorae are in prime use, they must have been in stockpile on Rhodes for some time before being gathered for this particular shipping venture. The wear on the jars themselves complicates matters further. The original catalogue cards from the excavation made frequent notations of ancient, worn breaks, including holes worn through the walls of some vessels. Such wear might be assumed to be the normal result of simple wave action over the centuries. Surprisingly, a survey of all shipwreck publications (monographs and journals) in the library of the American School of Classical Studies in Athens showed only four such holed vessels.[46] Of course, one can always turn a jar to show only the good side to the camera! More convincingly, a late 4th century Lesbian jar from a group of well preserved jars thrown into a pit at a small agricultural site near modern Cherson (Ukraine) shows the same sort of wear as seen on the Kyrenia amphorae.[47] Such wear, therefore, could occur on land and during a jar's ancient period of use. The other 'old breaks' – completely worn off rims, worn down handle breaks, etc. – on the Kyrenia jars could also represent wear and tear from years of use. The Kyrenia jars were either carrying goods that could still be held in such damaged containers or they were empty and headed for recycling. The tempting notion of a cargo of empty, old, decrepit amphorae is called into question by extensive experimentation by Susan Katzev showing that empty amphorae will pop to the surface and hundreds of empty amphorae might have enough buoyancy to rip off any restraining cover.[48] At this point the interpretation remains open pending further study of the distribution of signs of wear on jars and fragments throughout the cargo.

Repackaging to Offset Need for Local Amphora Production

Another ramification of the re-use of amphorae whether as refilling for reshipment or simply for storage, is the possibility that re-use of imported jars could supplant the need for local production. This idea is raised by Peña echoing an idea already floated by John Riley concerning the disappearance of local amphora production from later Hellenistic Berenike.[49] Such re-use, if on a sufficiently large scale, could explain the absence of any known Attic amphora type as the successor to the SOS and à la brosse types of the Archaic period. Although there is widespread assumption of exports of Athenian oil (some of which may have moved in Panathenaic amphorae),[50] there is no known Attic transport amphora type after the early decades of the 5th century. Various candidates are all better reattributed to other producers.[51] As noted earlier, the packaging of wine in Hellenistic Egypt was partly dependent on the re-use of emptied, re-resinated, imported amphorae; however, in this case local re-use co-existed with local production.

TYPE B AND C RE-USE
The Greek world shows certain important differences from the Roman world in the area of re-use of amphorae, either unmodified for a non-shipping purpose especially storage

(Type B re-use), or modified to serve as something other than a container altogether (Type C re-use).

Type B Re-use: Storage vs. Packaging

As more amphora assemblages are studied not just for the presence of major classes of amphora stamps (e.g., Rhodian, Thasian, Knidian) but for the wider range of identifiable types, amphorae produced within at least the general region of the site increasingly appear to have played a strong role in local storage and very localized movements of goods. Hence, the so-called Nikandros group amphorae dominate assemblages between Ephesos and Miletos (the production sites are not known, but they must be in that general area),[52] successive local amphora types dominate assemblages around the Troad and these types were rarely exported.[53]

In some cases it appears that the decision to use an amphora for storage purposes prolonged its use-life considerably. The best example of this phenomenon is seen in the collection of ten amphorae found in the narrow side room of a house constructed in the latter half of the 4th century BC and destroyed near the mid 3rd century near the Silen Gate on Thasos. Few of the jars are closely datable, but the one Chian amphora is of a form dating no later than the second quarter of the 5th century and the other jars are of forms that are most commonly paralleled in the late 5th century.[54] Elsewhere, too, intact jars tend to be the older, often by some decades, rather than the most recent pieces in deposits, suggesting that those jars curated for storage purposes lasted longer than was otherwise the case. For example, an entirely intact amphora in well R13:11 at the Athenian Agora shares a stamp with a large fragment found in a bothros likely closed by the construction of the Maussolleion at Halikarnassos and must, therefore, date before 351 BC, and possibly even earlier.[55] Other amphora fragments and finewares, however, make a closing date after ca. 325 BC more likely for R13:11. On a broader scale, Gerald Finkielsztejn has drawn attention to the fact that the most up to date fragments at Maresha, initially abandoned ca. 112 BC and entirely so by 108 BC, are small broken bits of stamped handles. The complete or nearly complete jars are decades older than the time of abandonment. A further element of practice to be drawn from Finkielsztejn's work is the preference for thicker-walled, western Mediterranean amphorae for such storage purposes. Such jars are significantly over-represented in the 'in situ' counts as compared with Aegean jars.[56]

Type C Re-use: Drainage, Fill, and Other Construction Features

Type C re-use refers to the use of amphorae or parts thereof for purposes other than storage or shipping. For example, one finds rows of Aegean amphorae buried in an inverted position in foundation levels of buildings, amphorae or sherds supporting a well shaft, and amphorae as the primary material for walls. Examples of inverted amphorae arranged in the subfloor levels of houses are relatively common in northern Greece, including Mesembria, Thasos, and Abdera.[57] A later, 3rd-century example is the Hôtel du Soleil deposit on Rhodes including 137 inverted Rhodian amphorae.[58] One of the best series of late 4th and early 3rd century B.C. amphorae in Athens was reconstructed from amphorae used as fill in the bedrock to support tiles a well shaft.[59]

In some cases, large numbers of amphorae have been found roughly aligned to create walls often of uncertain purpose. Perhaps the most influential example is the so-

43 Pulak *et al.* 1987.
44 Porticello, see Eiseman & Ridgway 1987; El Sec, see Cerdá 1987.
45 Lawall in press b.
46 A Punic amphora from the El Sec wreck (Cerdá 1987, pl. 18, no. 671); one possible example from the Bacoli wreck (Scognamiglio 1993, 156, fig. 7); and possibly two examples from the Mattoni wreck (Galli 1993, figs. 3 and 4). No such wear is illustrated in Zemer 1977, or in volumes of *Archeonautica, Cahiers d'archéologie subaquatique*, or various conference volumes on underwater archaeology.
47 I thank Valerya Bylkova for showing me the amphorae from the Belozerskoe excavations (see frontispiece of this paper).
48 S. Katzev, personal communication.
49 Peña 2007, 63; and Riley 1979, 120.
50 E.g., Reger 1994, 159-160; Valvanis 1986.
51 Lawall 1995, 223-225; responding to Grace 1971, 78 and 1953, 101-102, no. 147.
52 Lawall 2004a; 2005; Cankardeş Şenol 2001 on Metropolis material; Jöhrens 2004 on finds at Didyma.
53 Panas & Pontes 1998; Lawall 1999 and 2002 [2003].
54 Grandjean 1992, 575-581; cf. Garlan 1992, 211-213 and Empereur 2001.
55 Vaag et al. 2002, 95, no. A84, pl. 6, with discussion of the date of the bothros, p. 85.
56 Finkielsztejn 2002, p. 230, fig. 2; discussion pp. 231-231.
57 Τσατσοπούλου 1996, 918 fig. 2; for other examples see, from Abdera, Prakt 1956 fig. 46.a-b; and from Thasos, ADelt 1982[1989], 309, pl. 20 and ADelt 1979, 322, pl. 142.a.
58 Illustrated by Grace 1979, fig. 63. Another basement deposit with inverted amphorae is published by Φιλήμονος–Τσοποτού 2004, 65-66, note 250, pl. 23.
59 This is deposit F17:3, see Lawall 2004b, 447.

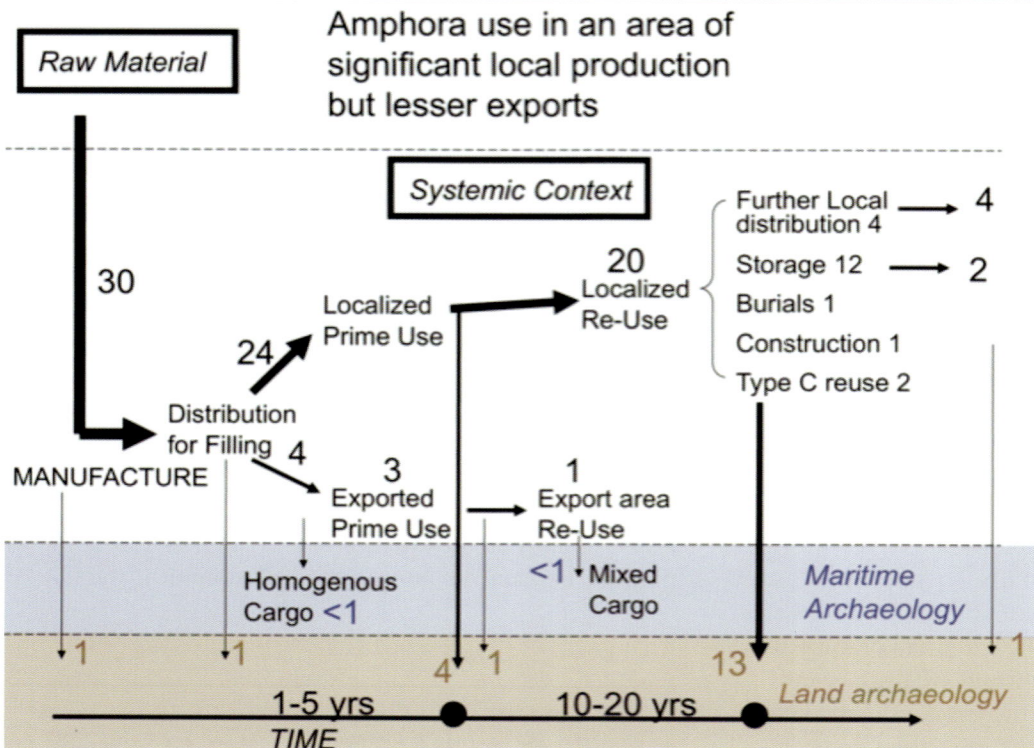

Fig. 4 Flow Diagram for Greek amphora use – regional production and distribution.

called Villanova deposit on Rhodes: a series of ca. 500 jars, mostly from the fabricant Diskos, arranged in two courses on the coast near ancient Ialysos.[60] Amadeo Maiuri's original publication of this deposit notes the presence of overfired pottery in the same area in support of seeing the site as a production center despite the appearance of multiple fabricant stamps (and even various imported amphorae). If it is a production site, then the 'fence' could represent a stockpile of jars accumulating over a number of years, jars that for whatever reason were never distributed. A similar structure has recently been illustrated from Akanthos,[61] and Gérald Finkielsztejn has reported similar uses of Classical period, Aegean amphorae used for constructions at Akko.[62]

And yet, despite these relatively early examples of amphora walls, the re-use of amphorae in construction features appears to become more common with increased exposure to the Roman or western Mediterranean world. Many of the Lamboglia 2 and Dressel form 6 amphorae inventoried in Athens were found in construction contexts for road-beds and well-shafts.[63] The latest Hellenistic

levels in the Tetragonos Agora at Ephesos, too, include large neck fragments of western Mediterranean amphorae embedded in a street surface perhaps for some function concerning drainage. Another example of re-use of western amphorae in the east is seen in the drainage channels near the Maison des Comédiens at Delos in which Maña C amphorae were converted to pipe segments by cutting off the bases and inserting the base of one into the mouth of the next.[64] Indeed, a significant problem in the study of the early appearance of Roman amphorae in the East and the Romanization of eastern trade is the valid comparison of quantities of these well-preserved pieces obviously selected for their robustness with quantities of eastern amphora sherds.[65] The use of Aegean amphorae for such construction purposes may have increased to a point of significance only after exposure to this Roman behavior (this is only a preliminary impression).

Type C Re-use – Modification of the jar
Type C re-use can also include individual amphorae that

have been modified for purposes entirely different from their original function as a transport container. Peña has already mentioned the example I published earlier of an archaic amphora cut down so that its base could be used to hold paint.[66] Archaic Greek amphora fragments are also noted as basins for plaster in shaft graves at Abusir.[67] Narrow, tapering amphora bases are sometimes pierced for use as a funnel. Amphora handles may be used to support molds in metal-working.[68] In Athens, the process of ostracism often enlisted amphora sherds (though black-glazed sherds show the name more clearly). Complete or partial amphorae were often used in Archaic and Classical burials; however, this practice declines sharply in the Hellenistic period.[69]

MODIFYING THE MODELS

From the foregoing considerations, it is possible to suggest some modified models for amphora use in the Greek world. As noted in the introduction, various research interests emerging more strongly perhaps in the world of Greek amphora studies encourage some changes to the basic arrangement of these diagrams. I have left aside the variable of reclamation; this is not a phenomenon that I have considered to any extent in this paper. I have also left out the labels of locales 1, 2, 3, and 4 because they are not so useful in the current study's contrast between amphorae primarily involved in local circulation as opposed to those involved more commonly in long-distance shipping.[70] I have added a distinction between the maritime and land archaeological records. For the case of the producer aiming at intensive, long-distance exports, I have also increased the initial number of produced amphorae to have a few more numbers to allocate, without being tempted into an impression of false precision, and to reflect the greater scale of production of such producers. Finally, I have added an early step of distribution for filling after the point of manufacture. This last addition reflects the interest in Greek amphora studies in various events between the potting of the amphora and its entry into the stage of consumer use as a container of some sort of agricultural product. In the accompanying diagrams I have distinguished between the case for a region producing amphorae largely for regional distribution (e.g., the situation for Ephesos and vicinity) (Fig. 4) and the case for a region producing largely for long distance shipping (e.g., Rhodes or Thasos) (Fig. 5). The third diagram, based on the regional distribution producer,

assumes a major destructive event interrupting the use and reuse process (though not a permanent abandonment of the site) (Fig. 6).

Emphasis on Regional Distribution

The first flow diagram emphasizes localized distribution. Even for this scenario of smaller scale production, I include some minor loss in the period of distribution from the kilnsite to the filling stations; small scale of production need not have meant that the jars were produced at the agricultural sites themselves. A small portion might well be shipped out as the primary portion of a cargo; however, I am assuming a very slim chance of this particular cargo ending up in the maritime archaeological record.[71] Over an average prime use period of up to roughly five years,

60 Maiuri 1924; a similar line of amphorae on Rhodes is published by Φιλήμονος–Τσοποτού 2004, 62-63, pl. 18b with reference to another such structure on Rhodes near Οδός Κάναδα though this is only one line, with the amphorae placed vertically, upright, with the necks broken off.

61 Τρακοσοπούλου–Σαλακίδου 2004[2006]b, 166, fig. 14.

62 Finkielsztejn pers. comm. April 2007.

63 Böttger 1992, 315-318 notes that 43 of 64 pieces from known contexts come from channels and other constructions related to water movement; see too Costaki 2006, fig. 65 (=Knigge 1991, 66, fig. 59) for Dr. 6 or Lamboglia 2 amphora placed upside down over a channel; Costaki 2006, 404-406, fig. 68 (=ArchDelt 31 1976 B1, 29, pl. 33b) Dr. Ia or Ic amphorae laid across a drain channel.

64 Wolff 2004, 453.

65 Cf. Will 1997 rejecting any such difficulty.

66 Lawall & Jawando 2002.

67 Smoláriková 2007, 192.

68 Rose 1998, 80-81; and a similar phenomenon is attested on Rhodes, see Zimmer 1999.

69 For necropoleis with substantial use of amphorae for burials in late 6th and 5th centuries, see Knigge 1976 (Kerameikos); Μυλωνάς 1975 (Eleusis); and Καλτσάς 1998 (Akanthos).

70 Locale 1 is the place of manufacture; 2 is the distribution path; 3 is the place of primary use; and 4 is other locations of use; see Peña 2007, 324.

71 On this point, however, the idea that these figures are only rough orders of magnitude bears repeating: If ancient shipping accidents followed Venetian patterns, there was roughly a 1 in 20 to 1 in 30 chance of wrecking; and yet Gibbins (2001, 208) estimates that we 'see', in the archaeological record, only wrecks resulting from roughly 1 in 500 sailings – and this only in the intensive shipping routes supplying Monte Testaccio. Such numbers are too small to represent with precision in the flow diagram, nor is that desirable in the sense that the models presented here are intended as simplifications to guide further research.

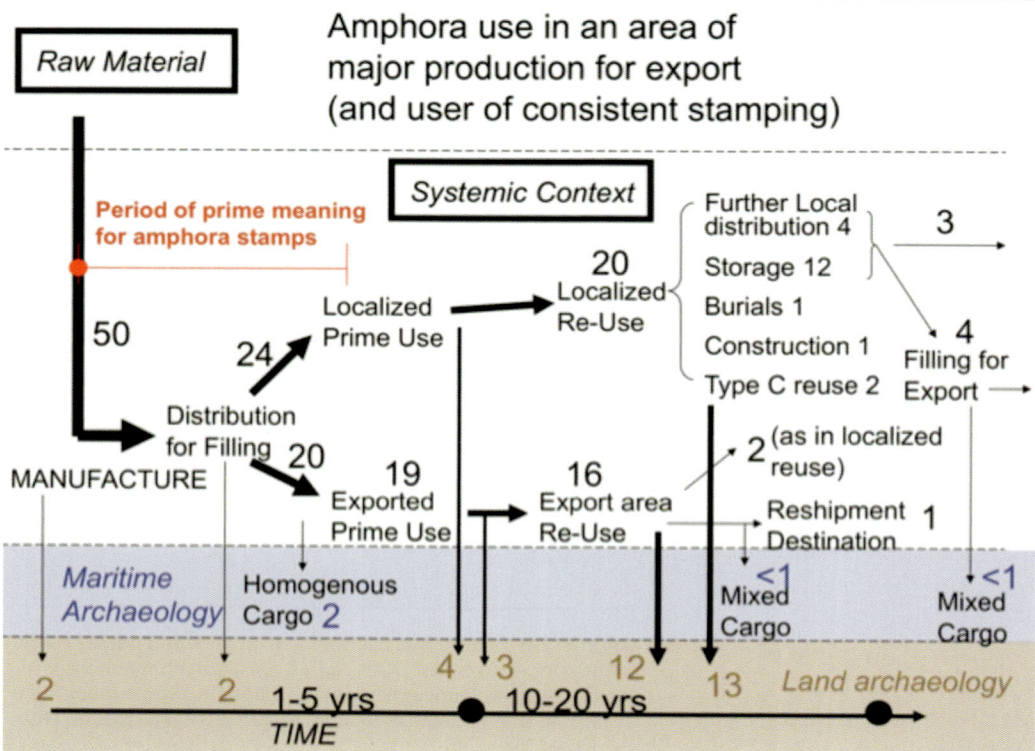

Fig. 5 Flow Diagram for Greek amphora use – production aimed at long distance shipping.

relatively few jars enter the archaeological record either in the local region or in more distant importing centers. This scarcity of jars rapidly leaving the systemic context reflects the lower numbers of jars within the last decade or so of many deposits' accumulations (see above). The further uses of the jars, mostly for storage with some for onward local distribution, burial containers, construction projects, etc., span the next decade or so, with the majority of this material entering the archaeological record as roughly ten to twenty year-old vessels/fragments. Vessels in reuse as static storage containers could easily last even longer in the systemic context; hence the few jars continuing from 'storage' reuse beyond this main period of discard.

By way of contrasting Greek and Roman discard patterns, this entry of Greek amphorae into the archaeological record is relatively sporadic with brief windows of large scale availability for discard. In the Roman setting it seems that jars are coming into availability for discard in large numbers over a longer period of time starting shortly after production. Hence, the single, thick

arrow coming down from the main re-use stage reflects well the sudden nature of Greek discard. Perhaps the behavioral difference to be drawn from this contrast is that Greeks tended to use jars more for local storage with very few alternative uses. By contrast, Romans may have emphasized a wider range of secondary uses with more varied, more frequent, and more consistent chances of the jars entering the archaeological record over a broader time frame. As a result, as noted earlier, 'new' jars are fairly common in closed Roman period deposits (when such data is available) while 'new' jars are in the minority in earlier Hellenistic and earlier contexts.

Emphasis on Exports

For the second flow diagram, I am imagining a production center like Rhodes or Thasos with a significant component in long-distance shipping and a very active routine of amphora stamping. There still needs to be sufficient production for local regional needs,[72] so I have increased overall production to add in a substantial export

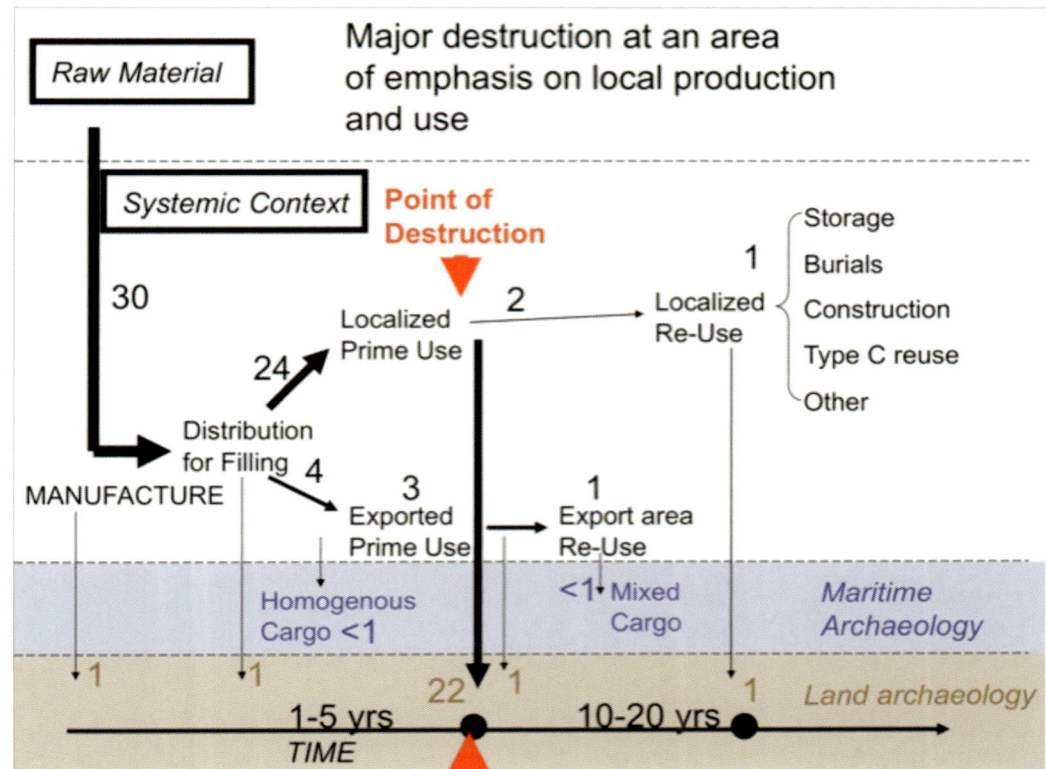

Major destruction at an area of emphasis on local production and use

Fig. 6 Flow Diagram for Greek amphora use – incorporating a major destructive event into the process envisioned in Fig. 5.

component. The dot and line projecting from the point of manufacture indicates the prime period of importance for amphora stamps and emphasize the fact that whatever problems were being solved by stamping must have existed within this initial phase of the amphora's life. The determination of the reasons for stamping has proven to be a complex problem, and reference to flow diagrams such as this one may help clarify the conditions that must be satisfied by any hypotheses.[73]

The portion allocated to recovery or potential recovery in maritime archaeological context is slightly higher than the portion allocated in the regional distribution graph. This increase indicates that with a greater quantity devoted to maritime export, there is a greater, yet still fairly small, chance of the jars ending up in a shipwreck.[74] This entry into the maritime record should happen earlier in the jars' use-life for homogeneous cargoes, later for mixed cargoes.

For local/regional use of amphorae, in this setting of greater emphasis on exports, later re-use as export shipping containers becomes an added possibility. While this

possibility exists even for areas without this emphasis on export, it seems stronger in an area where exports are more the norm.

With the larger scale of production and exportation, more jars should enter the land record from production and stockpiling sites, and there should be a greater chance of shipwrecks having such jars as a their main cargo. Once these jars reach their destinations, their uses largely resemble those seen already in the local region. I note here that despite having only one prime-use export

---

72 Stamping was not carried out more for jars being exported than for jars for local use, see Bresson 1986.
73 Recent discussions of the purposes of stamping all focus on the local context having recognized the difficulties faced by anyone trying to use the stamps for administrative purposes very far into the export process, see Lawall 2005 (to solve organizational problems caused by increased scale of production); Garlan 2000 (civic, fiscal purpose); Finkielsztejn 2006 (certification of capacity).
74 See above, note 71.

location illustrated, portions of cargoes may well have been dropped off at different ports, perhaps even transshipped to other carriers. I do not imagine though that this process would take multiple years, but the one section labeled here as 'exported prime use' should be thought of as the general universe of export destinations. Later refilling and reshipment of these exported jars as part of mixed cargoes is a possibility. Again the emphasis on use in storage should tend to delay final deposition so that there are few very new jars in any major short-duration discard location and a much larger portion of older jars. Hence, whether in the export contexts or the local region there should be a significant delay for many jars before they entered the archaeological record.

Catastrophes

In the two previous diagrams, I have characterized the entry of amphorae into the archaeological record as a slow process in the initial phases of use followed by more frequent discard well into the period of use. A major catastrophe, such as a destruction caused by human agency or a natural disaster, will catch not only many of the older amphorae in secondary uses but also an unusually large number of newly imported jars. Since an unusual number of such jars will now be lost from the systemic context, fewer jars of these types will be available for later re-use. Hence for some period of time after a major disaster, there may be a skewing of the archaeological record towards more consistently up to date amphora types. Thus major disasters affect not only the pottery in use at the time of the event but also what would or would not be available for discard in subsequent decades.

PROBLEMS FOR THE FUTURE

Regardless of the many debatable points in these diagrams, their ultimate importance may lie in the process of their development. The challenges raised by this sort of approach to the Greek amphora record are similar to those enumerated by Peña for the Roman side. Comparison among assemblages needs to be carried out with greater attention to the practices and other contextual variables creating that assemblage. Greater attention is also needed when observing and recording clues to the life histories of amphorae (fragmentation, but also excessive wear, unusual holes, etc.). And this importance of observation and recording pertains to both land and maritime assemblages.

Other problems are more specific to the case of Greek amphorae: situating processes of stamping and other markings within flow diagrams, issues of primary and irregular contents, and simply refining chronologies to the point that more evidence becomes available for histories of accumulation. Both chronological study of Greek amphorae and the interpretation of the data they provide for the ancient economy seemed more straightforward before the appearance of *Roman Pottery in the Archaeological Record*.

Iconographic Evidence for the Handling and Use of Transport Amphorae in the Roman Period

BY JOHN LUND

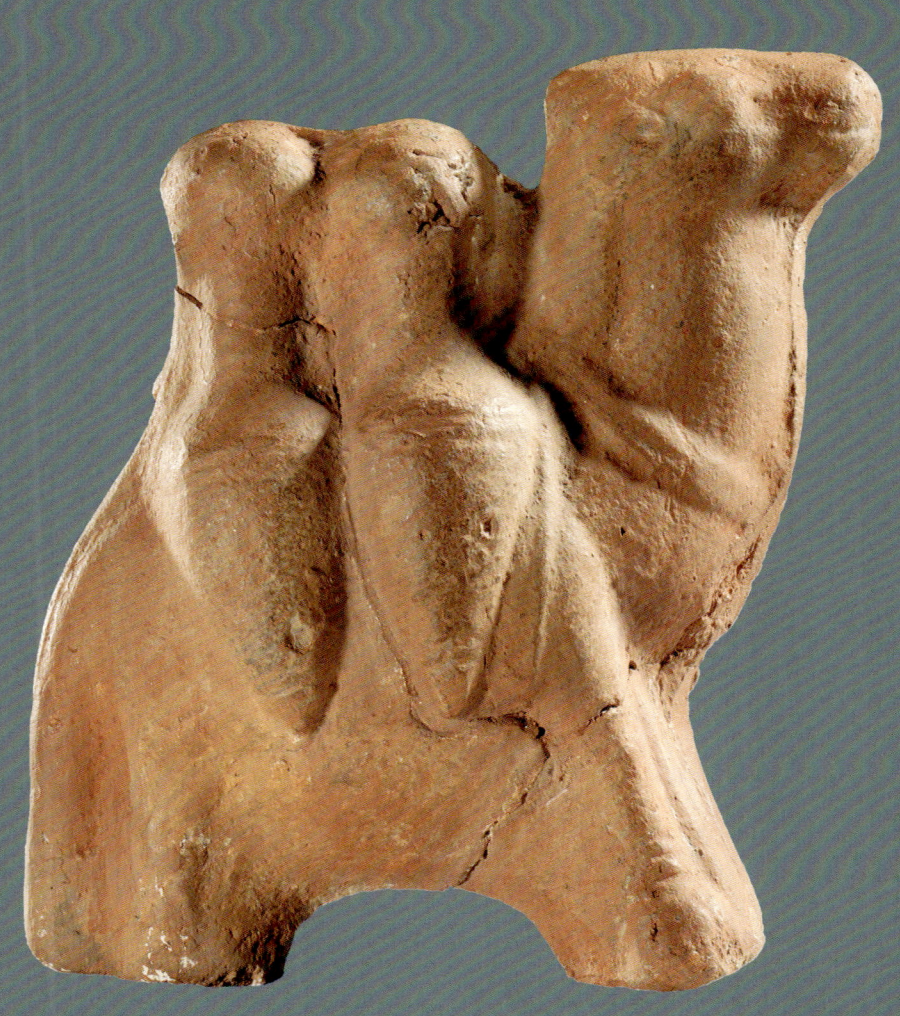

Iconographic Evidence for the Handling and Use of Transport Amphorae in the Roman Period

BY JOHN LUND

The purpose of this contribution is to review some of the iconographic evidence from the 1st century BC to the 3rd century AD for the handling of transport amphorae, with a view to examining how this kind of material can contribute to our understanding of the daily use of such vessels. The topic was chosen in consideration of Theodore Peña's inclusion of "Representational Evidence" among the sources for behavioural practices involving Roman pottery.[1]

Carolyn Koehler's discussion of the "Handling of Greek Transport Amphorae" and other scholars' treatments of various aspects of the Roman iconographic evidence constituted the starting points for the present study,[2] which is intended as an overview of a vast topic that has not so far been comprehensively investigated. Images of isolated amphorae and of those handled by gods, deities and skeletons are beyond the scope of this paper, but Nilotic scenes populated by dwarfs and pygmies are included, even if they play out in a twilight zone between imagination and "reality".[3]

Peña's model of the ceramic life-cycle of pottery ("Manufacture", "Distribution", "Prime use", "Reuse", "Maintenance", "Recycling", "Discard" and "Reclamation") provides a convenient framework for the following review of the iconographic evidence.[4]

MANUFACTURE

A few images show Roman potters at work, but none is involved in the making of amphorae.[5]

DISTRIBUTION BY SEA

There is, however, good iconographic evidence for the sea-borne distribution of transport amphorae.[6] Transport amphorae were normally stored below deck on large merchant vessels, but a mosaic dated to the 3rd-4th centuries AD from Tebessa in Algeria depicts a ship with thirteen stoppered amphorae packed in two rows on the deck.[7] Further examples include a fragmentary relief in the Villa Wolkonsky in Rome,[8] a sarcophagus relief from Rome dated to the second half of the 3rd century AD,[9] and a relief found near S. Maria in Capella in Rome.[10]

Images of smaller crafts and rowing boats carrying amphorae are also common. A wall painting from Pompeii shows two pygmies in a boat laden with amphorae.[11] A similar scene appears on two mosaics with Nilotic scenes: one dated to the first half of the 2nd century AD in the Terme di Nettuno at Ostia,[12] and another at Mérida in Spain, dated to the 3rd century AD.[13] A relief on a sarcophagus from the Severan period depicts two amphorae in a small vessel towed by a rowing boat.[14]

A mosaic from Ostia shows the transfer of amphorae from a larger to a smaller ship, evidently intended to transport them to a secondary landing-place,[15] and a 2nd century AD relief in Stockholm has a man pouring the contents of an amphora into some sort of container on a smaller vessel (Fig. 1).[16]

Having reached the end of the sea-journey, the amphorae were off-loaded, and a 3rd century AD relief from Ostia illustrates *tabularii* recording amphorae as they are carried off a ship.[17] A similarly engaged person is seen on another relief from Ostia,[18] and a fragmentary relief from Rome shows 13 amphorae stored next to a man sitting behind a desk with an inkstand. A small roof is indicative of an outdoor location, but it is hard to say without the missing part of the relief whether it depicts the recording of incoming amphorae at some storage facility in a harbour, or perhaps even at a stall selling amphorae.[19]

DISTRIBUTION BY LAND

An amphora filled with oil might weigh up to 100 kg, and one filled with wine up to half of this,[20] and the next stage involved transporting the amphorae onwards over land. One way of doing this over short distances was for two men to carry the amphora on a pole,[21] as seen on a shop

---

1 Peña 2007, 18.
2 Cf. Koehler 1986, which is also based on other sources than iconography. For the Roman period, see Zimmer 1982a *passim*; Blázquez Martínez *et al.* 1991; Hornig 2005-2006; Friedman 2005-2006; Bounegru 2005-2006; Calament 2007 and the publications referred to below.
3 Cf. Dasen 1994; Meyboom & Versluys 2007, 171: "Nilotic scenes in the Roman world are more or less realistic pictures of Egypt at the time of the annual flooding of the Nile". Though historically

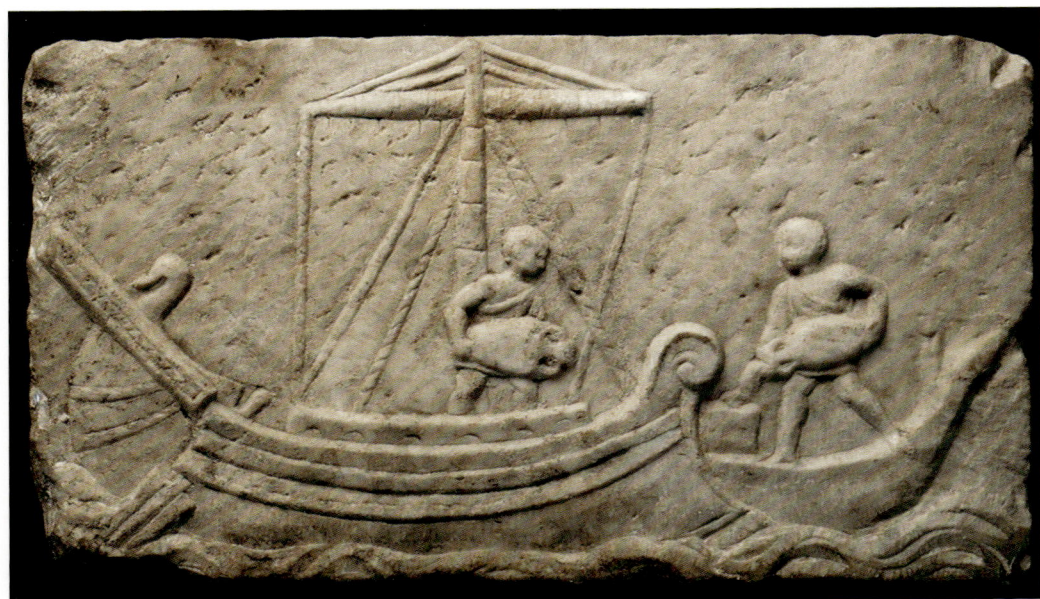

Fig. 1 Marble relief of unknown provenance showing two men transferring amphorae from a merchant vessel to a smaller craft. Photo courtesy The Museum of Mediterranean Antiquities, Stockholm.

incorrect, the term pygmy is used below for both categories as is often done with Nilotic scenes, cf. Meyboom & Versluys 2007, 173-177.

4 Peña 2007, 6-16.

5 Two wall paintings from Pompeii: Zimmer 1982a, 42 and 199 no. 143 and Peña & McCallum 2009, 59-63; a motif on an African Red Slip Ware jug from the first half of the 3rd century AD: Mackensen 1993, 64-65 fig. 12.1; a tomb relief from the early 2nd century AD in the Virginia Museum, Richmond: Zimmer 1982a, 42 and 199-200 no. 144.

6 Blázquez Martínez *et al.* 1991. The identification of the Latin names of vessel types involved is beyond the scope of this paper, cf. e.g. Höckmann 1994 and Bounegrou 2005-2006.

7 Dunbabin 1978, 74, 126, 272 pl. 59; Blázquez Martínez *et al.* 1991, 326 fig. 5; Tchernia 1997, 127; Pékary 1999, 52-54 no. DZ-13; Friedman 2005-2006, 128 fig. 5; Bounegru 2005-2006, 137 fig. 2.

8 Pékary 1999, 298-299 no. Rom-V 12.

9 Roma, Catacombe di Pretestato, Museo i.n. 925: Amedick 1991, 58 and 145 no. 143 pl. 47.3; Pékary 1999, 248-249 no. Rom-Ci 19; Friedman 2005-2006, 128 fig. 6.

10 Pékary 1999, 280-281 no. Rom-M 24; Another example is seen on a mosaic from the Maison des Muses at Althiburus in Tunisia dated to the second half of the 3rd century AD. Musée de Bardo i.n. A 168: Ennaïfer 1976, 66 note 285 pls. 40-41; Dunbabin 1978, 127, 153 and 248 Althiburus no. 1 (a). A ship carrying amphorae is also seen on a mosaic in L'édifice des Asclepieia at Althiburus: Ennaïfer 1976, 94-101 ship no. 24 pl. 94; Dunbabin 1978, 127, 136, 153 and 248 no. 1 (c) pl. 122; Pékary 1999, 362-363 no. TN-48 ship no. 24, and on a mosaic found at Bad Kreuznach in Germany dated at AD 234, Rabold 1995, 228 fig. 5; Pékary 1999, 16 Db-1. Cf. further a fragmentary relief from Ostia: Pékary 1999, 198-199 no. I-O 41b), and a mosaic from the Piazza delle Corporazioni at Ostia: Becatti 1961, 81-82 no. 127 pl. 182; Blázquez Martínez *et al.* 1991,

325 figs. 3-4; Pékary 1999, 190-191 no. I-O 16; Friedman 2005-2006, 131-132 fig. 16.

11 Napoli, il Gabinetto Segreto: Pékary 1999, 176-177 no. I-N 21; Bounegru 2005-2006, 138 fig. 5.

12 Becatti 1961, 59-60 no. 74 pl. 118; Basch 1987, 111 fig. 206; Blázquez Martínez et al. 1991, 323-324 fig. 1; Pékary 1999, 200-201 no. I-O 48; Versluys 2002, 43-45.

13 Dasen 1994, 598 no. 52.a pl. 479; Höckmann 1994, 429-431 no. 11 fig. 12; Pékary 1999, 58-59 no. E-7b.

14 Karlsruhe, Landesmuseum: Amedick 1991, 15 note 38 pl. 5.3; Pékary 1999, 26-27 no. D-44. See further a lost wall painting with a Nilotic scene in the Casa di Sallustio, Pompeii (VI 2,4): Versluys 2002, 114-115.

15 Becatti 1961, 74 no. 106 pl. 181; Blázquez Martínez et al. 1991, 324 fig. 2; Höckmann 1994, 426-427 no. 2 fig. 3; Tchernia 1997, 131; Pékary 1999, 188-189 no. I-O 10; Boetto 2001, 126 fig. 7; Friedman 2005-2006, 131-132 fig. 17; Bounegru 2005-2006, 137-138 fig. 3.

16 The Museum of Mediterranean Antiquities, i.n. MM 1975:1: Peterson & Winbladh 1976, 71; Pékary 1999, 338-339 no. S-2; Bounegrou 2005-2006, 138 fig. 4.

17 Roma, Museo Torlonia: Basch 1987, 463-465 fig. 1037; Tchernia 1997, 119; Pékary 1999, 290-291 no. Rom-M 55; Giulia Boetto in: Descœudres (ed.) 2001, 408 no. VII.2; Friedman 2005-2006, 132 fig. 18.

18 Roma, Museo Torlonia: Basch 1987, 463-465 fig. 1038; Pékary 1999, 290-291 no. Rom M-56; Boetto 2001, 403 no. IV.3; Friedman 2005-2006, 132 fig. 19.

19 Roma, Musei Vaticani, Galleria dei Candelabri III, 20 (138) (Porte Marancia): Zimmer 1982a, 219-220 no. 179.

20 Martin-Kilcher 1994, 525.

21 As had been done centuries earlier in Greece, cf. Koehler 1986, 58-60 fig. 10.

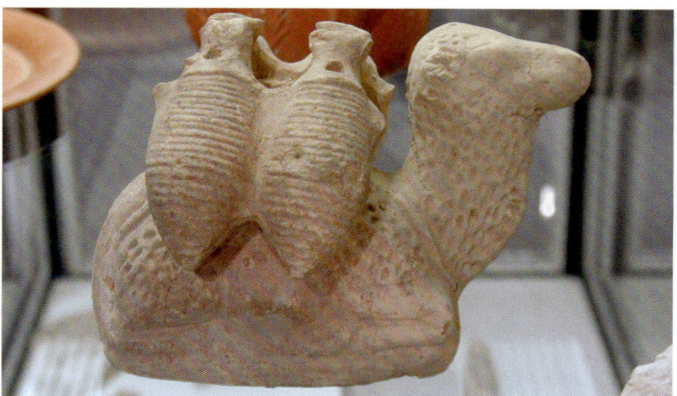

Fig. 2 Terracotta figurine showing a resting camel with amphorae, allegedly from Bosra. Photo courtesy The Museum of Ancient Art at Aarhus University.

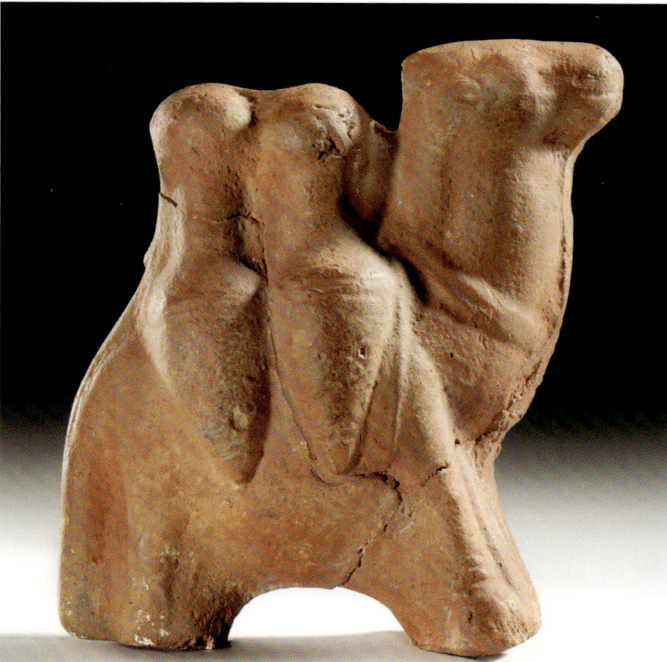

Fig. 3 Terracotta figurine of a standing camel laden with amphorae, allegedly from Lower Egypt. Photo by John Lee, the National Museum of Denmark.

sign in Pompeii (VII 4, 16) which obviously predates AD 79,[22] and on a 2nd century AD wall painting from Augst in Switzerland, where a Dressel 20 amphora is involved.[23] However, most of the relevant images involve the use of pack animals.

According to Colin Adams, epigraphic evidence shows that camels were primarily used in Egypt for the long distance transportation of goods,[24] and quite a few terracotta figurines (not only from Egypt) represent camels carrying amphorae, such as a resting camel allegedly from Bosra in Syria (Fig. 2).[25] Egyptian terracotta figurines commonly depict a standing camel laden with amphorae (possibly of the so-called Biconical type) (Fig. 3),[26] occasionally substituted by a horse.[27] According to Egyptian customs documents the average load for camels carrying wine was 4 *keramia*,[28] by which is presumably not only meant a measure corresponding to either 9 or 12 litres but also the amphorae themselves.[29] We can only guess at the contents of the amphorae shown on the terracotta figurines; wine is a possibility, but it cannot be ruled out that they are supposed to carry water.

Donkeys and mules have nearly the same carrying capacity as camels, but they were apparently mainly used for transporting goods over shorter distances in Egypt.[30] Mules carrying amphorae appear on a Campana relief with a Nilotic scene from the 1st or early 2nd century AD[31] and on a relief with yet another Nilotic scene from ancient Gorsium in Pannonia, dated to the 2nd century AD.[32] Roman representations of amphorae transported on wagons are by contrast hard to come by, and the epigraphic evidence from Egypt suggests that "pack animals were always more common and widely used than wagons" there.[33]

DISTRIBUTION III: STORAGE

Several images illustrate the storing of amphorae. On a relief from the 2nd century AD, we see a man carrying an amphora possibly of the Brindisi type to a storeroom with an overseer and six similar vessels stacked on top of each other.[34] One side of a sepulchral altar from Aquileia shows six similarly stacked amphorae, perhaps of type Dressel 6A.[35] Another side shows a standing man supporting an amphora on his shoulder – a motif reminiscent of a type of Egyptian terracotta figurine from the Late Hellenistic period (Fig. 4).[36] The amphora may be an Egyptian version of the Dressel 2-4 type.[37]

THE SELLING OF AMPHORAE AND THEIR CONTENTS

There are relatively few Roman illustrations of the selling of amphorae or their contents.

A sepulchral altar in the Louvre, dated to the end of

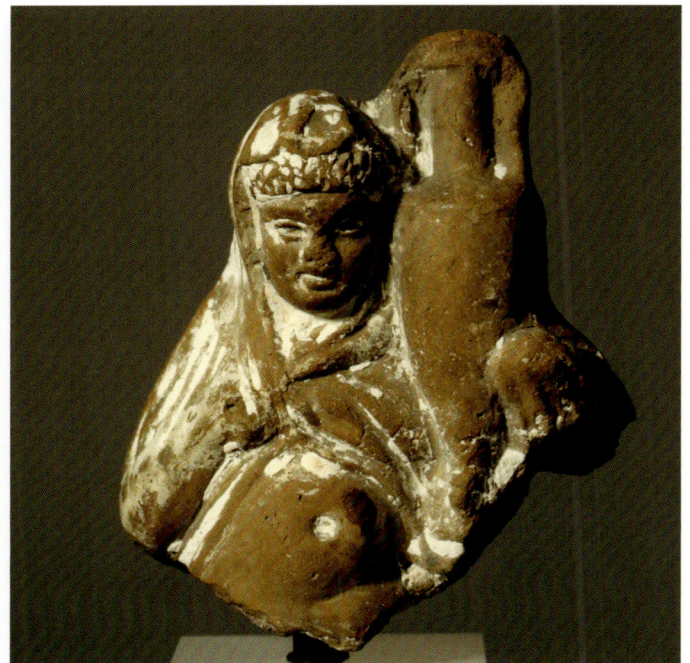

Fig. 4 Terracotta figurine of a standing man carrying an amphora on his left shoulder, acquired in Egypt. Photo courtesy the Ny Carlsberg Glyptotek, Copenhagen.

the 1st or the beginning of the 2nd century AD, shows a man with a purse in his right hand, who carries 4 amphorae (of two different types) on a pole.[38] He is arriving at (or departing from?) a storeroom with five amphorae lying about on the floor. The purse is suggestive of some commercial transaction.

A scene on an Okeanos mosaic from Bad Kreuznach dated to AD 234 seems to show the selling of amphorae in the open, in front of a *macellum*,[39] whereas a funerary relief in Augsburg dated about AD 200 takes us into a wine merchants' office,[40] in which South Gaulish amphorae – bound in straw – stand on a shelf above a row of wooden barrels. Another side of the same relief shows a person who dispenses a liquid to a customer in a *taberna* with shelves with wooden barrels and amphorae.[41]

A fragmentary terracotta relief from the Necropolis of Isola Sacra at Ostia dated to the period between Hadrian and Marcus Aurelius depicts a *taberna* with a row of transport amphorae standing on a shelf above a man at a counter, who pours a drink for a customer.[42] The name LUCI[....]ONDUS N[...]O is written on a tabula ansata, from

which four jugs are hanging. Peña observed that three amphora types seem to be involved (Africana 1 Piccolo, Tripolitanian 2/3 and Dressel 20), which are all thought to have been containers of olive oil.[43] A counterpart relief – likewise from the Isola Sacra Necropolis – shows a taberna with a man standing behind a counter on which is written

22 Zimmer 1982a, 222-223 no. 184; Koehler 1986, 58 note 44.
23 Martin-Kilcher 1994, 520 fig. 247, 525 and illustration on cover; cf. also Egyptian terracotta figurines, Fischer 1994, 211-212 nos. 389-390 pl. 37.
24 Adams 2007, 50-55.
25 Århus, The Museum of Ancient Art at Aarhus University, i.n. 524 (allegedly from Bosra); see further Pisani Sartorio 1994, 31-32 fig. 20 (from Aphrodisias).
26 The Danish National Museum, Collection of Classical and Near Eastern Antiquities i.n. 3128 acquired in 1886, allegedly from Lower Egypt. See also Calament 2007, 737 note 4 and the references there cited. For the amphora type, see Tomber & Williams 2000, 43 note 15.
27 See for instance Fischer 1994, 414 no. 1107 pl. 117.
28 Adams 2007, 80.
29 Cf. the quotation of the 3rd century AD jurist Ulpian quoted by Peña 2007, 48-49.
30 Adams 2007, 56-64; see further Vossen 1984.
31 Roma, Museo Nazionale i.n. 58192: Klaus Parlasca in: Helbig Führer III⁴, 76-77 no. 2164 i); Versluys 2002, 88-89 fig. 40.
32 Versluys 2002, 215 fig. 137.
33 Adams 2007, 65.
34 New York, The Metropolitan Museum, i.n. 25.78.63: Zimmer 1982a, 224 no. 187. For the Brindisi type, see Peacock & Williams 1986, 82-83 Class 1 and for the other types referred to below, see "Roman Amphorae: a digital resource": http://ads.ahds. ac.uk/catalogue/resources.html?amphora2005.
35 Zimmer 1982a, 200-201 no. 145 identified as a pottery workshop. Stored amphorae are also seen on Egyptian terracottas, cf. Breccia 1930, 44 no. 167 pl. 25.9 and Calament 2007, 737 note 2 fig. 1. For the amphora type, see Peacock & Williams 1986, 98-101 Class 8.
36 Copenhagen, Ny Carlsberg Glyptotek, i.n. Æ.I.N. 516: Fjeldhagen 1995, 143 no. 126.
37 Cf. Tomber 2006b, 153-155 Type 28.
38 Paris, Louvre, i.n. MA 2134: Zimmer 1982a, 223 no. 185.
39 See *supra* note 10 and Raber 1995, 326-327 fig. 4.
40 Röm. Mus. Augsburg, i.n. Lap. 376: Martin-Kilcher 1994, 539-540 fig. 255; Marlière 2002, 146-147 no. R47 fig. 175.
41 Martin-Kilcher 1994, 539-540 fig. 256; Wamser *et al.* 2000, 360-361 no. 94.
42 Museo Ostiense, i.n. 5859: Floriani Squarciapino 1956-1958 [1959], 193 pl. 5.2; Erika Simon in: Helbig Führer IV⁴, 14-15 no. 3004; Kampen 1981, 57-58 and 144 no. II 18 fig. 36; Zimmer 1982a, 217-218 no. 175. For the term taberna, see Langner 2002, 326.
43 Peña 1999, 23. For the amphora types, see Peacock & Williams 1986, 153-154 Class 33, 169-170 Class 37, and 136-140 Class 25.

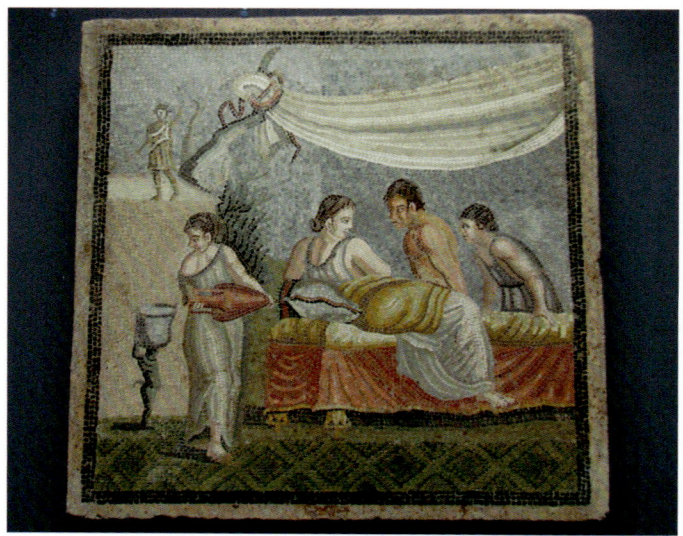

Fig. 5 A mosaic from Centocelle near Rome dated to the 1st century AD in the Kunsthistorisches Museum, Wien. Photo by the author.

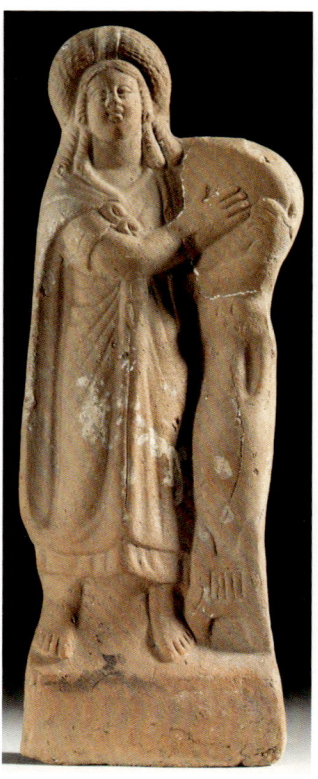

Fig. 6 Terracotta figurine of a woman holding a tambourine and standing next to an amphora on a small tripod, allegedly from Lower Egypt. Photo by John Lee, the National Museum of Denmark.

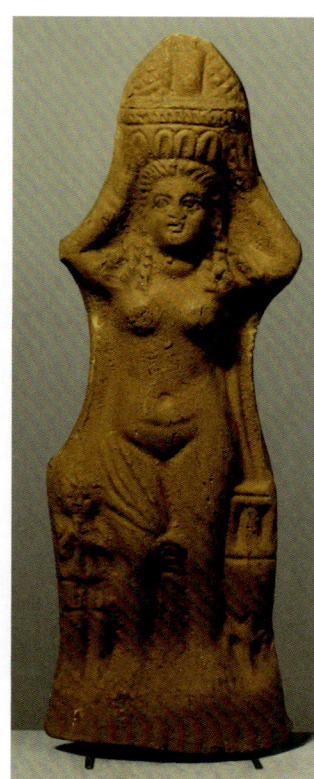

Fig. 7 Terracotta figurine of a woman flanked by an amphora in a tripod, acquired in Egypt. Photo courtesy the Ny Carlsberg Glyptotek, Copenhagen.

the name LUCIFER AQUATARI[US].[44] He faces towards a woman customer in front of a large pithos, and a wine amphora of South Gaulish type stands on a shelf. The name AQUATARI[US] is at times taken to imply the selling of water,[45] but Ostia was well supplied with water outlets and fountains,[46] and wine cannot be ruled out.[47]

PRIME USE

The iconographic documentation of prime use mainly consists of representations of dining and wining, such as wall paintings from Pompeii[48] and the Villa Farnesina,[49] and a mosaic from Centocelle near Rome (Fig. 5)[50] – all dated to the 1st century AD. On two of these we see an attendant[51] pouring wine from an amphora into a large bowl to be mixed with water.[52] A *velum*, trees and other props show that the banquets take place in the open, and this is also the case with the picnic shown in the *tablinum* of the Casa dei Dioscuri in Pompeii, where an amphora rests against a tree.[53]

Other paintings may show later stages of such outdoor parties. An amphora is placed in a stand close to the diners in a Nilotic scene in Pompeii,[54] and a painting from the Columbarium of the Villa Pamphili shows an orgiastic dance, in which a reveller lifts an amphora into the air.[55] A mosaic dated to the 3rd century AD from the

Aventine Hill in Rome has a somewhat similar motif: dancers and musicians surround an amphora placed in a tripod stand in an outdoor setting,[56] and stucco reliefs in the so-called Basilica Sotterranea outside the Porta Maggiore in Rome show outdoor revellers with amphorae lying about.[57] A mosaic from Dougga dated from the mid 3rd century AD shows two attendants with amphorae pouring wine for two men.[58]

Several types of Egyptian terracotta figurines represent persons with amphorae connected with the Isis cult,[59] for instance a woman holding a tambourine and standing next to an amphora (possibly of the Dressel 2-4) type fixed in a small tripod (Fig. 6).[60] Another type shows a woman next to an amphora carrying a basket on her head (Fig. 7),[61] and still others represent priests and other cult personnel with

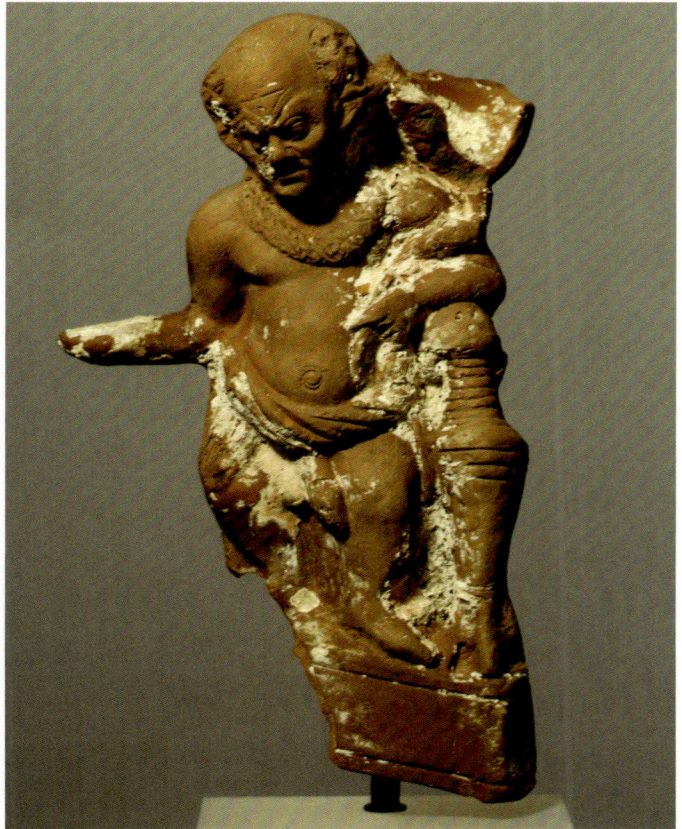

Fig. 8 Terracotta figurine of an elderly man whose left arm is resting on a transport amphora, acquired in Egypt. Photo courtesy the Ny Carlsberg Glyptotek, Copenhagen.

one or more amphorae (Fig. 8).[62] One is reminded of the Latin author Apuleius' (XI, 9-11) description of an Isiac procession in which an amphora was carried about.[63]

A glass cup with a painted decoration from the third quarter of the 1st century AD depicts a scene set in a Nilotic landscape (Fig. 9).[64] A woman grasping a transport amphora

44 Floriani Squarciapino 1956-1958 [1959], 192-193 pl. 5.1; Zimmer 1982a, 218 no. 176. For the amphora type see Peacock & Williams 1986, 142-143 Class 27 and Martin-Kilcher 1994, fig. 136.7-9 and 360-364 Gauloise 4.

45 Museo Ostiense i.n. 5858; Floriani Squarciapino 1956-1958 [1959], 192; Erika Simon in: Helbig Führer IV[4], 14-15 no. 3004; Kampen 1981, 57-58 and 143-144 no. II 17 fig. 35; Ellis 2005, 114.

46 Schmölder 2001.

47 Zimmer 1982a, 218: "Als sicher kann jedoch gelten, daß in dem gezeigten Laden nicht nur Wasser verkauft wurde"; Peña 1999, 23.

48 Wall painting from the Casa dei Casti Amanti (IX 12,6): Dunbabin 2003a, 53-56 fig. 26; Stehmeier 2006, 41-42 fig. 1.

49 Roma, Museo Nazionale, i.n. 1128, B5; Bragantini & de Vos 1982, 130 pl. 40; Beasom 2009, 41 fig. 7.

50 Kunsthistorisches Museum, Wien, AS Inv.-Nr. II 9; Clarke 1998, 97 fig. 30; Beasom 2009, 41 note 134 fig. 8.

51 Dunbabin 2003b.

52 A wine-pouring attendant is also shown on North African lamps from the 2nd century AD, see Deneauve 1969, 171 no. 743 (Carthage); Bussière 2000, 334 no. 2695 pl. 71 (from Tebessa). Both are signed by the lamp maker C MAR EVP.

53 Pompeii, Casa dei Dioscuri (VI 9,6/7): Versluys 2002, 120-121 fig. 65. Also a mosaic from the late 3rd century AD with Nilotic landscape in the Graeco-Roman Museum of Alexandria: Dasen 1994, 599 no. 53h) pl. 481; Daszewski 2005, 1145 note 8 fig. 4 (Tell Timai, ancient Thmuis).

54 Napoli, Museo Nazionale i.n. 113196, from Pompeii, Casa del Medico (VIII 5,24): Dasen 1994, 598 no. 46b) pl. 476; Versluys 2002, 138-140; Clarke 2007, 163-164 fig. 5; Meyboom & Versluys 2007, 178-182 fig. 2.

55 Roma, Museo Nazionale: Bernhard Andrae in: Helbig Führer III[4], 464-465 no. 2490; Dasen 1994, 597 no. 43; Meyboom & Versluys 2007, 186-187 fig. 4.

56 Roma, Musei Vaticani, Atrio del torso, i.n. 902: Klaus Parlasca in: Helbig Führer I[4], 210-211 no. 264.A; Versluys 2002, 458; Dunbabin 2004, 170; Savarese (ed.) 2007, 105; Meyboom & Versluys 2007, 192-193 fig. 10. For Greek amphora stands, see Koehler 1986, 61-62.

57 Mielsch 1975, 118-119 no. K 16 III; Dasen 1994, 599 no. 56 pl. 483; Versluys 2002, 61-63.

58 Tunis, Bardo Museum: see Dunbabin 1978, 123, 257 no. 5 pl. 114 and Blanchard-Lemée et al. 1996, 76-79 fig. 48; for two threshold mosaics with similar motifs from Oudna, see Dunbabin 1978, 123, 266 nos. 6c) and 4; for the latter see Ben Abdallah et al. 1998, 73-74 fig. 30.

59 The Collection of Classical and Near Eastern Antiquities, The National Museum of Denmark, i.n. 3533, acquired in 1890, allegedly from Lower Egypt. For other examples, see Dunand 1979, 35-36 and 96-98; Fischer 1994, 354-355 kat. 887 pl. 93; Fjeldhagen 1995, 122 no. 105; Calament 2007, 738-739 figs. 4-10.

60 The Collection of Classical and Near Eastern Antiquities, The National Museum of Denmark, i.n. 3533, acquired in 1890, allegedly from Lower Egypt.

61 Copenhagen, Ny Carlsberg Glyptotek, i.n. Æ.I.N. 379, Fjeldhagen 1995, 117-118 no. 99. For a discussion of this and related types, see Calament 2007, 739-740 figs. 11-13.

62 Copenhagen, Ny Carlsberg Glyptotek, i.n. Æ.I.N. 486, Fjeldhagen 1995, 114 no. 96. The amphora is readily identifiable as Egyptian, but it is not easy to pinpoint its exact type, see Tomber & Williams 2000, 43-45 fig. 2. For further terracotta figurines with the same motif, see Fischer 1994, 216 no. 402 pl. 39, and 212-213 nos. 392-393 pl. 30; Calament 2007, 741 figs. 16-17.

63 Griffiths 1975, 212-215; Calament 2007, 740-741.

64 Nenna 2008. I am grateful to Marie-Dominique Nenna for permission to reproduce her drawing.

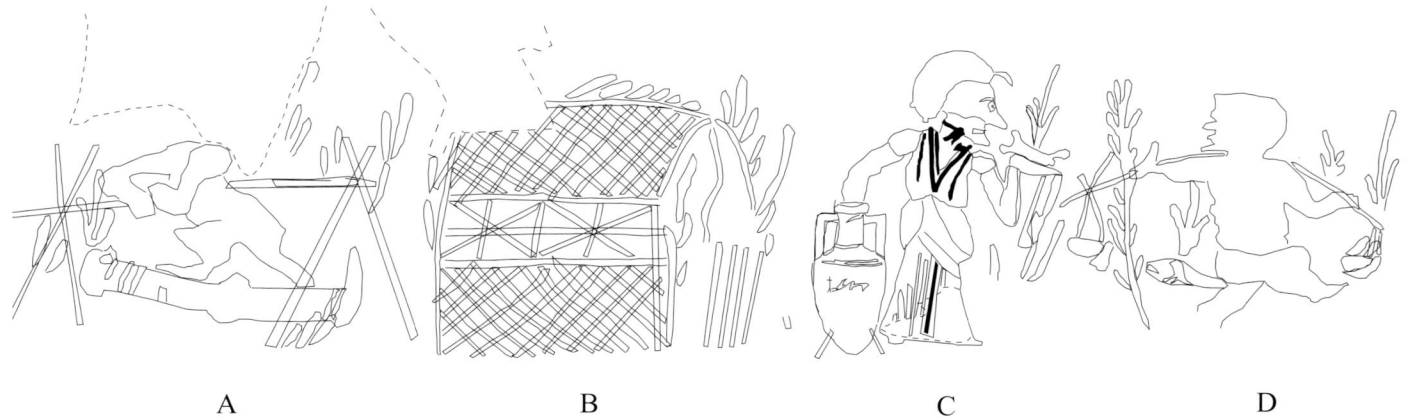

Fig. 9 A glass vessel with painted decoration, possibly originating in a workshop in Italy, showing a woman (C) with a transport amphora in a Nilotic landscape. She stands outside a hut (B) and seems to offer wine to the man on her right (D). In a private collection, provenance unknown. Drawing courtesy Marie-Dominique Nenna.

of the Dressel 2-4 type[65] stands in front of a hut. She looks towards a running man whom she seems to offer wine.[66] Perhaps the (lost) prototype for this burlesque enigmatic motif might have served as a source of inspiration for the North African lamp manufacturer Gaius Iunius Draco, who used a somewhat similar woman with an amphora as a discus motif (Fig. 10).[67] He and other North African lamp makers also produced rather similar lamps with a man holding on to the amphora (possibly of the Kapitän II type).[68]

REUSE

A lost wall painting from a drink and food outlet at Pompeii shows two men filling amphorae from the contents of an enormous oxen skin, carried on a wagon drawn by two mules. The nature of the liquid is not evident, but Thomas Fröhlich may be right in observing that the scene might illustrate the delivery of wine to the establishment.[69] If so, then the scene represents amphora reuse. Another possibility is that it shows the primary filling of amphorae with wine brought from a winery.[70]

Pictures of "reuse of amphorae as packing containers" may be impossible to detect in the iconographic record, but other instances of secondary use are attested. A tomb relief in Ostia from the late 1st century shows a workshop scene with two men holding a saw and a bisected amphora lying on a small podium between them. A complete amphora

is seen in the background.[71] One is reminded of the fresco from the Tomb of Trebius Iustus on the Via Latina near Rome, which may show a man carrying mortar in an amphora cut in half.[72]

Mention can also be made of a mosaic with a Nilotic scene found between the Farnesina Villa and Ponte Sisto, which i.a. depicts a pygmy who windsurfs on a floating amphora holding on to a provisory sail tied to its handles.[73] And a pygmy "holding a spear in his right hand and the top of an amphora as a shield in his left hand in front of a hippotamus" is shown on a curious 3rd century mosaic from Rome with a Nilotic scene.[74]

DISCARD

An enigmatic scene on a wall-painting from the Caseggiato del Ercole at Ostia dated to the late 2nd or first third of the 3rd century AD depicts two men arguing over a broken amphora in front of a magistrate.[75] It may be logical to place this image at the end of the "Prime Use", but it might alternatively be placed under Peña's heading "Discard and Reclamation".[76]

CONCLUSIONS

A number of tentative conclusions can be reached on the basis of the reviewed evidence.

1) The relatively many representations of amphora

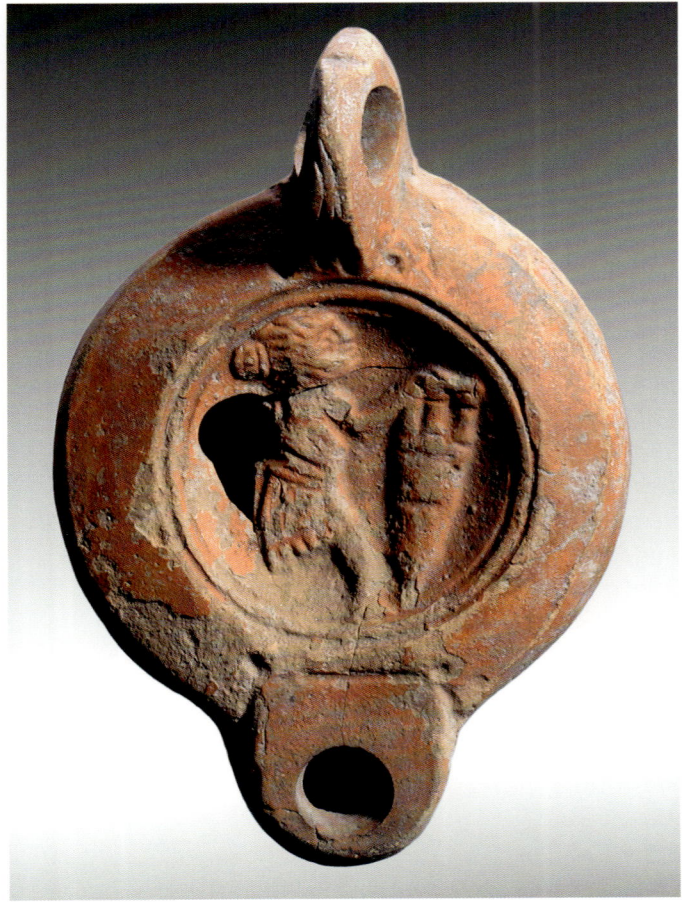

Fig. 10 A woman with a transport amphora on a terracotta lamp from Sidi Daoud or El Hauaria in North Africa, made by the lamp manufacturer Gaius Iunius Draco. Photo by John Lee, the National Museum of Denmark.

transport by sea as well as by land – as well as of their storage and selling – suggest that this category of vessel was regarded as a token of transport and trade in Antiquity, much as it is today. The images of amphorae in smaller vessels including rowing boats are good illustrations of the cabotage and redistribution, which was an important element in the maritime distribution of goods in the Roman period.[77]

2) Roman representations of prime use seem invariably to show amphorae as wine containers, even if as is well known, amphorae could carry many other commodities in the ancient world, and other illustrations show types which were used for olive oil.

3) The images of prime use of amphorae consistently have an outdoor setting. This might be surprising to someone inclined to think of ancient banquets as indoor events,[78] but there is in fact ample other evidence to show that picnics and other kinds of feasts in the open were common phenomena in the Roman world.[79] This iconographic evidence may go some way towards explaining why surveys often result in the uncovering of numerous amphora fragments in the open landscape.[80]

65 Nenna 2008, 18-19 figs. 4 and 6. For the amphora see Peacock & Williams 1986, 105-105 Class 10.
66 Nenna 2008, 23-27.
67 The Collection of Classical and Near Eastern Antiquities, The National Museum of Denmark, i.n. ABc 397: Lund in press b.
68 Peacock & Williams 1986, 193-195 Class 47. For these lamps see Lund in press b; Bonifay *et al.* 2004, 33 note 47 questions the identification, because the Kapitän ll type is usually thought to have emerged in the late 2nd century AD, i.e. after the lamps in question. But evidence from Mons Claudianus suggests that the type was already circulating in the Antonine period, cf. Tomber 2006b, 165 Type 50; see further Hayes 1983, 98, 144 type 37 and 160 Table 13 and Outschar 1998, 20.
69 Caupona (VI 10,1 room b): Fröhlich 1991, 216-217 fig. 1 and 221 note 1255.
70 Thus Marlière 2002, 22-23 fig. 12.
71 Ostia, Museo Ostiense, i.n. 138: Zimmer 1982a, 140-141 no. 58; Paola Olivanti in Descæudres (ed.) 2001, 415 no. VIII.6; see Martin-Kilcher 1994, 379 fig. 153, where reference is made to a similarly bisected and re-used amphora from Augst of the type Keay 1B.
72 Peña 2007, 141-142 fig. 6.5.
73 Roma, Museo Nazionale, i.n. 125535: Klaus Parlasca in: Helbig Führer III⁴, 429 no. 2481; Dasen 1994, 598 no. 51 pl. 477; Pékary 1999, 286-287 no. Rom-M 44; Versluys 2002, 78-79 fig. 28; Hornig 2005-2006, 119 fig. 7. See also a mosaic in the Museo Nazionale, i.n. 124698 from Collemancio at Assisi, Klaus Parlasca in: Helbig Führer III4, 22-23 no. 2128; Dasen 1994, 598 no. 52b); Versluys 2002, 173-174.
74 Roma, Museo Nazionale i.n. 171: Klaus Parlasca in: Helbig Führer III⁴, 332-333 no. 2403; Dasen 1994, 599 no. 53b) pl. 481; Versluys 2002, 76-78. This practice is paralleled on a mosaic in the necropolis of Isola Sacra in Ostia, Dasen 1994, 598 no. 51a) pl. 478; Clarke 2003, 210-212 fig. 123; Hornig 2005-2006, 119 fig. 7.
75 Ostia, Antiquarium i.n. 10099a: Mielsch 2001, 119-120 fig. 145; Stella Falcone in: Descæudres (ed.) 2001, 425 no. XII.5; Peña 2007, 55-56 fig. 4.1.
76 Peña 2007, 12-16.
77 Nieto 1997.
78 For dining place settings, cf. Dunbabin 2003a, 36-71 and for some representations of indoor banquets, see Clarke 2003, 223-245 and Serena Vendito in: Aßkamp *et al.* (eds.), 244-245 nos. 6.1 and 4.
79 Dunbabin 2003a, 50-52 and *passim*; Stehmeier 2006.
80 See Lund 2007. A further explanation is offered by Peña 2007, 37.

4) Surprisingly many images are set in a Nilotic landscape and involve pygmies. It is difficult to account for the popularity of the latter other than by pointing to the fact that the vessels might have served as convenient scales indicating the restricted size of the pygmies. Moreover, liberal wine consumption seems to have fitted well with the imagined lifestyle of these people.[81] Still, this is hardly the whole explanation, since amphorae are also shown on a considerable number of Egyptian terracotta figurines, which seem to relate to daily life.

In sum: the iconographical record confirms much that is already known – yet also contains certain surprises. Some images have details which tend to confirm that they are more or less accurate reflections of the real world. Representations of camels carrying amphorae are thus limited to Egypt and the Middle East, and pictures of wooden wine barrels seem restricted to the western part of the Roman Empire.[82] Moreover, it is possible in several cases to recognize the general amphora type involved even if the specific variant usually eludes us, and Egyptian amphora types are regularly seen on Egyptian terracotta figurines, whereas those of a South Gaulish type are shown on images from Gaul.[83] Images of the Dressel 2-4 and of the Dressel 20 type occur where such amphorae actually circulated, and this may even be true for the Kapitän II type. This suggests that the craftsman (and presumably also the buyer) was familiar with the types in question,[84] but the whole issue is complicated by the fact that some of the pictures may represent reuse rather than prime use and even – particularly in the case of Egypt – the transport of empties to the winery.[85]

Yet the images do not reveal the whole story. John Tamm, who compared images of silver vessels on Campanian wall paintings with the preserved silver ware from the Early Imperial period, reasonably concluded that: "The paintings, although providing a plausible representation of actual vessels, did not produce a 'photographic' record".[86] There is no reason to believe that wine consumed indoors did not come from transport amphorae, but perhaps such vessels were not included in images of indoor dining because they seemed no match for the luxurious silver service employed there – or simply because the wine was normally transferred from the amphorae to large craters and mixing bowls before the party began.

81 Cf. Clarke 2007 and Meyboom & Versluys 2007, 205.
82 On wooden barrels see Martin-Kilcher 1994, 485-487 and the rich iconographic documentation in Marlière 2002, 124-157.
83 See Marlière 2002, 190-192.
84 See further López Monteagudo 2001-2002.
85 Kruit & Worp 2000, 86-87, citing PCair Zen IV 59741. I am grateful to Mark Lawall for drawing my attention to this possibility.
86 Tamm 2005, 73; see also Langner 2002, 355 and Dunbabin 2003a, 56.

ACKNOWLEDGEMENTS

I wish to thank Jan Stubbe Østergaard for putting me on the track of images of transport amphorae on Roman sarcophagi at the beginning of my query, and J. Theodore Peña for drawing my attention to a number of representations and references that I might otherwise have missed. I am grateful also to Roberta Tomber for clarifying the find contexts of amphorae of the Kapitän II type at Mons Claudianus.

Amphora Fragments Re-used as Potter's Tools in the Rural Landscape of Panskoye

BY SØREN HANDBERG

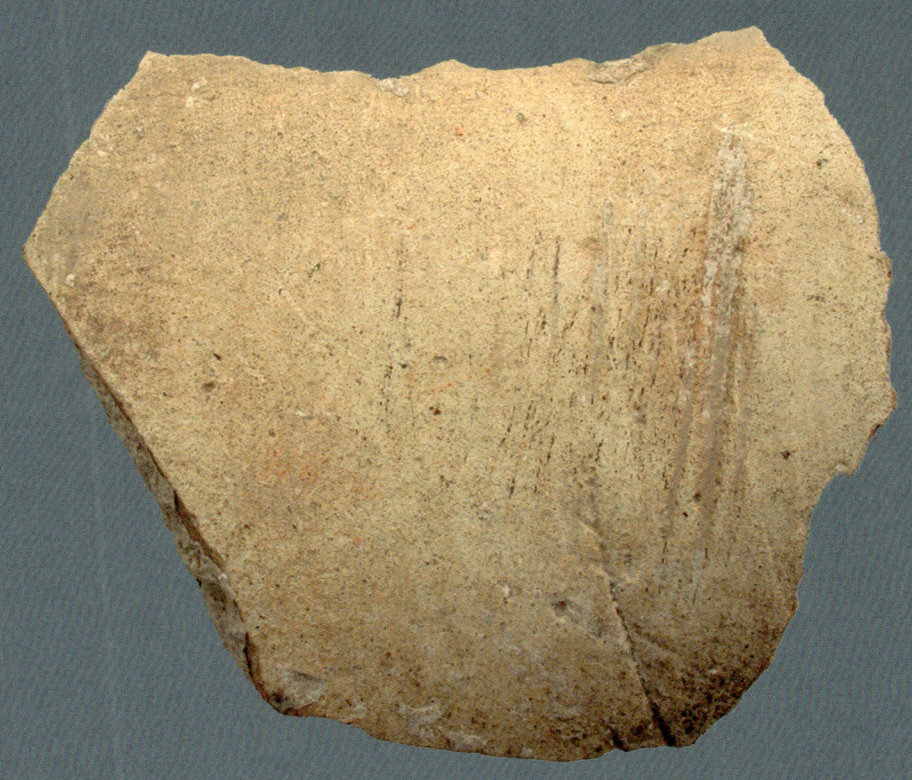

Amphora Fragments Re-used as Potter's Tools in the Rural Landscape of Panskoye

BY SØREN HANDBERG

The aim of this paper is to draw attention to a specific type of re-use of Greek transport amphorae: amphora fragments re-used as polishing tools likely associated with pottery manufacture. Even though the value of abrasion study and use-wear analysis has been recognized for a long time on a methodological level, implementation of these analytical tools on a practical level has been limited, especially within the sphere of Classical and Hellenistic Greek pottery.

During the months of May 2007 and May 2008, the Danish National Research Foundation's Centre for Black Sea Studies, in collaboration with the Groningen Institute of Archaeology (GIA), conducted an intensive survey of the rural landscape surrounding the Greek settlement of Panskoye and the Džarylgač Lake on the Tarchankut peninsula in Northwestern Crimea. The Džarylgač Survey Project (DSP) aimed at investigating the rural landscape around the Džarylgač Lake on the border of the distant chora of Tauric Chersonesos in modern Ukraine.[1] Approximately 15 km² of ploughed fields in the plains towards the sea as well as uncultivated areas on the inland slopes have been systematically surveyed (Fig. 1).

Several fragments of re-used late Classical and/or early Hellenistic transport Amphorae of various types were found in several of the surveyed areas. Three types of re-use could be recognized. The first group is not very numerous and consists of body and handle fragments with drilled holes presumably used as net- or loomweights. The second type of re-use is represented by only one fragment, which was used as a cutting board (Fig. 2). The third and largest group of re-used transport amphora fragments consists of handles and toes, which had been re-used as a kind of polishing tool. One handle fragment had been re-used twice, first as a weight and subsequently as a polishing tool. Out of little more than 238 amphora handle and toe fragments collected during the survey, sixteen pieces exhibit clear traces of having been re-used in this way (Fig. 3-4). All 16 fragments display a worn and faceted surface on one or both

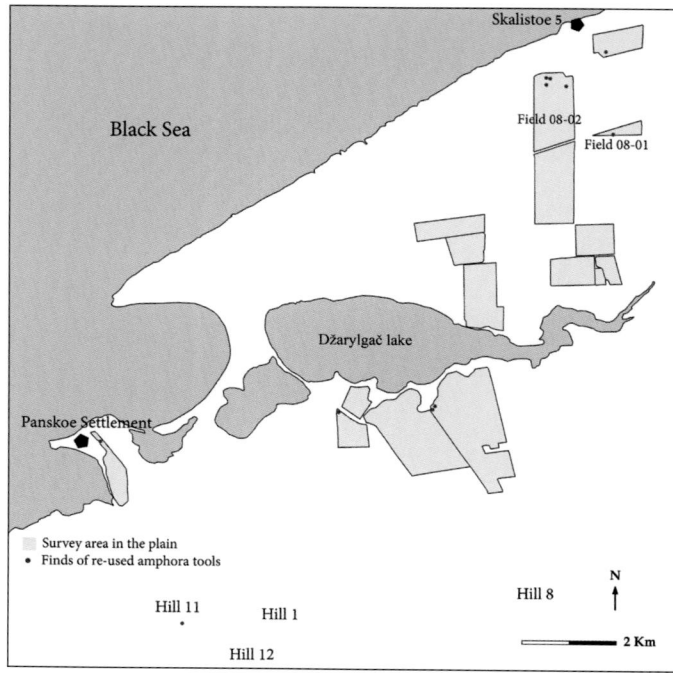

Fig. 1 Distribution map of re-used amphora tools in the rural landscape of the settlement of Panskoye.

ends of the handle or the underside of the toe. The worn parts vary considerably in size but are usually smooth with many multidirectional striations, which indicate that they must have been continuously used to polish something. Similar types of re-used amphora handles, although from the Roman period, were dealt with briefly by J.T. Peña.[2]

SITES

The main result of the Džarylgač Survey Project has been the identification of a dispersed network of minor sites and settlements in the area around the Džarylgač Lake and on the coastal plains as well as on the low inland hill plateaus.[3] The discovery of substantial traces of house structures with associated household pits on the inland hills deviates substantially from previous interpretations of land use in the area. Until now it had been widely believed that Greek occupation was restricted to the area along the coastline in smaller and larger fortified settlements such as Panskoye, Masliny, Kardža, Skalistoe 5 and the *apoikia* of Kalos Limen at the modern city of Černomorskoe west of the survey area. Traditionally, the Tarchankut peninsula is

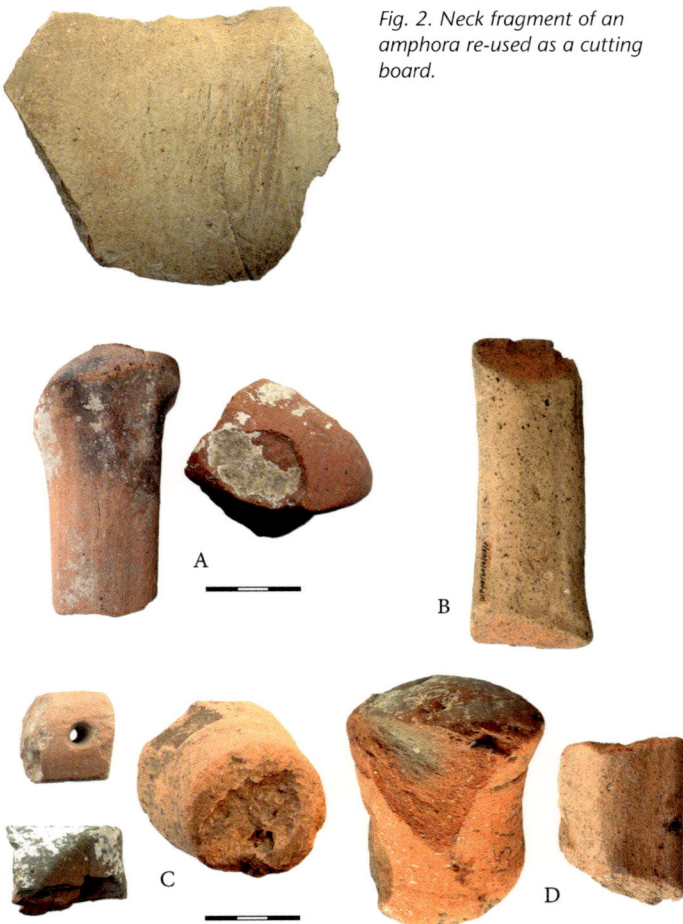

Fig. 2. Neck fragment of an amphora re-used as a cutting board.

Fig. 3 Examples of re-used amphora tools. A: Site close to Panskoye; B: From kurgan group in Field 08-01; C: Larger site in Field 08-02; D: Settlement on Hill 11-1.

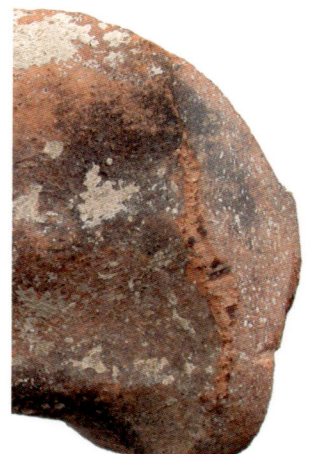
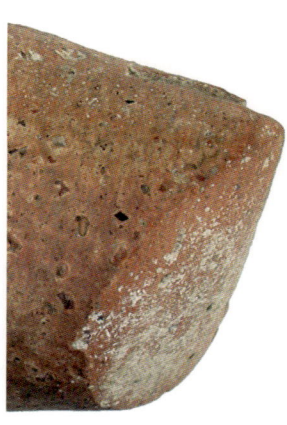

Fig. 4 Close up of the polished area on two amphora handle fragments.

grains found *in situ* in an amphora in Complex U6 suggest that amphorae were re-used as grain containers.[6]

All the re-used amphora tools were found in connection with identified settlements except for one handle tool, which was found at the site of three ploughed out kurgans in field 08-01. However, considering the small size of this field, a settlement may very well have been situated outside the surveyed area. Not surprisingly, the largest concentrations of re-used amphora tools were found at three larger sites: Panskoye, a site in field 08-02 south of the fortified settlement of Skalistoe 5, and a site on Hill 11-1. All three can be dated provisionally to the late Classical and early Hellenistic periods. Although no architectural remains were observed in the ploughed fields in the plain, substantial remains were identified on the inland hill

regarded as belonging to the distant chora of Chersonesos from around the middle of the 4th century BC. This area has been equated with the plain (πεδίον) mentioned in the famous inscription from Chersonesos, the so-called Oath of Chersonesos (IOSPE 12 401)[4], which relates that it was primarily used for agricultural purposes to cultivate grain and grapes.

The use of the area around Kalos Limen and Panskoye for agricultural purposes has been made probable by the finds of a cadastral system, a farmhouse with a pithos storeroom east of Kalos Limen[5], and the identification of a storage room of amphorae in Building Complex U6 at Panskoye. Charred

1 For the settlement of Panskoye see Hannestad *et al.* (eds.) 2002 and for the necropolis Stolba & Rogov, forthcoming. For the whole of the Tarchankut peninsula in the Classical and Hellenistic period see e.g. Randsborg 1994 and Vnukov 2001.
2 Peña 2007, 152-153, 205 fig. 7.6.
3 A full publication of the survey is currently being prepared by members of the survey team. For a preliminary account see Бильде *et al.* 2007, additional information can be found at http://www.pontos.dk/field_projects/survey.
4 Stolba 2005a.
5 Щеглов 1967.
6 The Chersonesean amphora Ad 10, cf. Janušević & Ščeglov 2002.

plateaus. Remains of probably six above-ground stone structures were found on Hill 11-2 approximately half a kilometre south of the site on Hill 11-1, and as many as eleven structures may be identifiable on Hill 12. Geomagnetic survey as well as a few small-scale excavations revealed that many household pits were situated close to the above-ground structures. Although no excavations were undertaken on Hill 11 the excavations of some of these pits on Hill 1 and Hill 8 showed that the pits probably served as storage facilities. These types of household pits are very common in the Black Sea area. On Hill 8 a Chersonesean amphora was also found on the floor of an above-ground structure.

A good example, of relevance to the re-used amphora tools presented here, comes from the Scythian-Greek settlement of Nikolaevka 2 on the northern side of the Dniester estuary south of Odessa. Here was found a household pit (no. 9) covered by an ash heap, which seems to have been dumped on top of the pit, containing eight amphorae, mostly Heraclaean, datable to the 4th century BC. On the basis of remains of charred pieces of wood found on top of the pit, the excavator proposed that the pit was originally closed with a wooden cover.[7] This pit is a good example of the way in which these household pits were used as storage facilities, whatever the amphorae originally contained. Interestingly, all of the amphorae were missing the toe and at least five were missing one or both of their handles, but they evidently still served as storage vessels. The excavation publication does not specify the context in more detail and no re-used amphora tools are mentioned, but here we might have a case of deliberate removal of amphora handles and toes to be used as tools.[8]

FUNCTIONS

The fact that the tools were found at different sites across the whole surveyed area suggests that they were related to a common practice performed in the early Hellenistic period in the rural hinterland of Kalos Limen and Panskoye. Considering the rural character of the area it would be natural to connect them in some way to agricultural work, although they cannot readily be associated with any specific activity. The occurrence of these tools on the site on the Plateau Hill 11-1 perhaps suggests that they were used in a daily domestic activity, perhaps in connection with the preparation of food. In food preparation they might have been associated with the grinding of salt. Salt was presumably extracted from the salt lakes near the

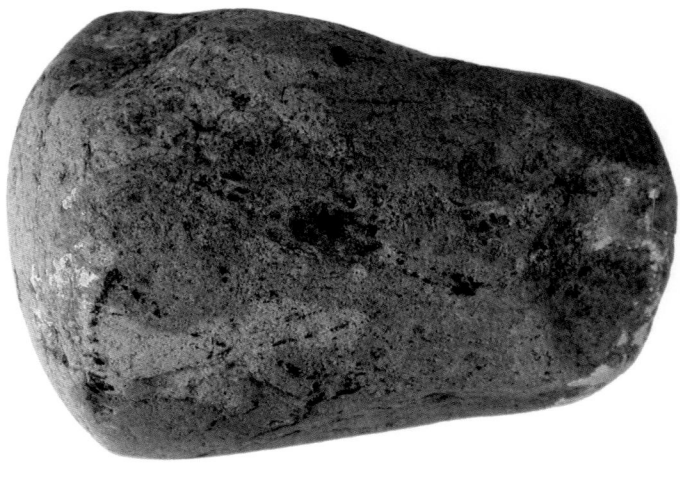

Fig. 5 Example of a grinding stone from the Džarylgač Survey Project.

settlement of Panskoye. Salt collected in such a fashion would have been very coarse and thus needed to be ground.[9] However, numerous grinding stones were found in the surveyed area which could also have been used for this purpose (Fig. 5). Although some osteological evidence for sheep breeding was found during the excavations on the Hill plateaus, the suggestion put forward by Peña, based on a sentence from Columella, that amphora handle tools could have been used for scabbing of animals is questionable. The handle tools discussed by Peña might have had this function, but it is difficult to associate the multidirectional striations, which are observed on the DSP amphora tools, with this specific task. One might also suspect that the tools could have been purposefully worn down to be used as tools for leather working. They might have been used to smooth the leather or create relief ornamentation on wet leather. Flint flakes and tools of various kinds were found at the larger settlements identified during the survey. Although the dating of these pieces is problematic, they could be interpreted as tools for bone and leather working. Such a workshop dating to the 4th century BC and containing many flint tools has been identified at the Thracian settlement of Helis in Bulgaria, and stone and bone implements, allegedly used for leather working, have been discovered at the Greek city of Nikonion on the Dniester liman.[10]

All of the interpretations presented above remain largely

speculative. One interpretation, which may be more likely, is that the amphora fragments were used as polishing tools in the process of pottery manufacture. In Mesoamerica pottery fragments with abrasions similar to the ones found on the amphora handle tools have been interpreted as potter's tools. The Mayan settlement of K'axob in northern Belize provides very convincing evidence for the use of broken pottery pieces in pottery manufacture.[11] On the basis of microscopic use-wear analysis as well as subsequent experimental replication of the K'axob pottery, 31 pottery fragments could be identified as having been used in various phases of the potting process. These 31 fragments were contextually associated with a domestic pottery workshop containing a kiln. Five basic functions of the tools were recognized: smoothing, scraping, incising, polishing and drilling. By visual comparison alone the abraded areas of the amphora handle tools are best comparable to the traces left on the K'axob tools that were used for polishing. The lustrous appearance and slight concavity of the polished areas as well as the presence of multidirectional striations are all characteristic features of the K'axob polishing tools. In addition, the K'axob potter's tools were made of fragments of utilitarian vessels presumably, at least in part, due to their abrasion resistance. This can be compared to the fact that only fragments of transport amphorae show traces of having been used as polishing tools in the surrounding area of Panskoye. Efforts to classify the K'axob polishing tools and observations made during the replication of the pottery also demonstrated that the shape of the tool was not an important factor in the selection of polishing tools. This accords well with the variety in the types of the amphora handle tools.

Furthermore, as previously mentioned, many flint flakes were found in the areas surveyed by us. At K'axob the highest concentration of obsidian blades on the whole site was found in the area of the workshop, which suggests a connection between ceramic tools, lithic flakes and pottery production. We know that pottery production took place in the survey area. Small domestic pottery kilns have been found at Panskoye I and Masliny further to the northeast on the Tarkhankut peninsula. The kiln at Panskoye I was found in *Room 7* in building complex U6 together with a pile of *grog*, and a limestone plate presumably used in its production. Vladimir F. Stolba has pointed out the existence of a small group of polished handmade pots.[12] Polishing tools have also been found in the late Archaic pottery

workshop in Pantikapaion. I.D. Marčenko has published a fragment of a finger from a marble sculpture, which according to him was used to smooth the surface of the pottery produced in the workshop. Marčenko states that several such tools were found during the excavation and it is reasonable to assume that this praxis continued in the late Classical/early Hellenistic period.[13]

The comparative evidence from K'axob and Pantikapaion speaks strongly for an interpretation of the re-used amphora handle tools as potter's tools, which were perhaps primarily, but not necessarily exclusively, used for polishing or smoothing handmade pottery. If this interpretation is accepted we would have to regard the find spots of these tools as sites for household pottery production.

The more or less contemporary existence of multiple, small, household pottery production sites within a comparatively limited area should not surprise us. A similar pattern was observed by Joseph C. Carter following the survey of the Metapontine *chora*.[14] Carter has argued that, in the Metapontine region, the location of water sources dictated the locations of pottery workshops. Access to water may also have been a determining factor in the location of the household pottery workshops around the Džarylgač Lake. Easy access to water in the form of natural springs or water concentrations close to the surface was facilitated by the Sarmatian and Pontic limestone formations at certain places where the hills meet the plain as well as in the area

7 Мелюкова 1975, 12.
8 Another recently discovered re-use of amphorae comes from the site of Zavetnoe 5 near Akra in the Eastern Crimea. Here the lower parts of amphorae, found in a storage pit for grain, were apparently used as shovels. In addition, the site also yielded polishing implements of both stone, bone and ceramics. For some published examples, see Соловьев & Шепко 2004, 14 fig. 18-19 and 23 fig. 32. I am grateful to the director of the survey, Sergej Solovyov, for kindly sharing this information with me.
9 For the importance of salt in Antiquity in the Western Crimea see Кутайсов 2004, 42-43, although the evidence for the Classical and Hellenistic periods is meagre.
10 For Helis, see Stoyanov *et al.* 2006, 15-17; for Nikonion, see Sekerskaya 2001, 86.
11 López Varela *et al.* 2001; López Varela *et al.* 2002. A similar use of ceramic fragments in pottery manufacture has also been observed at Gordion in Anatolia, see Henrickson 2005, 125.
12 Stolba 2002, 180 with further references. See in particular Hannestad 2005.
13 Марченко 1967, 152, fig. 1.2.
14 Carter 2006, 33 and 150.

close to the northern coastline.[15] Considering the overall low density of off-site pottery scatter observed in the entire surveyed area, it is not surprising that the amphora handle tools are related to sites. It is, however, noteworthy that tools were only found on sites at the northern borders of the fields south of Lake Džarylgač near the water. To the north of the lake all the amphora handle tools appear to form a cluster close to a spring south of Skalistoe 5. However, our current knowledge of the organization of pottery production in the Western Crimea is limited. No ceramic tools, or any other kind of tools, are reported from the two larger Hellenistic pottery workshops in Chersonesos. Only one pottery workshop has been reported in the estuary of the Bel'bek river north of Sevastopol in the Chersonesean home *chora*, but this complex unfortunately remains unpublished.[16] One amphora handle tool was found in the "halo" of the settlement of Panskoye I U6, where the manufacture of handmade pottery is proven, and three more come from Panskoye II less than 2 km. south of Panskoye I.

The situation outlined above raises a new possibility for understanding the landscape around Kalos Limen and Panskoye in the early Hellenistic period. The question of the identity of the people who inhabited the Chersonesean *chora* is a topic of continuous contention in scholarly work on Chersonesos. When the Dorian colony was founded, traditionally in 422/421 BC, a few indigenous Taurian settlements existed on the Herakleian peninsula less than 10 km. south of Chersonesos.[17] Around the middle of the 4th century BC the Chersoneseans expanded their chora to include the peninsula where they undertook a large scale division of the land into *kleroi* and constructed fortification walls. This confiscation on the part of the Greeks is supposed to have caused the expropriation and eviction of the Taurians from the peninsula, who then settled on the Sapun Hill east of the Peninsula. On the basis of a line in the famous late 2nd century BC decree of Diophantos (IOSPE I2, 352) mentioning the Taurians as "τούς δέ παροικούντας Ταύρους", D. Pippidi has argued that from the time the Herakleian peninsula came under Chersonesean possession, the Taurians formed a dependent population who tilled the Greek farmland.[18] The Taurian settlements on the Sapun Hill have never been fully published, but from what has been reported they seem to be identical to the settlements identified by the DSP on the inland hill plateaus.[19] Similarly a mix of Greeks and indigenous Scythians, or Hellenized Scythians, at Olbia in the period from the 5th to 3rd

centuries BC, have been discussed on the basis of a passage from Herodotus, who mentions the Ἕλληνές Σκύθαι (Hdt. IV.17) and the later so-called Protogenes decree (IOSPE I2, 32) mentioning the "μιξέλληνες".[20]

The intensive surveys undertaken during the DSP provide us with the opportunity to evaluate whether an indigenous population was involved in the cultivation of the land in the distant chora of Chersonesos. Here the amphora tools may play an important part. We only have very scarce information regarding the distribution and frequency of the handmade pottery in the home *chora* of Chersonesos, but on the basis of an unpublished report of the Tarchankut and lower Bug expedition Eugenij Ja. Rogov mentions a very low percentage of handmade pottery amounting to less than 4% of the ceramic assemblages.[21] The frequency of handmade pottery on the smaller rural sites identified by us is, on the contrary, very high. Here the percentage of handmade pottery in the assemblages varies from 28% at the site with the lowest frequency of handmade pottery to more than 82% at the site where most handmade pottery was found. Taking into account the fact that we have more direct evidence for the production of handmade pottery in the distant *chora* of Chersonesos in the form of the previously mentioned kilns at Panskoye I and Masliny, as well as the much higher frequency of handmade pottery in this area, and if we are correct in disassociating handmade pottery with Greek settlers, then we perhaps have better evidence for the involvement of an indigenous population in the agricultural work in this area than on the Herakleian peninsula. The ongoing surveys being conducted in various parts of Crimea by Ukrainian and Russian archaeologists may, in the future, clarify whether a high frequency of handmade pottery can be directly correlated to a presence of similar polishing tools.[22]

---

15 Смекалова 2007.
16 The workshop is mentioned by G.M. Nikolaenko (2006, 170) who refers to an unpublished report from 1903 by N.M. Pečenkin.
17 Кравченко 2005.
18 Pippidi 1975, 72-74, but see also Saprykin 1998, 245-246 with further references.
19 Zubar'-Kravčenko 2003.
20 Damyanov 2003; for a broader discussion of the term mixhellenes, see Von Bredow 1994.
21 Рогов 2002, 142.
22 For a recent overview of surveys in the Crimea, see Stolba 2008 and Smekalova 2008.

Depositional Patterns and Behavior in the Athenian Agora: When Disaster Strikes

BY KATHLEEN LYNCH

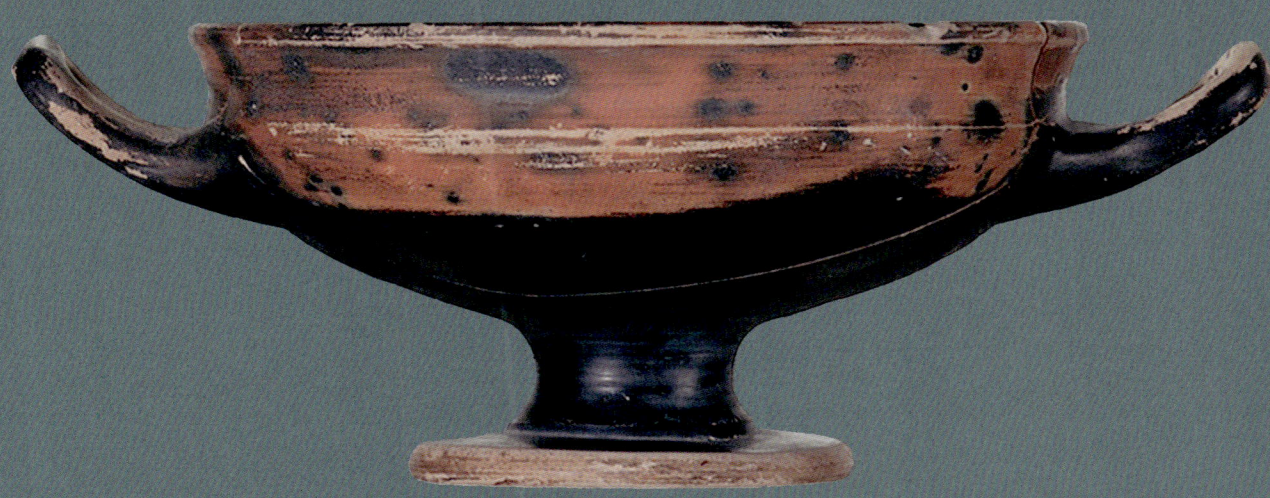

Depositional Patterns and Behavior in the Athenian Agora: When Disaster Strikes

BY KATHLEEN LYNCH

Recycling and conservation form a major theme of J. Theodore Peña's *Roman Pottery in the Archaeological Record.* His discussion and case-studies emphasize the investment ceramics represent, and his discussions assume that Roman users desired to conserve resources and reduce waste.[1] There is no reason to imagine Greek producers and consumers were much different. His investigation of re-use highlights the problems archaeologists face while trying to extrapolate original use and users from dumped deposits. A pot might have gone through a variety of primary, secondary, and even tertiary use contexts before discard, and even then the discarded material might be reclaimed for further use. The analysis of the life of a pot as a "system" imbues a sense of pragmatism to its life course or "use-life". We are left with the impression that producers and consumers made decisions affecting the life cycle of a pot based predominantly on economy and practicality.[2] However, unlike the biological phenomena that the term life cycle implies, human behavior is often "highly complex and somewhat messy".[3] Sometimes humans do things for illogical or even emotional reasons.

This paper presents one case-study in which unexpected human behavior may account for the peculiar life cycle and early discard of an assemblage of pottery: the 22 deposits from the Athenian Agora excavations that contain debris from the clean-up following the Persian destruction of Athens in 480 BC. Twenty-one of these deposits were the topic of an article by T. Leslie Shear, Jr. (1993).[4] Unlike typical refuse dumps, these deposits contain some complete and barely used objects. Athenians returning to their houses after the war made the decision to discard valuable resources, and such a choice should remind us that not all depositional behaviors can be predicted and modelled.

The excavations of the Athenian Agora have contributed significant studies of the typology and chronology of Greek pottery.[5] The backbone to these studies consists of a sequence of closed deposits, mainly wells filled in with debris after the well's use has ended.[6] Owing to the continuous occupation of the site, excavated stratigraphy is complicated and fragmented, rendering closed deposits valuable keys to the identification of contexts and to the development of pottery over time. Athenians routinely used open, defunct wells as refuse pits, sometimes filling them up slowly over decades, but in other cases, filling them in rapidly using fill of homogeneous character and date.[7]

In 479 BC, Persian troops sacked Athens under the command of Xerxes' general Mardonius. Not only do we have archaeological evidence for the sack, but Herodotos (9.13.2) claimed that Mardonius "burned Athens…, and if anything at all was left standing of the walls, or the houses, or the temples, he hurled it down and reduced it to heaps of rubble". This destruction produced both the famous *Perserschutt* on the Athenian acropolis[8] and the fragmentary architectural elements that would eventually be incorporated into the northern acropolis wall.

After the defeat of the Persians at Plataia, the Athenians, most of whom had fled to refuge sites, returned to their devastated city. Thoukudides (1.89.3) relates that the Athenians "… prepared to rebuild the city and the walls. For only short stretches of the circuit wall had been left standing, and most of the houses were in ruins; though a few survived, in which the Persian nobles themselves were quartered". Thoukudides emphasizes that the Athenians concentrated on rebuilding the city walls, but domestic clean-up and rebuilding must have proceeded apace because people needed places to live. The evidence for discard of pottery during this clean-up phase offers surprising insight on the clean-up mentality among post-war Athenians.

At the time of the Persian Wars, many Athenian houses featured household wells.[9] A conservative estimate is that at least half of the wells filled in after the Persian Wars were domestic in context although all deposits contained some debris originating in the households of Athens. Only a few of these wells can be associated with remnants of domestic architecture,[10] but this is owing to another character of clean-up behavior: in several instances it is clear that Athenians leveled the late Archaic houses to build anew.[11] Wells could also be associated with sacred, public, and as discussed below, commercial activities. Contributions to the fill may have come from more than the primary users of the well, thus resulting in a deposit from mixed primary use origins.[12] As a result, it is difficult to say with confidence that the contents of each deposit equate to the contents of only one household. I have argued, however, that the most recently excavated Persian destruction deposit, well J 2:4, did preserve only one household's pottery and contained little or no debris from the Persian destruction from outside the house.[13]

Fills of similar character characterize the Persian destruction deposits. The deposits include 17 wells and five pits or trenches (the location of each is marked with a star on the plan, Fig. 1). Shear presented evidence for both the homogeneity of contents and date of these deposits and linked their formation securely to the clean-up following the Persian destruction. Excavators have also noted occasional thick strata of debris corresponding in character to the Persian destruction deposits.[14] In addition, road pits or gullies were filled in with similar debris.

Each of the wells was put out of use by filling up the shaft with a large quantity of pottery, building debris, stones, or other material, and most were excavated carefully enough to distinguish strata within the fill. In general, fills consist of a period of use deposit at the bottom: this comprises pottery dropped into the well during use and refuse discarded into the well. Well owners did periodically clean out the period of use deposit as is indicated by the foot holds on the sides of some wells allowing access to the bottom, so an absence of period of use deposit does not necessarily mean the well was new when it went out of use.[15] In the Persian destruction deposits, the next stratum above the period of use sometimes consists of intact, or nearly complete, pottery.[16] In well J 2:4, delicate

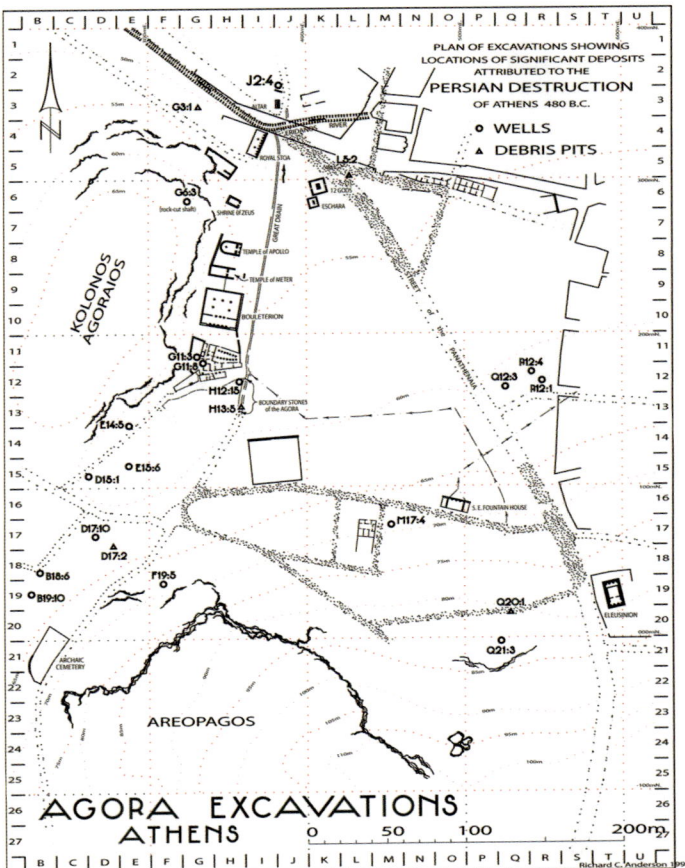

Fig. 1 Plan of the Athenian Agora ca. 480 BC with Persian destruction debris deposits marked. After Shear 1993, fig. 1; courtesy Agora Excavations.

1 Peña 2007, "A Model of the Life Cycle of Roman Pottery", Chapter 1, 6-16.

2 Peña 2007, 13-14 discusses the assumptions and limitations of this model.

3 Peña 2007, 16.

4 For the 22nd deposit, well J 2:4, see Lynch 1999 and Lynch forthcoming.

5 Brann 1962; Sparkes & Talcott 1970; Moore & Philippides 1986; Rotroff 1997; Moore 1997; Rotroff 2006a.

6 Sparkes & Talcott 1970, 43-46.

7 Peña 2007, 283. Pottery used to fill in a defunct well is, technically, re-use in that the discarded pottery is re-used to make the well safe.

8 Hurwit 1989, 63 and note 74; Hurwit 1999, 141-142; Lindenlauf 1997, 46-115. On the chronology of these Acropolis fills, see Stewart 2008.

9 Camp 1977, 102-104. Some wells, such as those associated with the Archaic buildings beneath the Tholos (G 11:3; G 11:8), were possibly civic or public; Thompson 1940, 25-26, 28-32; Shear 1993, 449-453, fig. 8.

10 Shear 1993, 405-406: B 19:10, B 18:6, D 17:10, H 12:15, Q 21:3.

11 Shear 1993, 406.

12 Shear 1993, 384.

13 Lynch 1999, 28-53, and forthcoming, chapter 2.

14 For example, fills associated with the Old Bouleuterion, see Shear 1993, 472-477.

15 For example, H 12:15, Shear 1993, 453-455 fig. 7. See also the discussion in Sparkes & Talcott 1970, where it is assumed that owners cleaned out their wells periodically, and that the presence of large numbers of water jars in the period of use fill of Persian destruction deposits signifies an interruption that prevented the owner from maintaining the well.

16 In addition to J 2:4, see also G 11:3, Shear 1993, 449-451 fig. 8; H 12:15, Shear 1993, 453-455 fig. 7.

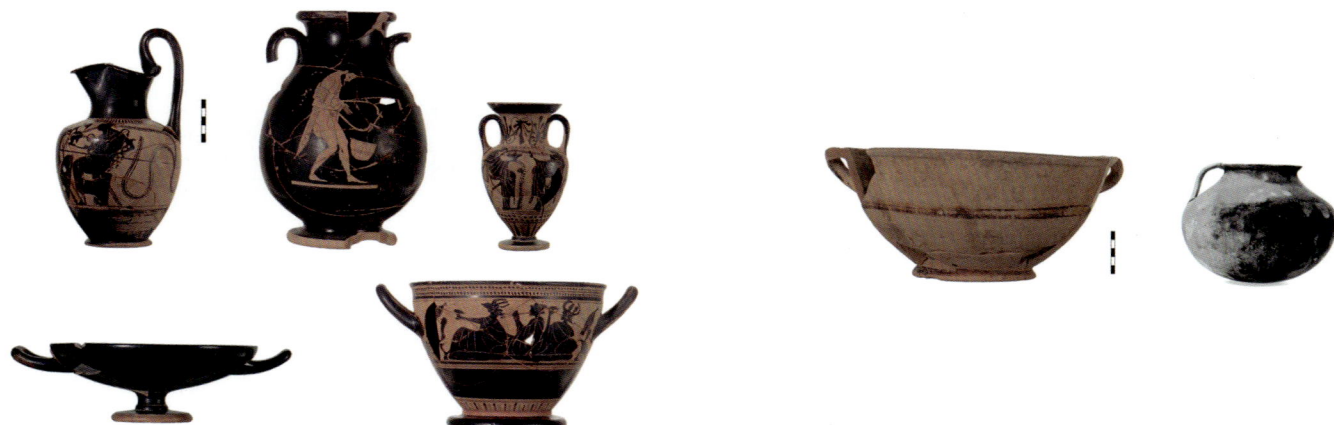

Fig. 2 Selection of complete or intact vessels from well J 2:4. Left side, Top row: P 32415, P 32418, P 32416; bottom row: P 32417, P 32413. Right side: P 32488, P 32407. Courtesy Agora Excavations.

cups and table amphorae mend up almost complete (Fig. 2). In fact 11 of the 22 Persian destruction deposits preserved complete or intact fine ware vessels including drinking cups. This observation of complete pots helps to refine Shear's statement that, "There can be no doubt that, in many instances, the pottery was subjected to heavy breakage before it came to be dumped into the wells and pits here under discussion". [17] While his statement is true – much of the pottery in these deposits was subjected to breakage – a significant and meaningful portion was not. It is this portion that illustrates unanticipated behavior. Not only are these complete objects that do not belong in wells – you cannot fetch water with a kylix – they do not appear to have been broken before deposition. Had they been broken above ground, their condition would be more fragmentary, especially missing handles and delicate body fragments, and the fragments would be more dispersed in the deposit. Instead, these objects were tossed into the well undamaged and formed a pocket above the period of use.

The Rectangular Rock-cut Shaft (G 6:3) and the Stoa Gutter Well (Q 12:3) also preserved complete cups and lekythoi.[18] These deposits display typical Persian destruction characteristics but were primarily filled with the stock of potters' shops. The Rectangular Rock-cut Shaft is not a well, and it was already in use as a refuse dump at the time of the Persian wars; only its upper fill is debris from the Persian destruction.[19] The Shaft contained over 200 inventoried objects including 104 complete or nearly complete black-

figured lekythoi and hundreds more fragments stored with the uninventoried pottery. Many of the lekythoi bore identical imagery by the same hand, and the fill contained multiple examples by the same or other hands. Similarly the Stoa Gutter Well contained over 300 inventoried objects including 155 complete or nearly complete black-figured lekythoi, also with hundreds more uninventoried.[20] These black-figured lekythoi point to a commercial establishment: a pottery sales shop specializing in lekythoi and drinking vessels produced by one or more workshops.[21]

Sally Roberts described the Stoa Gutter Well deposit as "the contents of various pottery workshops destroyed at the time of the Persian sack of Athens",[22] and Eugene Vanderpool said of the Rectangular Rock-cut Shaft, "The masses of broken pottery…suggest that the dump was used by near-by potters' shops for disposing of their broken, mis-fired, or otherwise unsaleable wares. This view is borne out by the finding in the well of mis-fired pieces of pottery".[23] These views are somewhat misleading. There is no evidence that these deposits should be associated with the *production* of pottery. Peña's careful delineation of what constitutes production debris draws attention to these deposits' lack of wasters, kiln equipment, or other detritus of production.[24] The Rectangular Rock-cut Shaft did contain broken firing rings, flat, donut-shaped separaters used to stack pots in a kiln.[25] These rings, few in number, may have been used to stabilize pots brought in from the kiln to the shop. The misfires that both Roberts and Vanderpool adduce

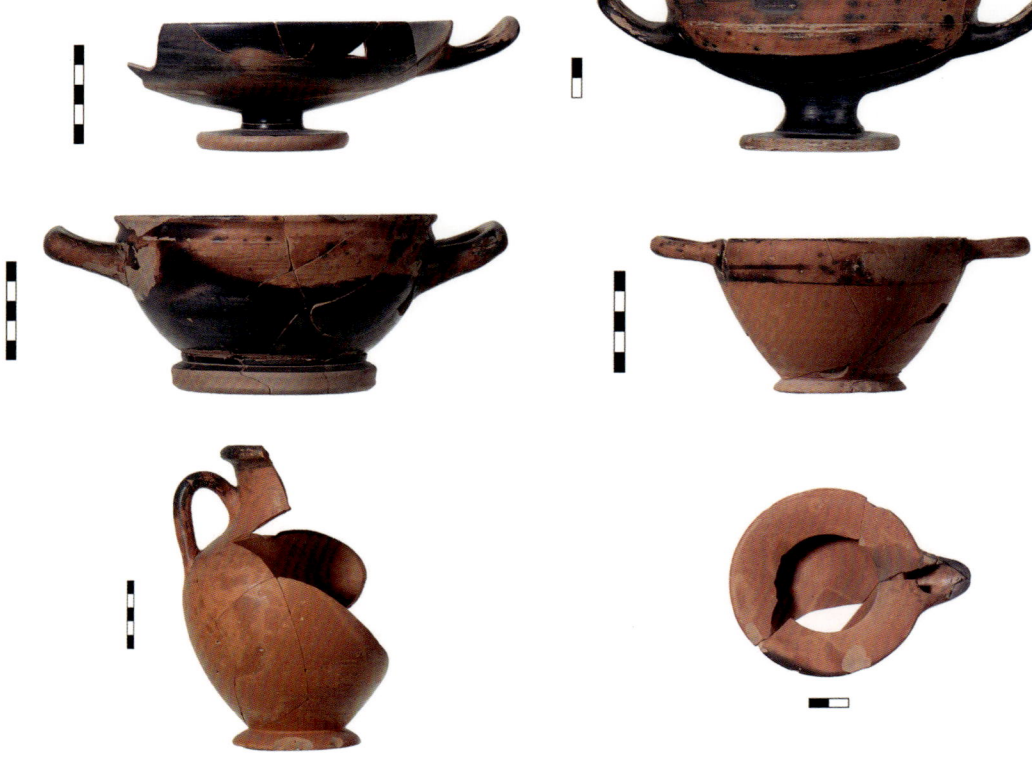

Fig. 3 Selection of mis-fired vessels from well J 2:4. Top: P 32478, P 32479, Middle: P 32472, P 32477, Bottom: P 32757, L 5982. Colors range from red to orange to greenish-yellow. Courtesy Agora Excavations.

as evidence for production are unevenly fired pieces, and subsequent study has shown that Athenian consumers happily bought and used far worse such as the assortment of drastically misfired complete pots from well J 2:4 (Fig. 3).[26] Instead, the shops associated with the Rectangular Rock-cut Shaft and the Stoa Gutter Well must have been the Agora store fronts or distribution sites for selected pottery workshops. Potters made the pottery elsewhere in the city, then brought it to the Agora for sale. And yet not all the material in the Stoa Gutter Well need have been intended for sale. The inventoried objects include only 11 pieces of red-figure and over 300 pieces of black-figure with hundreds more uninventoried black-figure fragments. The number of red-figured vessels, and the shapes, dates, and painters in the red-figured component parallel those of the domestic deposit J 2:4. Since the Stoa Gutter Well also contained domestic objects such as lekanai and cooking ware, the red-figure in the Stoa Gutter Well – including the famous Gorgos Cup – was most likely not for sale, but was the property of the shop owner, who probably lived on the premises.[27]

17 Shear 1993, 388.
18 Roberts 1986, many examples, but especially nos. 36 and 38, pl. 7, black-glazed cup-skyphoi, with only a few breaks.
19 Vanderpool 1938, Vanderpool 1946; Francis and Vickers 1988.
20 Roberts 1986.
21 Μπαζιωτοπούλου–Βαλαβάνη 1994 discusses a kiln with finds from both the CHC Group and the Cock Group, two stylistically related workshop groups found in both the Stoa Gutter Well and the Rectangular Rock-cut Shaft.
22 Roberts 1986, 4.
23 Vanderpool 1946, 266.
24 Peña 2007, 291-292, plus case-studies.
25 Vanderpool published one fragmentary example and restored one as an unidentified object: Vanderpool 1946, 327-328 no. 303 pl. 66; and See Monaco 2000 and Μπαζιωτοπούλου–Βαλαβάνη 1994, 50 and fig. 6.
26 Roberts 1986, 4 nos. 4, 18, 38, and 81; Vanderpool 1946, 266 nos. 75, 219, and 220.
27 For the Gorgos Cup, see Moore 1997, 317-318 (with additional bibliography), no. 1407 pl. 130. These commercial deposits document commercial activity in the area that would become Classical Agora late in the fourth quarter of the 6th century BC. For the debate on when the Classical Agora became the civic and commercial center of Athens, see most recently Papadopoulos 2003, 280-297.

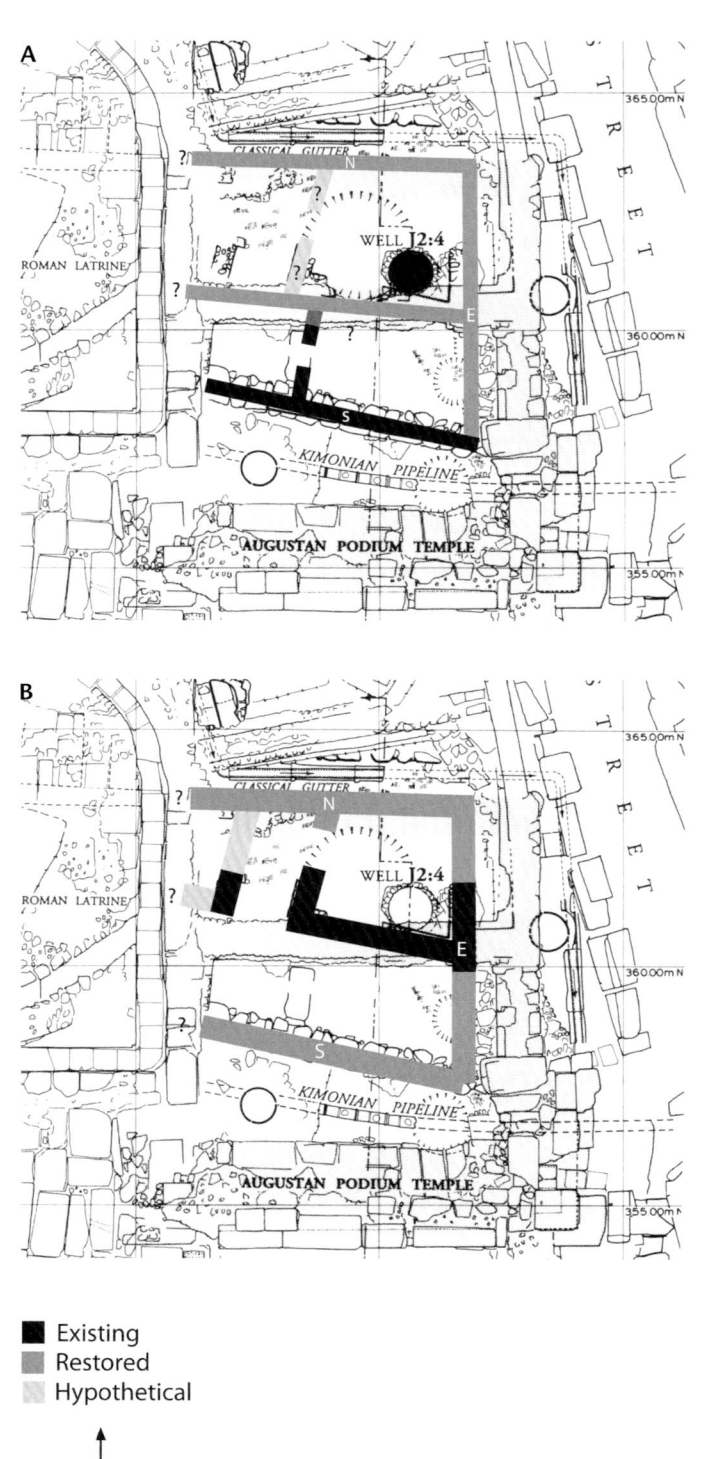

Existing
Restored
Hypothetical

N

Fig. 4 Restored plan of the House of Well J 2:4 a) at the time of the Persian destruction of Athens, and b) after Post-War renovations.

The Roman General Sulla's destruction of Athens in 86 BC, another example of a similar manmade disaster, provides a useful comparison. Deposits of debris generated by the Sullan sack do occur, but there is a longer lapse between destruction and rebuilding. (Does it take longer to rebuild when you are the loser?) Even the deposits deemed "earliest" in the post-Sullan clean-up effort are characterized by highly fragmentary pottery.[28] The Sullan deposits do not show the same discard of complete, functional vessels, and the clean-up did not proceed as quickly as that after the Persian sack.

The far-reaching post-Persian clean-up behavior demonstrated by the closure of functioning domestic and commercial wells and discard of useable pottery is paralleled by extensive architectural rebuilding. In six cases for which we can associate domestic architecture and a deposit, the later house was rebuilt on a different plan.[29] In three cases, the Archaic well was filled in with destruction debris, then sealed by a floor of the rebuilt house. For example, well Q 21:3, which would have been in the courtyard of its Archaic period house, was sealed under the *andron* of the Classical period house. Well J 2:4 and two other wells were sealed by walls of the Classical period running on top of them. The footprint of the house of well J 2:4 stayed the same; the Classical phase house used the Archaic foundation (Fig. 4.a-b). This house must not have suffered complete destruction, but survived well enough to be reconstructed without its courtyard well. As Shear notes, "Builders of the Classical period took no cognizance whatsoever of the location of Archaic wells. … [it is] as if they set their new structures upon a *tabula rasa* from which the Archaic predecessors had been quite literally swept away".[30]

In sum, the unanticipated behaviors seen during the Persian destruction clean-up include: houses rebuilt on new lines, wells filled with broken but also with some useable pottery, and the closure of the wells themselves, which may be the most unexpected of all. Clean water is the lifeblood of a city, particularly after a disaster, and if most of the wells were privately owned, intentionally putting them out of use denotes a significant loss of investment to the homeowner. Shear presents evidence showing that these wells had not "gone dry" or become defunct because of a collapse.[31] In well J 2:4, intact, unbroken cooking ware provides evidence for an existing water level at the time of discard. The thin-walled pots must have hit the water and sunk down as opposed to being tossed in on top of a pile, which would have meant certain breakage.[32] John Camp has attributed a 7th-century BC episode of well closures to drought,[33] but something more powerful than drought must have initiated the closing of these late Archaic wells. But who closed the wells and why. Here are three possibilities, which but are not exclusive of each other:[34]

1. The Athenians choked or poisoned the wells as they left so that the Persians could not use them.

2. The Persians choked or poisoned the wells as they left so that the Athenians could not use the water on return.

3. The Athenians filled the wells in during the post-war clean-up and reconstruction period.

1 and 2 are practical war-time strategies. If you are going to choke off a well (literally, to fill it in so that the water table cannot be reached), then you are going to use large masses of material, presumably, readily at hand because you are in a hurry. Herodotos records several instances of choking wells as a battle strategy.[35] In fact, some of the deposits do have deep fills of gravelly bedrock, which is easily dug in the Agora, in addition to ceramics. However, in some cases, this dumped fill of gravelly bedrock is accompanied by broken architectural members, roof tiles, or mudbrick.[36] Architectural fragments amongst the dug bedrock had to have been deposited after the destruction of the city, or possibly during, but not before. Therefore, option 1, that the Athenians choked the wells on their way out of town, seems less likely.

Joins of fragmentary pottery from top to bottom of the fills seem to argue against the Persians choking off the wells (Option 2). In well J 2:4, there is a deep layer of dug bedrock above the pocket of complete fineware. However, fragments from incomplete objects join across the dug bedrock. These joining fragments of fragments seem to argue for the entire fill being deposited over a short period of time. That is, the complete fineware went in first with one or two shovels-full of broken pottery, then the dug bedrock was used to fill in the bulk of the shaft, with the remaining fragments of broken pottery being thrown in at the top. The Persians likely would have wanted to fill up a well just enough to eliminate future use without expending unnecessary effort in such tasks as digging bedrock. The gravelly fill makes more sense as a by-product of post-war rebuilding activities that required foundations cut into the marly bedrock.

If the Persians had filled in the well, then 1) the effort to dig bedrock for fill seems extraordinary, and 2) the idea that they tossed complete pots and some of the fragments into the well makes little sense.

Of course, there are ways other than "choking" to render a water source unusable. For example, it is possible that the Persians dumped human or horse feces into the wells. Unfortunately, flotation analysis of the soil from well J 2:4 was inconclusive, and perhaps future excavations will offer more evidence to test this hypothesis.[37]

Option three, that the Athenians filled in the wells themselves during the clean-up, is the least logical, but may be the best explanation. In fact, a combination of 2 and 3 is possible: that the Persians rendered the wells unusable, causing the Athenians to fill them in upon return. Another clue to depositional behavior comes from a further category of Peña's system: refuse dumps. Archaeological and literary evidence attest to *koprones*, public pits for the disposal of household debris, but both date mainly to the 4th century BC.[38] However, the stratigraphy of well J 2:4 preserved some indirect evidence for the existence of refuse dumps in the late Archaic period: the oldest and most worn pieces of

---

28 Rotroff 1997, 34-36; Rotroff calls these "pure" Sullan debris deposits, see 35, note 127.
29 Shear 1993, 405-406: B 19:10, B 18:6, D 17:10, H 12:15, Q 21:3; and Lynch 1999, 71-81 (J 2:4).
30 Shear 1993, 406.
31 Shear 1993, 403-405.
32 For example: P 32404, an intact chytra.
33 Camp 1977, 50-51, for a 4th century BC drought, 147-149.
34 Shear 1993, 417, offers variations on these options, but he is not able to determine which is most probable.
35 Poisoning wells constitutes a well-known and heinous act of war used throughout history. Herodotos (9.49) says that the Persians choked the Greeks' water source near the battlefield of Plataia. At 4.120 and 140 the Scythians choked wells to prevent the Persians from using them. Xenophon, *Hell* 3.1.18, describes choking of wells by Spartans during an attack on a Persian city.
36 Shear 1993, 403-404. See especially pit L 5:2, Shear 1993, 459-461.
37 In more modern times, in the 1939-1940 Winter War, the Finns poisoned wells with manure as they retreated in front of the Russian advance, Trotter 1991, 68. 21st century examples include wells poisoned with chicken carcasses or diapers in Israel "Settlers suspected of well attack", BBC, 13 July 2004, http://news.bbc.co.uk/2/hi/middle_east/3891531.stm, and wells poisoned with dead animal and human carcasses in Darfur, Prunier 2005, note 60.
38 Thompson 1959, 101-102; Young 1951, 194-195; Owens 1983; Ault 1999.

pottery – from ca. 600 – were at the top of the well. We can hypothetically reconstruct the process of filling the well as this: the first objects to go into the well were the ceramics from the household's cabinets. Still needing more fill, dug bedrock was used to fill the majority of the shaft, probably from nearby reconstruction projects. At this point more of the damaged fragmentary pottery from the house was deposited, accounting for joins from top to bottom. This probably means the floors of the house were being tidied while the big loads of fill were being brought in. Finally, still needing more material, or perhaps the fill had settled some, a wheelbarrow load or so of supplemental debris brought from a refuse dump capped the fill. Thus, the oldest pieces came into the house from outside and cannot be associated with activity of the house. Instead this supplementary fill indicates access to and use of a nearby refuse dump.

Even more illogical but plausible is that whether the Persians poisoned the wells or not, the Athenians may have felt a sense of miasma, or pollution upon returning to their houses, which the barbarians had wrecked or even occupied. Without the archaeological evidence it is difficult to recognize the motivation for closing the wells as practical or conceived. The less ambiguous evidence of rebuilding houses with new plans suggests that homeowners wanted to start over, to clean the slate and start fresh; thus, the idea of throwing away perfectly useable pottery does not seem so far-fetched.

To the Persians we must attribute the damage to architecture, sculpture, but only *some* pottery. How did pottery escape breakage by the sacking Persians? Shear is right in saying that the majority of the pottery in the deposits is fragmentary. However, the complete, undamaged pottery is mostly fineware but includes some household and cooking ware. Is it possible that these complete pots were stored some place in the house out of the way of the attackers, in a locked storeroom such as we hear about in Xenophon's *Oikonomikos*,[39] for example? If we had only complete fineware, one might wonder if it was placed in the wells for safe keeping by the departing Athenians. Do the complete cooking ware and some complete household vessels from the same pocket of complete pots argue against this? Further, if the goal were to preserve valuables, I think we would find traces of other unrecovered objects such as jewelry and metal vessels, but we do not. And the Athenians won! They could have recovered the hoarded objects, but they did not.

This analysis of the formation of the Persian destruction clean-up deposits in the Athenian Agora permitted us to see a reflection of human behavior. The choice to discard functioning pottery after the war indicates that the Athenians were willing to waste these resources in the service of something greater. What they gained from this expense may have been a higher quality of life, or at least the perception of one. Renovated houses and a shift to a public water source, possibly of higher quality, combined with a psychological need to start a new life may explain the choice.[40]

In conclusion, according to Peña's system, the Persian destruction deposits exhibit "re-use" of pottery. Specifically, pottery is reused as structural fill to close the wells. If that is all we said, the picture would be sadly incomplete, for behind this "re-use" is a much more complex relationship between material culture and behavior that defies expectations.

Nevertheless, Peña's book has invited us to look at the human agency behind the life cycle of pottery. In most cases, that agency can be explained plausibly with reference to conservation of resources. Peña has provided us with a normative model. Now that we can visualize the norm, deviations should prompt us as interpreters to go beyond the logical.

---

39 Xen. *Oikonomikos* 8.2-910.
40 No public water sources dating to the second or third quarter of the 5th century to replace the late Archaic wells have been found yet, although the Kimonian waterline to the Academy did come through the Agora. It is possible that it was tapped at some point. Shear 1984, 49, note 101.

ACKNOWLEDGEMENTS
I wish to thank the Director of the Agora Excavations, Dr. John McK. Camp, for his support and permission to study deposit J 2:4 and the staff of the Agora excavation for their help doing so. I also thank the organizers for their invitation to give this paper and Ted Peña for inspiring us to think about pottery in new ways.

The Waste Stream of a Late Roman House:
Case Study of the Commissary Block in the Earthquake House at Kourion

BY BENJAMIN COSTELLO IV

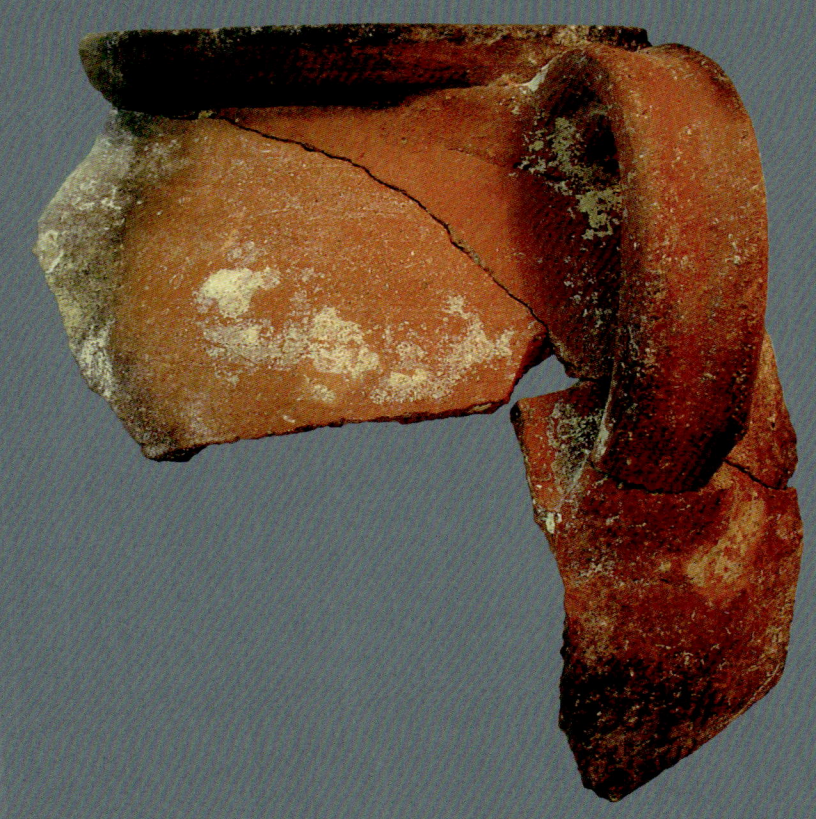

The Waste Stream of a Late Roman House: Case Study of the Commissary Block in the Earthquake House at Kourion

BY BENJAMIN COSTELLO IV

Of the various human behaviors that contribute to the formation of the archaeological record, perhaps the most universal among all cultures is the creation of waste material that must be disposed of. These discard processes, which have come to be known collectively as the "waste stream", include the deposition of material at the site of its creation (primary discard), the deposition of material away from its place of creation (secondary discard), and the temporary caching of material prior to discard with the prospect that it may be re-used in some capacity other than its primary use role (provisional discard).[1] In the Greco-Roman world such waste stream processes have begun to be examined at the settlement level, particularly in terms of certain very large, very 'high profile' examples including Monte Testaccio and the middens at Mons Claudianus.[2] Far more often, even for a well-preserved site like Pompeii, waste streams have been largely overlooked until relatively recently,[3] with the lack of attention paid to such processes being even more pronounced at the level

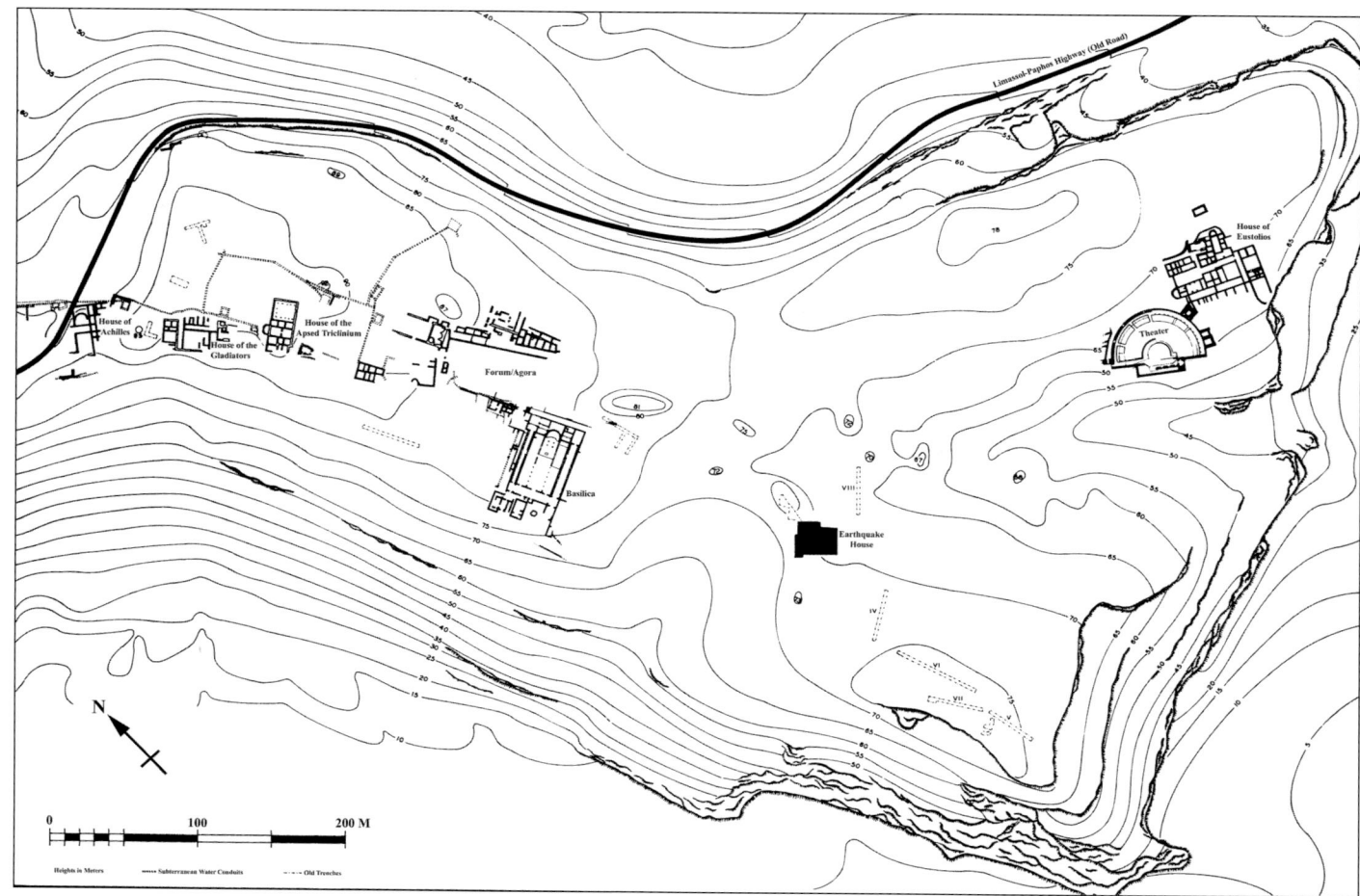

Fig. 1 Map of the Kourion Acropolis with the location of the Earthquake House (adapted from Mitford 1971, pl. 3).

of the individual household.[4] This paper offers a model for the study of the domestic waste stream of a house using the specific case of the so-called Earthquake House on the Kourion acropolis.

THE EARTHQUAKE HOUSE

The Earthquake House was likely built some time in the late 1st or early 2nd centuries AD,[5] and was destroyed along with the rest of the site by an earthquake at some point during the late 4th century AD. Following its destruction, Kourion was abandoned for approximately 20-30 years, before being reoccupied on a much smaller scale at the beginning of the 5th century. However, the site occupied by the Earthquake House appears to have been outside this resettlement zone, since no evidence of post-earthquake construction or attempts to salvage material preserved within the remains of the structure were discovered during its excavation.

In 1934, J.F. Daniel uncovered parts of the Earthquake House during his excavation of Trench III, whose finds included the skeletal remains of two individuals and numerous intact ceramic and metal artifacts whichappeared to confirm the destruction of the site by a massive earthquake in the late 4th century AD.[6] Despite these discoveries, excavation of Trench III was abandoned until 1984 when a team from the University of Arizona led by David Soren re-opened its southern end. The excavation of the Earthquake House revealed four distinct areas: the Main Block (Rooms 1,2,3,6,7, and 8); the Commissary Block (12,14, and 19), a courtyard and colonnade linking these first two sections (Rooms 15 and 18), and finally a large open courtyard (Room 11) (Fig. 2). Despite the recovery of five more skeletons and further numismatic evidence suggesting a link to an earthquake of 365 BC described by Ammianus Marcelinus,[7] the date of the house's destruction remains open to debate. However, the meticulous records and extensive retention of finds from the Arizona excavations allow consideration of a new issue that was not even a part of the original research design: the waste stream of the house in its late Roman period occupation. The best evidence for exploring this new issue comes from the Commissary Block, and since this is not a question or topic often considered in household archaeology in the Greco-Roman world, some methodological comment is needed before turning to the relevant data.

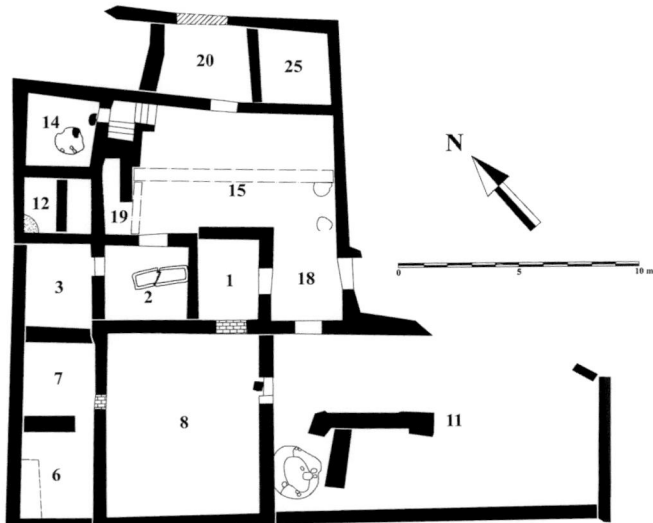

Fig. 2 Plan of the Earthquake House at Kourion, Cyprus (plan by author).

METHODOLOGY: EXPLORING THE WASTE STREAM

Archaeologically, two primary lines of evidence for the waste stream exist, the architectural and the artifactual. Each of these two categories is distinct and must first be

1 See LaMotta & Schiffer 1999, 21 for a general overview of formation processes. For other renderings of these processes see Hayden & Cannon 1983 and Needham & Spence 1997.
2 For the Greco-Roman world in general, see Dupré Raventós & Remolà 2000; Robinson 1993; Scobie 1986; Owens 1983. For Monte Testaccio see especially Rodríguez-Almeida 1984; Blázquez Martínez & Remesal Rodríguez (eds.) 1999 and 2001. For Mons Claudianus see Maxfield & Bingen 2001.
3 Exceptionally, see Maiuri 2002, 174-175, and Chiaramonte Treré et al. 1986, 21-54.
4 Cf. Peña 2007, 308-317.
5 Soren & Davis 1985, 296. The construction date was based on "imported and Cypriot Sigillata and a small quantity of fragments of early imperial lamps and early African Red Slip ware still to be studied".
6 Daniel Field Notebook p. 25. June 5, 1934: "Find clay pot, bronze pitcher, broken lamp, and part of another pot directly on the floor. Next to these, also on the floor, a human skeleton. This was not a burial. The person seems to have been standing when the house fell, and crushed where he stood. As there are no signs of fire an earthquake may have caused the disaster". Published in Soren & Davis 1985, 295 and Soren & James 1988, 80.
7 Amm. Marc. XXVI.10.15-19. For arguments against this link, see Lichcocka & Meyza 2001 and Fokaefs & Papadopoulos 2004.

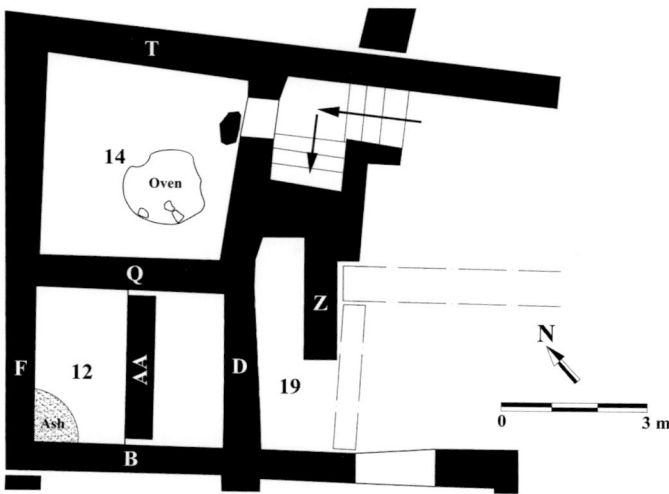

Fig. 3 The three rooms comprising the "commissary block" of the Earthquake House (plan by author).

examined individually utilizing specific methodology. Only after this initial analysis can the data sets be brought together and synthesized to provide a better picture of the general characteristics and processes that created a particular deposit.

Architectural Variables

A number of ethnographic studies have examined questions concerning the relationship between architecture and the discard of household waste.[8] This research has shown that refuse generated within domestic structures is normally cached as provisional discard within the structure before being removed into definitive discard.[9] In cases documented from the Greco-Roman world, this behavior often seems to have involved placing household waste into a built feature within the structure in a process that is classified by Peña as a form of provisional discard.[10] Such installations would then be emptied of their contents on a periodic basis, with the waste normally transported to a location outside the domestic space, although its deposition in some out of the way place within the structure itself has also been observed.[11] Based on these ethnographic observations, the plan of the Earthquake House was examined for architectural features or spaces that would have facilitated their use as areas for the disposal of household waste. Following this initial identification, material recovered from these likely

areas was studied in detail to determine if it possessed the characteristics of a deposit of this type.

One of the characteristics observed in discard deposits is elevated concentrations of artifacts, often of several different classes, within a relatively confined area. In order to compare concentrations of artifacts within locations of probable discard to the surrounding space, it was necessary to obtain three area calculations for rooms where such deposits were believed to exist. The first of these is the Total Usable Area, which was calculated by determining the total area of the room and subtracting from this the amount of space occupied by any built features within it. The second is the Total Available Area, which is the amount of space in the room that was open and unoccupied in which daily activities could be carried out. This was calculated by taking the Total Usable Area and further subtracting the area occupied by any elements of portable material culture that were determined to be in use at the time the structure was destroyed.[12] The third calculation is that of the amount of area utilized for discard. This final figure permitted the space for discard to be quantified as a percentage of the other two area measurements, as well as providing a basis for determining the density of material recovered within it.

Artifact Variables

A characteristic of the pottery from well preserved domestic waste deposits is its relatively intact nature. One of the best published examples is that of a pit excavated at the site of Gravina di Puglia in Southern Italy. The pottery was notable for having both a generally high level of completeness, when compared with other material recovered, and a relatively low level of brokenness.[13] Unfortunately, the determination of these two characteristics is relatively subjective, and to the knowledge of the author, no studies have been carried out to determine definitive figures that would allow overall levels of completeness and brokenness to be evaluated objectively.[14] Because of the nature of the assemblage recovered from the Earthquake House, overall levels of completeness and brokenness for particular vessels were imposed based on the complete specimens recovered as part of the in use assemblage. In this study, a very high level of completeness indicates a vessel that was either recovered whole, or was completely reconstructable, and vessels with a high level of completeness were normally > 90% reconstructable. A very low level of brokenness was only assigned to vessels recovered intact, with other levels being assigned based on the overall character of the sherds belonging to the vessel.[15]

In order to determine overall density of material recovered from a particular space, it was necessary to quantify the ceramic material recovered so that comparisons between probable discard and non discard areas could be made in terms of the overall density of material. The ceramic assemblage was examined and quantified by calculating the Estimated Vessels Represented (EVREP). Given the nature of the material recovered from the Earthquake House, EVREP was more suitable than other methods of quantification that have been proposed[16] and allowed the calculation of an average number of vessels represented by the material recovered. The methodology utilized for calculating the EVREP by the assemblage is as follows.[17] All sherds collected from the floor deposits and associated contexts were laid out, and joins were actively sought among them. In cases where joins were present, the sherds were grouped as belonging to the same vessel. The primary criteria for the identification of an individual vessel was the presence of a rim fragment, as all forms in the Cypriot repertoire have them, but not all forms possess bases and handles. Each rim fragment and its associated sherd family was assigned a Minimum and Maximum EVREP value of 1, which indicates a distinct vessel in the assemblage. Following this evaluation other diagnostic fragments (bases and handles) were examined, and joins were also sought for these among the material recovered. Unless these fragments had a attribute (i.e. fabric, decoration, etc.) that distinguished them as being unique from the previously identified vessels, they were assigned a Minimum EVREP value of 0, and a Maximum EVREP value of 1.[18] These values allow for the possibility that unattached diagnostic fragments could possibly belong to one of the previously identified vessels, but cannot be definitively linked to them (Minimum EVREP: 0), or could belong to a unique vessel where the main diagnostic feature, the rim, has not been preserved (Maximum EVREP: 1). Through this process, both a Minimum EVREP, which is equivalent to the minimum number of vessels (MNV), and a Maximum EVREP can be calculated and then averaged to provide a more realistic figure for the number of individual vessels the assemblage actually represents.

Data Synthesis
Following quantification, the individual vessels identified

were located spatially in the room based on the findspots recorded in the excavation notes. The EVREP was then divided by the appropriate calculated area, which allowed relative densities of material in EVREP/square meter to be determined for locations of probable discard in individual rooms. This density of vessels was then compared to the EVREP density recovered from the remainder of the room to determine if the concentrations were significantly different, indicating that a dissimilar set of behaviors led to their formation.

The final step in the process of identifying and tracing the household waste stream was to actively seek out definitive and probable joins to vessels recovered within identified discard loci. Such links were sought in adjacent

8 See Hayden and Cannon, 1983. For data and models largely developed through ethnographic research conducted on contemporary groups, predominantly in the New World, see Deal 1985 and Kamp 1991.

9 E.g., Hayden & Cannon 1983; Kamp 1991.

10 Provisional discard installations have a variety of names in the Roman world including *latrina, lacus and stercilinum* (Peña 2007, 308). In the Greek world, the term used for these types of installations is kopron (See Owens 1983 and Ault 1999 for discussion).

11 See Peña 2007, 274-6 for a discussion of general characteristics of domestic discard derived from ethnographic data. One of the primary studies of household waste installations of this type in the Greco-Roman world was conducted by Ault at the site of Halieis in Greece. In several houses he identified a number of stone lined earthen floor pits that were filled with a variety of residual material consistent with that generated as household waste (Ault 1999, 550-557).

12 Available area utilizes the maximum diameter for each vessel of the in use assemblage, which was recorded during the evaluation of the assemblage by the author.

13 Hayes in Small *et al.* 1994, 206-26.

14 Although Orton (1989, 97) provides formulae for the calculation of brokenness and completeness (Brokenness = Sherds/Estimated Vessel Equivalency (EVE); Completeness = EVE/Estimated Vessels Represented (EVREP)), he offers no correlation as to what the results obtained from this formula should equate to in terms of physical description (i.e. "X Value = Partially Broken," "Y Value = Very Complete," etc.).

15 In the case of the in use assemblage, sherds from the various classes of pottery (fineware, cookware, plainware, etc.) were normally quite large and were assigned an overall low level of brokenness.

16 See Orton *et al.* 1993 for a general overview of pottery quantification methods.

17 General methodology adapted from Orton *et al.* 1993, 172.

18 Sherds that possessed unique characteristics even in the absence of diagnostic fragments were determined to represent distinct vessels and were assigned a Minimum and Maximum EVREP value of 1.

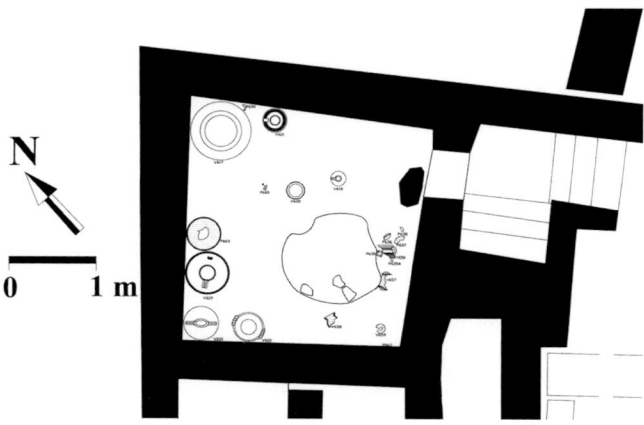

Fig. 4 Room 14 showing locations of in-use and residual vessels (plan by author).

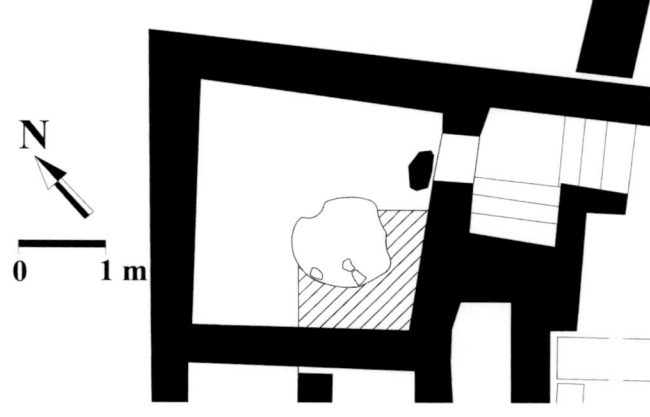

Fig. 5 Room 14 with hatched area indicating space used for provisional discard (plan by author).

spaces whose architectural characteristics (e.g. marginal space, limited access, etc.) indicated probable location where discard activity was likely to have taken place.

THE COMMISSARY BLOCK

The three-room group referred to as the Commissary Block focuses on Room 14, which is accessed from the central courtyard of the house via a short staircase. The artifacts in the room fall into two main groups. Eight complete or nearly complete vessels (Fig. 4), which were in use at the time the structure was destroyed, were recovered in the north and west area of the room. These vessels range from a large complete pithos (V617) in the northwest corner, to a Cypriot Red Slip Ware Form 1 dish (V622). This area of primary use is complemented by a scatter of discarded pottery around a large, hemispherical, mudbrick oven located in the southeast quadrant of the room. Just to the south, Room 12, accessible by the same staircase as Room 14, houses a large cistern whose assemblage attests to its use as a discard location for debris from various parts of the house including Room 14 during the final phase of the structure. Third, and finally, Room 19 to the east of Room 12 is a very small space (2.96 X 1.16 meters) that is accessed from the central courtyard. The staircase, currently preserved to the north, passing over Room 19 would have further limited the usable space in the room. Despite the cramped circumstances, the threshold of Room 19 was noted as being "well worn … indicating frequent passage

into and out of the room". Like the cistern in Room 12, Room 19 is also argued below to have served as a discard location serving both Room 14 and other parts of the Earthquake house. The three rooms of the Commissary Block provide architectural and artifactual evidence for a waste stream moving from the north and west parts of Room 14, to the southeastern part of that room, to either the nearby cistern (Room 12) or the nearby sottoscala (Room 19).[19]

Room 14

The starting point for exploring the discard processes of the Commissary Block is the area to the east and south of the oven in Room 14 where the hard packed earthen floor gave way to a looser, less compact soil. Measuring approximately 1.16 square meters, this area accounts for 17.90% of the total available space of Room 14 (Fig. 5).[20] The excavation notes concerning this part of the room record a large amount of material, which was initially interpreted as part of the in-use assemblage of complete and reconstructable vessels recovered along Walls F & T. Reexamination of this material shows that this was not the case. The vessels that were in use at the time of the quake have a very high to high level of completeness and a low to very low level of brokenness. In contrast, vessels recovered near the oven tended to have a moderate level of completeness in that they were partially, but nowhere near fully reconstructable, and a moderate to high level of brokenness. Thus, these vessels could not have been in use when the house was destroyed. Instead, these fragments represent debris created during the use life of the room that were deliberately "collected" in the marginal space created by the side and back of the oven, in a state of provisional discard awaiting either re-use or ultimate disposal. Within this provisional discard area, a notable difference is present between the vessels recovered on the east side of the oven, and those on the south. The vessels near the north end of the east side are relatively intact, displaying a moderate level of completeness, and an overall low level of brokenness with many larger fragments present. Based on their location, it is probable that this material was deliberately placed here as "clutter refuse", i.e. artifacts that retained some perceived value and were kept where they could be easily accessed.[21] In contrast, on the south side of the oven, vessel V658 possessed a moderate level of completeness, but also a high level of brokenness. Although most fragments belonging to this vessel were found to the south of the oven, a few were recovered on the northern side of the room in the general vicinity of the Gaza amphora V621. This indicates that V658 was in discard for a long period during which it became more fragmented and dispersed.

One of the characteristics of domestic refuse at Greco-Roman sites is the apparent diversity of material that they contain, as evidenced from the deposits recovered from the Villa Regina and Gravina di Puglia.[22] Material recovered from Room 14 of the Earthquake House is consistent with these examples, and although the majority consists of ceramic and faunal bone, glass and botanical remains do form a minor component. The Average EVREP for the entire room is 65, with twelve vessels (18.46%) having an overall level of completeness that indicates they were in use at the time of the earthquake. The remaining 53 vessels represent residual material present in the room, of which an Average EVREP of 27 (50.95%) were recovered in the space to the east and south of the oven, with the remaining 26 (49.05%) occurring throughout the rest of the room. Although the number of vessels is split almost equally between these two areas, a comparison of the overall density of the residual vessels recovered from them reveals a significant difference. In the main area of the room, the density of residual vessels equals 4.02/square meter, whereas in the area to the east and south of the oven, which is believed to have been utilized as a discard area for refuse produced in the room, calculations reveal a residual vessel density of 23.27/square

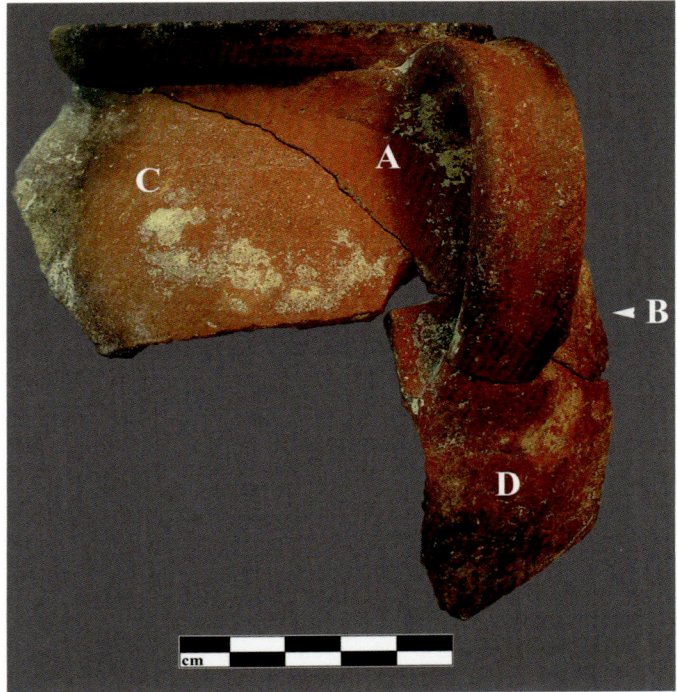

Fig. 6 Room 14, V657 (A) with joining fragments from Room 19 (B and C) and Room 12 (D) (photo by author).

meter.[23] The density of vessels in the proposed discard area is 5.78 times greater than the remainder of the room and appears to indicate that a different set of behaviors affected the deposition of material in this location.

The identification of this space as a discard area for waste material produced in the room is further

---

19 The walls of these rooms are preserved to a significant height, which prevented any cross contamination of artifacts between them.
20 The total area of Room 14 is 8.911 m². The built feature of the oven occupies approximately 1.293 m² (14.51% of the total area), with the in situ vessels occupying 1.14 m² (12.79% of the total area). Subtracting these figures from the total area of the room provides an "available" space of 6.478 m².
21 Hayden & Cannon 1983, 131.
22 De Caro 1994, 96; Small *et al.* 1994, 201.
23 Area used for these calculations does not account for the area occupied by the in situ assemblage, as these are based on the maximum diameter for the vessels, not the actual area they occupy on the floor surface, which is minor.

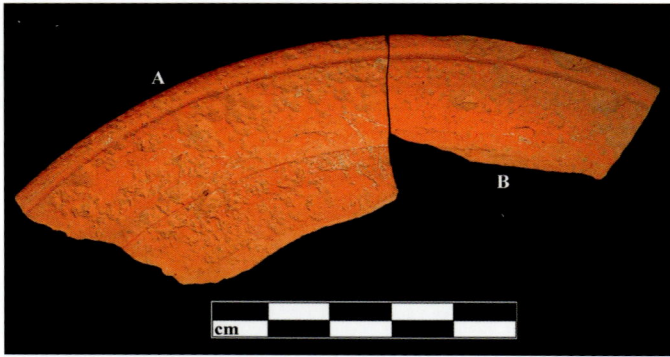

Fig. 7 Joining African Red Slip Form 67 rim fragments from Room 19 (A) and Room 14 (B) (photo by author).

strengthened by an examination of the faunal remains. This class of material generally forms a significant component of refuse deposits and is perhaps one of the easiest ways to identify areas where discard activity occurred.[24] In Room 14, a total of 347 faunal bone fragments were recovered from the floor and its associated contexts during the course of the excavation. Of this total, 159 fragments (45.8%) were recovered in the area to the east and south of the oven. Like the ceramic evidence, the density of the faunal material demonstrates a significant difference between the two areas of the room. In the main space, where 188 fragments (54.2%) were recovered, the faunal remains density equals 29.11 fragments/square meter, whereas in the probable discard area it increases to 137.0 fragments/square meter. The density inside the discard area is 4.7 times greater than that of the surrounding space, and mirrors the types of behaviors observed in the analysis of the ceramic material.

Both the ceramic and the faunal debris are thus interpreted as indicating that the material from the east and south side of the oven in Room 14 represents the provisional discard of waste created during the use of the room, which would have been eventually removed to a subsequent location. The nearby rooms 12 and 19 provide some evidence for the onward movement of debris from Room 14 through the waste stream of the Earthquake House.

Room 12: The Cistern

In the southwest corner of the cistern in Room 12, a deposit of fine ash mixed with bone and ceramic fragments rested on a relatively thin layer of fine, water-deposited silt that had accumulated during the use life of the installation. Soren and colleagues hypothesized that an earlier earthquake had damaged the cistern to the extent that it could no longer fulfill its prime use function, and then became a dumping area for household refuse.[25] Locating the origin(s) of this refuse is of central importance to the present task of documenting the waste stream of the Commissary Block.

The ceramic material recovered from the cistern's ash layer has a high percentage of cookware and lamps. Cookware and lamp fragments are similarly prominent in the material recovered from the provisional discard area of Room 14. This point of similarity at least raises the possibility that the cistern debris originated in part in Room 14. Supporting this possibility, a cookware fragment recovered from the cistern at roughly the same elevation as the ash layer, but strictly speaking outside its boundary, joined cookware vessel V657 from the east side of the oven in Room 14.[26] A second set of fragments from the cistern do not physically join, but almost certainly belong to cookware vessel P636 from the east side of the oven in Room 14. The fragments share similar fabrics, a heavy accumulation of soot on their interior and exterior surfaces, the same estimated rim diameter, and an overall similarity in rim profile. In addition, the cistern's ash layer also produced fragments of fineware vessels and other more utilitarian vessels including amphorae. Again, joining fragments indicate that Room 14 provided a portion of the residual material that was deposited within the cistern. Because the preserved wall elevations make very unlikely any random, post-abandonment movement of fragments from one room to the other, the cistern's fragments joining Room 14 vessels attest to the deliberate deposition of waste material from Room 14 into Room 12.

Despite the similar percentages of cook wares and bone and despite these cross-mends between rooms 14 and 12, differences between the two rooms' assemblages indicate that some material recovered in Room 12 was most likely derived from waste produced elsewhere in the house, and not just from the adjacent space. Other possible sources include the two small ovens along the east wall of Room 15/18, or, less probably, the large oven in the southwest corner of Room 11.

These possibilities, however, do not remove the demonstrable connections between Rooms 14 and

12. The reuse of the non-functioning cistern in Room 12 is consistent with Peña's observation, based on the ethnographic data, that "some domestic refuse is disposed of in out of the way places around the residential compound, with features that constitute an enclosed depositional basin, such as abandoned rooms, outbuildings, fixtures, and pits, particularly favored for this purpose".[27]

Room 19: The Sottoscala

Room 19, like the cistern in Room 12, was being used for the deposition of household waste when the house was destroyed. Soren and colleagues interpreted Room 19 as a general storage area on account of its marginal location, small size, and constrained space, all of which rendered it unsuitable for other household activities.[28] As noted earlier, however, the threshold leading into the space from the courtyard was surprisingly well-worn, so the room's function required access on a frequent basis. Since little material was recovered from the stratum contemporaneous with the house's final 4th-century activity phase,[29] Soren and colleagues postulated that Room 19 was used to store ephemeral material, possibly fodder for the mule stabled in the adjacent Room 2.

Although this initial interpretation makes sense, both the architectural and ceramic evidence indicate that, at the time of the earthquake, the space was not used for storage, but for discard within the house. The floor in Room 19 is roughly 40 cm below that of the threshold of the doorway. This difference would have made entering and exiting the space difficult, particularly if the individual was carrying goods to or from storage. Two other rooms in the Earthquake House, rooms 8 and 14, had floor levels that were well below the adjacent threshold. In both rooms, some form of step was provided in order to facilitate access.[30] Such a feature was not found in Room 19. Unlike a general storage area, which presumably would have required entry on a regular basis, access to a room used for discard would only have occurred when the space required cleaning out. The wear noted on the threshold of the room, rather than having resulted from repeated entry and exit, may be explained by people having frequently stood in the doorway to dispose of refuse.

Such an explanation is supported by the ceramic debris in Room 19. The material recovered from the lowest stratigraphic layer is contemporary with the latest use of the structure. The assemblage here is similar to

that found in the cistern in Room 12. As in the cistern, so too in Room 19 a greater percentage of the identified vessels is of a utilitarian nature than was seen in the discard assemblage of Room 14. The Room 19 material included two large pithos rims and numerous fragments of amphorae, indicating that the material was most likely derived from throughout the house. In quantifying the ceramic assemblage from this context, an Average EVREP of 34 was obtained, of which four (11.76%) preserved joins with vessels recovered in Room 14 (Fig. 6 and 7). Like Room 12, the preserved walls separating Room 19 from Room 14 would have prevented any later random movement of these fragments from room to room.

A striking feature of Room 19 in terms of this interpretation as a place for in-house discard is that the amount of material recovered from Room 19 is quite low when compared to other rooms in the house, or such refuse-collection loci documented elsewhere which are normally found filled or overflowing.[31] One possible explanation is that Room 19 may have been cleaned out shortly before the earthquake. Alternatively, the room may have been used primarily for the disposal of organic material, possibly animal waste produced by the mule in Room 2, with other, more durable household waste being deposited only occasionally. The positive, preserved

---

24 Only one cesspit at Pompeii has been investigated (Arthur 1993, 194-5) which yielded a quantity of faunal bone, although the total number of fragments has not been published. By far the best preserved feature of this type is the one from Gravina di Puglia, which yielded 1853 pieces of bone and shell (MacKinnon in Small et al. 1994, 243).

25 Soren et al. 1988, 173-4. Although the oven in Room 14 was the most likely candidate, the deposit in the cistern has not been definitively linked to this feature.

26 Kourion Excavation Notebook: 1986; Room 12, Locus 003 and Locus 005 (Unpublished).

27 Peña 2007, 276.

28 Soren et al. 1988, 175-176.

29 At the time of the excavation, three stratigraphic layers were identified in Room 19, all of which were interpreted as being earthquake debris. Research conducted by the author has demonstrated that this is incorrect, with the lowest layer consisting at least partially of fill deposited during the final phase of the structure.

30 In Room 14, the floor is 73 cm below the entrance threshold. In Room 8 the difference between the floor and threshold is approximately 43 cm.

31 E.g., Small et. al. 1994 and Ault 1999, 567-568.

evidence, however, makes it clear that Room 19 at least in part served as part of the waste stream fed by ceramic material in use and then provisionally discarded in Room 14.

CONCLUSIONS:

The evidence presented above reveals that Rooms 14, 12, and 19 of the late 4th century AD phase of the Earthquake House were linked parts of the household waste stream. Pottery and bone debris indicates that an area east and south of the oven in Room 14 served for the provisional discard of household waste at an early stage in this process. Rooms 12 and 19 provided loci for the discard of household waste, not only from the adjacent Room 14, as indicated by preserved cross-mends, but also from other areas of the house.

The results of this study clearly demonstrate that the domestic waste stream can successfully be tracked by utilizing a combination of architectural and artifactual evidence. Ethnographic data can be used to identify architectural features and spaces likely to be used for discard activities. In complement to this, an analysis of the general characteristics of the material (e.g. brokenness and completeness of ceramics, diversity of artifact classes, etc.) recovered from potential discard areas, as well as a higher overall artifact density compared to the surrounding area, can provide confirmation for a deposit of this type. The ceramic evidence can then serve as a guide for cross referencing/mending with material recovered from other spaces, which may provide further links in the chain of the domestic waste stream.

Although the sudden destruction of sites such as Kourion in some ways provides the ideal scenario for examining discard assemblages and behavior, it must be emphasized that without scrupulous collection and retention of material combined with the detailed recording of artifact findspots during excavation, the difficulty of identifying these types of deposits and recovering the information they contain is dramatically increased. Provided the initial data set is conducive to this type of analysis, the methodology outlined and utilized for this study provides a valuable tool that is not regionally, temporally, or contextually dependent and is readily transferrable to other sites that can help elucidate aspects of this little understood facet of daily life in the ancient world.

ACKNOWLEDGEMENTS
The author would like to thank the organizers for their invitation to participate in the workshop and series of papers that culminate in this volume as well as the Danish Institute in Athens for their hosting of this event and the financial support for travel to Greece. I would also like to thank the Cyprus American Archaeological Research Institute (CAARI) and particularly its director Thomas Davis for their sponsorship and financial assistance of my research while in Cyprus, the Cyprus Fulbright Commission and the A.G Leventis Foundation for providing the financial support and resources to collect the data integral to this project, the Cyprus Department of Antiquities, particularly its director Pavlos Flourentzos and the staff at the Kourion Museum in Episkopi for granting me permission to conduct this research and providing the facilities to carry it out, and David Soren for his permission to study the material recovered during his excavations. A special thanks is due to J. Theodore Peña, my advisor at The University at Buffalo, SUNY as well as Stephen Dyson and Bradley Ault for their guidance during the course of my research.

Olympia:
Roman Pottery in the Archaeological Record

BY ARCHER MARTIN

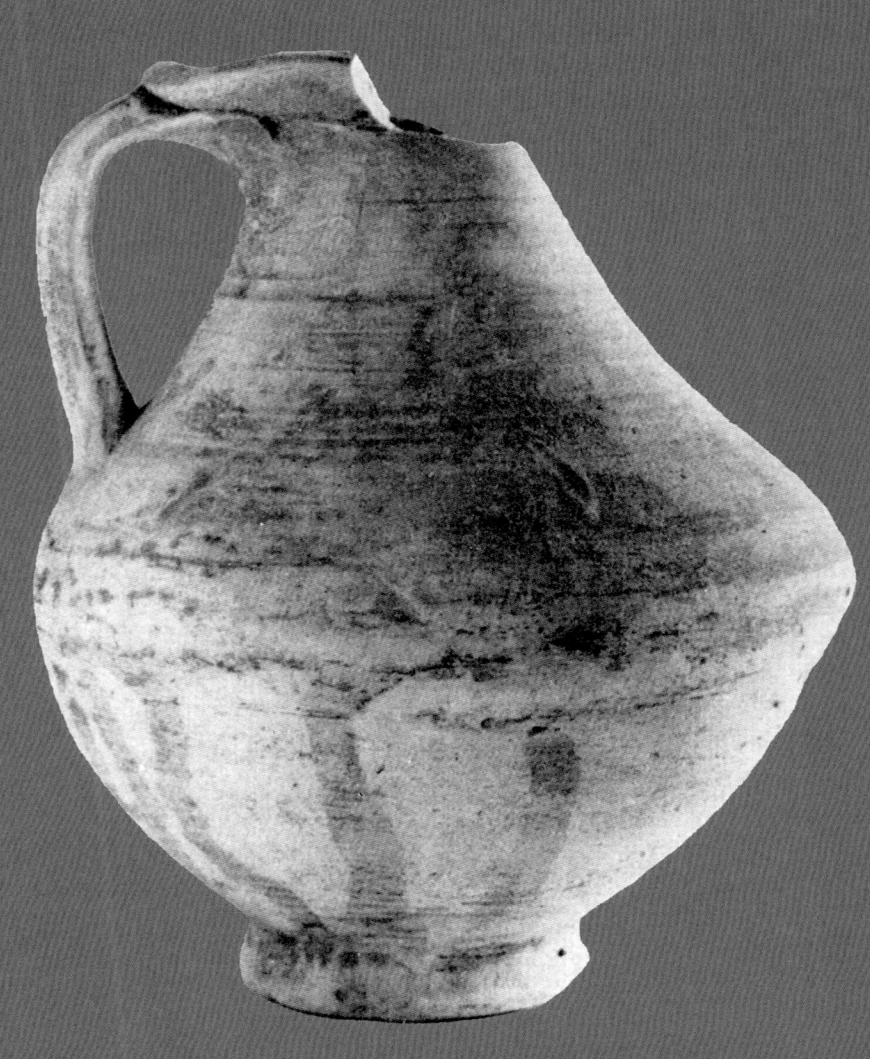

Olympia: Roman Pottery in the Archaeological Record

BY ARCHER MARTIN

INTRODUCTION

My intentions with this paper are to take Olympia as the case study of a site with an ample archaeological record not considered in Peña's book in order to see on the one hand, what elements it offers to illustrate Peña's model and, on the other hand, to determine how useful Peña's model is in understanding the ceramological record there. My evidence comes mostly from the large-scale excavation campaigns between the 1930s and 1960s, although to some extent I am able to bring in material discovered in the more recent excavations in the Southwest Building.[1] I consider the evidence that Olympia offers in the same order that Peña used.

MANUFACTURE

Pottery was certainly produced at Olympia. The best evidence concerns the period of the settlement that grew up on the site after the end of its use as a sanctuary.[2] In the north of the area there was a 5th-century[3] workshop (attested by a kiln, three connected basins and layers of production waste) that produced mostly storage jars and cooking pots. In the late 6th and 7th centuries lamps, for which moulds have been found, were made in a workshop located nearby. Pottery may have been made elsewhere at Olympia. On the one hand, various kilns (some of which must date to the time of the site's use as a sanctuary) were discovered in the older excavations,[4] and on the other there are over-fired pieces in the storerooms of the museum that should be wasters (unless they result from secondary burning). The kilns and the presumable wasters are unfortunately not clearly associated with one another in the records of the excavation. Furthermore, some of these kilns may have been used for tiles.[5] Thus, production at Olympia cannot provide any useful case studies at the moment for our purposes.

PRIME USE
"Vorratsecke" or "Kochstelle"

A pantry ("Vorratsecke"), excavated on 8-9 December 1953 in Room 17 of Guest House I south of the Kladeos Baths

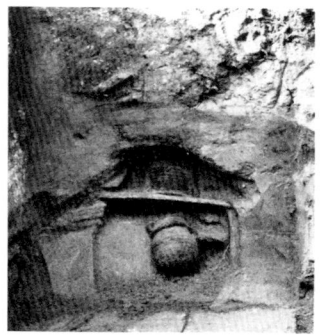

Fig. 1 The "Kochstelle" during excavation (Olympia-Bericht VI, Abb. 16).

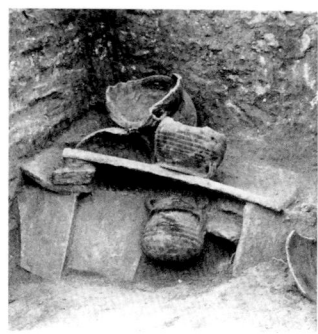

Fig. 2 The "Kochstelle" after excavation (Olympia-Bericht VI, Abb. 17).

(Figs. 1-3),[6] provides a rare example of a prime-use deposit. Here a collapsed set of shelves made of pieces of tile was uncovered beneath a layer of alluvial sand from a flood of the nearby Kladeos. Evidence for the date of abandonment of this deposit comes from the destruction layer beneath the alluvial sand: the most recent coin is Diocletianic, dating after AD 294.[7]

There is some confusion about the vessels discovered in association with the shelves. According to the excavation diary there should be six vessels from the find and two more from nearby. The entry for 9 November indicates three complete and three fragmentary cooking pots discovered in the "Kochstelle" itself (without specifying exactly where), and the entry for the next day refers to two more nearly complete, coarse, one-handled vessels found to the north of the "Kochstelle". Mallwitz writes in greater detail of a total of seven vessels from the pantry – a

---

1 As I was not able to return to Olympia to prepare this paper, I have had to rely on notes and illustrations that I made in the past and on published material.
2 Schauer 1991, Schauer 2002, Schauer 2010.
3 Unless otherwise stated all dates are AD.
4 Kunze & Schleif 1941, 33-34; Schleif & Eilmann 1944, 23-25; Schleif 1944, 66; Schauer 2002, 216.
5 Schleif & Eilmann 1944, 25; Schauer 2002, 215-216.
6 Mallwitz 1958, 39; Walter 1958, 67. In the excavation diaries and the pottery inventory the find is called the "Kochstelle", although the published excavation report refers to it more accurately as the "Vorratsecke". In citing indications in the diaries and inventory the term used there is given.
7 Walter 1958, 67.

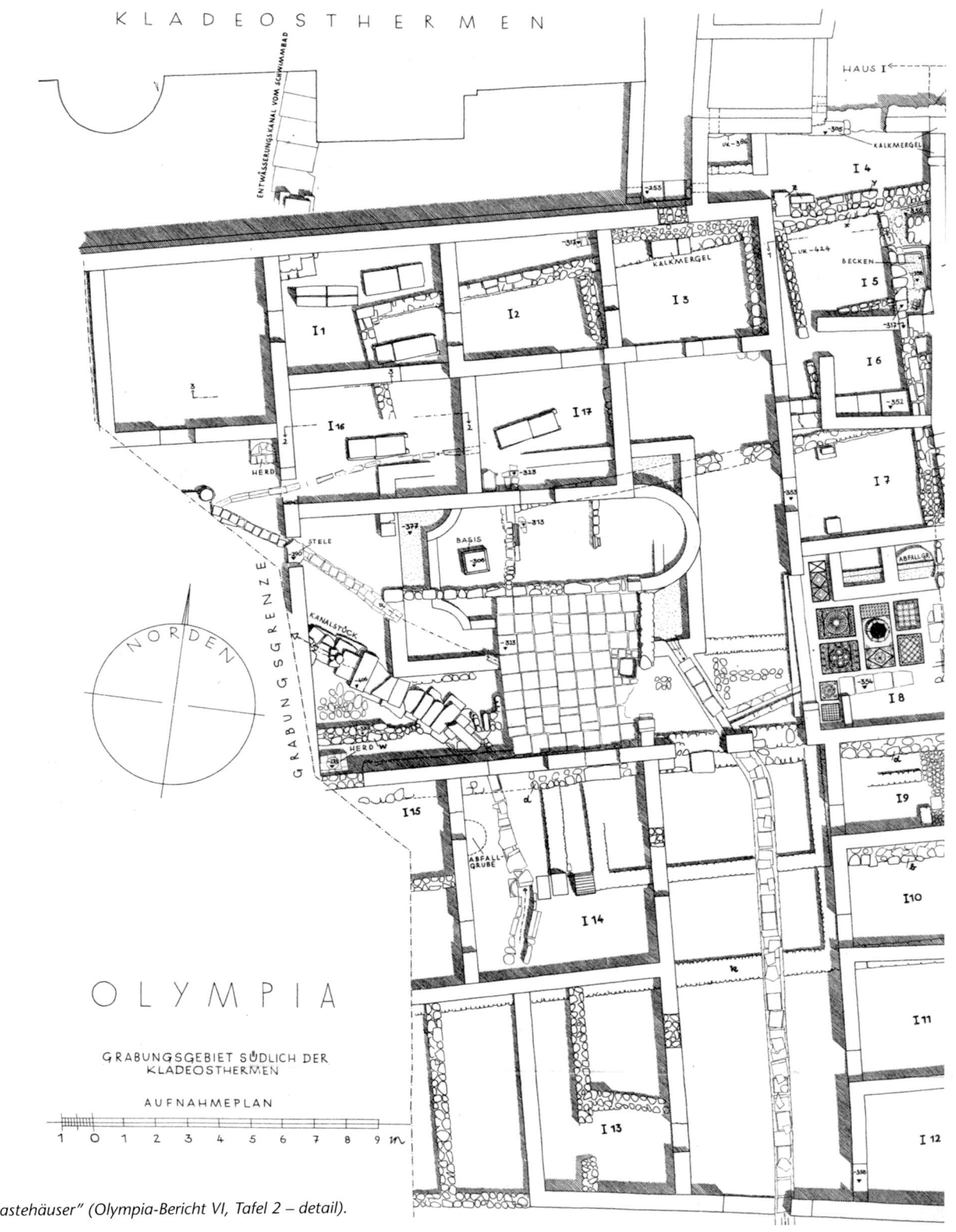

Fig. 3 Plan of the "Gastehäuser" (Olympia-Bericht VI, Tafel 2 – detail).

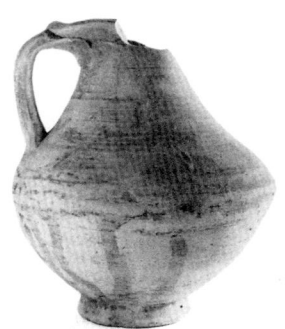

Fig. 4 Coarse-ware jug from the "Kochstelle": inv. n. K 967 (Olympia-Bericht VI, Abb. 59).

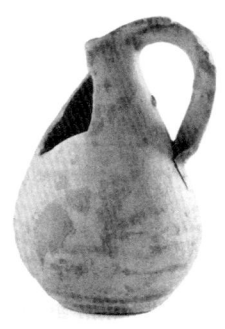

Fig. 5 Coarse-ware jug from the "Kochstelle": inv. n. K 1016 (Olympia-Bericht VI, Abb. 60).

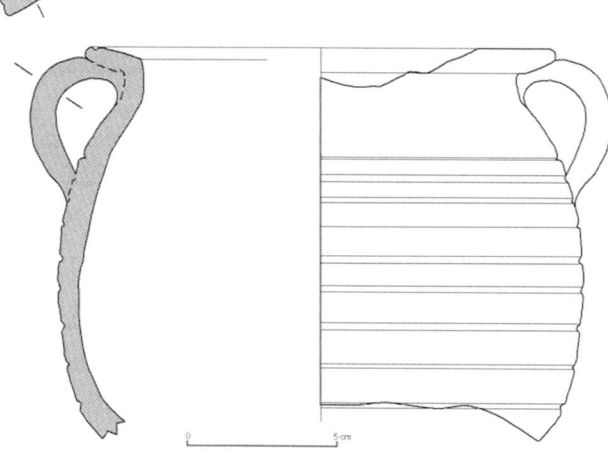

Fig. 6 Cooking pot from the upper level of the "Kochstelle": inv. n. K 1014.

whole and a broken cooking pot (one on top of the other) with a third lacking its base next to them on the tile shelf and two jugs and a small cooking pot with a pan set on it underneath the tile. Mallwitz does not mention, however, any further vessels as having been found nearby. Hans Walter, who dealt with the pottery from the excavations in the area south of the Kladeos Baths, says nothing about the overall number of vessels but presents photos of five vessels said to come from the pantry. Five vessels in the storerooms at Olympia are inventoried as coming from the *"Kochstelle"* and another as found in the alluvial sand in the room with the *"Kochstelle"*, while one of the five published by Walter is recorded as being from either the Guest House or the Byzantine Church.

The photo in Fig. 3 gives the most useful elements for identifying the vessels. On the upper level one can see the three vessels as Mallwitz describes them, and on the lower one the small pot with the pan. There is no sign of the two jugs (Figs. 4-5). These must be the two vessels found the following day to the north of the so-called "Kochstelle" - none of the other vessels in question is one-handled. Three vessels in the photo can be recognized immediately among those attributed to the *"Kochstelle"* in the inventory: the cooking pot on the upper level lacking its base (Fig. 6) (not published by Walter); the pan on the lower one (Figs. 7-8); the small pot (Fig. 9) on which the pan rests.

Graffiti on Sigillata

Of the more than 1000 vessels of sigillata and red-slip ware from the pre-1985 excavations at Olympia a small number presents graffiti: 22 inscriptions on 21 vessels, as well as one

somewhat dubious example on another vessel. Individually the graffiti have little to say, limited as they are to one or at most a few letters. Consideration of them as a group, however, proves able to shed light on the prime use of these vessels.

With two exceptions, all the inscriptions are written on the lower parts of the exterior of the vessels, either inside the ring-foot or around the outside of it. Marks in this position would be readily visible when the vessels were stored stood on edge with the rim toward the wall – thus owners or habitual users could find their items in a communal situation. The external graffito near the rim is on a low-walled vessel and would also have shown when stacked in a leaning position. The internal graffito, the questionable one, falls completely outside this sort of reasoning, which may argue for its being only casual scratches.

Most of the vessels belong to plain Italian sigillata, often of the shape *Conspectus* 3.[8] The exceptions are two Eastern Sigillata A vessels and an African red-slip Production C3 Hayes 50A/Lamboglia 40 dish (the one with the graffito near the rim).[9] Italian sigillata was the dominant fine ware at Olympia from the mid 1st to the mid 2nd century (with some 500 vessels attested), as was African red-slip ware from the 3rd century onward (of which Production C counts a similar number), while Eastern Sigillata A is well attested as a secondary presence alongside Italian sigillata, *Conspectus* 3, and the other types of Italian sigillata bearing graffiti, are those dominant in the overall assemblage at Olympia, and Hayes 50A is also extremely common there. In other words, nothing unusual appears to be singled out for graffiti.

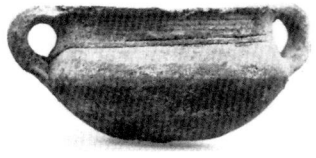

Fig. 7 Pan from the lower level of the "Kochstelle": inv. n. K 1015 (Olympia-Bericht VI, Abb. 56).

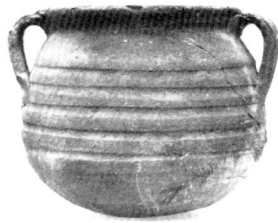

Fig. 9 Cooking pot from the lower level of the "Kochstelle": inv. n. K 1013 (Olympia-Bericht VI, Abb. 57).

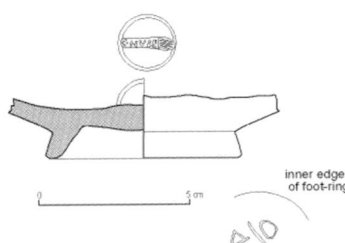

Fig. 10 – Italian sigillata base with the graffito ΔIO: inv. n. K 11766.

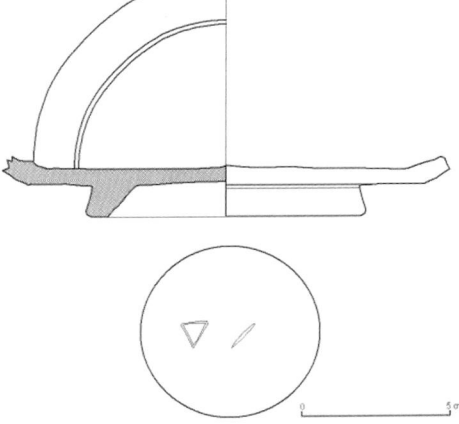

Fig. 12 – Italian sigillata base with the graffito ΔI: inv. n. K 11334.

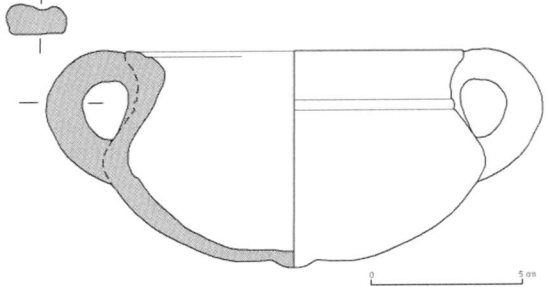

Fig. 8 Pan from the lower level of the "Kochstelle": inv. n. K 1015.

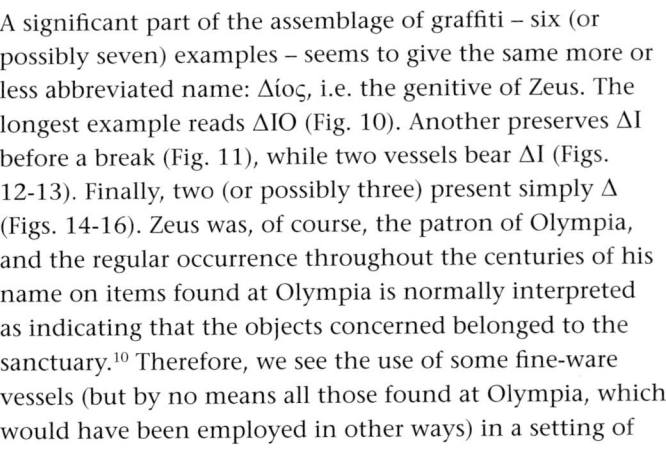

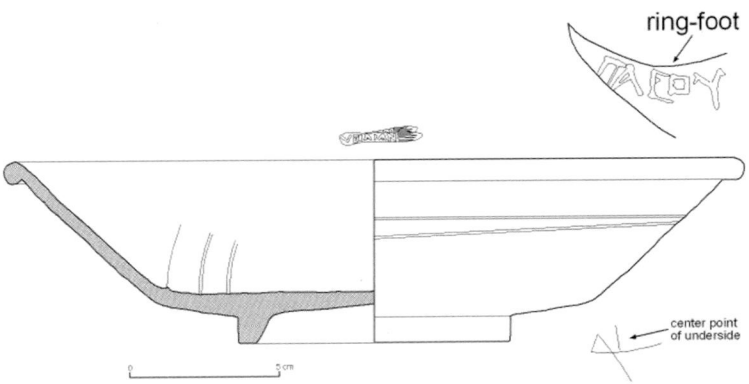

Fig. 11 – Italian sigillata base with the graffito ΔI[: inv. n. K 11661.

Fig. 13 – Italian sigillata dish with the graffiti ΔI and ΠΑΣΟΥ(?): inv. n. K 2940.

A significant part of the assemblage of graffiti – six (or possibly seven) examples – seems to give the same more or less abbreviated name: Δίος, i.e. the genitive of Zeus. The longest example reads ΔIO (Fig. 10). Another preserves ΔI before a break (Fig. 11), while two vessels bear ΔI (Figs. 12-13). Finally, two (or possibly three) present simply Δ (Figs. 14-16). Zeus was, of course, the patron of Olympia, and the regular occurrence throughout the centuries of his name on items found at Olympia is normally interpreted as indicating that the objects concerned belonged to the sanctuary.[10] Therefore, we see the use of some fine-ware vessels (but by no means all those found at Olympia, which would have been employed in other ways) in a setting of

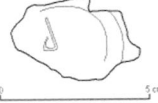

Fig. 14 Italian sigillata base with the graffito Δ: inv. n. K 13508.

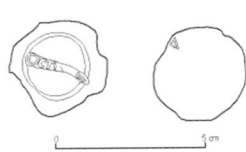

Fig. 15 Italian sigillata base with the graffito Δ: inv. n. K 11768.

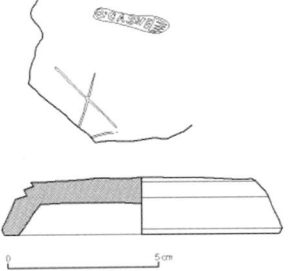

Fig. 16 – Italian sigillata base with the graffito Δ: inv. n. K 11358.

8 Conspectus, 56-57.
9 Carandini & Saguì 1981, 65-66.
10 Dittenberger & Purgold 1896, have examples of more or less extensive inscriptions of possession containing the standard genitive Δίος or its Elian equivalent Δίορ: n. 697-698, n. 704, n. 707, n. 709-711 (various objects); n. 760-807 (tiles); Groups 1-53 (weights).

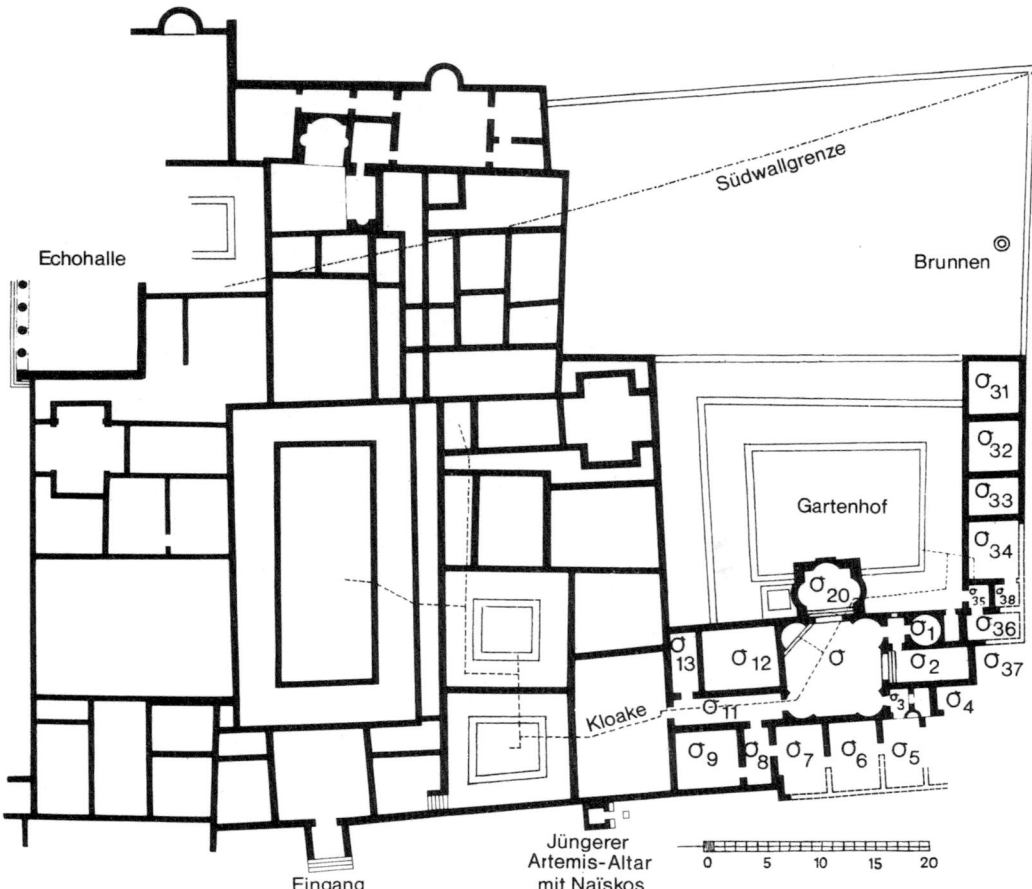

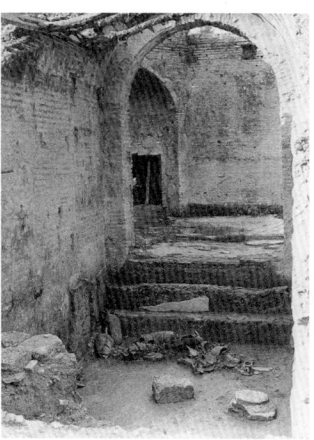

Fig. 18 Eastern Baths: The "Amphorenlager" after excavation (Olympia-Bericht IX, Abb. 37).

Fig. 17 Eastern Baths: plan (Olympia-Bericht IX, Abb. 29).

communal dining with an interest in identifying individual vessels. Since it is reasonable to expect that as in other cases the indication Διος indicates possession on the part of the sanctuary, it probably played a considerable role in this. Such a scenario is far from unlikely at a site that experienced enormous influxes of athletes and spectators for the Games and was frequented by pilgrims and priests at other times. It remains to be seen why an interest in identifying vessels existed from ca. 50 to 150, while there was so little need or desire to mark vessels in succeeding times – possibly there was a change of eating habits from individual vessels to ones used in common, lessening the need to identify ownership; perhaps at a later date individuals were no longer expected to provide their own vessels, meaning that there was no need to indicate ownership.

Reuse for the Same Purpose

One of the marked vessels, with two distinct graffiti, may attest to a more complicated situation, which could be considered reuse for the same purpose. One of the *Conspectus* 3 dishes bears both ΔI inside the foot ring and an especially heavily incised name around it (Fig. 13). The latter has been published as ΓΑΙΟΥ,[11] the Roman name well attested in its Greek version.[12] The graffito, however, seems actually to read ΠΑΣΟΥ, a less well known name with, however, some possible parallels.[13] There is no proof which of the two graffiti came first. It is likely, however, that ΔI was the original mark, written in a comparable way to the other graffiti, and that the new owner carved his name so deeply in order to draw attention away from ΔI. If so, the stratagem succeeded with Eilmann, who failed to notice the graffito ΔI.

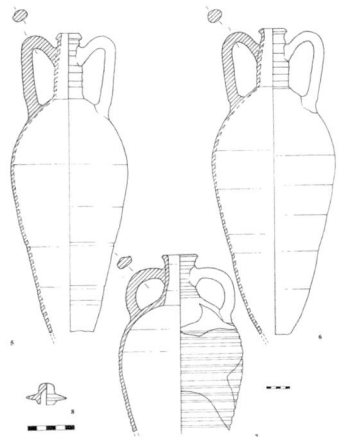
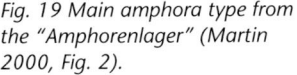

Fig. 19 Main amphora type from the "Amphorenlager" (Martin 2000, Fig. 2).

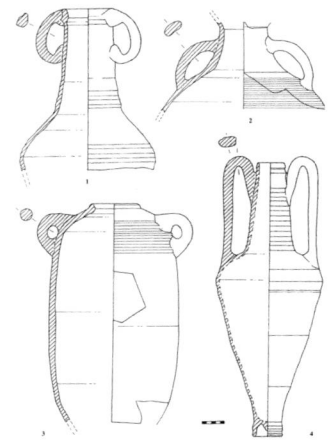

Fig. 20 Other amphorae from the "Amphorenlager" (Martin 2000, Fig. 1).

REUSE OR PROVISIONAL DISCARD OF AMPHORAE

The "Amphorenlager" was discovered in Room O2 of the Eastern Baths (Fig. 17). The excavation diary for 6 November 1965 says that a large number of mostly slender amphorae closed by small lids were found on the floor of a basin, and the entry for 8 November records the discovery of more amphorae on the floor of the same basin. The excavation report for those years, published nearly three decades later, after the deaths of both the excavator and his immediate scholarly heir, does little more than mention the find, although it says that the amphorae were deposited after the baths had suffered severe earthquake damage.[14] It represents undoubtedly more than a simple fill, as I thought when I first treated the assemblage.[15]

The published photo shows the amphorae lying in the basin in a disorderly fashion – some are lying flat in various directions and others reclining diagonally in a corner (Fig. 18). The situation recalls that of the *impluvium* in the Casa di Mestrius Maximus at Pompeii, where there are also amphorae pointing in various directions,[16] and it is tempting to opt for the same explanation: that the amphorae were being soaked and scrubbed for reuse. There is, however, no context in Room O2, as there is in the Pompeian example, of rows of containers near the basin to support the hypothesis. It is possible that we have here rather a case of provisional discard.

It has been possible to identify the "Amphorenlager"

finds in the storeroom, where twenty largely complete vessels were restored and inventoried and other un-inventoried pieces were labeled as coming from the "Amphorenlager". As the diary indicates, the main type of amphora is a slender vessel, of which there are eight nearly complete examples, as well as three pieces comprising the upper part of the amphora. Six lids are also preserved. The "Amphorenlager" assemblage is the most important attestation of this type (Fig. 19).[17] The better known types of amphorae suggest a date for the assemblage around 400 (Fig. 20).[18] The most recent one, Egloff 172 produced in Middle Egypt and dating from the late 4th to the mid 6th century, is represented by two examples. There is one example of Carthage Late Roman Amphora 4 in Majcherek's type 2 from Gaza dating to the later 4th century. Carthage Late Roman Amphora 2, from the Aegean area and datable between the 4th and the 6th centuries or later, is also present with one example. The most frequent of the typologically well known amphorae is Kapitän II/Niederbieber 77, of which there are two nearly complete examples, the bodies of two more, as well as four rims with varying amounts of the upper part of the vessel and two base fragments with some of the lower body. This type, considered to be of probable Aegean origin, circulated in the Mediterranean throughout the 3rd and 4th centuries and still occurs in the East into the 6th.

Many of the vessels in the "Amphorenlager" were emptied by knocking off the toe. All eight of the nearly complete examples the slender amphorae lack the toe, and the excavation diary indicates that the lids were still

---

11 Eilmann 1944, 89 fig. 61 (which gives the false impression that the strokes that would make up ΓΑΙΟΥ are much stronger than the others he does not mention).
12 See Fraser & Matthews 1997, 96, for examples.
13 Πασός appears in a signature at the Paneion of El-Kanais in Egypt, where it is considered theophoric – Bernard 1972, no. 87, and also at Thebes – Baillet n.d., no. 2097 (which I could consult through the PHI Searchable Greek Inscriptions); Πασοῦς occurs at Tomis in Scythia Minor – Stoian 1987, no. 120(5). My gratitude goes to Mark Lawall for his help with this name.
14 Kyrieleis 1994, 25.
15 Martin 2000, 429-430.16
16 Peña 2007, 88-91 with Fig. 3.5.
17 See Martin 2000, 430, for a discussion of this type.
18 See Martin 2000, 429-430, for a discussion of the chronologically significant vessels found in the "Amphorenlager".

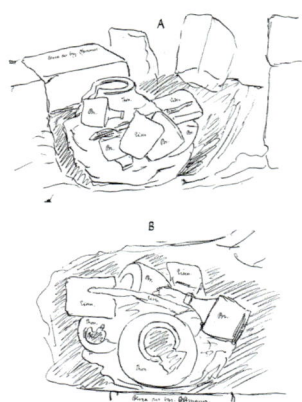

Fig. 21 Hoard found north of the temple of Zeus in 1877 (Völling 1995, Abb. 1-2).

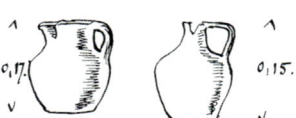

Fig. 22 Vases from the hoard found north of the temple of Zeus in 1877 (Völling 1995, Abb. 4 – detail).

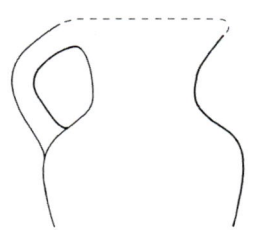

Fig. 23 Vessel containing a hoard found in a late-antique house in 1880 (Völling 1995, Abb. 9).

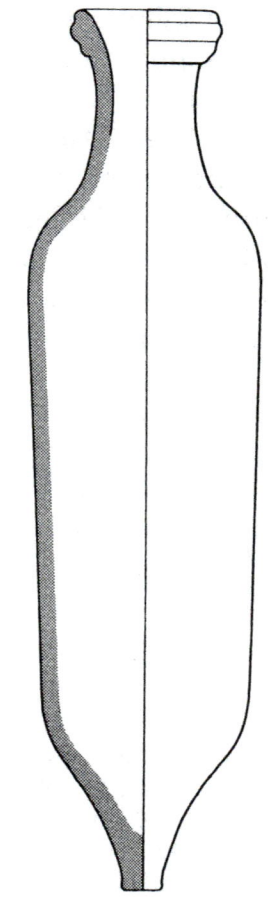

Fig. 24 Spatheion containing a hoard found in 1941 (Völling 1995, Abb. 10).

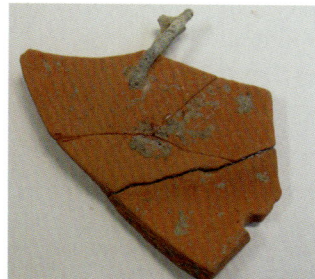

Fig. 25 African Red-Slip sherd with clamp: inv. n. K 11875.

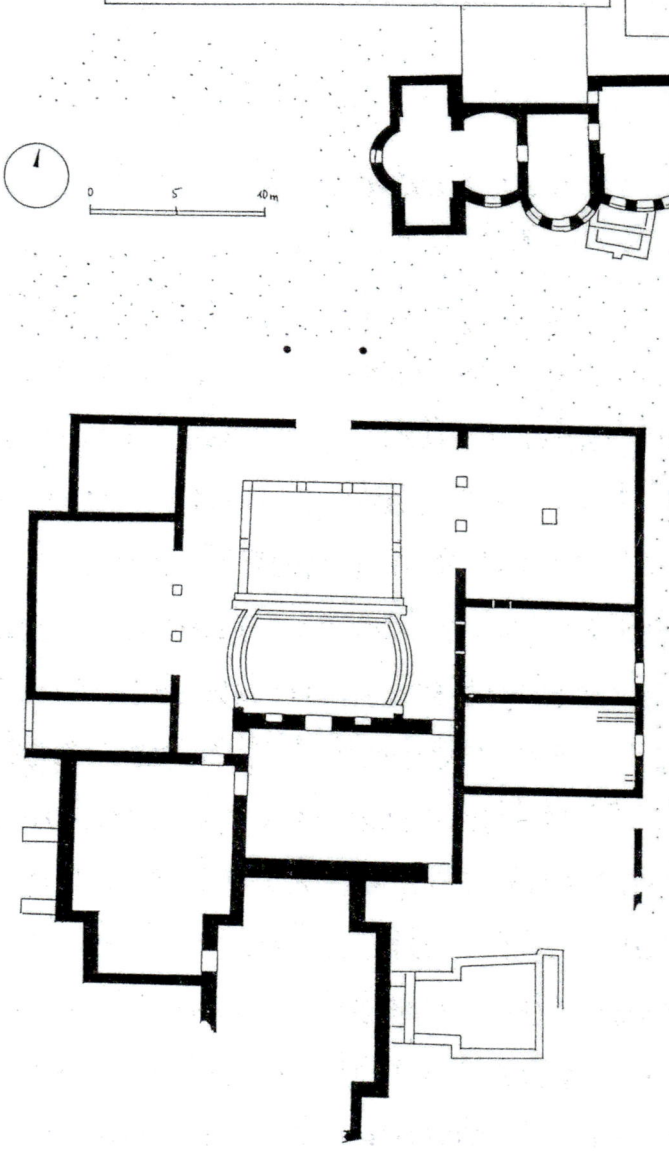

Fig. 26 Plan of the Leonidaion Baths and the Southwest Building (Sinn, U., G. Ladstätter, A. Martin & T. Völling 1994, Abb. 2).

in place in the necks. It is unclear in other cases whether the bases were removed deliberately in antiquity or lost subsequently. Any future reuse of those vessels emptied in this way to contain liquid would require the base to be stopped as well as the mouth.

REUSE OF VESSELS TO CONTAIN HOARDS

The most notable hoard attested at Olympia was a mixed one of bronze and iron objects and coins ranging from the 4th and 5th centuries to the 6th contained in or grouped around four ceramic vessels.[19] It was discovered in 1877

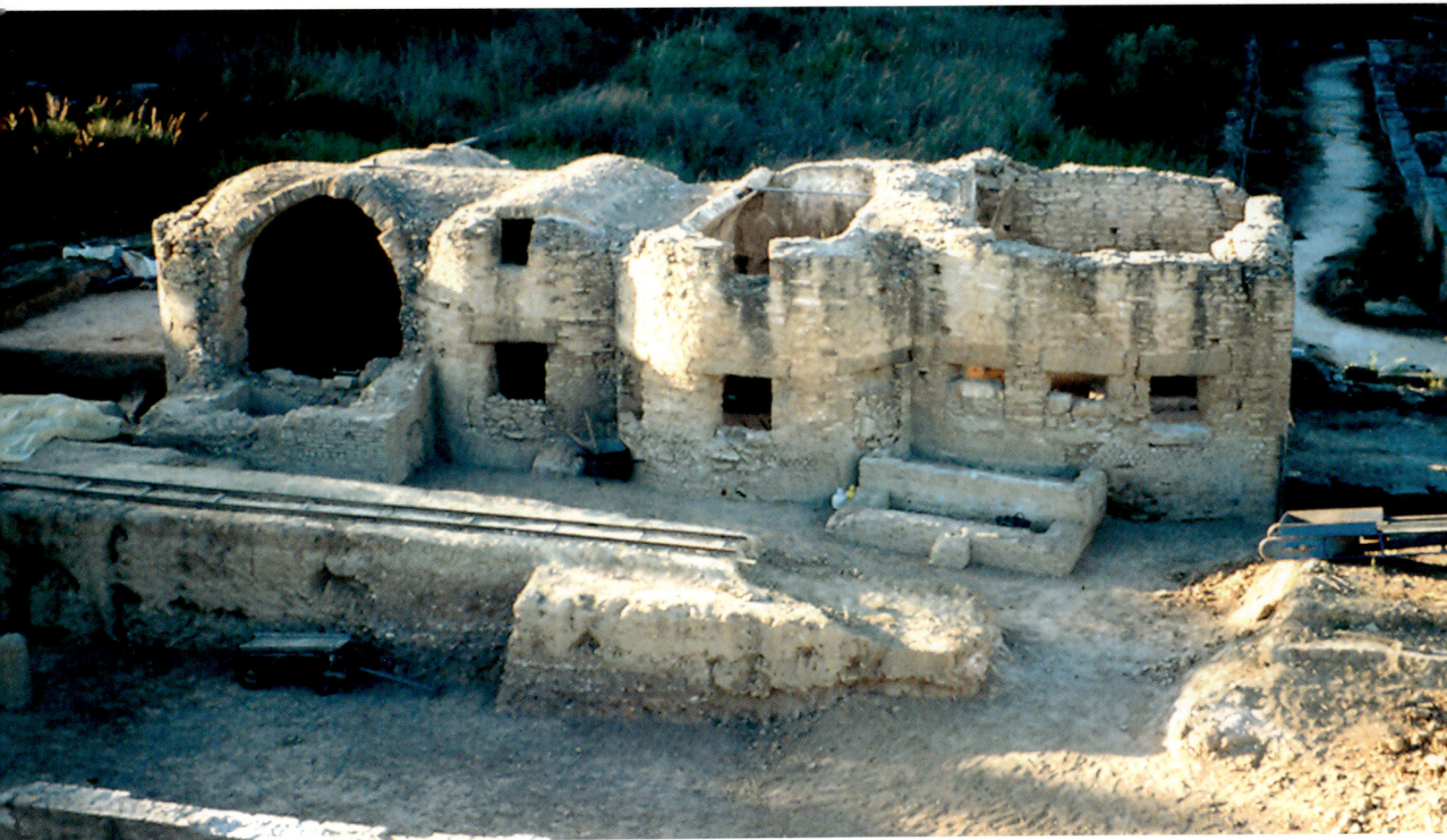

Fig. 27 – View of the Leonidaion Baths.

north of the temple of Zeus. On the basis of the notes and drawings in the excavation diary, most of the objects could be identified in the storerooms. Unfortunately, these do not include the clay pots, which are known only from the rather attractive drawings made at the time of the excavation (Figs. 21-22).

The early excavation diaries give the sketch also of a vessel, found in 1880 in a house of the late-antique settlement, that contained a hoard of what are described as tiny copper coins (Fig. 23).[20]

A spatheion without handles that was found in 1941 contained a hoard of bronze coins. The most recent were struck under Justinian and the Ostrogoth king, Totila,[21] who reigned from 541 to his death in 552 (Fig. 24).

MAINTENANCE

The sigillata and red-slip ware from the older excavations provides six examples of maintenance to keep vessels in use through repair. They all involve the drilling of holes to house clamps. In one case the clamp survives, although only one of the two pieces to be joined does (Fig. 25). The repairs concern almost exclusively African red-slip ware (two Hayes 50A/Lamboglia 40 vessels[22] in Production C3, one unidentifiable piece in Production C3, one Hayes 58B[23]

19 Völling 1995, 425-450.
20 Völling 1995, 452.
21 Völling 1995, 453-454.
22 See note 9.

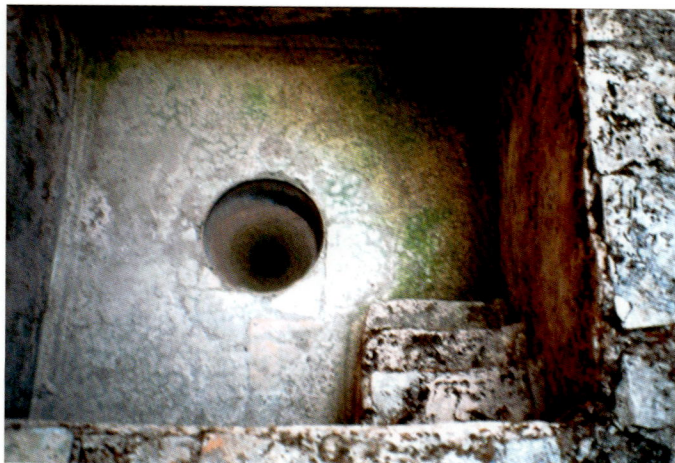

Fig. 28 – Vat installed in the Leonidaion Baths.

in Production D1, one unidentifiable piece in Production D1), with only one vessel in Italian sigillata (*Conspectus* 3).[24] This is curious because, as has been noted, African and Italian products are present at Olympia in approximately equal quantities. Did imported tableware become more valuable in later centuries and therefore more worth repairing?

RECYCLING

Pottery was also recycled in architecture at Olympia. In the Leonidaion baths (Fig. 26-27), for example, an opening at the center of the vault of the westernmost room was lined with the neck of a Kapitän II amphora.[25] When a wine-pressing operation was installed in the complex, the lower part of a large vessel was placed in a depression in the bottom of the vat in the second room from the east (Fig. 28). Systematic investigation would certainly give other examples of pottery recycled in various ways in architectural settings.

DISCARD

A probable case of provisional discard in an abandoned room can be seen in the Southwest Building (Fig. 26). In the westernmost room of the main block there, the southern door in the eastern wall was blocked, and the space was filled to the height of several meters in a single filling episode, as joins between pieces from different levels show. The material has been sorted only in a preliminary fashion,

but a 6th-century date appears likely, i.e. not long before the abandonment of the late-antique town established on the site of the sanctuary. The layer was covered to the top of the standing walls by sterile alluvial sand. This recalls the situation attested at Wadi Umm Hussein,[26] where abandoned rooms (in one case with a blocked doorway) were used for discarding rubbish during the last phase instead of locations off site as before.

CONCLUSIONS

At the beginning of this paper, two questions were asked. The first was what elements Olympia offers to illustrate Peña's model. It supplies a surprisingly large number, covering almost all the model's phases, which suggests that it will fit other sites too. The second question was how useful the model is in understanding the ceramological record at Olympia. Once again, the answer is highly positive – it has provided the stimulus and the means for a better understanding of the record at the site. These answers show what an important work Peña's is.

---

23 Carandini & Tortorella 1981, 81-82.
24 See note 8.
25 Sciallano & Sibella 1991, 99.
26 Peña 2007, 288-290 with reference to original publications.

ACKNOWLEDGEMENTS
I wish to record my gratitude to the Deutsches Archäologisches Institute and its representatives who invited me to work on material from Olympia and favored my research over the years, in particular Ulrich Sinn, the head of the project on Olympia in the Roman period and late antiquity. I am very grateful to Susanne Bocher (DAI Olympia), who kindly photographed the African Red-Slip ware piece with the clamp for me , and to Christa Schauer, who gave me copies of her articles, which otherwise would not have been accessible. My thanks go also to my student, Vittorio De Stefano, who prepared my pencil drawings for publication.

Repair and Recycling in Corinth and the Archaeological Record

BY KATHLEEN WARNER SLANE

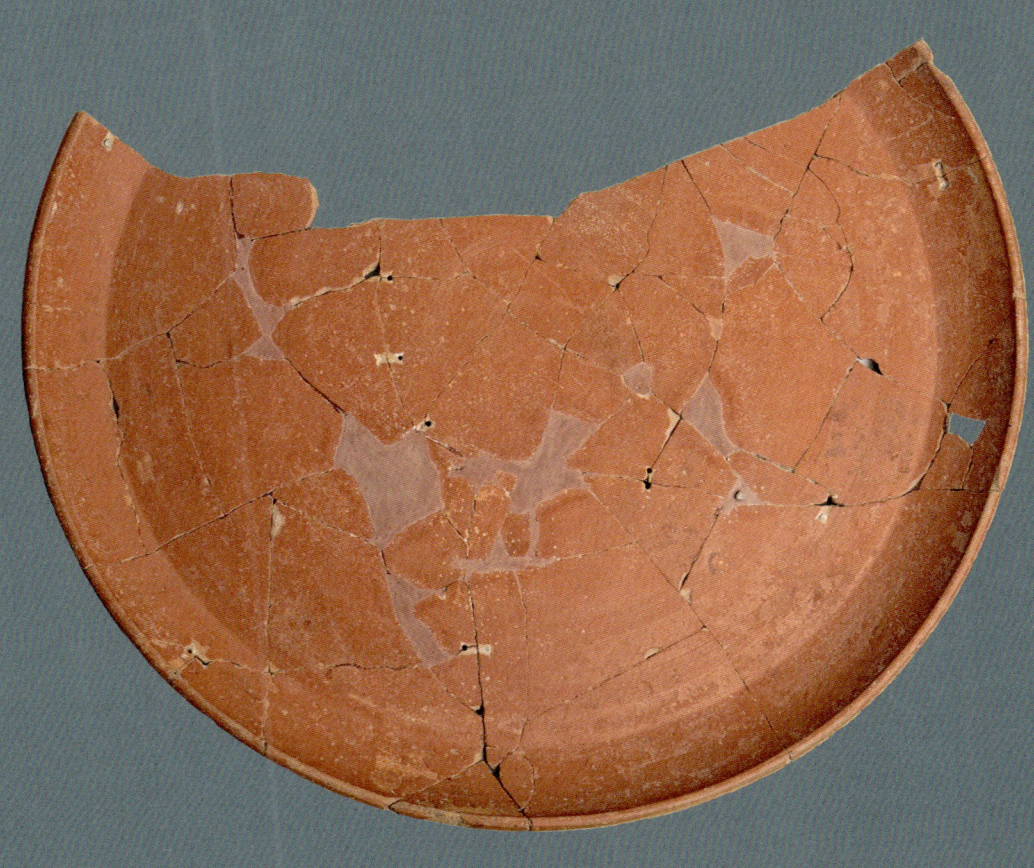

Repair and Recycling in Corinth and the Archaeological Record

BY KATHLEEN WARNER SLANE

	Reading 1 (out)	Reading 2 (in)	Reading 3 (out)
Lead (Pb)	95.334 ± 0.261	94.679 ± 0.264	93.482 ± 0.275
Tin (Sn)	2.565 ± 0.136	3.052 ± 0.144	2.606 ± 0.134
Iron (Fe)	0.935 ± 0.095	1.134 ± 0.102	2.533 ± 0.134
Titanium (Ti)	0.126 ± 0.019	0.185 ± 0.015	0.263 ± 0.022
Chromium (Cr)	0.165 ± 0.020	0.175 ± 0.014	0.177 ± 0.019
Vanadium (V)	0.161 ± 0.018	0.065 ± 0.011	0.130 ± 0.018
Zirconium (Zr)	0.041 ± 0.019	0.038 ± 0.019	0.066 ± 0.019

Table 1.

Reading Peña's *Roman Pottery in the Archaeological Record*, I recognized several phenomena that I had previously noted without thought. My initial impression was that what I had seen at Corinth resembled in many respects what he was reporting, in particular from central Italy, but differed in others. I was therefore delighted at the opportunity presented by this conference to look in more detail at the Corinthian evidence. Like several other speakers, I began by collecting all of the instances of repairs that I could find in Corinth;[1] in doing so I also encountered several cases of reuse. My goal in this paper is to present these Corinthian cases of repair and reuse, to suggest the chronological limits of such reuse, and to determine whether there is evidence of systematic reuse that warrants caution in interpreting the archaeological record.

Under the general heading "maintenance" (defined as the "upkeep or repair of a vessel so that it can continue"... in use), Peña identified four activities: cleaning, resurfacing, filling/patching, and bracing.[2] The repairs I could identify are primarily Hellenistic and early Imperial, and they occur on both coarse and fine wares. Unlike the Italian examples, Hellenistic repairs at Corinth seem to remedy flaws in manufacturing. One of the most interesting is a large decorated pithos excavated from a well west of Oakley House.[3] It is 1.85 m high and 0.96 m at the greatest diameter. Elizabeth Boggess suggested that it was intended to be sunk into the ground to just below the decorated zone at its point of maximum diameter. On opposite sides of the vessel there are two major areas of repair in which two cracks meet or cross each other, and there is also a minor crack with a single clamp. The mended cracks are not conterminous but simply end, unlike the cracks that develop when a vessel is dropped and broken into pieces. They are also essentially horizontal or vertical. It is most likely that they developed along lines of weakness as the pithos dried, perhaps in the kiln. The cracks had been mended with lead clamps, of which 21 are preserved, 16 on the vessel and 5 separately

inventoried.[4] The clamps are of varying lengths and about 0.015 m in width. They consist of a flat strip, placed on the inside of the pithos, two circular struts that filled holes drilled in the side of the pithos on either side of the crack, and a beveled outer strip also attached to the struts and tying them together. A similar but considerably smaller lead clamp was employed to repair a crack in the lip of a Hellenistic kantharos, which threatened the adjoining handle.[5]

Mending with clamps is also attested during the Roman period for pithoi and for Pompeiian Red Ware. The only pithos preserved of a row of pithoi set up in Building 7 in the 2nd or 3rd century was also mended with a clamp (Fig. 1.a-b). The repair was not visible at the time of excavation and was probably buried below the floor level in antiquity; I cannot determine when the crack occurred. A single clamp, 0.09 m long and 0.012 m wide, is preserved. The material is reddish brown, apparently iron, broken by a series of irregular cracks more or less parallel with the long sides. Both the inner and outer strips have a half-round profile and appear to have been formed in a mold. The form is therefore different from the clamps on the Hellenistic pithos. The composition of this clamp was measured July 3, 2008, using a Niton XRF analyzer on loan to Corinth and the results are presented in Table 1.[6] The material was uniform throughout the clamp. It consisted of lead with a significant admixture of tin and iron, and trace elements.

In discussing repairs that extended the use-life of vessels, a reminder that some vessels survived for a long period without being repaired is useful. More than half of a large Italian sigillata platter (C-1985-113a, b) of mid-Augustan date was broken in at least two large pieces

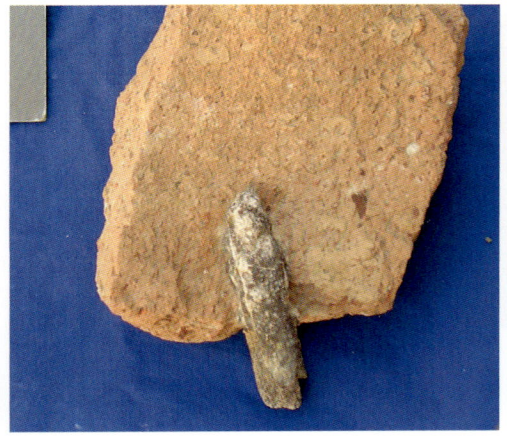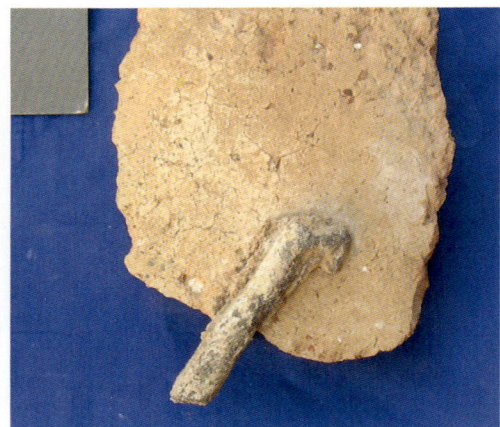

Fig 1.a-b Pithos from building 7 with clamp (inside and outside) (1:3).

(now mended from multiple smaller ones) before it was discarded in a mid-2nd century context east of the Theater: it was never mended but must have survived intact until it was broken and discarded c. 150.[7] The supposition is reinforced by a second, nearly complete Italian sigillata platter found in a "cellar" beside the Lechaion Road in 1929;[8] the chronology of a context excavated so long ago is more uncertain, but the notebook reports a coin of Tiberius and the plan shows three one-handled Corinthian pitchers of a type dateable in the 2nd and 3rd centuries (unfortunately not inventoried). The diameters of these two platters mark them out as special, one is 0.454 m in diameter, the other over 0.60, and the evidence presented here demonstrates that they were carefully preserved by their owners. Because they were not manufactured until a generation after the arrival of the Roman colonists and because such very large vessels were difficult not only to manufacture but also to transport, they are likely to have been specially ordered rather than acquired in a local shop.

Two equally large Pompeiian Red Ware platters were found in Tiberian or Claudian contexts and also must have been imported during the Augustan period. Both had been mended in antiquity, however. One (C-1977-212, Fig. 2), 0.63 m in diameter, had broken into at least three large pieces. It was repaired by cutting shallow, dovetail beddings in the inner surface of the platter and mending with lead clamps, two of which are preserved on the back. A second Pompeiian Red Ware platter, C-1976-64, also apparently broken during use rather than cracked in firing,

was mended in the same way.[9] The same difficulties of manufacture and transport apply to these vessels as to the Italian sigillata platters discussed above. I find it difficult to conceive that anyone would have acquired these vessels as "seconds" and therefore think that they broke and were mended in Corinth rather than in Italy. That two Pompeiian Red Ware platters broke within half a century while the Italian sigillata platters were preserved intact for

---

1 Because the Corinth inventory database is not searchable, I was limited to searching my own database of east of Theater material and physically examining the inventoried pottery in storage.
2 Peña 2007, 209.
3 Boggess 1970.
4 Boggess 1970, 74.
5 C-2005-20 was studied by Sarah James as part of her PhD dissertation (University of Texas-Austin, 2010) on Hellenistic pottery from the Panaghia field.
6 Two measurements were taken on the outside strip and one on the inside strip of the clamp; the second measurement on the outside was of the melted material outside the mold. The analyzer also reads antimony, palladium, silver, aluminum, molybdenum, niobium, bismuth, selenium, tungsten, zinc, copper (one reading on inside 0.061 ± 0.025), nickel, cobalt, and manganese, which were all below the limits of detection. The spectra also show calcium as a significant component presumably because we had not cleaned the metal before testing. I thank Nicol Anastasatou, Corinth conservator, for her assistance with the measurements.
7 OCK 183.0; dated c. 15-10 BC in Slane 2004b, fig. 5.
8 O-C 1814c = OCK 1941.2; dated c. 15-10 BC in Slane 2004b, fig. 5 and p. 36 (diam. 0.60 m).
9 Wright 1980, 153 no. 74 fig. 5, diam. 0.454 m. A second platter found with it shows no sign of repairs.

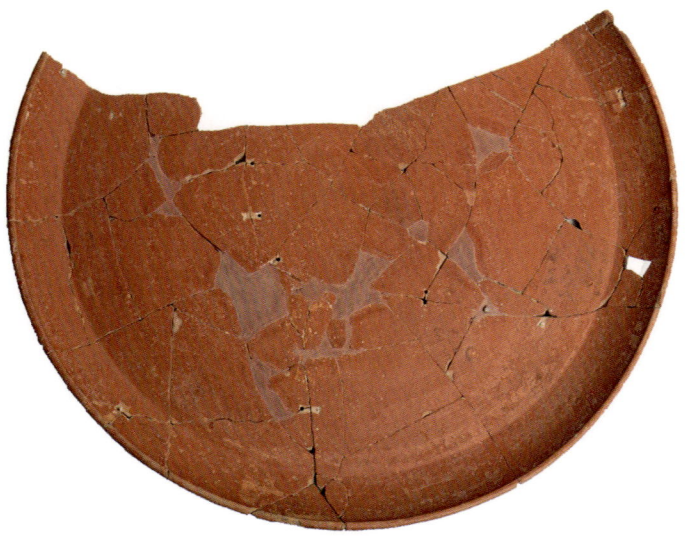
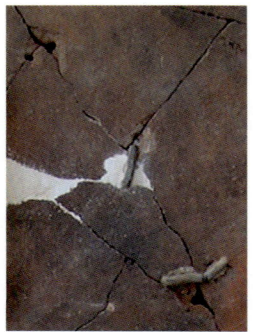
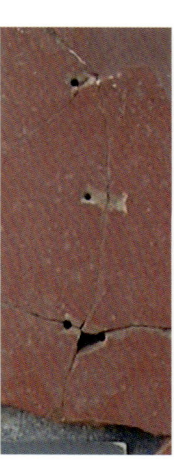

Fig 2.a-c Pompeiian Red Ware platter (C-1977-212) with details of dove-tail clamp cuttings.

several generations may well reflect the fact that cooking vessels are more likely to break than table wares.

All of the repairs discussed so far leave a circular hole on either side of the break. Single holes, by contrast, are evidence of use rather than maintenance. One instance is a Corinthian A amphora of the late 4th century BC that has a lead bung at the point of maximum diameter.[10] The placement suggests that the hole served to half-empty the amphora, and the presence of the lead bung shows that drawing off the contents took place on multiple occasions (otherwise why have a stopper?). The same may be true of a single hole, 0.005 m in diameter, drilled below the mid-point of a Gaza amphora (C-1959-278, Fig. 3.a). Neither hole is a standard feature (it does not appear on numerous other examples of the same type), and both would cease to be useful when the level of the contents dropped. Were the remaining contents then decanted into another container? On the other hand, an otherwise identical single hole in the shoulder of a fractional Palestinian amphora (C-1981-191, Fig. 3.b) is not placed for removing the contents. (The latter is too far from the break to have been a repair hole for a clamp.) David Adan-Bayewitz has suggested that such holes, which may appear in multiples, provided a source of air to equalize the interior pressure and facilitate flow when the contents were being poured from the mouth (as does puncturing a can on two sides of the top in modern use or

the hole Athenians of the Roman period cut in the shoulder of an amphora reused as a bucket).[11] As Peña had already seen, such evidence indicates that holes were drilled to enhance the way a vessel functioned as well as to repair it. In all of the instances cited here, the hole must have been drilled from the outside of the vessel (see below).

I also found two examples of rectangular holes cut in the walls of coarse wares. C-1934-1972, a closed vessel (a pitcher or amphora?) in local cooking fabric, preserves a slit cut from the outside perpendicular to the wheelmarks. It seems suitable for a repair accomplished by passing something like a strip of leather or lead through the wall, perhaps flattening it to keep it in place (Fig. 4.a-b). But on the best-preserved example, the Spanish amphora C-1974-186, the slots are horizontal and were chiseled from the outside in pairs that are not related to any broken edge (Fig. 5). One pair and parts of two others are preserved, placed at regular intervals around the neck. Peña, who noted the existence of the third set on this vessel during our visit to Corinth, suggested that these holes allowed some kind of soft cover to be tied in place. The two examples thus seem to attest two different activities: the alteration of the Spanish jar may have been made while it still contained its primary contents, garum, or when it was reused for something else, but the other vessel had been broken before the hole was cut.

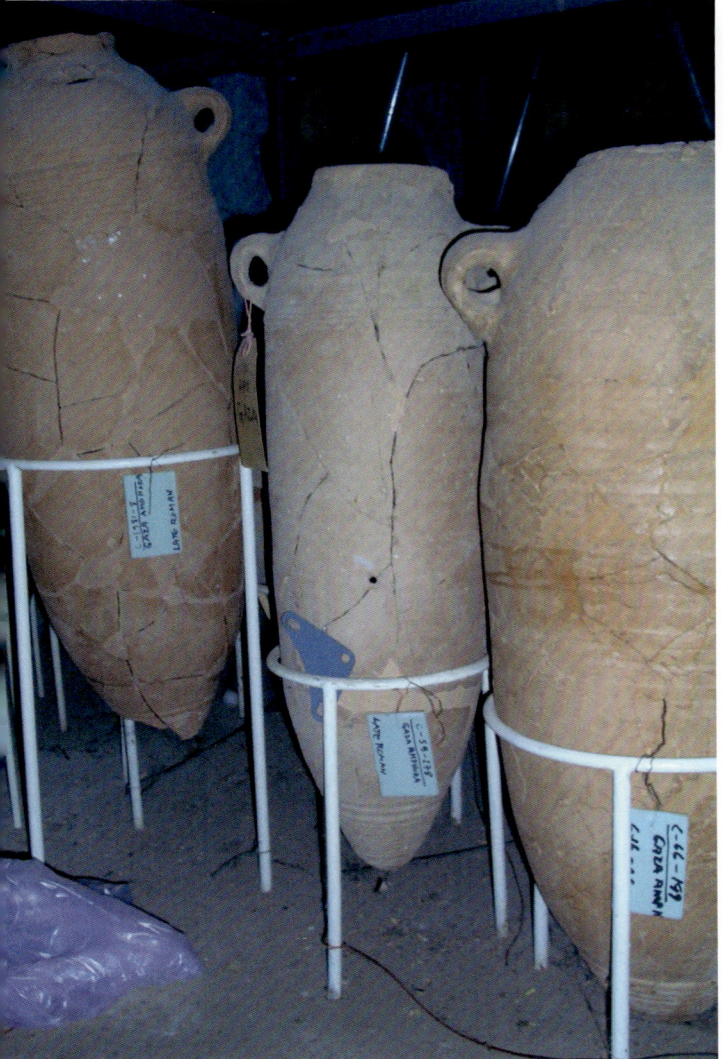

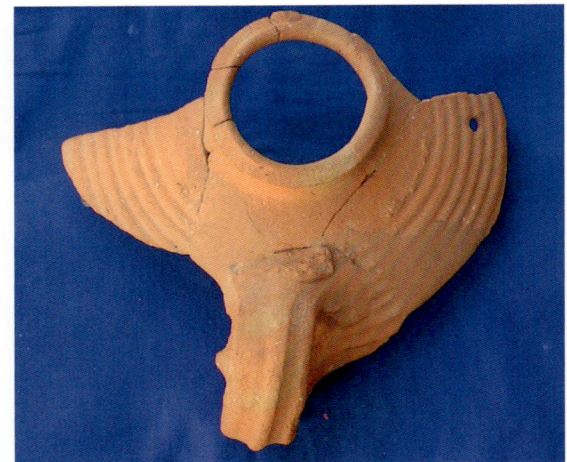

Fig. 3.b Fractional Palestinian amphora (C-1981-191) with hole drilled in shoulder (1:3).

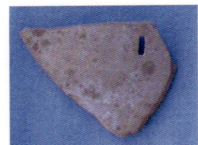

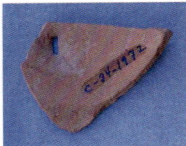

Fig. 4.a-b Closed vessel in cooking fabric (C-1934-1972) with cut slit (1:3).

Fig. 3.a Gaza amphora (C-1959-278) with hole drilled in wall.

The reuse of amphorae as burial containers was documented by Peña from Italy, North Africa and Spain.[12] Examples from Corinth extend the practice into the eastern Mediterranean. Sixth-century Gaza amphorae were reused in both the Lerna Hollow cemetery and the Panaghia field;[13] their size and cigar-shape make them suitable as containers for infants. There are some earlier instances as well. The earliest example of the reuse of amphorae as burial containers that I know of is a 2nd- or early 3rd-century Knidian jar in the destruction debris of Building 3 east of the Theater. It held the carefully arranged corpse of

10 C-1963-689. Robinson 1969, 9-10, pl. 2.2; Riley 1979, under D85, p. 142. I thank Carolyn Koehler for permission to bring it up in this discussion.

11 Adan-Bayewitz 1986, cited by Peña (2007, 67); Robinson 1959, *passim*, discussed by Peña (2007, 136-137, fig. 6.3).

12 Peña 2007, 164-170, sections 6.22-6.23.

13 For such a burial of an infant, placed in a rock-cut grave in the Lerna Hollow cemetery, see Wiseman 1967, 34-35, pls. 14.c-d (grave 6, with the upper half of the amphora shattered on top of the grave cover). The graves in the Panaghia field are unpublished. Additional examples which might be overlooked: Rudolph & Sheehan 1979 report an amphora body (African - KWS) from Porto Cheli that held a child's burial, grave 5, 300, no. 10, 309, with fig. 4, 307.

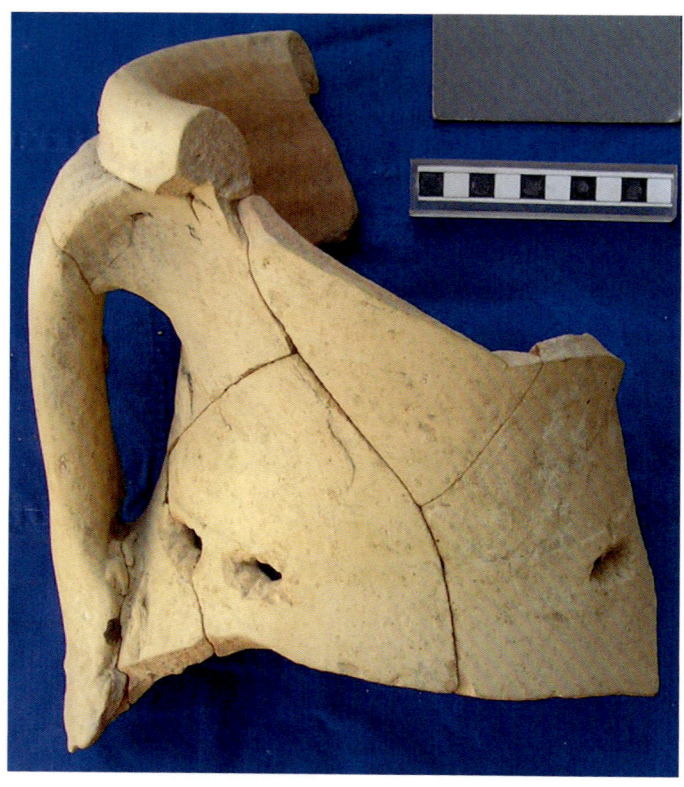

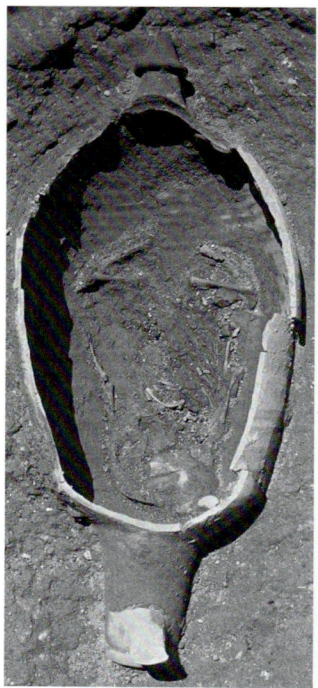

Fig. 5 Rectangular holes in pairs on a Spanish amphora, probably to serve as anchors (1:3).

Fig. 6 Right. Roman Knidian amphora (C-1985-90) used for infant burial.

a child (Fig. 6) and is notable for not being in a cemetery.[14] The vessel was oriented with the broken handle upward, and the regular break on the right (visible in a photograph in *Hesperia*) seems to mark where the amphora was broken open to receive the corpse. Two of five subsidiary graves associated with the Late Square Tomb to the northeast of the city were also amphora burials, perhaps dating as late as the early 5th century.[15] In another instance among the graves excavated by Robinson along the modern aqueduct on the north edge of the city, the lower third of a Dressel 6 amphora was reused as a container for a cremation urn.[16] Other types of vessels could also be reused as burial containers. Robinson's Painted Tomb contained a local pitcher reused for a late cremation burial: the neck and handle had been roughly knocked off and a buff dish of a type used as a lid for cremation urns had been sealed over the opening.[17]

During the Roman period pottery vessels were reused for a wide variety of miscellaneous purposes that seem unlikely to have much impact on the pottery record as a whole.

There are several examples of small vessels reused as paint-pots: a bank (C-1986-111), a thin-walled cup (C-1988-100b), and a fine-ware bowl (C-1936-1849). One also finds vessels with a small hole cut in the floor to allow them to be used as funnels or strainers (C-1936-2105, and C-1990-80 from the Building 7 amphora deposit mentioned below). In addition, both fine and coarse vessels might be chipped down to be reused as gaming tokens and lids (Fig. 7.a-d).[18] The feet of two fine-ware dishes, one of Italian sigillata and the other of Boeotian Red Slip ware (C-1962-226, C-1934-1835, early 2nd and 6th century respectively), were carefully chipped away from the upper part of the vessel, with the result that the stamped decoration in the center of the floor became more conspicuous. I had supposed that they were reused upside down as saucers, but other conference participants suggested that they were lids or stoppers, with the stamped side up. One Eastern Sigillata A plate floor had been reused as a scratch pad (C-1936-1872, Fig. 8).

Peña is right to emphasize that Amphorae in particular were systematically recycled. Type A and B reuse, in which

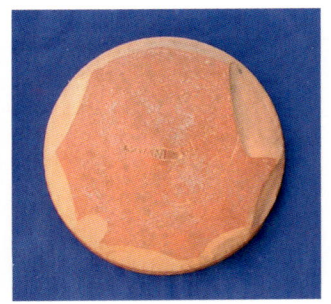 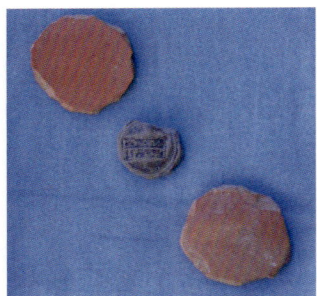 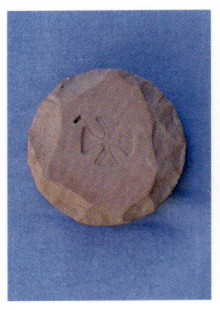 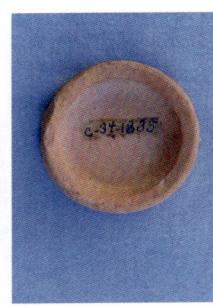

Fig. 7.a-d Vessels cut down for use as lids or tokens. a. C-1962-226; b. C-1936-1875, C-1935-200, C-1936-1876; c and d. C-1934-1835. (1:3).

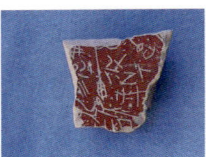

Fig. 8 Interior of Eastern Sigillata A plate fragment (C-1936-1872) reused on both sides as a scratch pad. (1:3).

the vessels are used "as is", can therefore be difficult to recognize. Dressel 6 or Dressel 2-4 amphorae were placed across the mouths of manholes to close them (one in Forum Southwest, at least two east of the Theater).[19] Peña discussed a published context from Corinth in which 26 fractional amphorae (also some funnels and pitchers, and a few other vessels) seem to have been collected for reuse.[20] Since the circumstances have already been discussed twice, there is no need to belabor them here. He remarked quite fairly that the suggestion of reuse is plausible but cannot be proven.

Type C reuse, involving modification of the vessels, is more easily documented. The Spanish garum jar discussed above is one example. Amphorae reused as burial containers, also discussed above, fall into this category, but most such uses are architectural or industrial. The reuse of Niederbieber 77/Kapitän II amphora necks as drain pipes is relatively well-known, at least in the East.[21] They were also reused as bellows at Corinth (Fig. 9.a-b) and Ephesos.[22] In both cases the necks were carefully separated from the bodies and the handles were usually discarded; for the bellows, a hole drilled a few centimeters from the join of the neck provided air, and heavy vitrification of the mouth proves it had been held in a fire.

Corinth also provides several instances of the reuse of amphorae as parts of water installations and sewer systems. In one instance excavated by Robinson, the upper half of an amphora like G197 (C-1962-176) was placed upside down near a lined basin; sherds placed beneath it partially blocked the neck opening and a square tile was the cover (Fig. 10.a-d). The lower body had been chipped away and the neck and handles carefully removed. When it was found a terracotta water pipe was still inserted through a large hole cut on one side. A corresponding but

14 Williams & Zervos 1986, 137-138, no. 8 (C-1985-90), pl. 30; fig. 1 on p. 130 shows the position of the amphora (burial 1985-1) in the room.

15 Slane, in preparation, pl. IV.6a, c. A Forlimpopuli amphora (a late 1st- to early 3rd-century type) had been divided at the shoulder and was found buried below the floor of the tomb against its north wall (LST-Γ); no bones were preserved. In LST-δ two related 3rd-century amphorae were placed end to end and may have contained two children. None of these amphorae was inventoried. Their location suggests the burials are related to the Late Square Tomb (early 5th century) rather than to the earlier Chamber Tomb with Sarcophagi (2nd and 3rd century) as the date of the amphorae might indicate.

16 Ibid., grave 39. Peña had documented amphorae reused as ossuaries or sarcophagi in the West, but only cooking pots reused like this Dr. 6 amphora, Peña 2007, section 7.2.4.

17 Ibid., PT-B-59 and PT-B-60 (C-1962-978 and C-1962-977 respectively).

18 Among many examples, including some stored with the context pottery: C-1935-200, a gaming counter chiseled from a local gray-ware cup with stamp; C-1936-1875, a lid chiseled from African Red Slip Ware; C-1936-1876, a lid chiseled from an amphora wall; and C-1935-725 nfc, i.e. "cooking ware not for cooking" pitcher base chiseled to use as a lid; lot 1983-83 contains six such stoppers. Although the second and third examples might have been imported as lids (see Peña 2007, 154-157), the first and fourth are local products and served different purposes.

19 For one of the latter, see Williams & Zervos 1983, 18, 22, no. 61 (C-1982-83, an Italian Dressel 2-4), fig. 3 (location), pl. 9.

20 Peña 2007, 97-98 (s.v. Korinth); it was published in Slane 2004a.

21 Cf. Peña 2007, 180, 6.26.

22 The Niederbieber 77 amphorae discussed by Outschar (1993, 46-52), show the same pattern of vitrification around the rim as those in Corinth and are therefore also likely to have been reused a bellows rather than being wasters.

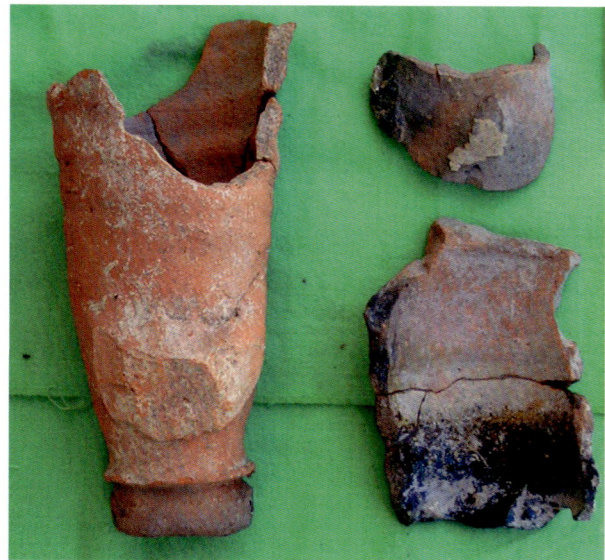

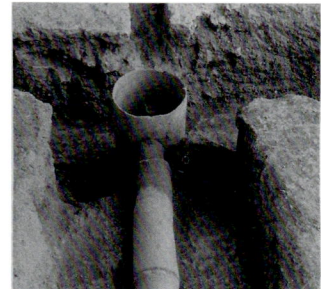
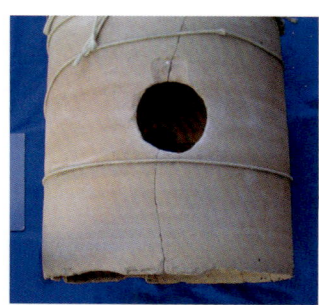
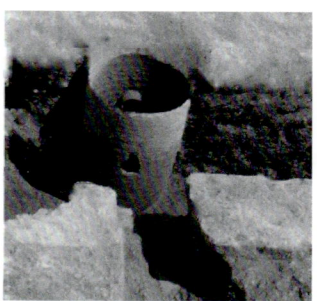
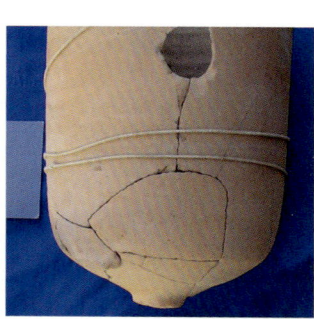

Fig. 10.a-d Amphora reused upside down as a connector in a pipeline (two views in situ 62-62-31 and 62-62-36 and two views of the amphora C-1962-176).

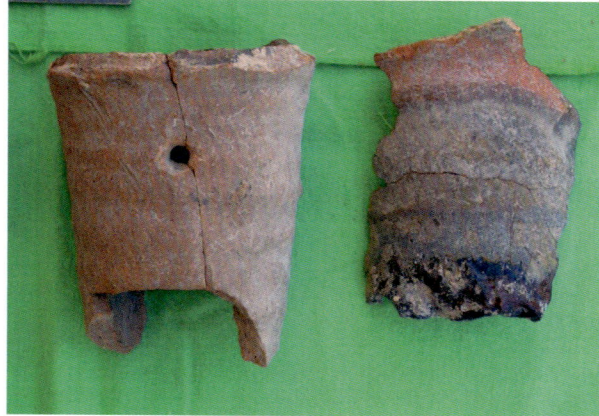

Fig. 9.a-b Niederbieber 77 amphora necks reused as bellows (lot 1988-68) (1:3).

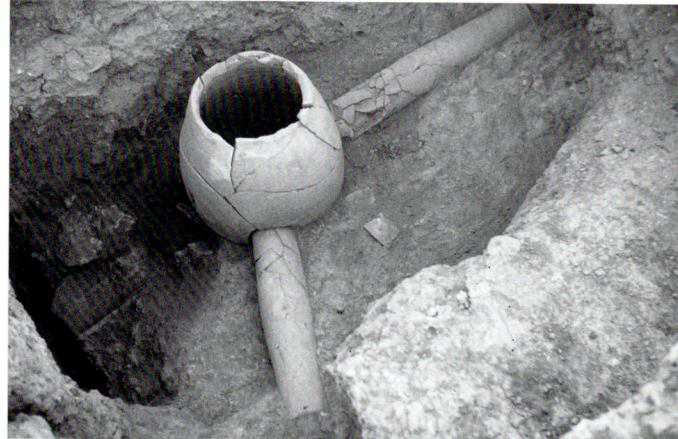

Fig. 11 Dressel 6 amphora behind shop XV of the South Stoa.

smaller hole had been chipped out of the opposite side; square depressions of unknown purpose were chiseled adjacent to and above the holes. Single amphorae placed as connectors or settling basins in pipelines have also been recorded behind shop XV of the South Stoa (Fig. 11) and in the Panaghia field.[23] Dressel 6 amphorae were reused as downspouts and sewer pipes in and around the long rectangular building southeast of the Forum (C-1975-151 and C-1975-150).[24] Instances of such reuse by cutting largish holes in the sides of amphorae are better attested at Corinth than holes cut in the sides (rather than the

shoulder) to empty the contents;[25] interpretation may depend on the context.

The area east of the Theater also provided evidence of amphora bodies cut into strips, of several different widths, and systematically broken into small, rectangular pieces (Fig. l2.a-b).[26] Several types of amphorae are involved:

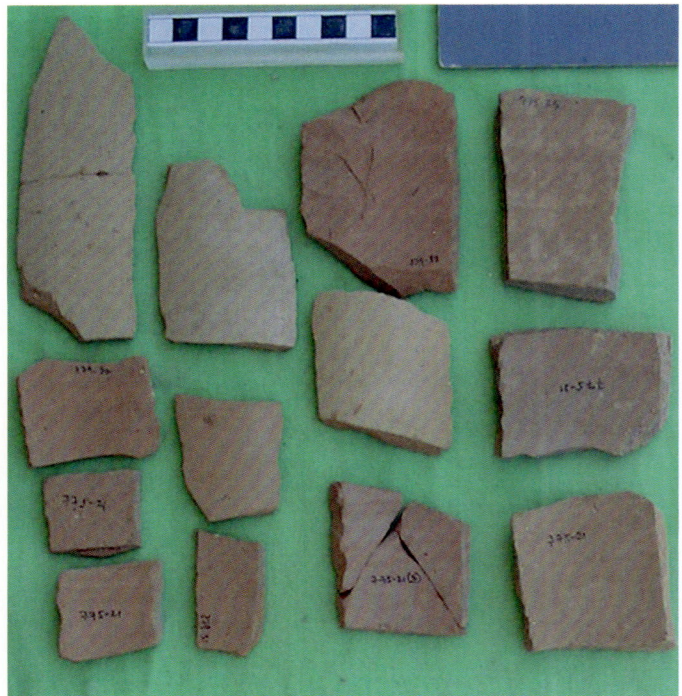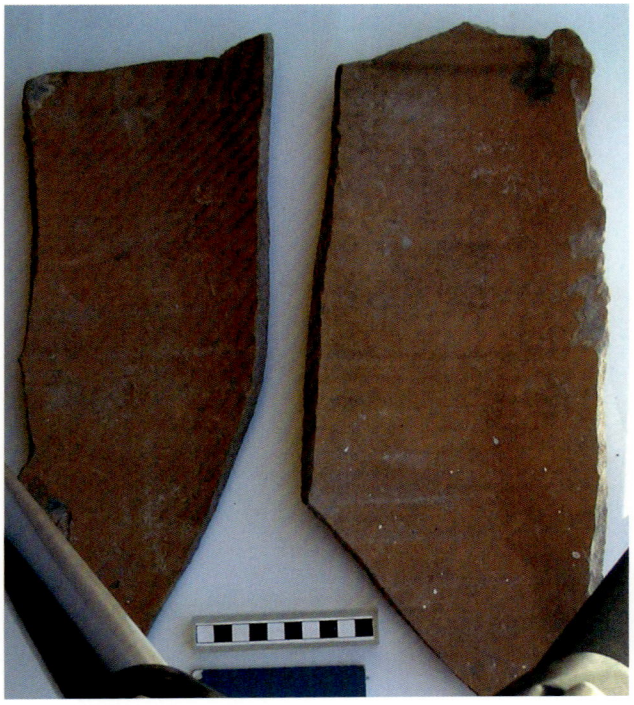

Fig. 12.a-b Amphora bodies cut into strips and broken to be used in as backing for wall plaster, in floors or as ostraka.

more or less cylindrical bodies were most desirable and their tops, handles, and toes (the diagnostic, countable features) have been removed. The purpose of such strips is uncertain. Peña had suggested that long strips might be *ostraka*,[27] but the systematic breakage of the east of Theater examples seems to indicate another use. One possibility is chinking in rubble walls, but examination of standing walls across the site at Corinth did not reveal any examples of such "cut amphorae" used as chinking.[28] A second possibility is that they were set on edge in the floor of a basin; however, the basins preserved at Corinth have floors paved with diamond-shaped tiles. A third alternative, suggested by Charles Williams, is that they might have been used against the face of a rubble or pisé wall to level it before plastering.[29] A related use is as a backing for mosaic *emblemata*: the glass panels from Kenchreai are reported to have been mounted in a resinous plaster against a background of amphora sherds.[30] Such uses might have been more common than we realize. Once the plaster disintegrated, how could one recognize this reuse? Nevertheless, that is an unlikely explanation for the east of

23 Cf. Broneer 1954, pl. 16.5; this appears to be a Dressel 6 amphora chopped off at the shoulder. The line in the Panaghia field is unpublished.
24 Robinson 1962, 112, pl. 33c; see also Williams & Fisher 1976, especially 131-132 and fig. 3 (128); the two amphorae mentioned above come from yet a third, unpublished, example associated with this building. At the conference I also illustrated an example of a deep plain-ware basin with vertical wall that had been reused to receive water from a downspout and in which a large hole had been drilled for the insertion of an outflow pipe (C-2002-54); see Williams, in preparation.
25 For the latter, see Peña 2007, 67-69 and, for an interpretation as urinals, see 138-140, section 6.4.
26 In lot 1985-79 (Fig. 12.a), for instance. Similar pieces come from the context pottery of South Stoa shop XXI (Fig. 12.b). The presence of such "cut amphorae" in excavated contexts is clearly from a secondary use rather than from their initial purpose as containers, and I ultimately decided to exclude them from the east of Theater quantification project.
27 Peña 2007, 160-164, section 6.20.
28 In the Roman and Byzantine walls I examined, tile rather than pottery was the chinking material. For cut amphorae reused as chinking in house walls, see Costello, this volume.
29 Personal communication 1992.
30 Ibrahim *et al.* 1976, 2 figs. 9-11 with pl. IV A.

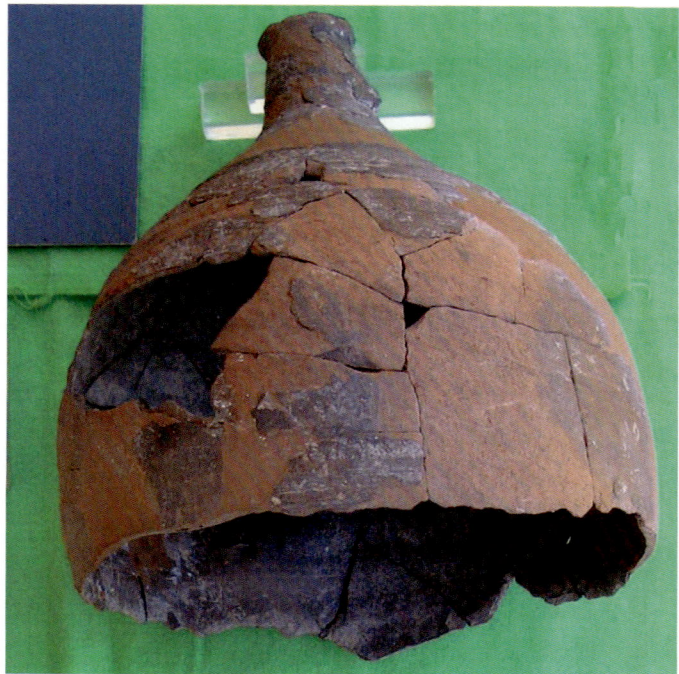

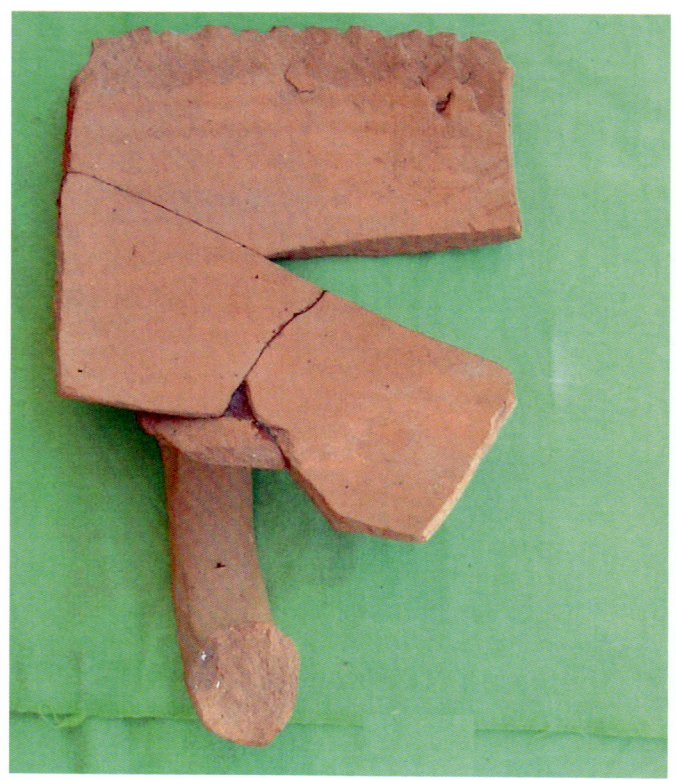

Fig. 13.a-b Amphora tops drilled and split off to reuse as funnels. A second-century micaceous water jar (lot 1981-50) and a sixth-century LR Amphora 2 (Lot 1982-107:1) (1:3).

Theater or South Stoa "cut amphorae" because many of the strips are complete or mendable, which suggests they were processed where they were found.

One of the most persistent modifications of amphorae was to cut the top away and reuse it as a funnel. A micaceous water jar and a LR Amphora 2 were cut down by drilling a series of more or less contiguous holes around the circumference at the shoulder or belly; the top was then knocked off (Fig. 13.a-b). Earlier examples such as a Coan amphora, C-1985-218, and an imitation Rhodian, C-1987-104, show a similar horizontal line of splitting but lack clear evidence that holes had been drilled to provide a breaking line. A Gaza amphora (C-1981-194, Fig. 14.a-b) has such a line, but it continues evenly around the base of the handle to include it: a funnel with a handle. In the future it will be possible to distinguish such reuse by examination of the break:[31] it is always horizontal (rather than transverse as it would be if the vessel had been dropped) and shows a series of small, overlapping chips on the interior surface.

Peña refers to "substantial undisturbed deposits of refuse that include significant amounts of pottery . . . including the substructures of buildings, cisterns, wells, pits," etc.[32] His passing reference to such deposits underplays the significance of such fills especially in the Roman period. The filling (and topping up) of wells and cisterns is well known in Athens and Corinth, beginning as early as the Geometric period and continuing through the 3rd century AD (the Dressel 6 amphorae referred to above). They are commonly recognized as sources of mendable pottery, and this is not limited to vessels that may have been reused as buckets: a glance through the Athenian Agora groups A-M shows a wide range of mended, more or less complete vessels.[33] What is specific to the Roman period is large-scale "construction fills" of similar composition by which building substructures and terraces are filled in.[34] These fills consist of densely packed, mendable sherds and are a different phenomenon from the setting of whole amphorae for terraces and drainage projects as discussed by Peña,[35] of which none have so far been found at Corinth. In the Corinthian examples cited below many mendable vessels

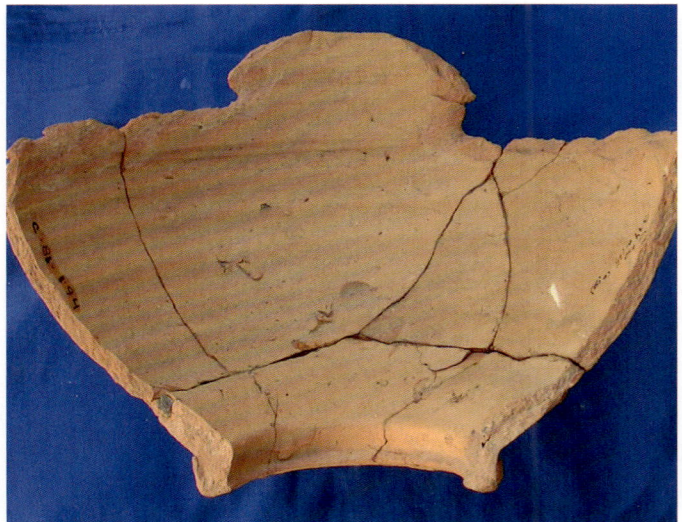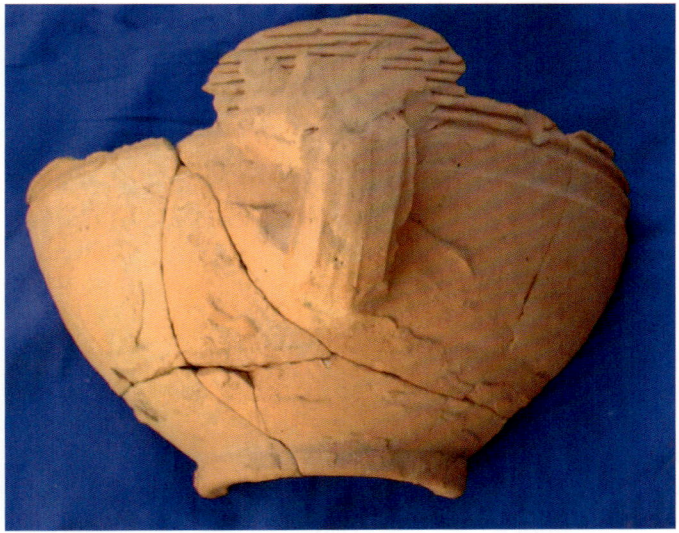

Fig. 14.a-b Top of a Gaza amphora (C-1981-194) drilled and split off, including handle, to reuse as a funnel.

have been found, but the sherds of a single vessel are dispersed both horizontally and vertically through the fill.

How to understand such groups lay at the beginning of Peña's investigation of how the archaeological record is formed. Such groups have been, in fact, preferred in quantified studies because the amount of material is large: 50-100 kg is common at Corinth and elsewhere,[36] and between 1983 and 1990 the excavations east of the Theater at Corinth produced 15 deposits of 100-500 kg; on the eastern edge of the area, and in front of and behind the theater cavea wall, three units of more than 1000 kg were recorded. Deposits from behind the South Stoa, from the core of the South Basilica, from an early Roman building in Forum Southwest, and the filling in of the quarry at the east and west ends of Temple Hill are other Corinthian examples.[37] Influenced by John Hayes's dates for the Stoa and Basilica groups, such deposits have been referred to as "clean-up of AD 77 earthquake debris,"[38] but the east of Theater excavations have demonstrated that not all such deposits are of that date. Whether all might be clean-up of earthquake debris is another question. In addition to size, these "construction fills" are characterized by large quantities of mendable pottery, and stratigraphically, by having been dumped as a short-term project rather than having accumulated over time (as would be the case for Peña's "refuse disposal", i.e. garbage dumps on vacant

land or middens.) It is worth noting that Corinthian construction projects were attuned to civic needs, including status-advertising projects of the elite, rather than simply to the necessity of rebuilding after an earthquake, although that was sometimes a motive.[39] For such large amounts of pottery to be available for construction projects, however, it seems likely that there was a source, that is, that such large quantities would not be collected ad hoc for each project. And the fact that so much of it is mendable is a

---

31 Cf. Peña 2007, 148, section 6.12.

32 Peña 2007, 283, see also 254, section 9.2 and in general, Chapter 10 Discard and Reclamation.

33 Thompson 1934; Robinson 1959.

34 I exclude "destruction debris" usually from earthquakes, found essentially in situ; such deposits are normally no more than 0.60-0.75 m deep and may occur at any time. Nor do I mean to imply that the practice begins suddenly: both the terrace north of the South Stoa at Corinth and the Middle Stoa fill in the Athenian agora are earlier, smaller scale examples of the practice. The former at any rate is not particularly sherd-rich.

35 Peña 2007, 181-192, section 6.27.

36 Slane 2003; see also Tomber 1988, 1993, Riley 1979, Fulford and Peacock 1984, Reynolds 1995 (appendices), for instance.

37 South Stoa and South Basilica, see Hayes 1973; the 1977 fill from Forum Southwest and the quarry fill are unpublished.

38 Slane 1986.

39 E.g., Hayes 1973; east of Theater terrace buildings.

good indication that it has not been moved many times or selectively reused. It also seems to me an argument against the systematic scavenging of discarded pottery postulated by Peña for Rome.

Two instances of selective reuse involve material of very small size but are likely to be significant because of their probable ubiquity and extent. First, Charles Williams has suggested that quantities of pre-Roman ceramics were incorporated into Roman pisé in Building 3 east of the Theater,[40] thus selectively adding Archaic or classical sherds to a Roman context. This observation is supported by the large quantities of Classical fine-ware sherds (with little or no accompanying coarse-ware fragments) found in other contexts, for instance in the northwest room of Building 5 where, in 35% of the Roman lots containing 100 or more pre-Mummian sherds, the average sherd weight is less than 5 grams and none of the fragments join.

Second, Ruth Siddall has recently demonstrated that all mortars and hydraulic cements from a series of Roman baths at Corinth contain large quantities of recycled (crushed or ground) orange ceramics in a size range of 1-3 mm.[41] She points out that the "pozzolanicity" of clay aggregate mimics volcanic tuff and is affected by firing temperature (600-900° preferred), composition (kaolinite is best), and grain size. She calculates that the proportion is about 750 kg of crushed ceramic per cubic meter of cement and argues that the scale indicates organized collection and processing as part of the construction industry. The identifiable ceramic aggregate includes both pottery and brick, much of it imported judging from the quartz and feldspar tempers. She further suggests that the pottery was systematically selected on the basis of its suitability as a reactive aggregate, perhaps simply by color (buff fabrics are largely absent).

In summary, the Roman period provides more evidence than other periods for the reuse and recycling of pottery at Corinth. There is evidence that unusually hard-to-replace or valuable vessels were repaired, including as a way of salvaging work in the potter's workshop. Throughout the Roman period more or less whole vessels were recycled on a small scale, particularly for domestic or light industrial uses, and some were employed ad hoc for use in water installations and drains. By far the most important reuse yet documented was "construction fills" (though Siddall's research is beginning to highlight the massive volumes of pottery in opus signinum). Such large-scale re-use is largely limited to the Roman period. Contents and functional classes vary from unit to unit but are broadly repetitive for a given phase. There is no reason to suspect that they are systematically deficient (or enriched) in a way that would distort our view of Roman trade.

---

40 Williams & Zervos 1987, 20.
41 Siddall forthcoming.

ACKNOWLEDGEMENTS

I am particularly grateful to the organizers and to the Danish and Finnish Institutes of Archaeology in Athens for their hospitality during the conference. My debt to Charles Williams and Guy Sanders, past and current directors of Corinth, for on-going discussions of the behavior that led to the formation of particular contexts, is profound. Site photographs and the large image of C-1977-212 are courtesy of the Corinth excavations; I thank Ioulia Tzonou-Herbst and James Herbst for their help with these. The remainder of the photographs are mine. Unless otherwise stated all dates are AD.

Reusing Pottery in the Eastern Desert of Egypt

BY ROBERTA TOMBER

Reusing Pottery in the Eastern Desert of Egypt

BY ROBERTA TOMBER

J. Theodore Peña's influential book *Roman Pottery in the Archaeological Record* provides a classification system for the identification and interpretation of pottery reuse at all stages of its lifecycle, from production to final discard. The evidence for reuse from the Eastern Desert of Egypt is widespread and in some cases can be seen as the product of general behavioural patterns that might be identified in diverse contexts; in others the behaviour is more specific to individual circumstance.

The ecology of the Eastern Desert presents a dichotomy. On the one hand the desert can be seen as an inhospitable environment, remote by days from the more fertile areas of the Nile Valley. At the same time it was an area rich in mineral resources, metals and stones, including decorative stones prized by Imperial cities and Emperors. On the Red Sea coast, ports facilitated the lucrative trade with Africa and the East and therefore were a magnet for more exotic imports from both the Roman and non-Roman world. Some small-scale agricultural gardens, particularly for vegetables, could be maintained in the desert,[1] but settlements peopled by soldiers, merchants, workers and their families required a substantial and constant supply of imported foodstuffs to support their Roman lifestyle.

Amphorae were a vital means for provisioning the desert and they consisted entirely of pottery imported from outside the region, since the nearest production areas lay in the Nile Valley. Here we will look at the evidence for reuse from four sites: the quarries at Mons Claudianus and Mons Porphyrites, and the ports of Myos Hormos (modern Quseir al-Qadim) and Berenike. Importantly, all share the arid environment that offers remarkable preservation including organic assemblages and written texts, both of which contribute to our understanding of reuse.[2]

QUARRY SITES: MONS CLAUDIANUS AND MONS PORPHYRITES

Mons Claudianus was excavated by an international team under of the aegis of the Institut Français Oriental

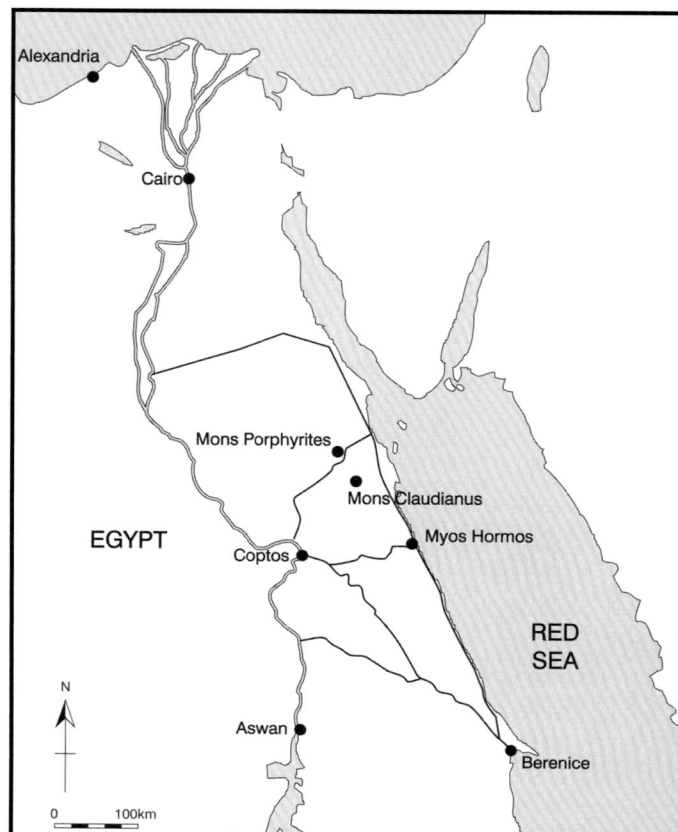

Fig. 1 Location map.

d'Archéologie between 1987 and 1993. This fortified settlement, located to extract the granodiorite from nearby quarries,[3] had occupation layers dating between the late 1st and the early 3rd centuries. One of the most prolific features was a large rubbish dump (up to 1.8 m high, 18 m wide and 75 m wide) – the southern *sebakh*.[4] This feature dates primarily to the Trajanic period, although there was dumping activity and some reworking of the *sebakh*, and therefore disturbance between layers, until the Antonine period.[5]

Approximately 9,000 *ostraca* were collected from the site as a whole, and their gradual publication is providing a detailed picture of life in the settlement and quarries inhabited, according to one *ostracon*, by 917 individuals on one day during the Trajanic period.[6] The *ostraca* occasionally refer to ceramic vessels, particularly as containers to bring foodstuffs to the site from the Nile

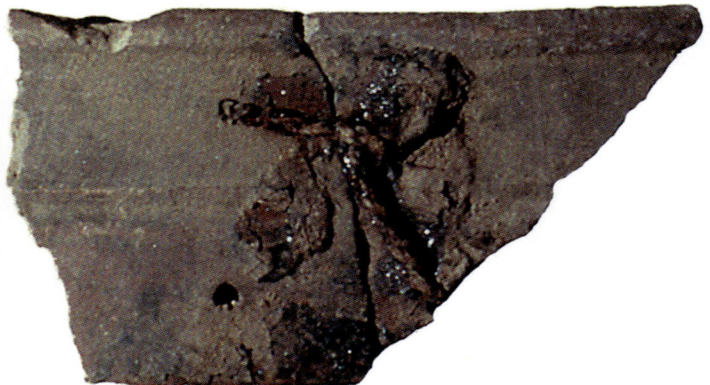

Fig. 2. Two bowl sherds joined by threading a string through four pierced holes that were then covered with a black substance (Scale 1:2).

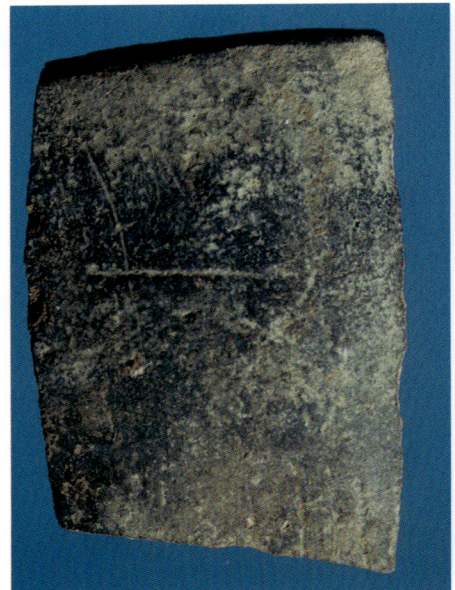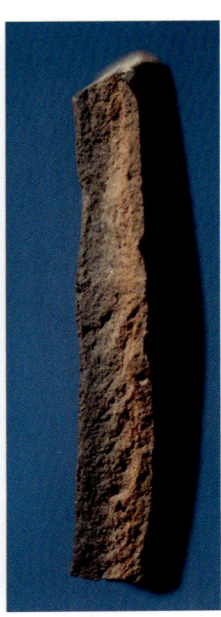

Fig. 3 Surface view of reworked sherd showing its applied black surface (left); fresh break including the reworked edge showing the exposed core (right) (Not to scale).

Valley. In some cases they contained not their primary or original contents, but secondary goods – such as water[7] or meat.[8] The latter is particularly interesting, providing continuity with Pharaonic times when it was a primary content of amphorae.[9]

This need to provision the site is reflected in the quantities of amphorae, comprising up to 76% of the assemblage. Percentages of this size are normally associated with port sites, but here the amount exceeds 65% through-out the entire sequence at the main Claudianus site.[10]

Despite the large quantities of pottery found on site, examination shows that care and attention was taken to mending some vessels, such as the small coarse ware bowl shown on Figure 2 that was perforated, joined with a string and subsequently covered in a pitch or bitumen type substance. Mended pottery is known throughout the Roman world, although apart from *dolia*, examples are rare and most frequently recorded on finewares.[11] The Claudianus example indicates that pottery was at a premium and could not be thoughtlessly discarded.[12] This conclusion is strengthened by examination of table ware assemblages, showing some of the vessels to be reworked from the more plentiful amphorae. The quality of these reworked vessels was high, so they were not immediately recognised as such, but detailed examination identified two main features for recognising them: 1) wheel marks were not parallel to the rim; 2) where a core existed it was not always enclosed but sometimes had been sliced off leaving the core area exposed as seen on Figure 3.

At Claudianus a complete sequence of manufacture, by sizing down amphorae and other larger vessels, could be identified. When amphorae were resized, the spike and lower walls of the Nile silt 'Amphore Egyptienne 3'[13] were used as the basis. Most of the spike was removed, sometimes leaving a small portion of it to form a base, with rounded or conical-shaped walls forming a bowl or beaker (Fig. 4).

1 Van der Veen 1998.
2 This contribution relies primarily on published data, particularly from Bailey 2007; Thomas and Tomber 2006 and especially Tomber 2006a and 2006b.
3 Peacock *et al.* 1994.
4 For *sebakh* more generally in the eastern desert, see Ballet 2003, 222-224.
5 Maxfield & Bingen 2001.
6 Cuvigny 2005, especially p. 334.
7 Bingen 1997, 118-119, O. 280.
8 Bülow-Jacobsen 1992, 127, O. 139.
9 Hope 1977, 24.
10 Tomber 2006b, 197, table 1.4.
11 Peña 2007, 248-249.
12 Tomber 2006b, 182.
13 Empereur & Picon 1992, fig. 3; Tomber 2007.

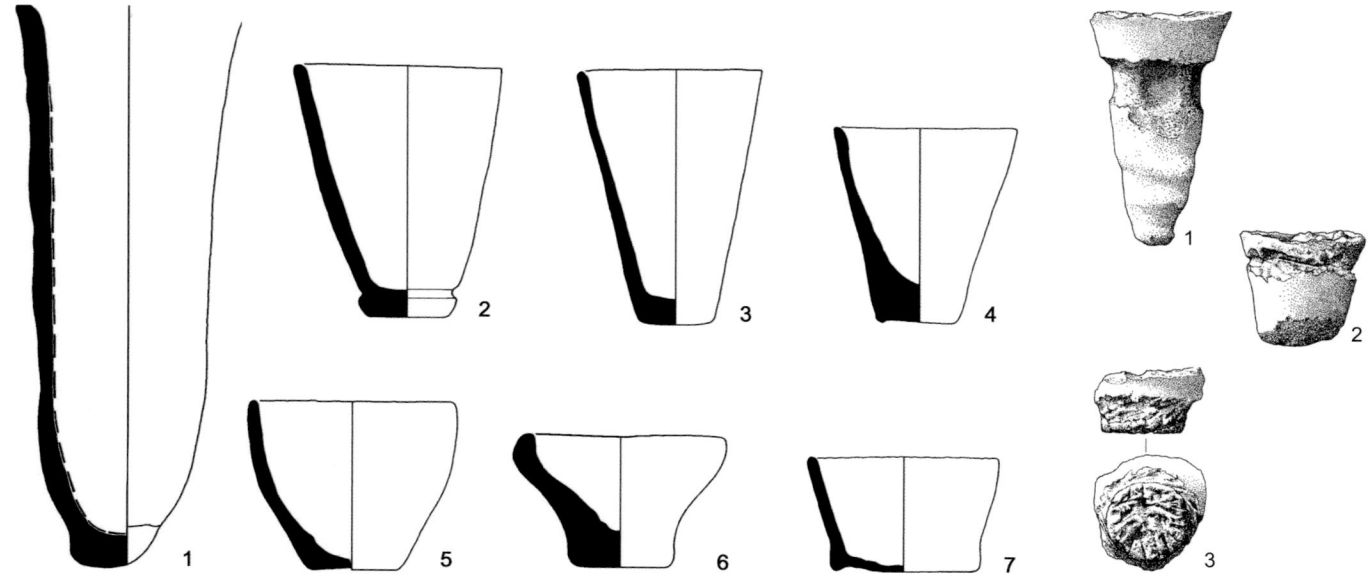

Fig. 4 A range of beakers and bowls reworked from amphorae (nos. 1-6); no. 7 is a sized down table ware vessel (Scale 1:4).

Fig. 5 Cutting down and shaping of amphora spikes (Scale 1:4).

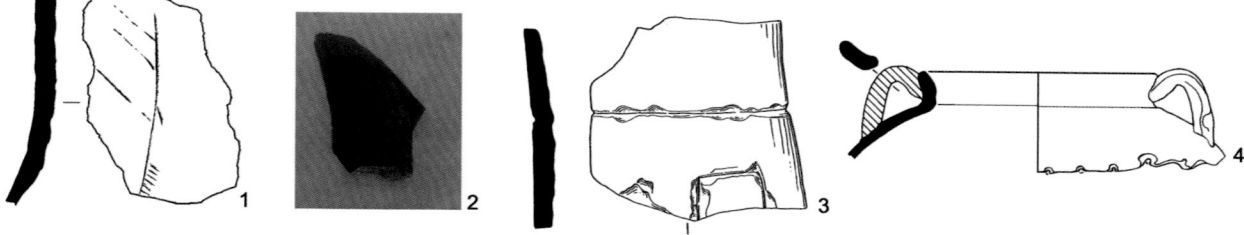

Fig. 6 Marking out sherds prior to cutting (nos. 1-2); cutting marks on sherd (no. 3); perforated holes to create a serrated edge for breaking the vessel (no. 4) (Scale 1:4).

Removal of the spike and resizing of the walls seems normally to have been undertaken with a chisel and stages in the removal of the spike are shown on Figure 5; in other cases an edge was perforated with small dots in order to facilitate breaking, as in "tear on the dotted line" (Fig. 6, no. 4). Rare sherds with charcoal lines suggest that the vessel was marked before cutting (Fig. 6, nos. 1-2). In addition to drinking vessels, funnels were another functional type that was repeatedly formed (Fig. 7). Archaeologists and papyrologists living on sites throughout the Eastern Desert continue this tradition today by sizing down mineral water bottles for numerous uses – from funnels to pencil holders and vases.

Once a new vessel was created it was finished off in a number of different ways. Some of the vessels are rough and may have been unfinished; others, but not all, were smoothed over and covered with a black substance presumed to be either pitch or bitumen (see Fig. 3). There seem to have been two likely sources for this black lining on site: either reheating of accumulated deposits in the toes of amphorae from their original lining (which can be very thick and glassy) or the importation of bitumen with its nearest natural source at Gebel Zeit near Suez.[14] Three mid-3rd century pottery leases from Oxyrhynchus describe lining jars with pitch, but here as in other documents it is not specified whether the pitch derives from wood or mineral.[15] A programme of scientific analysis would be fruitful if samples could be made available.

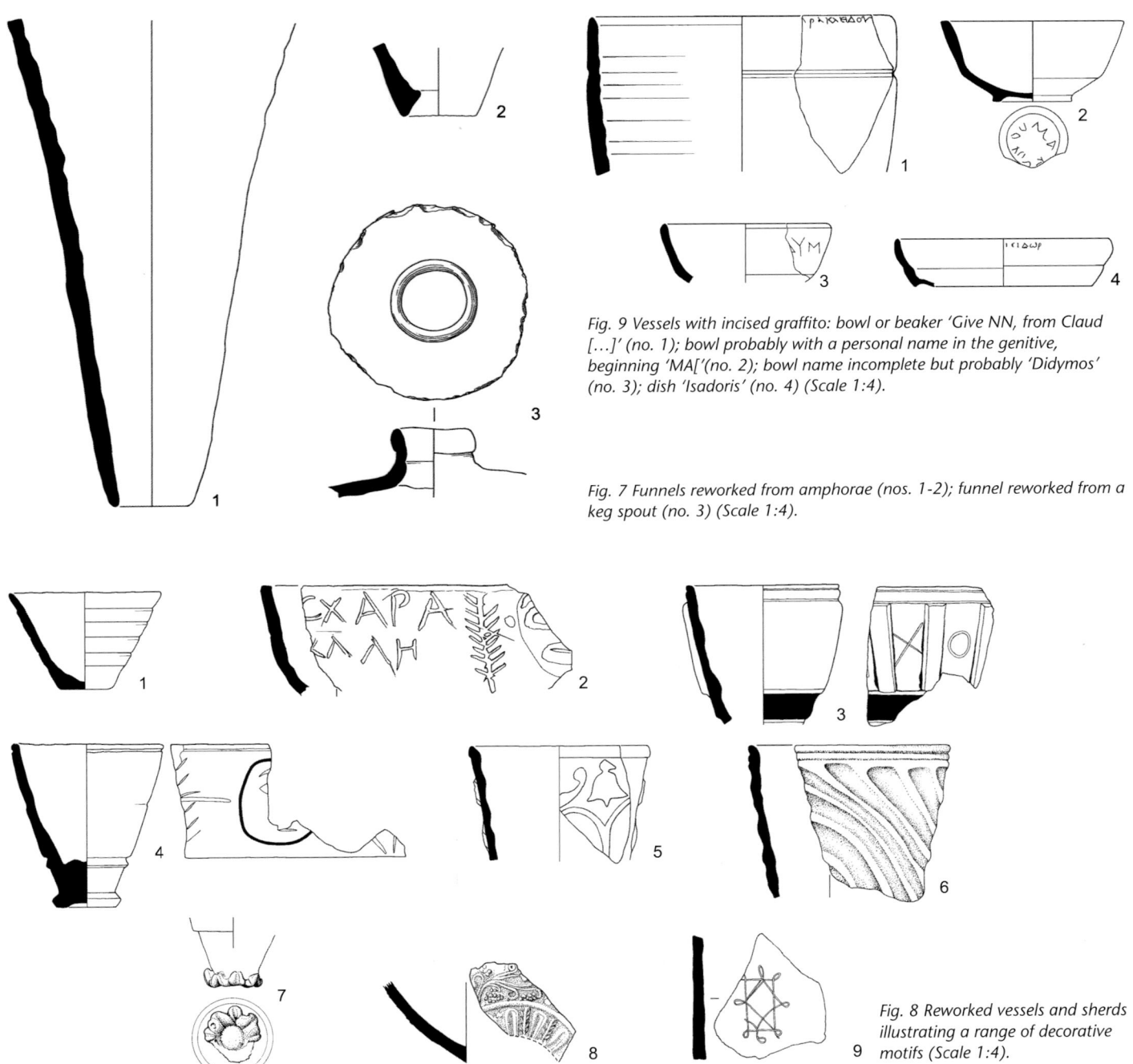

Fig. 9 Vessels with incised graffito: bowl or beaker 'Give NN, from Claud […]' (no. 1); bowl probably with a personal name in the genitive, beginning 'MA['(no. 2); bowl name incomplete but probably 'Didymos' (no. 3); dish 'Isadoris' (no. 4) (Scale 1:4).

Fig. 7 Funnels reworked from amphorae (nos. 1-2); funnel reworked from a keg spout (no. 3) (Scale 1:4).

Fig. 8 Reworked vessels and sherds illustrating a range of decorative motifs (Scale 1:4).

As shown on Figure 8, a wide range of decorative techniques were applied to these vessels, including incising and excising to form relief decoration, sometimes emphasised with red, white or black colouration (nos.

14 Harrell & Lewan 2002.
15 Cockle 1981, 94.

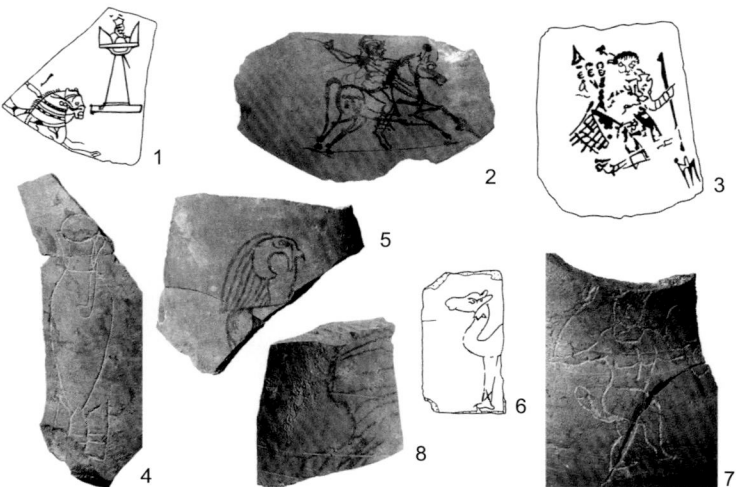

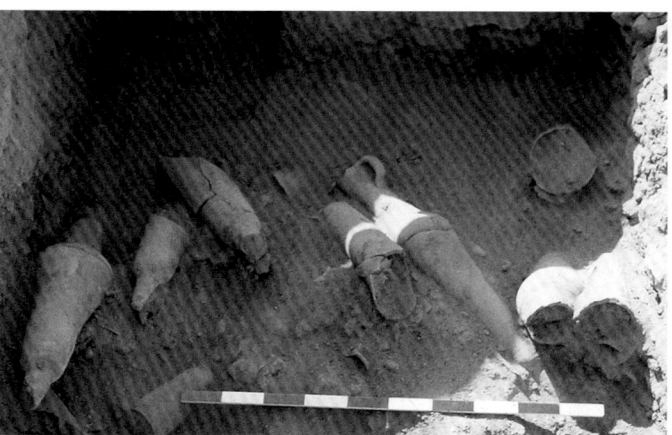

Fig. 10 Pictorial graffiti: inscribed circus horse and altar (no. 1); inscribed cavalry horse and rider (no. 2); inscribed retiarius (no. 3); incised amphora and ladle on a pot stand (no. 4); inscribed Horus (no. 5); inscribed camel (no. 6); incised macrophallic figure (no. 7); inscribed phallus (no. 8) (Scale 1:4).

Fig. 11 Discarded amphorae at Mons Claudianus inside the fort (area Fort West I).

3-4). Perhaps the most elaborate is no. 8, one of two vessels imitating a mould-made bowl. Certain motifs recur, including one that may be a palm frond (nos. 2, 4), while written inscriptions (not always literate, e.g. no. 2) are another recurring motif. The latter, sometimes with a human face (no. 4), reinforce decoration as a means by which to personalise drinking vessels in what would otherwise have been a regimented environment. This need to personalise or identify vessels can also be seen from the ordinary, non-reworked assemblage, where drinking vessels particularly are inscribed with a name (Fig. 9).

Similarly the desire for artistry is evidenced by the many sherds used as sketching pads, with Roman themes well represented – here a *retiarius*, cavalry and circus horses and an amphora are illustrated (Fig. 10, nos. 1-4). Egyptian and desert themes are epitomised by Horus and a camel (Fig. 10, nos. 5-6), with phallic symbols representing a more universal motif (Fig. 10, nos. 7-8).

The need to personalise and create a free time activity in an environment with few external diversions may have been the prime motivators behind this industry. Nevertheless, the quantity of reworked vessels in comparison to other pottery types provides insight into their function and use. Although present throughout the sequence, they are somewhat more common during the Hadrianic, Antonine and Severan periods representing

2.6%, 1.4% and 0.8% respectively of the total assemblage, in contrast to a maximum of 0.4% for the earlier phases.[16] A plausible explanation for this is that while the supply of amphorae was by necessity renewed throughout the life of the site (and later costrels, flat-sided flagons or pilgrim flasks, which were also used to bring foodstuffs), other wares were refurbished in smaller quantities. This might account both for the restricted number of vessel types that are markers from the Hadrianic period onwards[17] (although other factors could contribute to this), and for the corresponding increase in reworked wares. If fewer new coarse wares were sent to the site, inhabitants may have been motivated to improvise vessels for cooking and the table. We might envisage a site that was initially well provisioned, but where ceramic vessels other than amphorae gradually became increasingly scarce.

The quarry workers at Claudianus had the skills and dexterity with tools to produce vessels of a high standard.[18] Amphorae were discarded in abundance around the entire site, many complete or semi-complete (Fig. 11); scavenging (and therefore disturbing) dump deposits such as the Southern *Sebakh* would have provided another source.

Not only were vessels made from amphorae, but a range of other functional objects were fashioned from amphora spikes and body sherds. Identifiable objects formed from spikes include a range of stoppers in different sizes, both well finished and rough (Fig. 12, nos. 1-5) and incense burners (Fig. 12, no. 6). Objects of more obscure function include spikes that were hollowed out and squared-off (Fig.

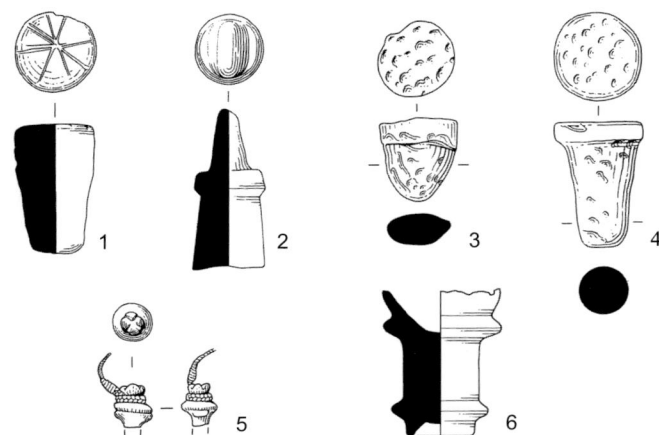

Fig. 12 Stoppers reworked from amphora spikes (nos 1-5); incense burner reworked from an amphora spike (no. 6) (Scale 1:4).

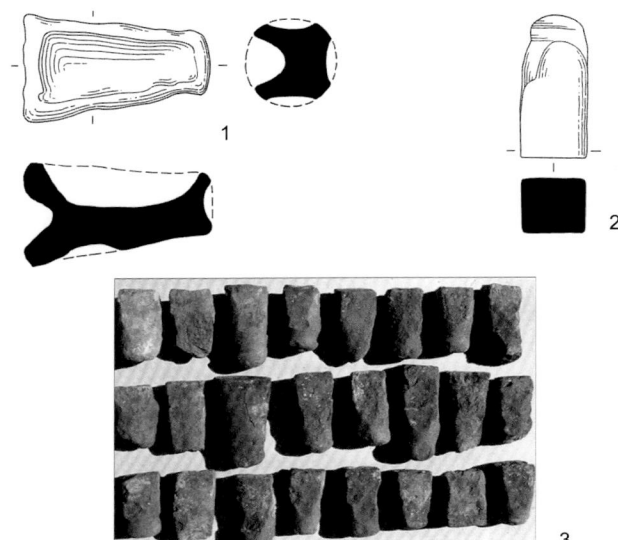

Fig. 13 Reworked amphora spikes of unknown function: hollowed (no. 1) and squared-off (nos 2-3) (nos. 1-2. scale 1:4; no. 3 not to scale).

13). Twenty-nine of the latter occurred, of which 22 were found together in a single deposit within the fort. These 22 weighed between 84-160 grammes, with 13 between 100-125 grammes. They may have been used as weights or, as suggested by Donald Bailey, gaming pieces.[19]

Body sherds were suitable for the ubiquitous round discs that could be used both as stoppers and gaming pieces, and of course for the *c.* 9,000 ostraca. Some relatively large rounded sherds were pierced around the edge; their function was unknown until one from Porphyrites was recovered with a piece of string still laced through the holes, clearly indicating its use as a stopper (Fig. 14, no. 1).[20] In other instances sherds and complete vessels were used as stoppers in conjunction with a plaster seal (Fig. 14, nos. 2-4).[21] These are ubiquitous throughout Egypt, probably originated elsewhere and were not part of the Claudianus industry described here.

Sherds were also pierced for labels (Fig. 15, nos. 2-3); again, one with an intact string from Quseir (not illustrated here) confirmed its function. Further uses for reworked sherds were as lamp covers (Fig. 15, no. 1), and a rather remarkable incense burner made from cementing an amphora body sherd with mud into the neck of an AE3 amphora (Fig. 15, no. 4).

Mons Porphyrites, another quarry site in the Eastern Desert, was situated to exploit the Imperial Porphyry between the 1st and early 5th centuries. Here, too, reworking of amphorae is noted with a similar range of objects[22] and vessels, although vessels were produced on a

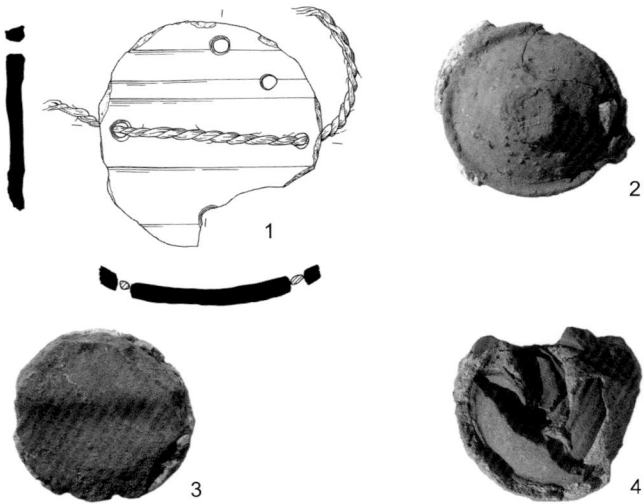

Fig. 14 Amphora stoppers: rounded sherd with string threaded through perforated holes (no. 1); rounded sherd covered with plaster (no. 2); complete bowl covered with plaster (no. 3); sherds covered with plaster (no. 4) (Scale 1:4).

16 Tomber 2006b, 197, table 1.4.
17 Tomber 2006a, 215.
18 I thank Adam Bülow-Jacobsen for this suggestion, *ibid*. 182.
19 Tomber 2006a, 297.
20 Bailey 2007, 308.
21 Thomas & Tomber 2006, 241-242.
22 Bailey 2007.

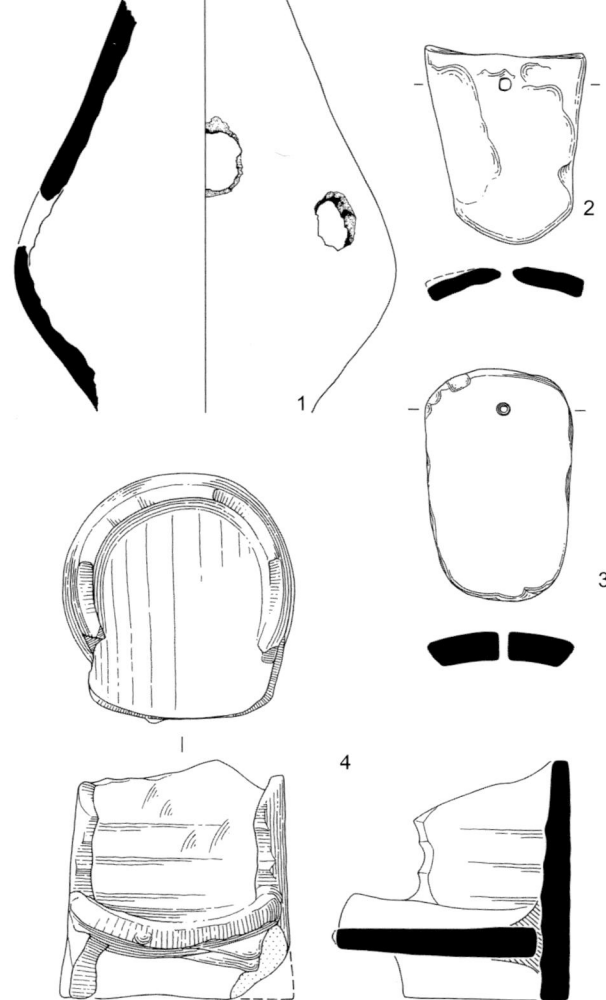

Fig. 15 Amphora sherds reworked for lamp cover (no. 1); labels (nos. 2-3); incense burner (no. 4) (Scale 1:4).

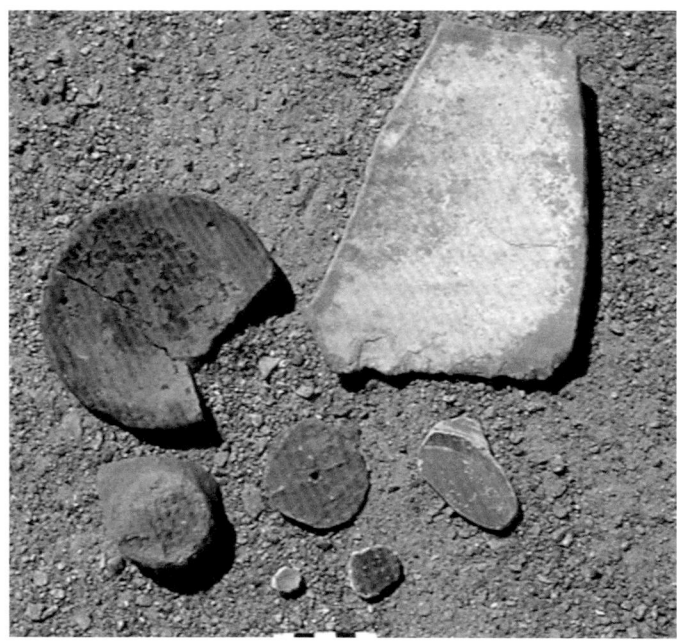

Fig. 16 Reworked sherds, including gaming pieces found on a mountain pass between Mons Porphyrites and Badia.

much smaller scale than at Claudianus and their decoration less lavish. This may be because, as suggested by the excavated deposits, the site was replenished more regularly than at Claudianus.[23] One especially poignant assemblage of gaming pieces came from an isolated building on the mountain pass between Badia[24] and the fort at Mons Porphyrites and emphasises again the bleakness of the environment, enlivened by game playing (Figure 16). The structural reuse of amphora spikes and mortar to build an oven was also recorded at Porphyrites.[25]

At present this reworking industry in the Eastern Desert is unique in its systematic reuse of pottery, undoubtedly

facilitated by the surplus of amphorae, the deficit of other wares, the skill of the quarry workers and an environment with few external diversions. All of these features provided a suitable milieu that encouraged reworking, but the actual spread of the technique can be attributed to the movement of personnel between the two sites. In 1993 David Peacock noted the presence of porphyry – numerous small working flakes and a few larger blocks at Mons Claudianus, from which he suggested that personnel were shared between the two sites with Mons Porphyrites functioning as the centre for quarries in the area.[26] His conclusions have since been strengthened by *ostraca* from Mons Porphyrites that mention two of the same *architektones* (men responsible for planning and organising the engineering and transport of the quarries) also known from the Claudianus *ostraca*.[27] Whether the individuals responsible for the reworking technology originated at Poprhyrites or Claudianus is more difficult to determine, but certainly the technique was more widespread and had more impact at Claudianus.

PORT SITES: MYOS HORMOS AND BERENIKE

The association between reworked amphorae, quarry skills and their concentration at Mons Claudianus and

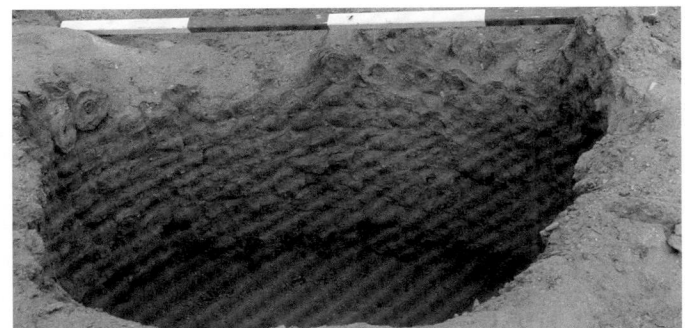

Fig. 17 Oven lined with amphora spikes at Myos Hormos.

Porphyrites is further strengthened by the lack of systematic reworking at the port sites of Myos Hormos and Berenike, where "round cut" sherds for gaming pieces[28] and stoppers are the only recurring examples. Other types of reuse are evident, though, such as the reuse of foreign amphorae for Egyptian products at Berenike where an Italian amphora is stoppered with an Egyptian plug,[29] and an *ostracon* refers to local wine in a foreign amphora.[30]

Like at Porphyrites, amphora spikes and mortar were used for the construction of two ovens (Fig. 17).[31] The most conspicuous reuse of amphorae, however, comes from the excavation of the silted harbour at Myos Hormos, where an extensive deposit comprising hundreds of intact or near intact vessels in upright to supine positions was revealed (Fig. 18).[32] These vessels were used to consolidate the muddy area between sea and land and for the construction of a jetty. Mostly amphorae, but also including Roman and non-Roman coarse wares, the vessels were packed with soil and overlaid by a floor, all of which contained sherds of the same date (including plentiful amounts of Eastern *Sigillata* A), from the late 1st century BC into the early 1st century AD.

Parallels for the use of amphorae for consolidating ground, in diverse contexts including other harbours and harbour structures, have been noted throughout the Empire. Examples particularly from northern Italy (the Po Valley and the Venice region), and southern France were published by Pasavento Mattioli[33] in the proceedings of a conference devoted entirely to this subject. Recently Bernal *et al.* have mapped the distribution of fluvio-marine drainage installations and their map spans from Cadiz and Zaragoza in the West to Terracina in central Italy.[34] Quseir extends this phenomenon to the other end of the Empire. Regional variations exist in the detailed application of these features, with timber for example being used in tandem with amphorae in the West, where it was more readily available than in the Eastern Desert. Amphorae, however, were a resource uniformly available throughout the Empire and therefore ideal for shared technology.

Many of the published examples date to the same period as Quseir or at least are restricted to the early Roman period; late Roman examples are less common. This appears to be a successful technology that was widely utilised during the early Roman period with complete or semi-complete amphorae providing excellent load-bearing properties.[35] It serves to underline one of the more general observations made by Peña, of the scale and problems of rubbish discard in Antiquity,[36] for in addition to being a viable means for consolidation and drainage, it provided a constructive way to use discarded amphorae.

Certainly rubbish continues to be a problem today in Egypt and, as at Mons Claudianus,[37] is deposited on the rooftops of buildings. Cairo has a tradition dating back to around 1900 of sorting and recyling rubbish for resale. The system was initiated by an oasis people (the *wahiya*), who collected and sold household waste for fuel; since the arrival of the *zabbaleen* ("garbage collectors") from Upper Egypt around 1950 the system has been more formalised and the *wahiya* are middlemen for the *zabbaleen*, arranging the rights to particular buildings and

23 Tomber 2001, 297.
24 Badia is *c.* 6 km. south-east of the main fort as the crow flies.
25 Peacock 2007, 13.
26 Peacock 1996.
27 I am grateful to Valerie Maxfield for drawing my attention to the evidence for movement of personnel. Bingen 1992; Van Rengen 2007, 409.
28 Elsewhere in the Eastern Desert an enigmatic group of sherds published by Gillian Pyke reworked into 't', 'v' and 'y' shapes may have served a similar function (Sidebotham *et al.* 2002, 221, pl. 28, 3).
29 Wendrich *et al.* 2003, 78.
30 Bagnall *et al.* 2000, 18.
31 Thomas & Masser 2006, 132.
32 Peacock & Blue 2006.
33 Pesavento Mattioli (ed.) 1998; see also Peña 2007, 182-192 for a detailed summary of Pesavento Mattioli.
34 Bernal *et al.* 2005, fig. 7.
35 Blue & Rey da Silva in press.
36 See also Ballet *et al.* 2003 for a range of papers supporting this same premise.
37 Maxfield & Peacock 2001a, 446.

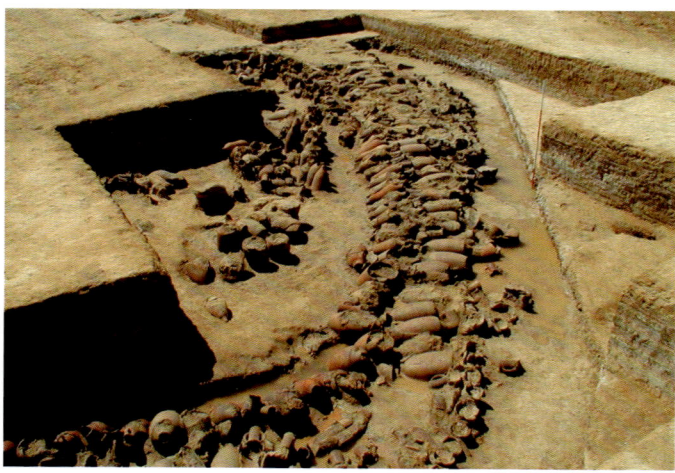

Fig. 18 Mons Claudianus jetty constructed from amphorae.

routes for the *zabbaleen*. The *zabbaleen*, mostly Copts who live in Muqattam, an eastern suburb of Cairo, take on the task of sorting rubbish into different materials before being sold on.[38] More recently the government has attempted to modernise these arrangements by offering contracts to foreign refuse collectors who in theory would work with the *zabbaleen*. Whether such arrangements can be as successful as the more traditional methods has yet to be determined.[39]

While it is not suggested that such a formalised arrangement existed for refuse disposal in the Ancient world, this modern example nevertheless demonstrates an attitude towards discarded objects that may well have been prevalent in the past, when discarded material was regarded as having some use. A similar attitude is gaining prevalence today, as seen by the range of recycled items that are not only available but considered desirable.

The reuse of pottery in the Eastern Desert was a response to both scarcity and abundance. What is the effect on the removal of pottery from the primary record through recycling? Claudianus and Prophyrites can be viewed as fairly closed systems, since the supplies they received were intended for consumption on site and would have been expended in full there. The port sites are an entirely different matter, where goods flowed in and out, but we have no way of estimating the proportion of items intended as terminal or transit. It seems unlikely that the large number of amphorae and other vessels used for the amphora deposit were intended for transit, since the *ostraca* indicate that items for export were fairly strictly regulated,

and instead should be seen as a positive way of disposing of discarded amphorae. This is further supported if we examine the composition of the Quseir amphora deposit, with Amphore Egyptienne 3 and Campanian Dressel 2-4 the most common types, in reference to amphorae distribution throughout the Indian Ocean. Egyptian products carried in AE3 seem not to have been a significant item for Roman trade with the East and are distributed only in small numbers, while in contrast Campanian amphorae are one of the most common amphora types exported throughout the Indian Ocean. Without quantification of the amphora deposit, it would seem that selection for it was unrelated to demands further down the line.

What then of the effect of recycling pottery on the quantified data that we as pottery specialists collect today? At Claudianus reuse removed some amphora bases from the quantified data, but they re-entered the record as different types of vessels. Again, at Myos Hormos recycling did not remove these amphorae from the site. In both cases, though, reuse significantly affected the quantities and profiles of individual loci or context, making an overall assessment of the pottery from the site as a whole important when evaluating specific loci. The real interest of reuse or recycling pertains to achieving a fuller and more vivid biography of the artefact in question and therefore a better insight into past behaviour and culture.[40]

38 Assaad & Garas 1994, 1-4; Volpi 1997, 14-16.
39 Rashed 2002.
40 Gosden & Marshall 1999.

ACKNOWLEDGEMENTS

I would firstly like to thank the organisers for inviting me to participate in this very stimulating seminar and for their hospitality in Athens. The written paper has benefited enormously from discussions with Valerie Maxfield regarding the relationship between Mons Claudianus and Mons Porphyrites, while both Dario Bernal and Lucy Blue provided useful information and bibliography on the structural reuse of amphorae. The individual illustrations were the work of many, acknowledged in the original publications; here I record my thanks to Tony Simpson who skilfully reorganised them into the figures seen here. Unless otherwise stated all dates are AD.

Mended in Antiquity:
Repairs to Ceramics at the Athenian Agora

BY SUSAN I. ROTROFF

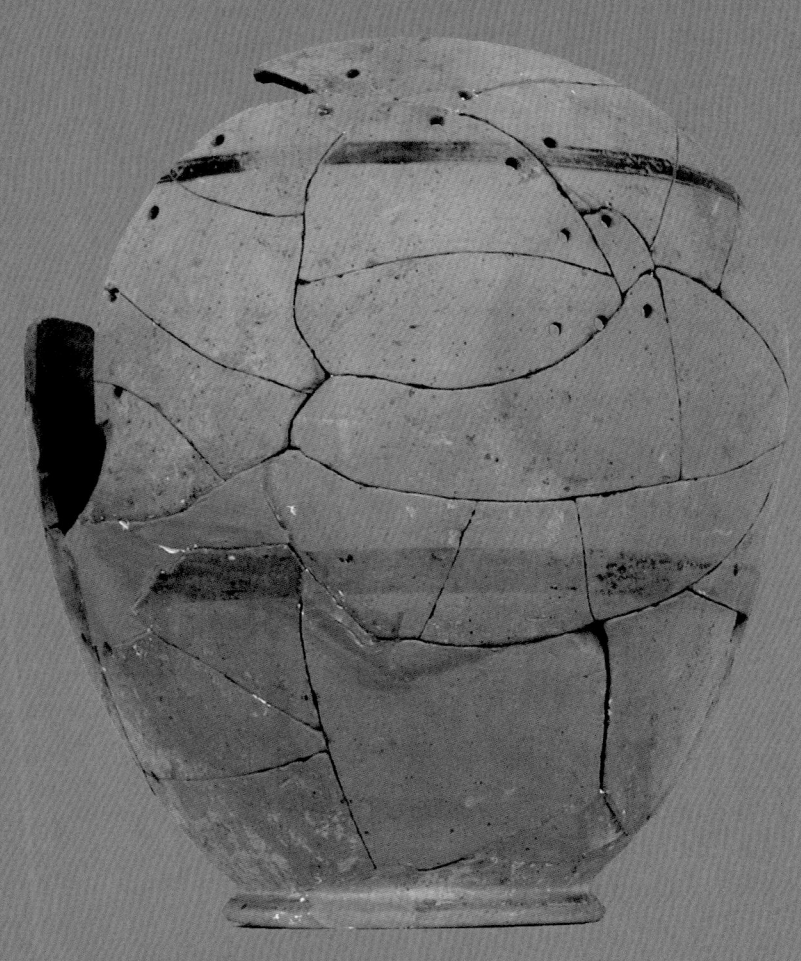

Mended in Antiquity:
Repairs to Ceramics at the Athenian Agora

BY SUSAN I. ROTROFF

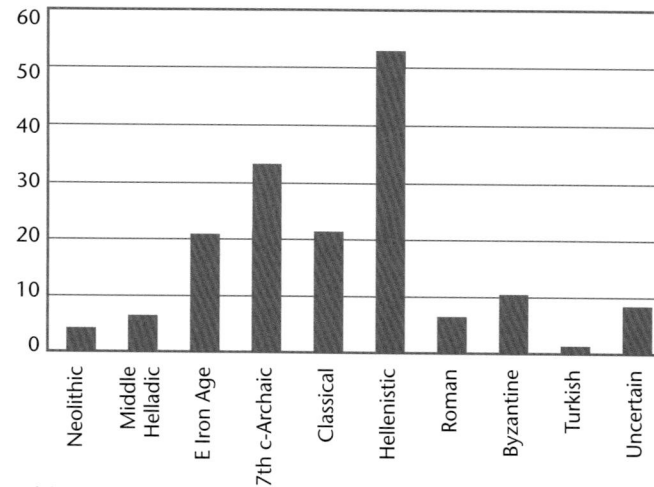

n = 160
Uncertain: eight objects that are too fragmentary for dating or where the probable date spans more than one period (e.g., P 19223, the handle of a krater of Archaic or Classical date, or P 4393, an unidentified transport amphora of Classical or early Hellenistic date).

Fig. 1 Dates of mended vessels.

Among the phenomena that detour a pot along its route from the kiln to the midden is its reclamation through repair. Anyone who has worked with ceramics has encountered ancient mends. They have warranted brief mention in handbooks of Greek and Roman pottery[1] and somewhat longer treatment in the case of particular (usually figured) vases,[2] but it is not until recently that serious inquiry has been made into the methods of and motives for ancient repairs. Much of the impetus has come from conservators, whose observations are enriched by a professional knowledge of materials and personal experience with repair. A pioneering study by Maya Elston, in 1990, based on her work at the Getty Museum,[3] is now joined by several important essays by both archaeologists and conservators, a number of them arising from a 2006 conference on ancient and modern restorations,[4] and Gianpaolo Nadalini has contributed one of the few studies to discuss the variation in repair choices and practices in different corpora, including both museum collections and excavation inventories.[5] Ted Peña's lengthy discussion of ancient repairs to Roman pottery in the context of the formation of the archaeological record examines yet another facet of this neglected subject.[6] In the New World, Louise Senior's 1995 study of mended pots in ethnographic and archaeological collections investigates the relationship between repair and value.[7]

One of the factors that hamper study of ancient repair is a lack of data. The anecdotal publication of random mends leaves us without a sense of the scale of the practice and of its variability over time, over different classes of pottery, and in method. The present study, focusing on ancient mends from the Agora excavations in Athens, will provide an overview of the practice as it is documented at a single site over many centuries. This lays the foundation for comparative studies with other collections, which, it is to be expected, may tell quite different stories. I will also discuss the thorny question of the motive behind the repairs, an issue that is intertwined with the identity of the mender (or commissioner of the mends) and the place where the mends were undertaken. Here one can only speculate, but with the Agora data as a base, I explore some suggestions made by others who have pondered these matters.

DESCRIPTION OF THE AGORA MENDS

The Agora Excavations were inaugurated in 1931 in order to locate and investigate the civic center of the ancient city of Athens. In the course of those excavations, uncounted millions of potsherds have been unearthed and over 35,000 pieces of pottery have been entered into the excavation inventory. They stretch from the Neolithic to the modern period and come from contexts ranging from funerary to ritual and domestic. Among them are 160 certain or highly probable instances of ancient repair, about one-half of one percent of the inventoried pottery.[8] There are also about 20 clamps no longer attached to pottery, which make it possible to investigate the technical aspects of mending more thoroughly. Few comparative statistics are available, but those that are suggest that this low incidence of repair is fairly standard. Nadalini reports only about ten mends out of hundreds of lots of (mostly local) vessels excavated at Gela in 2002-2003,[9] and repairs to sigillata imports excavated at the settlement and fort at Piercebridge, in Britain, amounted to something over one percent.[10] Among vessels assigned to specific workshops or hands, a little less than half a percent of the known output of the workshop of the C Painter and around one percent of the vases associated with the Phiale Painter and the Achilles Painter show evidence of repair.[11] Museum collections present the special challenge of distinguishing between ancient and undocumented modern mends. It seems, however, that about one-half to one percent of the red-figure cups in the Leipzig Antikensammlung display ancient repairs and about one percent of the sigillata in the Museum of London.[12] These figures provide an interesting foil to another statistic reported by Nadalini, that 20% of the ca. 40 kraters by Euphronios in the Louvre have been repaired, probably in antiquity, a figure that suggests special circumstances. With this exception, however, it appears that mending was a recurrent but rare phenomenon.

CHRONOLOGY

All but a few of the mended vessels in the collection can be dated at least to a period and often much more closely, and it is rare for a mended pot to be found in a context much later than its date of manufacture. We are speaking here, of course, in terms of archaeological time, reckoned in quarter-centuries at the least. Nonetheless, it seems that mends were not frequently made to vessels generations old and that mended vessels did not continue in use for many generations.

Indisputable instances of mending in the collection range from the Middle Helladic period to the Turkokratia; four late Neolithic vessels with drilled holes are too fragmentary for certainty, but they too were probably mended in antiquity.[13] These instances, however, are not evenly spread over that span (Fig. 1). Early Bronze Age repairs are known elsewhere,[14] and their absence at the Agora is probably the result of the very low representation of that period in the excavation's ceramic corpus. The Middle Helladic figures are remarkable, given the small size of the collection (perhaps about 80 inventoried pots), giving a very high incidence of repair (over seven percent). This makes the absence of a single Mycenaean repair among 450 or more inventoried vessels all the more surprising. Rising affluence or possibly the contexts of the Late Bronze Age material, almost all of which comes from burials, may play a role here.

From the Protogeometric period onwards, however,

mends are regularly documented. The high number of Hellenistic instances (52) can in part be explained by the fact that I have personally examined all of the Hellenistic pottery. It is difficult, however, to account for the low numbers of Roman mends (a mere six), given the large size of the Roman collection. Possibly pottery was cheaper or replacements more readily available than they had been in previous periods. Large-scale production and massive trade in high-quality table ware in the Roman period might have had such a consequence. The low numbers of Byzantine and later mends may reflect the relatively small number of objects inventoried for these periods, this in turn a reflection of the chronological prejudices of Agora scholars. In what follows, I will concentrate on the vessels of Archaic through Hellenistic date, where the sample is largest (109 items), though I will make occasional reference to the earlier and later material.

---

1 Richter 1923, 59, 63; Richter 1946, 35; Charleston 1955, 16; Frel 1973, 6; Noble 1988, 175; Hemelrijk 1991, 254-5; Spivey 1991, 138; Cook 1997, 240; Boardman 2001, 161-2. See also Rice 1987, 303.

2 E.g., Nogara 1951; Bizzarri 1962, 59; Moore & Bothmer 1972, 9-11; Vos 1981, 33-4; Snow 1986; Connor 1996, 367-8.

3 Elston 1990.

4 Pfisterer-Haas 2002; Dooijes & Nieuwenhuyse 2007; Schöne-Denkinger 2007; and Nadalini 2007.

5 Nadalini 2003.

6 Peña 2007, 213-249; see also Marsh 1981, 227-228 for a concise discussion of mends to sigillata found in London.

7 Senior 1995.

8 Ancient repairs have usually been at least noted, if not described, in the inventory records. The mends discussed here were collected by means of a search of the electronic inventory for relevant terms (clamp, rivet, hole, drilled, etc.). A few additional examples where mends had not been described in the record were found by chance; others no doubt remain undetected, but probably not many.

9 Nadalini 2003, 201.

10 Ward (1993, 15, 19) reports 74 vessels with traces of mends among a maximum of 5543 vessels at Piercebridge.

11 Brijder (1983, 40) reports 13 mends in an inventory of about 275 vessels from the C Painter's workshop. I am grateful to John Oakley for the figures for the Phiale Painter (two mends among ca. 200 vases) and Achilles Painter (four mends among over 400 vases attributed to or associated with the painter).

12 Pfisterer-Haas 2002, 51; Marsh 1981, 227.

13 P 14590, P 26979, P 14738, P 26993 (Immerwahr 1971, 29, 33, 34, 39 nos. 56, 88, 100, 138 pls. 5, 7, 9, 68). Cf. better preserved instances found at Franchthi: Vitelli 1993, *passim* (figs. 21:p, 35:a, 47:k, and 59:c offer particularly good examples).

14 E.g., Mylonas 1959, 40 no. 50 fig. 132.

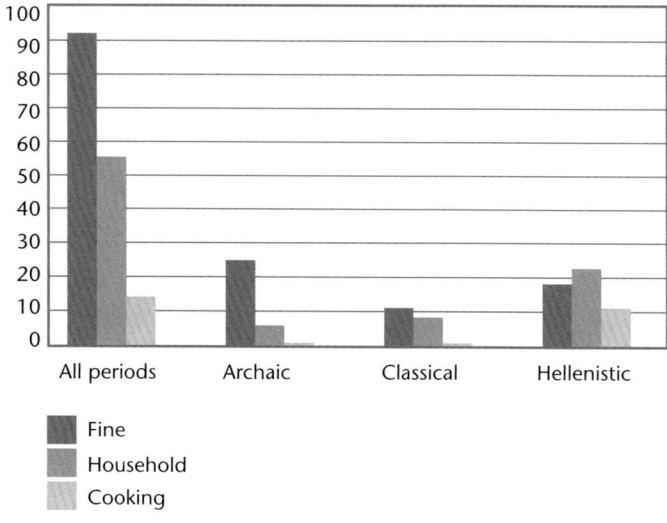

Fig. 2 Categories of pottery mended.

Fine
Household
Cooking

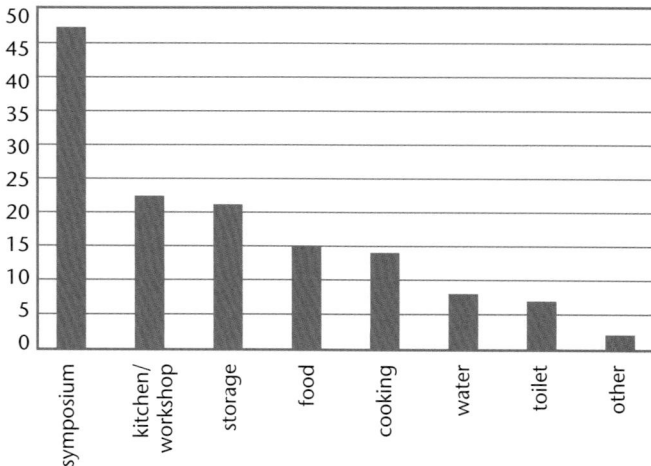

n = 136 vessels where function could be inferred with some certainty. Other: a Panathanaic amphora and a public measure.

Fig. 3 Functions of mended vessels, Middle Helladic to Roman.

TYPES OF POTTERY MENDED

Fine table ware is an obvious candidate for repair. Although the little evidence we have about the price of decorated pottery suggests it may not have been significantly more costly than some plain ware, its aesthetic qualities, its uniqueness, and its association with the symposium and the boudoir might reasonably enhance its value for its owner. Taken as a whole, the Agora collection seems to match these expectations, for there are more repairs to fine vessels (91) than to utilitarian ones (69, including 55 of household and 14 of cooking fabric) (Fig. 2).[15] Examination of the data from the best-documented periods, however, suggests an evolution in this behavior. The figure for mended fine pottery of the Archaic period (25 vessels, mostly figured, but some black-gloss ware) is over four times as high as that for household ware (6 vessels), and cooking ware is almost absent (1 vessel). By contrast, the numbers for fine and household mends of the Classical period are almost equal, and in the Hellenistic period utilitarian pottery was mended significantly more frequently than fine pottery (34 as opposed to 18 vessels). Also in contrast to earlier times, Hellenistic cooking vessels were mended in some numbers: I have identified 11 instances. Assuming that these figures reflect a real trend rather than some bias in the sample, the lower technical and aesthetic quality of fine ceramics produced in the Hellenistic period might be a factor here. Still, it surprises me that

there is no instance of a repair to a moldmade relief bowl, a shape that was generally both finely crafted and attractively decorated. Perhaps the answer lies in the mold technology, which would have made the production of virtually identical vessels possible over a relatively long period of time; replacements would have been easily found. The fact that there is evidence for repair to a mold for a relief bowl[16] suggests that the means of production was more valued than the product.

The Agora material appears to support the frequent claim that pottery is more often mended far from its place of origin than in the locale where it was manufactured.[17] Twenty-seven of the Agora repairs are to imported vessels, concentrated in the Hellenistic and Roman periods, when imports were far more numerous than they had been earlier. The raw statistic is not very revealing, but the numbers begin to bear meaning when seen in the light of the composition of the pottery assemblage as a whole. In the Hellenistic period, where comparative figures for imports are available, it appears that about 12% of the inventoried wheelmade fine ware was imported.[18] By contrast, 39% of the Hellenistic fine-ware repairs are to imports (7 out of 18); if our small sample is representative, imports were more than three times as likely to be repaired as local vessels. Repairs to imports are also frequent among Hellenistic cooking pots: 45% (5 of the 11 examples) in comparison to 35% of imports in the total inventory of Hellenistic cooking ware.[19]

In terms of function, nearly a third of the mended vessels are shapes associated with the symposium: 20 drinking cups, 11 oinochoai and olpai, seven or eight table amphorae, six kraters, a stamnos, and a psykter, ranging in date from Middle Helladic to Roman (Fig. 3). Mended cups and kraters are also frequently encountered in museum collections.[20] This, however, may do no more than reflect the inordinately large proportion of Greek table ware devoted to the drinking of wine, documenting the large role that the symposium played in Greek life; proportionally, the frequency of mending may be no greater than for vessels of other functions. Also occurring regularly are, in declining order of frequency, repairs to: household-ware vessels used in the kitchen or workshop or on the farm (chiefly lekanai, basins, mortars, and beehives); storage vessels (pithoi, smaller storage bins, and household-ware table and transport amphorae); bowls, plates and platters for food service; and cooking pots. Water jugs and fine toilet vessels are represented in smaller numbers, in the former case probably because the production of a lasting and sturdy water-tight seal was a challenge and feasible only when breakage was minor (a hole that could be plugged or a fragment missing from the rim). In the Hellenistic period, where approximate figures for the ceramic collection as a whole are available, a surprisingly high proportion of the inventoried storage and utility vessels was mended (14% and 4% respectively). By contrast, the percentage of mends to symposium vessels is tiny (less than a tenth of a percent), a statistic that may reflect changes in the symposium suggested by other aspects of the Hellenistic assemblage.[21]

Repairs to cooking pots, although they are few, raise the issue of the practicality of a lead mend to the bottom of a vessel designed for use directly on the fire. Two mends are to the floors of chytrai, stewpots intended to hold liquid and to be in direct contact with the fire. The round bottoms of these vessels make them unlikely candidates for alternate use, as containers for dry goods, for example. Their repair offers an indirect piece of evidence for the efficacy of what look like challenging repairs.

METHODS OF MENDING

Ancient damage documented in the Agora collection ranges from holes requiring a simple patch, to cracks, detached handles, feet or rim fragments, and extensive breakage. In most instances, repairs were achieved by drilling pairs of holes spanning the break, then joining the fragments by lacing them together with a thong or string (the hole-and-lace technique), or with a lead clamp (the hole-and-clamp technique, in rare instances combined with a mortise-and-tenon system).[22] In slightly less than half of the Agora examples only the holes remain, and we are left to conjecture about the material that was used to bind the fragments together. When present, the clamps are of lead; there are no instances of bronze and no green staining around any of the holes. The Agora evidence therefore supports the observation made by others, that bronze mends are largely restricted to Etruria.[23]

Although string or a leather thong leaves no trace, there are a few instances where the hole-and-lace technique can be conjectured. A pair of unusual long narrow holes on a Protogeometric amphora (P 1043) suggest the use of a thong, and twine or a thong probably bound together the pieces of an Early Geometric amphora (P 6406), where a

---

15 Raw numbers are less useful than percentages that express the relationship between mends and the total number of vessels of a given type within the collection. Unfortunately, the Agora ceramics have not been quantified in a manner that makes this easily possible. It is certainly true, however, that more fine than household and cooking pottery has been inventoried, a fact that suggests caution in approaching these figures. For a statistical study of mends in a fully quantified corpus of pottery from the American Southwest, see Senior 1995.

16 P 16221 (Rotroff 2006b, 372 fig. 7).

17 Stähler 1983, 24; Arafat & Morgan 1989, 326-327, quoting personal comment of J. Boardman; Connor 1996, 368; Boardman 2001, 161; Cohen 2006, 62. For a more nuanced view, see Nadalini 2003.

18 Rotroff 1997, 5.

19 Rotroff 2006a, 61-63, Chart 7. The difficulty of distinguishing imports from local household-ware pottery makes the relative incidence of repair to such vessels impossible to evaluate.

20 Pfisterer-Hass 2002, 51; Elston 1990; John Oakley, pers. comm. Sept. 10, 2008.

21 Rotroff 1996; Rotroff 1997, 14-15.

22 I use Peña's terminology (Peña 2007, 232-234). Others have offered similar typologies. Dooijes & Nieuwenhuyse 2007, 16-17 figs. 3, 5: Type A (hole and clamp), Type B (hole and clamp combined with mortise and tenon). Nadalini 2007, 29-32 fig. 2: a lingotto (hole and clamp), alveolare (hole and clamp combined with mortise and tenon).

23 Williams 1996, 251-252; Pfisterer-Haas 2002, 55-56; Bentz & Kästner 2007, 7.

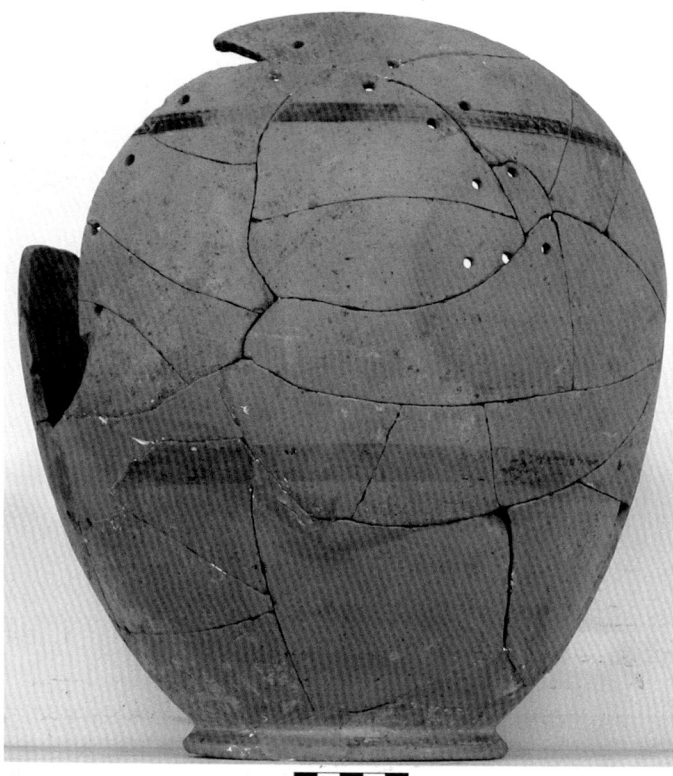

Fig. 4 Early Geometric table amphora (Agora inventory number P 6406)
(photographs by the author unless otherwise stated).

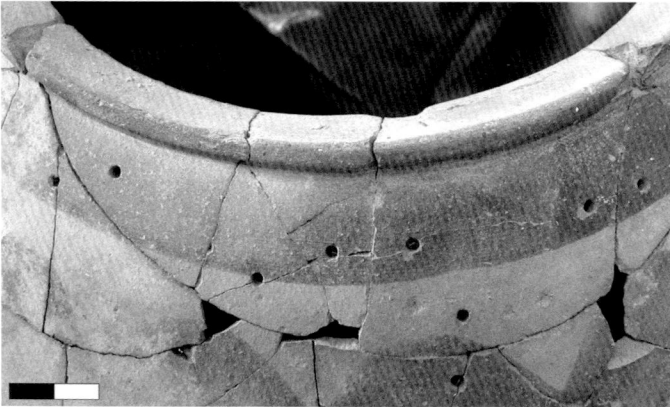

Fig. 5 Mended area of storage jar (P 16658).

series of closely-spaced holes along a break attest to the
need for extensive bracing (Fig. 4). The hole pairs end in
a row of three holes perpendicular to the break, perhaps
to accommodate some arrangement for tying off a thong
firmly at the end of the brace. String or thong mending
is not limited to early examples and can probably be
recognized on a late Hellenistic storage jar that served as
the final resting place of a dog (Fig. 5).[24] Two fragments
broken away from the rim, possibly to enlarge the mouth
to accommodate the deceased animal, had been mended by
drilling five pairs of holes. Clearly the vessel was complete
when buried, for the fragments would otherwise have been
dispersed. No lead clamps were found, however, either in
situ or in the nearby soil. I suspect that the dog's grieving
master used twine or thong to repair his coffin before
burial.[25] One advantage of the method is that it could be
performed in the household by anyone with a drill and a
length of lacing material.

Lead clamping, however, required special tools, skills,
and knowledge. Such expertise was available early on, for
lead clamps are found on four of the six Middle Helladic
vessels in the collection (two amphorae, a pithos, and
a plain-ware fragment).[26] An even earlier instance was
unearthed at Aghios Kosmas, on the Attic coast, where
an Early Helladic pithos was repaired with lead clamps.[27]
The Middle Helladic repairs use the same hole-and-clamp
technique as later repairs, but exhibit one peculiarity: while
later drill holes are straight-sided, all of the visible holes
on the Middle Helladic vessels are conical, two or three
times as large in diameter on the exterior as they are on the
interior (Fig. 6).[28] The same is true of Neolithic drill-holes
on mended pots at Franchthi,[29] and this similarity may
indicate the continued use of stone tools for the Middle
Helladic repairs. Later drilling can be remarkably fine; holes
no more than 2 or 3 mm in diameter are not unusual.

Of those instances where lead is preserved, the hole-
and-clamp method was by far the most common, with 60
examples ranging in date from the Middle Helladic to the
Hellenistic period.[30] The clamp itself consists of two straps
or bars spanning the break and joined at either end by a pin
running through the vessel wall. The strap is commonly a
flat rectangle, between 0.15 and 0.6 cm thick and between
0.4 and 1.7 cm. wide. Some of the thicker straps have a
slightly convex surface or beveled edges (Fig. 7, left), but
the thinner ones look like band-aids on the surface of
the pot (Fig. 7, right).[31] Other straps have a pronounced
half-round form, like half of a metal dowel (Figs. 8, 9),[32]
which is often bordered by a flat flange. Although the flat

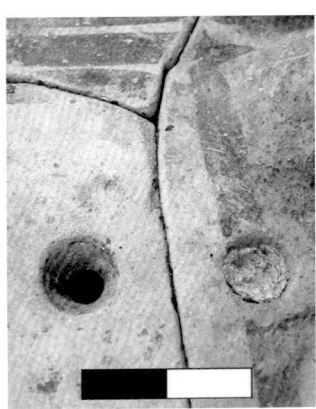

Fig. 6 Conical drill holes with lead of clamp preserved in one hole, Middle Helladic matt painted table amphora (P 10524).

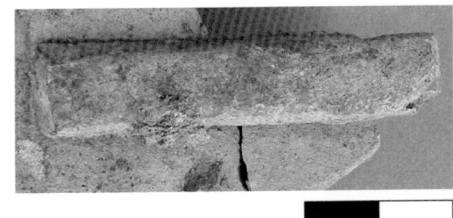

Fig. 7 Strap with beveled edges on a Classical household-ware basin (P 31130) and thin strap on a 5th-century household-ware table amphora imported from Corinth (P 21936).

strap is the more common, both flat and half-round forms are documented in all periods. As is the case with other material arts, the craftsmanship of clamps of the Archaic period and 5th century is superior; with few exceptions, straps are well-defined and often thin, and there is little excess lead.

The way (or ways) in which such clamps were created remains something of a mystery. The pins cannot have been inserted into the holes and bent and fused to create the join, for the ends of the straps project beyond the pins on both sides of the wall. The clamps themselves are seamless – there is no indication of separate parts having been hammered together; nor are there traces of significant

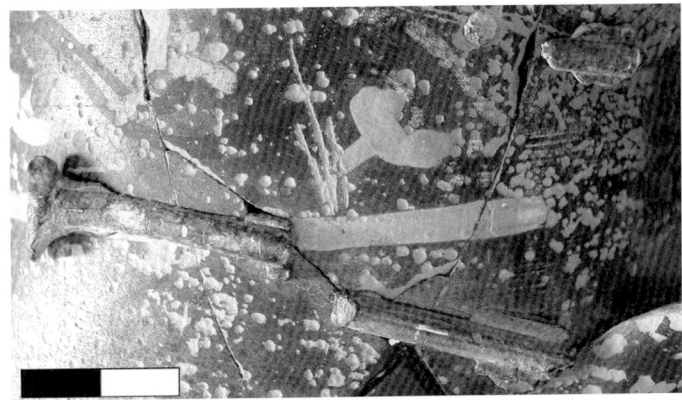

Fig. 8 Three half-round straps on a 3rd-century angular West Slope kantharos (P 6301).

24 P 16658 (Young 1951, 268 no. 1 pl. 83:c, d; Rotroff 2006a, 263 no. 172 fig. 28), deposit B 22:2 ("Fido's Grave," ibid. 346).
25 Cf. the famous Protoattic amphora from Eleusis (Μυλωνάς 1957, 4-5, 119).
26 P 10435 (Immerwahr 1971, 75-76 no. 271 pl. 18), P 10524 (Immerwahr 1971, 79 no. 301 pl. 20), P 13965 (Immerwahr 1971, 88-89 no. 358), P 9752.
27 Mylonas 1959, 40 no. 50 fig. 132.
28 P 10524 (Immerwahr 1971, 79 no. 301 pl. 20).
29 Vitelli 1993, e.g. figs. 9:i, 18:m, 21:p, 22:d, 35:a, 59:c, 91:g. Drill holes on the probable Neolithic mends at the Agora are also conical: e.g. P 26979, P 14738 (Immerwahr 1971, 33, 34 nos. 88, 100 pls. 5, 7).
30 No clamps are preserved on Roman pottery at the Agora, but many are known elsewhere; Peña (2007, 233-234) lists some of them. Lead clamps are also lacking on pottery of Protogeometric, Byzantine, or Turkish date in the collection.
31 P 31130; P 21936 (Sparkes & Talcott 1970, 339 no. 1480 pl. 62).
32 P 6301 (Rotroff 1997, 364 no. 211 pl. 20); P 527.

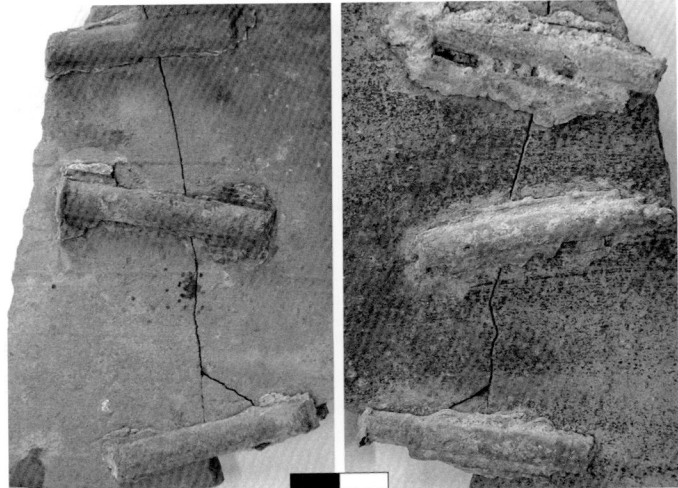

Fig. 9 Clamps with half-round straps on the outside (left) and inside (right) of a Hellenistic household-ware lekane (P 527).

heating to the surface of the pot. The pins that connect the two straps fit the holes precisely, indicating that the lead entered the holes in a liquid or a very malleable state. The strap too was at least sometimes in a liquid or pliable state when it came in contact with the vessel wall, as can be seen from the inner faces of detached straps, where a small ridge at about the center point is often visible, the impression of the break that the strap straddled.[33] It has been suggested that in some cases the clamps were cast in place, the mender creating small clay molds on either side of the vessel wall and pouring liquid lead into them.[34] Some of the Agora mends seem to show the results of such a procedure. Small protrusions of lead often extend beyond the strap, marking the points at which the mold was not tightly sealed against the vessel wall and the lead flowed beyond its confines (Figs. 8, 9). In a few cases one end of a strap widens into the shape of a nail head, possibly formed by a funnel-like mouth through which the lead was introduced (Fig. 8). Otherwise, however, there is no trace of this feature, and it is difficult to believe that the mender would have taken pains to remove it so regularly.

The pour hypothesis does not seem to fit all of the Agora examples. The thinnest of the lead straps, with thicknesses of 1.5-2.0 mm., simply do not look like castings: their edges and their rectangular shape are sharp and well defined, with little lead extruding beyond the borders (e.g., Fig. 7, right). One possibility is that the pins were formed by means of tiny pours of molten lead, while the straps were applied separately.[35]

Alternatively, Peña has suggested the use of lead putty (a mixture of white lead and linseed oil) for some Italian mends,[36] and it may be that this substance was used for some of the Athenian mends under consideration here. A mender would have worked lead putty into the drilled holes, then applied a layer of putty to the lower face of the thin lead strap that was to be placed on the two surfaces of the vessel. The putty acted as a glue binding the strap to the lead material within the hole; and the strap in turn acted as a protection and consolidant for the putty. As the mender pressed the straps down, the putty would sometimes squeeze out around the sides, but the strap itself would retain its discrete shape.

The use of putty might also explain some peculiarities of some of the clamps with half-round straps. For example, the half-round straps of the clamps on the interior of a brazier mended in the last quarter of the 5th century are bordered by a regular flat area (Figs. 10, 11).[37] This effect

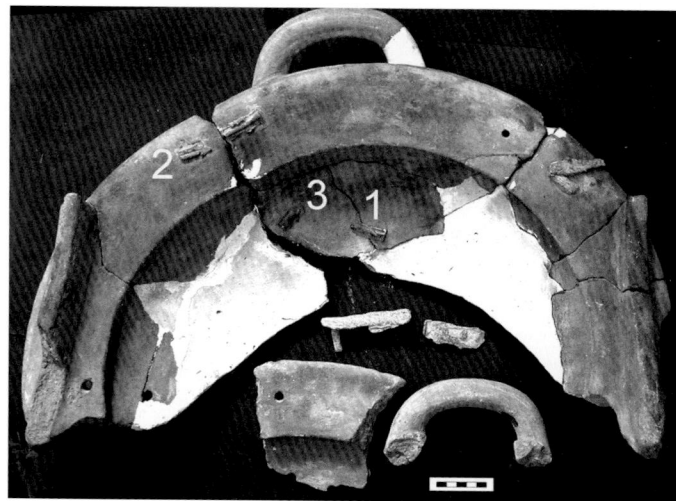

Fig. 10 Brazier of the last quarter of the 5th century (P 11015).

could have been achieved by drawing a tool over putty that had been spackled onto the surface, or by pressing a tool or a mold down into it. Such a process could explain the deep grooves that surround the half-round and divide it from the lead extrusion on a clamp on the outer wall of the same brazier (Fig. 11, right), and the stamp-like impression on two other stamps, where excess lead rises higher than the molded surface of the strap (Fig. 11, left and center).

The use of lead putty in Greek antiquity is conjectural, but such a substance is perhaps to be recognized in a puzzling material on the floor of a 2nd-century cooking pot.[38] It was found in a well outside the northwest corner of the agora square, among debris discarded by workers in metal, bone, and horn in the second quarter of the 2nd century BC. Only the lowest part of the pot is extant, a large fragment that was enjoying a second use as an artisan's mixing bowl. The substance in question is grayish-white, with pearlescent highlights, and the pattern of the deposit – a mound at the center and a ridge around the outside – suggests a thick substance that had been mixed, then abandoned to dry and harden. Preliminary analysis with a hand-held X-ray fluorescence instrument, undertaken by Amandina Anastassiades, has revealed a high percentage of lead.[39]

Most hole-and-clamp mends follow the patterns described above, but there are some anomalies. The straps of the clamps on a 3rd-century kantharos are unusually shaped,

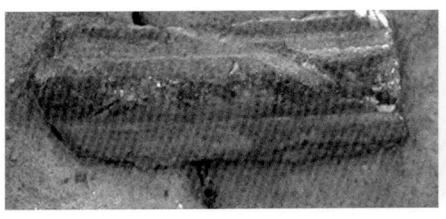 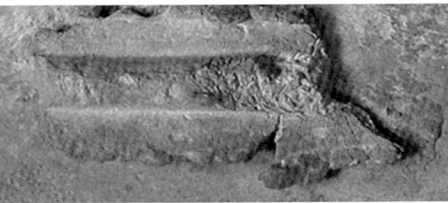 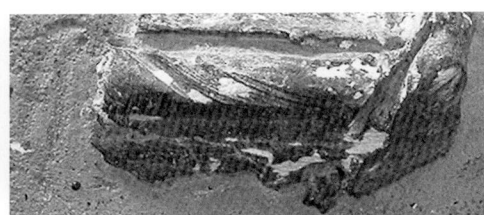

Fig. 11 Detail of clamps 1 and 2 (inside) and clamp 3 (outside) (at far right) of brazier P 11015.

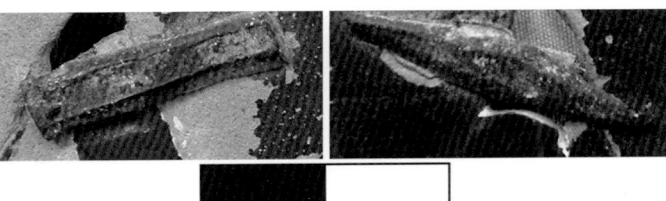

Fig. 12 Outside (left) and inside (right) of clamp on 3rd-century West Slope kantharos (P 20861).

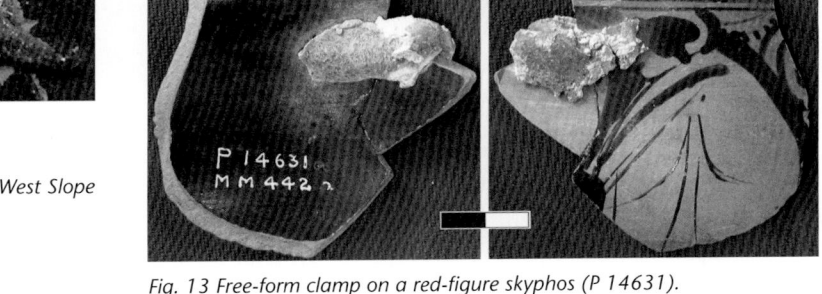

Fig. 13 Free-form clamp on a red-figure skyphos (P 14631).

with the edges sharply beveled on the outside, and lozenge-shaped on the interior (Fig. 12).[40] In the place of clearly defined straps, the mend on a red-figure skyphos has amorphous masses of lead, suggesting that it was carried out without the use of a rigid mold (Fig. 13).[41] The straps of the large clamps on a Hellenistic household-ware lekane have a strongly convex surface with regular longitudinal striations, as though they had been shaped with a toothed tool (Fig. 14).[42] Precisely the same feature

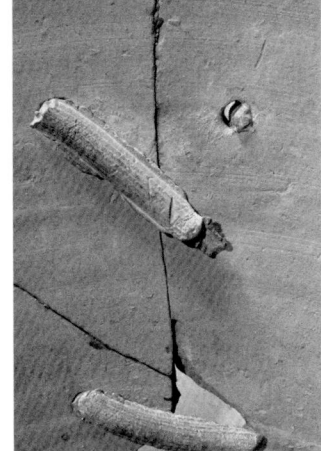

Fig. 14 Half-round straps with striations on a Hellenistic household-ware lekane (P 17041).

33 E.g., on clamps on P 830 (Moore & Philippides 1986, 172 no. 553 pl. 53); P 11015; IL 1856; noted also by Peña (2007, 241) on a clamp on an Italian black gloss plate/bowl.

34 Elston 1990, 58; Peña 2007, 238-239 (the form of the clamp is somewhat different); Schöne-Denkinger 2007, 25; Dooijes & Nieuwenhuyse 2007, 17; Nadalini 2007, 29.

35 This seems to be the procedure envisioned by Pfisterer-Haas (2002, 54) for some of the lead mends in Leipzig.

36 Peña 2007, 220, 222, and especially 241-242. For lead putty as known in the Renaissance and the 19th century, see Thornton 1998, 11.

37 P 11015 (Corbett 1949, 335-336 no. 99); for the shape, cf. Sparkes & Talcott 1970, 378 no. 2030 pl. 98.

38 Uninventoried vessel from lot ΛΛ 354; from well G 5:3. For the deposit, see Rotroff 2006a, 358.

39 X-ray fluorescence Niton XLt instrument, manufactured by Thermo Electron Corporation. I am grateful to Amandina for her investigations of the substance, which included experiments with mixing patterns. She is pursuing further analysis of the material.

40 P 20861 (Rotroff 1997, 261 no. 187 fig. 14 pl. 17).

41 P 14631 (Moore 1997, 304 no. 1298).

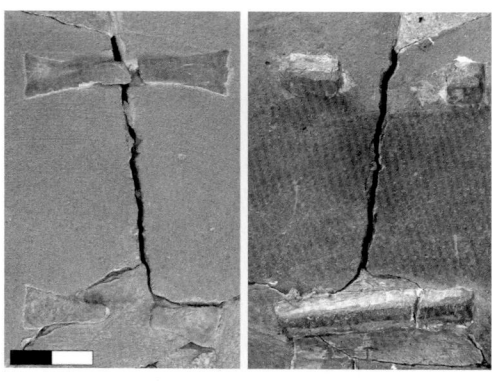
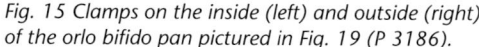

Fig. 15 Clamps on the inside (left) and outside (right) of the orlo bifido pan pictured in Fig. 19 (P 3186).

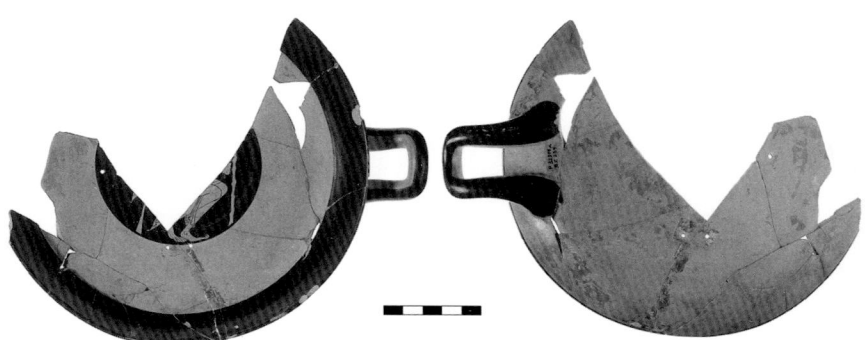

Fig. 16 Kylix painted by Euphronios, with drill holes for three clamps and traces of lead strip used as a seal (P 32344) (photograph Agora Excavations).

occurs on a clamp on a Sicilian skyphos of the Classical period and a 1st c AD Italian dolium at Piammiano;[43] whatever the production process involved, it was a standard and widespread one. And on an Archaic household-ware amphora, extensively repaired with clamps and patches, the inside strap of one of the clamps seems to bend and enter the drill hole, suggesting it was constructed by threading lead wire through one of the holes, a technique suggested for mends elsewhere.[44]

Eleven vessels were repaired with a different system, combining the hole-and-clamp procedure with a mortise and tenon (Figs. 15, 19).[45] In addition to drilling two holes, the mender carved a swallow-tailed sinking for the lead strap in the more visible of the two surfaces, so that the surface of the lead strap is flush with that of the vessel. The answering strap on the other, less visible side of the wall sits atop the surface in the normal manner. The close fit of the lead clamp to the cutting shows that here too the lead was applied as liquid or putty, but any overflow was trimmed away to preserve a smooth surface. The examples fall into two groups: two utilitarian vessels (a mortar and a household-ware stand) probably of Classical date and mended no later than the 3rd century BC;[46] and a concentration of nine fine- and cooking-ware vessels clustering in the late Hellenistic period. Although the earlier mends provide local precedent for this technique, the late Hellenistic clustering is remarkable, and I will return to it below.

The Agora collection preserves a single example of a mend using a fragment of a second pot, a practice well-attested for figured pottery in museum collections.[47] One handle and the foot had been broken away from a black-gloss Droop cup. The handles were reattached, but a new foot was supplied by a slightly larger lip- or band-cup and attached by a system of pins and straps.

The application of a filler or sealant would have been necessary if a mended pot was to be water-tight.[48] Traces of a white substance between a lead plate and the vessel wall in an unusual mend to a Hellenistic amphora may represent the remains of such a substance (P 24284, discussed in more detail below). A similar white material was used as cement on the handle of a cracked Classical (?) transport amphora (P 19538).[49] Indirect evidence for the effective use of filler comes from a 5th-century household-ware amphora, where the mend left a substantial gap in the wall, and only a filler could have rendered the vessel functional.[50] A different sealing technique was used on a red-figure cup painted by Euphronios in the last years of 6th century and found in Persian destruction debris (Fig. 16).[51] A fragment comprising about one third of the wall and rim was reattached with three widely-spaced clamps, and a strip of lead was applied over the break both inside and out. The strip itself is missing but has left clear traces on the part of the surface covered with intentional red gloss. There is no sign of it, however, on the black-gloss surfaces, suggesting that such a sealing technique could have been used frequently without leaving any trace.

THE MOTIVES FOR REPAIR

A repair without a doubt indicates that the pot had value for its owner; the nature of that value, however, is not easy to specify.[52] Attempted explanations – all of them

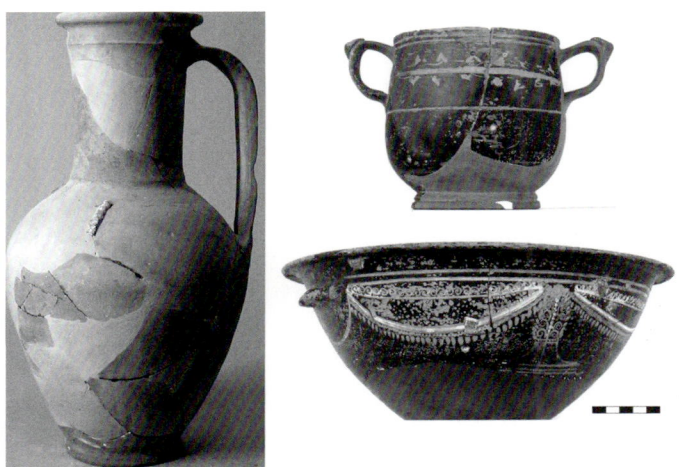

Fig. 17 Household-ware jug, West Slope kantharos, and West Slope bolster-krater from the Satyr Cistern (P 16281, P 16240, P 15166).

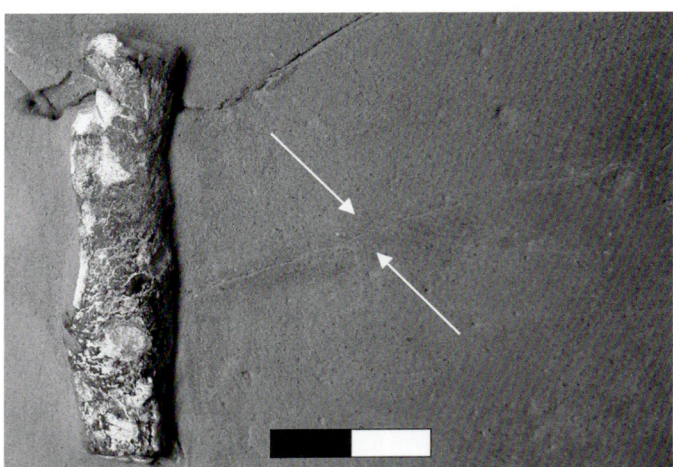

Fig. 18 Detail of mend to a household-ware jug; arrows indicate the location of the hairline crack (P 16281).

previously offered for mends in other times and places – can be classified as economic, functional, social, and personal, and it is instructive to hold these up against the data of the Agora mends.

The economic explanation, at its simplest level, maintains that cost was paramount in a decision to repair a broken pot.[53] A repair may have been cheaper than a replacement, but we are lacking the documentary sources that would allow us to test that hypothesis for the Agora mends. The vessels are largely of local production and some are of the simplest sort;[54] the differential between replacement and repair must have been tiny, an incentive only for the truly impoverished.

An economic motive may, however, have played a role at a different level: that of the potter or the seller of pottery. Roland Hampe and Adam Winter, writing of 20th-century potters in Southern Italy and Sicily, describe how pottery

of fill deposited by ca. 275 BC. P 27862 (stand), found in Room 5 of South Stoa I, layer B, deposited in the second half of the 3rd century, but with much earlier material (Agora field notebook T, 7255, 7258).

47 P 13817 (Sparkes & Talcott 1970, 263 no. 397 pl. 19). For other examples of mends using alien fragments, see Nogara 1951; Moore & Bothmer 1972, 9-11; Brijder 1983, 40-41 figs. 1:a and b; Noble 1988, 175 pls. XI, XII; Elston 1990, 63-65; Pfisterer-Haas 2002, 52.

48 As many have commented. Resin is often suggested: Vos 1981, 34; Noble 1988, 175; Elston 1990, 66; Hemelrijk 1991, 254. Nadalini 2003, 202 describes a brown discoloration along a break that may represent traces of a filler or adhesive.

49 Cf. a substance employed to mend a late Roman jug (Peña 2007, 229-231 figs. 8.8, 8.9). Hampe & Winter (1965, 61-62) observed the use of a cement made of quick lime, pulverized ceramic, egg white, and spit by S. Italian potters in the 20th century.

50 P 21936 (Sparkes & Talcott 1970, 339 no. 1480 pl. 62). A photograph taken before the vessel was fully mended shows the fully preserved clamp in place over a crack 2-3 mm. wide (Boulter 1953, 93 no. 106 pl. 34). A subsequent restorer broke and displaced the clamp to achieve a gapless repair.

51 P 32344 (Camp 1996, 251 no. 36 pl. 76; Cohen 2006, 62-63 no. 10 figs. 10.1-10.3, with excellent detail of the repair).

52 Senior (1995) focuses on the relationship between repair and value in both ethnographic and archaeological collections.

53 The caption to a photograph of a china mender in Afghanistan in the 1970s reads "The craft flourishes in a land where every coin counts; even the cheapest replacement may cost ten times as much as repair" (Michaud & Michaud 1973, 658-659). Boardman (2001, 162) characterizes mended imported vases in Italy as "too expensive to discard".

54 E.g., P 15974, a black-gloss skyphos (Fig. 24); P 23547 and P 18422, black-gloss olpai. None of these was considered worthy of inclusion in Sparkes and Talcott's authoritative publication of the black-gloss pottery from the Agora.

42 P 17041 (Rotroff 2006a, 274 no. 269, fig. 46, pl. 38).

43 Nadalini 2003, 198 fig. 4 (he suggests the strap was formed by a hot iron tool); Peña 2007, 225 fig. 8.7.

44 P 25279, from well R 12:3, extensively mended with clamps and patches, and discarded by ca. 500 BC. For the technique, see Nadalini 2007, 29; Peña 2007, 236.

45 P 3186 (Rotroff 2006a, 318 no. 699 fig. 89 pl. 72).

46 P 27217 (mortar, probably 4th-century; for the form, cf. Sparkes & Talcott 1970, 370 no. 1911 fig. 16 pl. 92), found in F 30:1, a layer

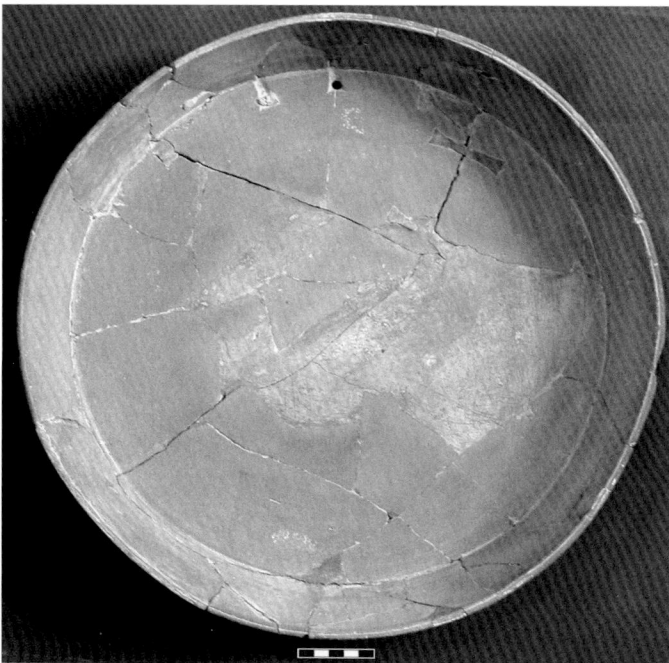

Fig. 19 Orlo bifido cooking pan mended with hole-and-clamp combined with swallow-tail tenons (P 3186).

damaged during production could be repaired – both with metal clamps and with cement – and then sold, sometimes even at the full price.[55] Their observations prompt consideration of clusters of repaired pottery in workshop dumps at the Agora. Perhaps potters and coroplasts did a sideline business in repairs, but it is also possible that some of these repairs were aimed at rectifying production damage. The best example is afforded by the Satyr Cistern, located to the south of the agora square and filled with the rubbish of two generations of potters and coroplasts.[56] Its lower, late 3rd-century fill contained four mended pots, as well as a large fragment of a moldmade bowl made in a broken mold that we may take as a proxy for a mend.[57] One of the mends is to an imported transport amphora, but the other three may be to the workshop's own products (Fig. 17). A clamp braces a hairline crack on a household amphora; the flaw is small enough that repair for sale seems feasible (Fig. 18).[58] A baggy kantharos is more extensively mended, with three clamps along a crack that runs from the rim to the lower body.[59] From what remains, it looks as though no part of the kantharos had actually broken away,

and that this was a brace rather than a full-blown repair; this cup too might have been deemed salable. A third mend involves the restoration of a large rim fragment to a West Slope bolster-krater.[60] No attempt has been made to disguise these repairs; if the mended vessels were intended for sale, whoever bought them would have known he or she was purchasing damaged goods. Perhaps the mended pot sold more cheaply, but the potter's time (or that of his slaves) spent making the repair may have been worth less than the reduced selling price.

A second case for entrepreneurial mending can be made for the nine late Hellenistic vessels repaired with swallow tail clamps sunk into mortises. All are of large, open shapes, particularly well crafted by the standards of their time, and most or all are imported. Most extensively repaired is a very fine *orlo bifido* cooking pan (Figs. 15, 19),[61] where a crack in the floor perpendicular to the edge was braced and a segment of the vertical wall reattached. Two clamps in the floor stabilized the crack; three more, with right-angle bends, joined the rim fragment to the floor, and two bound the fragment to the wall on either side. Several of the clamps are missing, revealing the channels that had been cut into the floor, and the unusually large holes (Diam. 0.65 cm.) drilled through the wall. On the inner surface, the preserved swallow-tail tenons are flush with the vessel wall, while the straps on the exterior are thick, flat, and rectangular, with irregularly beveled edges, and sit atop the vessel wall. Similar mends appear on five large Eastern Sigillata A plates of Atlante forms 2-4,[62] one on a gray-ware platter,[63] and two on imitation Pompeiian red-ware cooking pans.[64] Most or all of these vessels are imported. The *orlo bifido* pan is of a well-known type native to Italy.[65] The five ESA plates were made in the Levant, in the area of present-day Lebanon or Syria,[66] and the gray-ware platter comes from the region of Ephesos.[67] The imitation Pompeiian red-ware pans copy Italian cooking ware but their sources are uncertain. According to John Hayes, one is perhaps Cycladic; he characterizes the other as "local (?)",[68] but his query allows that it too could be imported. Forms and contexts indicate that these vessels are fairly restricted in date. Two (the *orlo bifido* pan and one of the ESA plates) are part of Thompson's Group E, deposited before ca. 110 BC.[69] Context dates another ESA plate within the first half of the 1st century BC.[70] Three more vessels (the Ionian platter, one ESA plate, and one of the imitation Pompeiian red-ware pans) come from a cistern system containing material of the 2nd and 1st centuries BC,[71] their forms allowing a date no earlier than the late 2nd. Another ESA plate and imitation Pompeiian red-ware plate are later, dating in the last decades of the 1st century.[72] The final member of the group (an ESA plate from the second fill of Well B 13:7) is contemporary or only slightly later.[73]

The convergence on Athens of unusually mended pots from opposite directions at about the same time is intriguing. If this mending technique is a home-grown innovation, it is strange that it is not repeated on local pottery. We might imagine a foreign craftsman, working in Athens but using a method learned in an apprenticeship elsewhere; the range of date, however, longer than the working life of a single person, makes that unlikely. If we expand the hypothesis to a workshop functioning over generations, we again meet the confounding fact that the technique was (probably) not applied to any but imported pottery. It is therefore tempting to believe that these objects were mended before export; but where? There is precedent for the technique in Archaic and late Hellenistic Etruria,[74] but I am unaware of any mends of this type in Ionia or the Levant; ESA plates mended at Tel Anafa display the standard hole-and-clamp method.[75] Another possibility is that the pots were mended en route – perhaps at Delos. Enormous collections of ceramics there demonstrate that the island served as an entrepot, receiving pottery from both East and West and shipping it on to other markets. Athens' close ties with the island and the similarity between the ceramic assemblages of the two cities in the late Hellenistic period suggest that many of Athens' imports reached the city through this route. It might be that goods damaged in transit to Delos were repaired there by middlemen before being sent on for sale as "seconds." But whether sufficient pottery passed through the island after the destruction of 69 BC to maintain this hypothesis is very much open to question.

In the private sphere, an owner might wish to prolong the use-life of a pot for reasons other than harsh economic

foot of which has been unobtrusively reattached by means of a lead pour; and P 7778 (Rotroff 2006a, 312 no. 640 fig. 82 pl. 68), a casserole with a single lead clamp in its floor. For the deposit, see Rotroff 2006a, 351. Menon's cistern, outside the southwest corner of the agora square and serving a coroplast's workshop, furnished two mended pots: P 28335 (Rotroff 1997, 248-249 no. 70 fig. 7 pl. 7), a West Slope cup-kantharos to which the high-swung handles had been reattached; and P 28074 (Rotroff 2006a, 270 no. 234 fig. 39 pl. 33), a household lekane with a braced crack or possibly attachment of a rim fragment. For the deposit, see Miller 1974 and (for the date) Rotroff 1997, 24-25.

57 See note 16 above.

58 P 16281 (Rotroff 2006a, 248 no. 37 fig. 7 pl. 7).

59 P 16240 (Rotroff 1997, 267 no. 240 pl. 22).

60 P 15166 (Rotroff 1997, 303 no. 582 fig. 41 pl. 54).

61 P 3186 (Thompson 1934, 419 no. E 140 figs. 106, 107; Rotroff 2006a, 318 no. 699 fig. 89 pl. 72).

62 P 3424, P 10892, P 11231, P 14963, P 22479 (Hayes 2008, 124-126 nos. 3, 5, 11, 12, 19 fig. 1 pl. 1).

63 P 6864 (Rotroff 1997, 399 no. 1573 fig. 95 pl. 124).

64 P 32039 (Hayes 2008, 289 no. 1824 fig. 56 pl. 91), P 33061.

65 Rotroff 2006a, 192-193.

66 Hayes 1985, 10; Slane 1997, 272.

67 Zabehlicky-Scheffenegger et al. 1996.

68 Hayes 2008, 121, 289; and Hayes' notes on the inventory card for P 33061. The fact that Hayes does not include P 33061 in his volume on fine-ware imports also implies his judgment that the piece was locally manufactured.

69 P 3186, P 3424 (Thompson 1934, E 140 and E 151). The dating of this deposit has been revised since its publication; see Rotroff 1982, 100, 110; Rotroff 2006a, 356.

70 P 14963, from well F 19:3; for the date of the context, see Hayes 2008, 298.

71 P 10892 (ESA plate) from the lower fill of cistern D 11:4; P 6864 (Ionian platter) and P 33061 (imitation Pompeiian red-ware plate) from the lower fill of draw shaft D 12:2. The cistern and draw shaft are separated by a tunnel only 50 cm. long and there were joins between pottery in the two fills. Pottery ranges from the 2nd to beyond the middle of the 1st century BC. See Rotroff 1997, 441-442 and Rotroff 2006a, 348-349. Hayes (2008, 126, under no., 19) dates the ESA plate to the early(?) 1st c BC.

72 Hayes 2008, 125, under no. 12 (ESA plate, 20-1 BC); 289, under no. 1824 (imitation Pompeiian red-ware plate, late 1st c BC).

73 Hayes 2008, 125, under no. 11 (late 1st c BC or later). For the date of the deposit, see Rotroff 1997, 435; Rotroff 2006a, 344; it does not extend much, if at all, beyond the turn of the era.

74 Louvre G 110, a late 6th-century krater by Euphronios, preserves a swallow-tail sinking (Nadalini 2003, 205 fig. 22; Nadalini 2007, 31-32 fig. 6). Unfortunately, its provenience is not known, but the use of sinkings or channels with straps of bar, rather than swallow-tail, shape is well-attested on figured pottery found (probably) in Etruria (e.g., Moore & Bothmer 1972; Vos 1981, 33-34; Snow 1986; no author 1990, 77, 108; Elston 1990, 56; Nadalini 2007, 31-32; Pfisterer-Haas 2002, 54). Peña (2007, 239-242) describes in detail a similar mend (again with plain straps) to a black-gloss Italian plate or bowl from Piammiano, north of Rome, probably of Morel forms 2272-2274 and most likely dated in the late 2nd century or the first half of the 1st century BC (Morel 1981, 158-159).

75 Slane 1997, 346 FW 451-FW 453 pl. 51.

55 Hampe & Winter 1965, 60-62, 198.

56 For a full discussion of the deposit and reference to further bibliography, see Rotroff 1994. Potter's debris also characterized cistern E 3:1, located on the road to the Kerameikos, with two mends: P 7761 (Rotroff 1997, 257 no. 144 fig. 11, with mend indicated by hatching, pl. 13), a West Slope bowl-kantharos, the

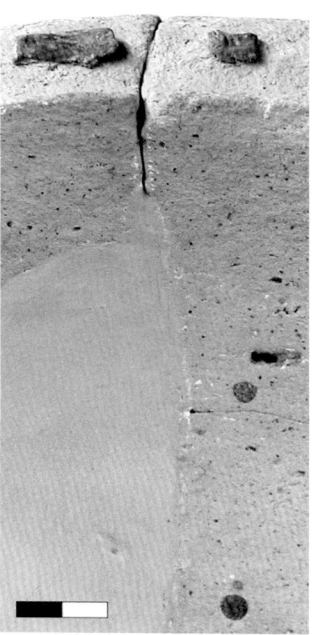

Fig. 20 Rim and inner wall of household-ware mortar, showing surface of pins, worn and flush with surface (P 18778).

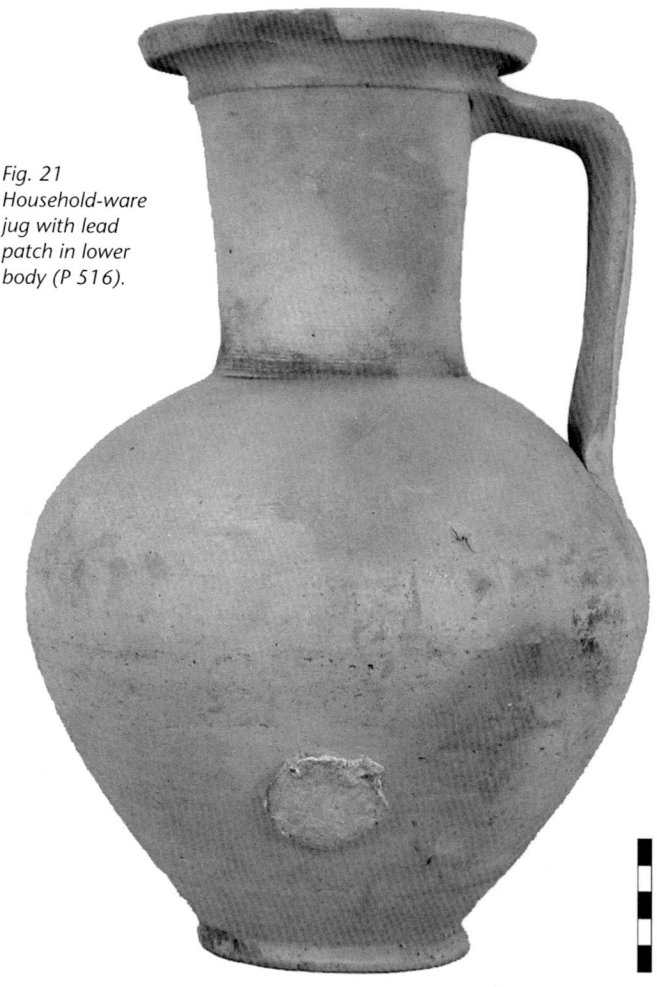

Fig. 21 Household-ware jug with lead patch in lower body (P 516).

necessity: frugality, inertia, attachment to a tool that has performed its function well or a possession with sentimental associations. If mending could be effected conveniently – by sending a servant or slave to the mender's establishment, or conceivably by a traveling "tinker"[76] – it would be natural to indulge a disinclination to discard something that could be made useful again at small cost. In the case of some vessels (like pithoi, which played the role of major appliances) replacement and reinstallation would have taken considerable time and trouble; even if repair were expensive, it may have involved less time and trouble than replacement. If frugality is the motive, the repair must be effective; that is, the mended pot must be able to continue to perform its original function. Most repairs to household-ware vessels probably fall into this category, and some provide positive evidence of continued functionality. Four clamps braced a crack in a remarkably large mortar, possibly of Classical date but found in a 2nd-century context (rare evidence, incidentally, for a long-lasting repair) (Fig. 20).[77] The straps are now missing from the clamps on the floor of the vessel, but the exposed surface of the pins, now flush with the floor, are worn smooth, attesting to years of use after the mortar's repair. Another example is provided by a jug with a large

lead patch, part of the fill of a Hellenistic well that may have accumulated during its use (Fig. 21);[78] apparently the patch was sufficient to render the jug water-tight and fit to draw water.[79]

A cluster of mended vessels provides a more specific context for such behavior (Fig. 22). A pair of mended household lekanai was found in Cistern M 20:1, filled in the wake of the Sullan sack of Athens in 86 BC. The contents include many vessels designed for unspecified industrial use and probably come from a nearby workshop.[80] A single clamp braces a crack just below the rim of one of the lekanai; damage to the other was more extensive, requiring three horizontally-set clamps just below the rim and a fourth in the lower wall. At least three more repaired vessels

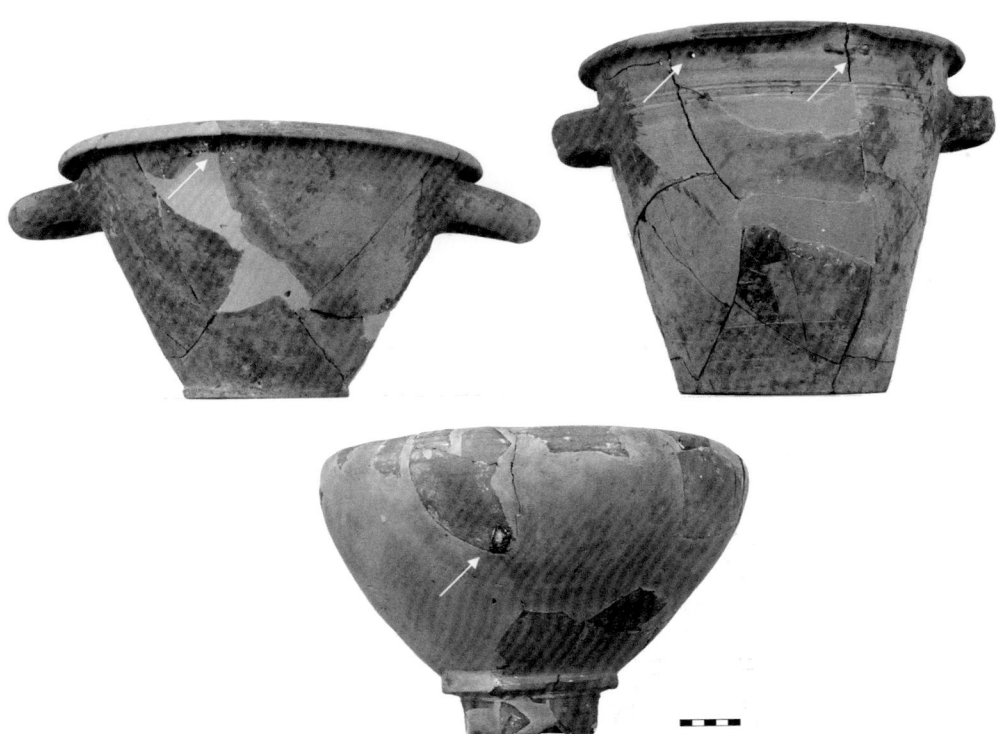

Fig. 22 Mended household ware from industrial debris in cisterns M 20:1 and N 19:1 (P 14457, P 14452, P 11894).

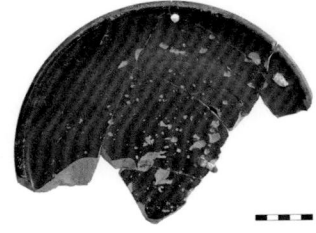

Fig. 23 Black-gloss plate of the early 3rd century, mended and pierced for suspension (P 29779).

(a funnel, a storage jar, and a fragmentary cooking vessel) were found in the nearby cistern N 19:1 among similar debris and possibly from the same workshop.[81] In these cases artisans with the appropriate tools, materials, and skills at their disposal may have found it more convenient to repair a working pot than to buy another. Slave labor might have made such repairs close to cost-free.

Even if rendered unfit for its original function, a mended pot could of course continue to be useful in another way. This is clearly the case with a 4th-century bowl with a panel of black-pattern spirals, which quality and decoration identify as table ware.[82] Two drill holes below a horizontal break witness the attempted reattachment of the rim. When this failed, the break was smoothed down, and heavy abrasion on the floor and a red deposit show that the bowl was subsequently used for grinding pigment. Another instance is provided by a Classical pithos (P 23105), put into service as a settling basin after the loss of its upper body, the reattachment of its bottommost section with eight or nine clamps, and the additional bracing of cracks.

76 Even today (summer of 2008), in increasingly affluent Athens, itinerant menders of metal cooking pots set up shop at the weekly markets in Ano Ilissia. It is worth considering whether there is any evidence for similar practices in antiquity.

77 P 18778 (Rotroff 2006a, 265-266 no. 195 fig. 33 pl. 27).

78 P 516, Hellenistic water jug, Form 1, found at a depth of 13 m. in the middle fill of well G 14:2. For the deposit, see Rotroff 2006a, 359.

79 Possibly also from a use fill is a more seriously damaged Archaic table amphora (P 25279), where two small holes in the lower body had been patched, a large tear-shaped fragment of the shoulder reattached and a crack braced.

80 P 14457 (Rotroff 2006a, 273 no. 260 fig. 44 pl. 36), P 14452 (Rotroff 2006a, 273 no. 265 fig. 45 pl. 37). For the deposit, see Rotroff 2000; Rotroff 2006a, 365.

81 P 11890 (Rotroff 2006a, 311 no. 632 fig. 81), cooking vessel; P 11894 (Rotroff 2006a, 260 no. 153 fig. 23 pl. 21), funnel; P 11892 (Rotroff 2006a, 261 no. 162 fig. 26 pl. 22), storage bin. All come from the upper fill of N 19:1 (Robinson's Group F, Robinson 1959, 10-21), which was deposited in the early 1st century AD but contained a large amount of much earlier, Sullan debris (see Rotroff 1997, 464; Rotroff 2006a, 368). The three mends may therefore be contemporary with the material from M 20:1 and all five may derive from the same source; see ibid, 65.

82 P 11808; cf. Sparkes & Talcott 1970, no. 82 pl. 4 for the shape.

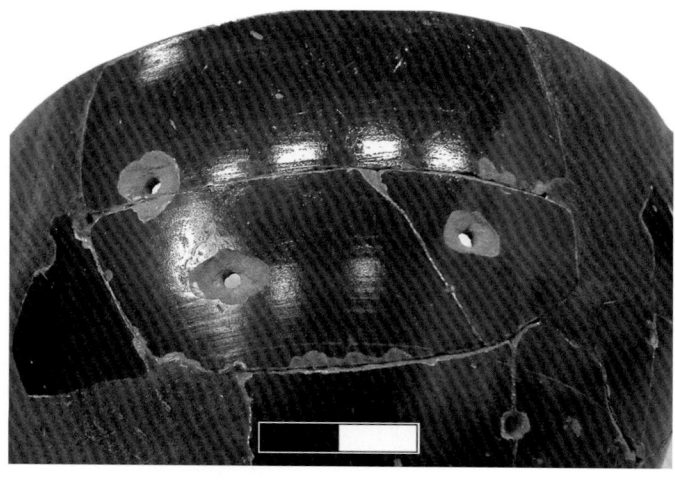

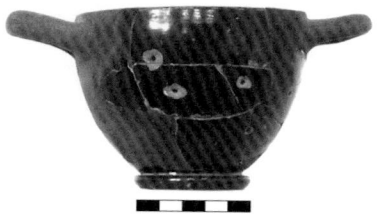

Fig. 24 Black-gloss skyphos of the second quarter of the 5th century, with drill holes for reattachment of large rim and body sherd (P 15974). The left handle is wrongly restored as horizontal.

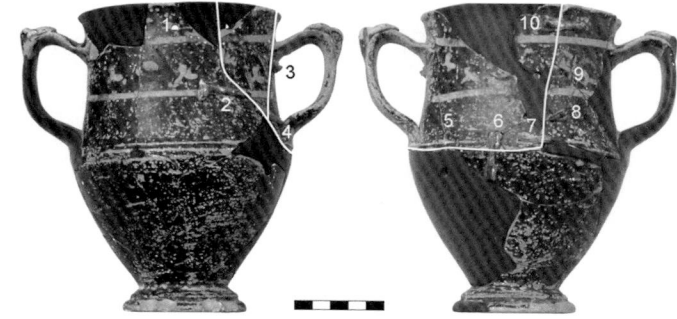

Fig. 25 West Slope angular kantharos; seven clamps and holes for three more for reattachment of two fragments (P 6310).

Some scholars, assuming that extensive repairs could not have rendered a broken wine container leak-proof, have concluded that the mended vessels underwent a more radical change of function.[83] No longer useful as tableware, they were displayed as badges of prestige – either in the home or in the tomb – enhancing the status of the owner as a person with access to or the taste for a certain type of goods.[84] Several commentators have noticed that the menders of red-figure vessels found in Etruria sometimes seem to have done their best to avoid the figures in placing their clamps, also sinking them in channels so that they would be flush with the vase surface and therefore less obtrusive,[85] an indication that the appearance of the vessel was as much a concern as its utility. Although the figured examples at the Agora are very fragmentary, they too suggest a concern with appearance, even though here the pottery in question was not imported.[86] On nine examples the placement of holes and clamps suggests that the mender respected the figures. Even when there is some overlap, only rarely does a clamp or hole seriously obscure a figure,[87] and perhaps unavoidably, due to the location of the break. But here, as also in Etruria, concern for appearance does not mean that the vessels were intended solely for display. It merely affirms what is obvious from the existence of figured pottery in the first place: that the decoration as well as the function of a vessel was appreciated.

In an examination of mended glass goblets of the 17th century, where the mends did not render the vessels functional, Hugh Willmott has suggested that repair might even have enhanced symbolic value, conveying the message that the owner was in possession of old vessels and by implication was a person of established wealth and status.[88] The Agora collection provides no evidence that bears on that issue, but it does include an object that may have been displayed as an antique curiosity. Lead clamps reattached a large fragment of the rim and floor of a black-gloss rolled-rim plate of the early 3rd century BC (P 29779, Fig. 23). A large hole had also been drilled through the rim; it was not part of the mend, for it is not part of a pair, and its purpose must have been to suspend the plate.[89] The plate was found in a context of the 4th century AD, and it is tempting to see it as an ancient vessel, perhaps unearthed by chance, repaired, and displayed by an antiquarian owner.

Perhaps the most potent reason for a repair is that the owner regards the broken object as irreplaceable. This assumes a personal affection for the vessel: the owner particularly liked the way it looked or felt or functioned. It might well be impossible to purchase a precise replacement for an imported pot (a fact that offers an

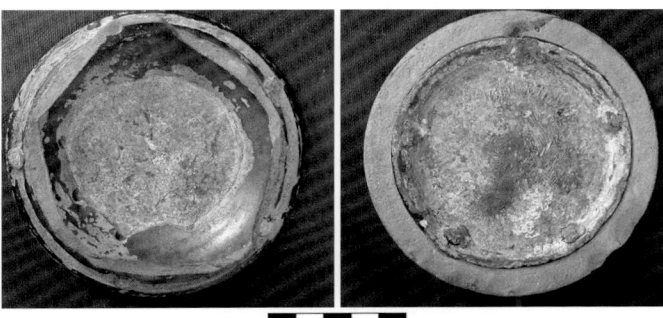

Fig. 26 Inside (left) and underside (right) of foot of Hellenistic amphora mended with lead plate and rivets (P 24284).

obvious explanation for their high incidence of repair), but passage of time would also make the replacement of local products impossible, especially in the case of table ware, where styles, techniques, and quality evolved quickly. A pot might also have had an association with a particular person, group, past event or situation, or activity that rendered it unique. Such situations are virtually impossible to demonstrate, but we might suspect something of the sort in cases where the effort devoted to repair seems out of proportion to the apparent value of the object mended. Such is the case with a black-gloss skyphos of the second quarter of the 5th century BC (Fig. 24).[90] Its shape and highly reflective gloss are certainly very fine, but nothing out of the ordinary for their time, and the vessel is both small and without any decoration. Nonetheless, four pairs of holes were drilled to reattach a large fragment of the rim and body, comprising most of one side of the cup. The large amount of chipping on the exit side of the holes suggests a mender inexperienced with the drill, perhaps the owner? A similarly disproportionate mend was made to a West Slope kantharos of the 3rd century, where part of the rim and one handle had broken away in two fragments (Fig. 25; see also Fig. 8).[91] The ten clamps employed in the reattachment seem excessive: the holes involved in drilling them can hardly have enhanced the viability of the vessel and the highly visible and crudely formed clamps do nothing for its appearance. A final case involves repair to a small Hellenistic table amphora, of which only the foot now survives (Fig. 26).[92] A first attempt at repair was designed to reattach the now missing center of the amphora's floor. This was initiated by drilling eight holes

around the perimeter of the break, presumably to install clamps for the attachment of the missing piece. When this failed – either immediately or after some time – the mender cut out a circle of lead, warmed it sufficiently to make it malleable and worked it with a small hammer until it exactly fit the contour of the underside of the foot; the tooling marks are visible on its surface. He drilled five holes through the foot, matching holes in the lead plate, threaded five lead rivets through them and hammered their ends flat on either side. It is likely that more extensive repair was also needed, as the flattening of the inner end of these rivets would have been impossible if the remainder of the pot was intact. Traces of a white material that could be the remains of an adhesive or filler can be seen between the plate and the remaining underside of the amphora, perhaps an attempt to create a tight seal. It seems as though only personal motives – whether desire to display a vessel with a particular cachet in a particular environment, or affection for an object with significant associations – could warrant

83 E.g., Furtwängler & Reichhold 1904, 82; Reichhold 1919, 10. Nadalini (2003, 199) expresses doubts about the ability of mended vessels to hold liquid.

84 As Willmott (2001, 103) argues for the display of mended 17th-century glassware; see also general remarks by Dooijes & Nieuwenhuyse (2007, 15, 18-19), who are interested in the relationship between physical and cultural transformations.

85 Nadalini 2007, 31-32; no author 1990 77, 108. Others, however, have observed disregard for the figures, both on vases in museum collections (Richter & Hall 1936, 138-139; Richter 1946, 35) and on figured pottery found at Olynthos (Robinson 1950, 59).

86 There are 13 mends to black-figure and 11 to red-figure vessels; breaks are located in the figured area of the vase on 15 of them.

87 P 1122 (Moore & Philippides, 1986, 255 no. 1270 pl. 89), black-figure tripod pyxis, hole drilled through leg of animal; P 13845 (Moore & Philippides 1986, 141 no. 321 pl. 33), Panathenaic amphora, hole drilled in figure of Athena; P 25324 (Moore & Pease 1986, 122 no. 159), early black-figure neck-amphora, hole drilled in animal figures, but close spacing makes avoidance of figures impossible.

88 Willmott 2001, 103.

89 Suspension holes, always in pairs, were sometimes made at the time of manufacture in the rims of decorated plates (e.g., Rotroff 1997, 325-326 nos. 827 832, pls. 69, 70), but never, as far as I am aware, on plain black-gloss plates.

90 P 15974; cf. Sparkes & Talcott 1970, 260 no. 362 pl. 17.

91 P 6301 (Rotroff 1997, 364 no. 211 pl. 20).

92 P 24284. The shape is the same as on Hellenistic table amphorae, though the diameter (10.8 cm.) is smaller than is usual for the shape. For amphorae with feet of about this size, see Rotroff 1997, 286-287 nos. 414, 418, figs. 25, 26, pls. 40, 41.

such an excess of effort. Unfortunately, the context of the object does not help; it was found during small excavations undertaken during the reconstruction or the Stoa of Attalos, in "mixed fill," a catch-all description for material with a wide range of date.

We will never know the reasons behind most of the ancient repairs we recover, and their small incidence will have made little impact on the makeup of the archaeological ceramic record. A greater knowledge of the basic data about the practice, however, can alert us to situations in which mending points to something out of the ordinary. The high percentage of mends to the Louvre's Euphronios kraters provides one instance; I offer a final anecdote from the Agora as another, and, interestingly enough, it also involves Euphronios. The mended cup that he painted (Fig. 16) comes from the Agora's largest concentration of repairs:[93] the Euphronios cup and another closely similar one, surely a pair, both of them now about half preserved, and, much more fragmentary, another red-figure cup, a black-figure amphora and stamnos, and a black-gloss lekanis lid. Perhaps a single event in which much pottery was broken created an impetus for the repair of the least badly damaged, whether through frugality or personal attachment to the vessels concerned. Here and elsewhere answers may elude us, but a better knowledge of the mending habit will at least alert us to ask the questions.

---

93 From an Archaic well north of the agora (Camp 1996, 242-252). The deposit will be published in full by Kathleen Lynch in a forthcoming Supplement to Hesperia.

ACKNOWLEDGEMENTS

I am grateful to the organisers for their invitation to participate in the conference and to Ted Peña for prompting me to look more closely at the Agora mends. Several colleagues contributed to this study and I thank them all: Brad Koldehoff, Bob Lamberton, Mark Lawall, Kathleen Lynch, Craig Mauzy, John Oakley, and especially Amandina Anastassiades, who shared with me her data base of Agora mends as well as the results of her study and analysis of the "lead putty" from well G 5:3. The Agora staff, and in particular Sylvie Dumont, helped with access to the material and brought several recently inventoried examples of ancient mending to my attention.

Roman Pottery in the Archaeological Record:
Some Follow-Up Comments

BY J. THEODORE PEÑA

Roman Pottery in the Archaeological Record: Some Follow-Up Comments

BY J. THEODORE PEÑA

I would like to begin by stating how gratified I am that my book, *Roman Pottery in the Archaeological Record,* has proved to be of interest to so many and such distinguished students of Greek pottery and Roman pottery in Greece and the eastern Mediterranean, more generally,[1] and to express my very great appreciation to the editors of this volume and organizers of the conference on which it is based, Mark Lawall and John Lund, and also to the Gösta Enbom Foundation, the Danish Institute at Athens, and the Canadian Institute in Greece for funding and hosting the event. The presentations made in the course of the conference and the contributions to this volume, most of which I have had the opportunity to read in draft form, have brought to my attention various views that I would not have considered on my own and a vast amount of relevant evidence, research, and bibliography of which I was and in many cases would likely have remained unaware, and for this I am indeed most grateful.

In writing the book it was my hope that it would inspire students of archaeological pottery – both in the Roman world and beyond – to explore how the generalizing, normative model of the pottery life cycle that it presents might be applied in specific cultural/chronological/geographical contexts to learn interesting things about both the pottery record and the past more generally. Of the various contributions to this volume, I would like to single out two – those by Mark Lawall and Susan Rotroff – as engaging this challenge in precisely the way that I had hoped might occur. In the case of Lawall's contribution, he has used his extraordinary knowledge of Greek amphorae to revise and elaborate the model with a view to capturing the specific circumstances of the life history of these vessels. Performing this exercise allowed him to discern several differences in the ways in which amphorae were used between the Greek world and the Roman world, account for certain features of the representation of Greek amphorae in refuse deposits, and articulate distinct models for the life

history of amphorae within regions oriented toward the production of foodstuffs for local consumption and those oriented toward their production for export. In Rotroff's case, she has reviewed in as systematic a fashion as the circumstances permit the pottery assemblage recovered in the American School of Classical Studies in Athens' excavations in the Athenian Agora for evidence for vessel repair. On account of the extraordinarily large size of this body of material she has been able to document in an impressively robust fashion variability in this practice by vessel type and time period. While some aspects of this picture could have been predicted *a priori* on the strength of logical considerations, others are entirely unexpected, and raise interesting questions about the ways in which the inhabitants of Athens used and regarded their material possessions.

I would also like to make specific note of the contribution by Elizabeth Murphy and Jeroen Poblome. This presents the results of a program of path-breaking research on pottery production, and had work of this kind been available to me when I wrote the book I would very probably have elected to engage the production phase of the pottery life cycle in something more than the cursory fashion in which I did in the book.[2]

Research published elsewhere since I consigned the revised book manuscript to the publisher in March, 2006 has advanced significantly our understanding of certain of the topics touched on in the book, while research still in progress at the time of writing promises to do the same. In late 2008 Kevin Greene published an article that provides a synthesizing overview of consumption and consumerism in the Roman Empire, furnishing a much needed set of conceptual constructs for considerations of the consumption of pottery and the pottery life cycle.[3] More recently, Nicholas Ray has completed a PhD thesis that presents an extended consideration of consumer theory and the forms of evidence for consumption in the Roman world, including pottery evidence, followed by a detailed analysis of the artifact assemblages from 12 houses at Pompeii with a view to elucidating various issues of consumption.[4] This represents an extremely welcome effort to wed general theory relevant to the study of material culture with a carefully designed empirical study, and we can look forward with great anticipation to the publication of Ray's results. Elsewhere, Ruth Siddall is carrying out a program of research involving the compositional analysis of mortars and cements from Roman Corinth that is providing important evidence for the practices involved in the recycling of pottery and other ceramics as reagents in these materials.[5] Finally, the appearance of the journal *Facta: a journal of Roman material culture studies*, edited by one of the editors of this volume (Lund) and two of the other conference participants (Daniele Malfitana and Poblome), constitutes an extremely important development, as it means that there is now a regular forum for the publication of research of the kind here under consideration.[6]

One aspect of the model presented in my book that I believe requires more careful consideration, perhaps leading to some more or less substantial revision, is the distinction between primary and secondary use and the conceptualization of artifact function on which it is based. In brief, the model posits that the producer of an artifact will have in mind some specific application or set of applications that it will serve or, alternatively, that the consumer who acquires a newly manufactured artifact will have some specific application or set of applications in mind for which to use it, and that we can employ this fact to identify – if only notionally – an artifact's primary use and, following from this, any secondary use or uses.[7] As it turns out – and as was completely unknown to me at the time that I wrote the book – the tendency on the part of those who manufacture and acquire artifacts to evaluate their suitability for performing a certain application or set of applications is an issue that has drawn the attention of philosophers, including Risto Hilpinen, Randall Dipert, and Johan Modeé, and a consideration of the treatment of these questions in the philosophical literature might permit a more soundly articulated approach to the definition of primary and secondary use.[8]

Turning to the broader issues addressed in the book, one also hopes that scholars will in the near future devote considerably more attention to the study of practices of refuse discard in the Greek and Roman worlds and the ways in which these shaped both urban and rural landscapes.[9] A particularly conspicuous example of this phenomenon has been documented at Ostia, where it appears that there was a systematic effort to raise ground level across effectively the entire city by as much as ca. one meter during the later first century AD through the importation and dumping of mixed refuse, quite probably debris resulting from the Great Fire of AD 64 at Rome.[10] This was presumably carried out with a view to raising the city somewhat higher above the

water table, which normally stood at a level only slightly below that of the natural ground surface.[11]

Roberta Tomber, in her contribution to this volume, employs information regarding the organization of refuse disposal in Cairo during the 20th century to good effect, and I would like to close by similarly introducing some comparative evidence from modern Egypt with a view to illustrating aspects of the two topics just raised. In this case, I am drawing on the well known description of Egypt composed by Dominique Vivant, Baron de Denon, one of the savants who accompanied Napoleon on his Egyptian expedition of 1798-1801 and subsequently the first director of the Musée du Louvre.[12] In writing about Balasse (Deir el-Ballas), a town located on the west bank of the Nile

---

1 Peña 2007. For reviews of the book that consider the question of whether or not it is likely to succeed in this regard, see Kolb 2007; Bes 2008; Freed 2008; Jackson and Greene 2008; Pryor and Slane 2008; Tomber 2008; Viitanen 2008.
2 See also Gibson and Lucas 2002, which presents interesting evidence regarding the incidence of various kinds of production defects in the pottery assemblage recovered in the excavation of the Roman pottery workshop at Greenhouse Farm, in Cambridgeshire. For a useful survey of the papyrological evidence for amphora production in Egypt during the Roman period, see Gallimore forthcoming.
3 Greene 2008.
4 Ray 2009.
5 Siddall 2006; http://www.ucl.ac.uk/%7Eucfbrxs/Homepage/rsresearch.htm. For a short characterization of some of the results of this work, see the contribution by Slane in this volume.
6 See Peña 2009 for a review of the first number of this journal.
7 Peña 2007, 8, 9-10.
8 For a critical survey of the treatment of these issues in the philosophical literature, see Modée 2007, 34-46.
9 See in this regard Ballet *et al.* (eds.) 2003, which I encountered only after I had submitted the book manuscript to the press. This volume contains extremely interesting case studies of practices of refuse discard in several cities in Roman Gaul, including Autun, Lyon, Nîmes, Aix-en-Provence, and Tours.
10 For this raising of ground level at Ostia, see Meiggs 1973, 64-65 and the various studies published in Meded 58 (1999), 61-97. There may have been a similar effort to raise the ground level over much of the neighboring hamlet of Vicus Augustanus during the first and/or second centuries A.D. See http://www.rhul.ac.uk/Classics/LaurentineShore/VicusAugustanus/VC_VicusAugustanus.html.
11 For a similar effort to raise ground level above the water table in a coastal area by the systematic importation and dumping of mixed refuse in contemporary Senegal, see http://www.nytimes.com/2009/05/03/world/africa/03garbage.html?_r=1)
12 Denon 1803.

River in Upper Egypt that is renowned for the specialized manufacture of water jars (known as Bâlâlis), he noted: "... they [the jars] are made at very little expense, and are sold so cheap that they are sometimes used to construct the walls of houses, and the poorest inhabitant may supply himself with them in abundance....The people make rafts of these pots, which have been described by every traveler into Egypt; they are thus carried down the Nile, part of them are sold on the way, and the remainder are embarked at Rosetta and Damietta [Rashid and Domyat, harbor towns at the mouth of the Nile] to be sent abroad....I have often been at Balasse, and have been astonished at the immense cargoes of these jars, which are either piled up on boats, or made into rafts, like the large floats of wood on our rivers, which are borne by the stream, and at the same time carry their owners, who dispose of them to good advantage".[13]

Freshly manufactured Bâlâlis were thus regularly employed for two completely unrelated applications – either as water jars or as structural elements – and a significant portion of those destined for export to non-local markets for the second of these two applications also served first as floats that supported the transport of their sellers down the Nile as far as its mouth. This interesting set of circumstances suggests just some of the sorts of complications that will need to be taken into account if we are to achieve a more satisfactory definition of primary and secondary use.

In another passage, Denon writes: "Our second expedition was to Meimund, a very rich village, with ten thousand inhabitants. Like all the rest, it is surrounded with dunghills and heaps of rubbish, which, in such a flat country as this, form so many hills, that may be seen at a considerable distance. Every evening each of these eminences is seen covered with people, who lie down upon it, and breathe its noisome vapours, smoking their pipes, and observing if all is quiet in the fields. These heaps of dung and rubbish produce many inconveniences, they obscure the houses, infect the air, and fill the eyes of the people with an acrid dust mixed with minute straws, which is one of the numerous causes of the disease of the eyes to which the people of Egypt are so much exposed".[14]

It thus appears that the rubbish middens surrounding villages such as the one in question constituted prominent landmarks, and that while they represented both a nuisance and a threat to the villagers' health, they also served positive purposes, since they provided a vantage point from which it was possible to keep watch on the fields surrounding the village, an activity that appears to have led to their emergence as popular spots for the inhabitants to relax and perhaps also socialize during the evening hours. It is not at all difficult, indeed, to imagine that the berm-like midden situated immediately to the south of the fort at Wadi Umm Hussein/Mons Claudianus termed by the excavators the South Sebakh might have been employed in a similar way by the inhabitants of this isolated outpost of the Roman Empire.[15]

---

13 Denon 1803, 231-32.
14 Denon 1803, 168.
15 For this feature, see Peña 2007, 285 fig. 10.3, 286

Bibliography

Bibliography

The abbreviations of journals
are in accordance with Projekt
Dyabola, Realkatalog des Deutschen
Archäologischen Instituts, Rom.

Adams, C. 2007
*Land Transport in Roman Egypt. A Study
of Economics and Administration in a
Roman Province.* Oxford.

Adan-Bayewitz, D. 1986
B. The Pottery from the Late
Byzantine Building (Stratum 4) and Its
Implications, in: Levine, L.I. & Netzer,
E. et al., *Excavations at Caesarea
Maritima 1975, 1976, 1979 – Final
Report*, QEDEM 21, 90-129.

Allison, P.M. (ed.) 1999
The Archaeology of Household Activities.
London.

Allison, P.M. 2004
*Pompeian Households: An Analysis of
the Material Culture*, Cotsen Institute
of Archaeology Monograph 42. Los
Angeles.

Amedick, R. 1991
*Die antiken Sarkophagreliefs I 4: Die
Sarkophage mit Darstellungen aus dem
Menschenleben. Vita privata.* Berlin.

Αναγνοστωπούλου-Χατζηπολυχρόνη,
E. 2004 [2006]
Σωστική ανασκαφή στην αρχαία
Μένδη, *AErgoMak* 18, 133-140.

André, B. 1973
*Le Paneion d'El-Kanaïs: Les inscriptions
grecques.* Leiden.

Annis M.B. 1988
Modes of Production and the Use
of Space in Potters' Workshops
in Sardinia: A Changing Picture,
*Newsletter Department of Pottery
Technology Leiden* 6, 47-77.

Arafat, K. & Morgan, C. 1989
Pots and potters in Athens and
Corinth: a review, *OxfJA* 8, 311-346.

Archibald, Z.H., Davies, J.K., Gabriel-
sen, V. & Oliver, G.J. (eds.) 2001
Hellenistic Economies. London & New
York.

Archibald, Z.H., Davies, J.K. &
Gabrielsen, V. (eds.) 2005
*Making, Moving and Managing. The
New World of Ancient Economies, 323-
31 BC.* Oxford.

Arnold, D.E. 1985
Ceramic Theory and Cultural Process.
Cambridge.

Arnold, D.E. 2005
Linking Society with the
Compositional Analyses of Pottery:
A Model from Comparative Ethno-
graphy, in: A. Livingstone Smith, D.
Bosquet & R. Martineau (eds.), *Pottery
Manufacturing Processes: Reconstitution
and Interpretation*, BAR International
Series 1349. Oxford, 15-21.

Arnold, P. 1990
The Organization of Refuse Disposal
and Ceramic Production within
Contemporary Mexican Houselots,
American Anthropologist 92, 915-932.

Arnold, P.J. 1991
*Domestic Ceramic Production and
Spatial Organization: a Mexican Case
Study in Ethnoarchaeology.* Cambridge.

Arthur, J.W. 2003
Brewing Beer: Status, Wealth and
Ceramic Use Alteration among the
Gamo of South-Western Ethiopia,
WorldA 34, 516-528.

Arthur, P. 1993
Le città vesuviane: problemi e
prospettive nello studio dell'exologie
umana nell'antichità, in: Franchi
dell'Orto, F. (ed.) *Ercolano 1738-
1988, 250 anni diricerca archeologia*,
Sopreintendenze Archeologica di
Pompei Monografie 6. Roma, 193-199.

Assaad, M. & Garas, N. 1994
*Experiments in Community
Development in a Zabbaleen Settlement*,
Cairo Papers 16.4. Cairo.

Aßkamp, R., Brouwer, M.,
Christiansen, J., Kenzler, H. &
Wamser, L. (eds.) 2007
*Luxus und Dekadenz. Römisches Leben
am Golf von Neapel.* Mainz.

Ault, B.A. 1999
Koprones and Oil Presses at Halieis:
Interactions of Town and Country
and the Integration of Domestic and
Regional Economies, *Hesperia* 68, 549-
573.

Ault, B.A. 2005
*The Excavations at Ancient Halieis II:
The Houses – the Organization and Use
of Domestic Space.* Bloomington &
Indianapolis.

Ault, B.A. & Nevett, L.C. (eds.) 2005
*Ancient Greek Houses and Households:
Chronological, Regional, and Social
Diversity.* Philadelphia.

Бадалъянц, Ю.С. 1970
Родосские амфорные клейма из Нимфея [Rhodian Amphora Stamps from Nymphaion], *VDI* (3), 113-126.

Badoud, N. forthcoming
La cité de Rhodes. De la chronologie à l'histoire.

Bagnall, R.S., Helms, C. & Verhoogt, A.M.F.W. 2000
Documents from Berenike I: Greek Ostraka from the 1996-1998 Seasons, Papyrologica Bruxellensia 31. Brussels.

Bahn, P. 1989
Bluff Your Way in Archaeology. Horsham.

Bailey, D. 2007
Fired clay, Plaster and Miscellaneous *Objects,* in: Peacock & Maxfield, 297-327.

Baillet, J. n.d.
Inscriptions grecques et latines des tombeaux des rois ou syringes à Thèbes. Le Caire.

Balfet, H. 1958
Poterie artisanale en Tunisie, *CahTun* 23-24, 317-347.

Ballet, P. 2003
Dépotoirs culturels, domestiques et "industriels" dans la chôra égyptienne à l'époque romaine, in: Ballet *et al.,* (eds.), 219-230.

Ballet, P., Cordier, P. & Dieudonné-Glad, N. (eds.) 2003
La ville et ses déchets dans le monde romain: rebuts et recyclage. Actes du colloque de Poitiers (19-21 Septembre 2002), Archéologie et histoire romaine 10. Montagnac.

Basch, L. 1987
Le musée imaginaire de la marine antique. Athènes.

Μπαζιωτοπούλου-Βαλαβάνη, Ε. 1994
Ανασκαφές σε αθηναϊκά εργαστήρια αρχαϊκών και κλασικών χρόνων, in: Coulson, W.D.E. *et al.* (eds.), *The Archaeology of Athens and Attica under the Democracy.* Oxford, 45-54.

Beasom, P.T. 2009
Oculi Sunt in Amore Duces: the Use of Mental Image in Latin Love Poetry, Ph.D. Dissertation, University of Cincinnati.

Becatti, G. 1961
Scavi di Ostia 4: Mosaici e pavimenti marmorei. Roma.

Beck, M.A. 2006
Midden Ceramic Assemblage Formation: A Case Study from Kalinga, Philippines, *American Antiquity* 71, 27-51.

Beck, M.E. & Hill, M.E. 2004
Rubbish, Relatives and Residence: The Family Use of Middens, *Journal of Archaeological Method and Theory* 11, 297-333.

Ben Abdalla, Z., Hen Hassen, B., Maurin, L., Van Ysendyck, L. & Zaccaria, C. 1998
L'histoire d'Uthina par les textes, in: Ben Hassen, H. & Maurin, L. (eds.), *OUDNA (UTHINA). La redécouverte d'une ville antique de Tunisie.* Bordeaux, Paris & Tunis, 37-91.

Bentz, M. & Kästner, U. 2007
Vorwort, in: Bentz & Kästner (eds.), 7-9.

Bentz, M. & Kästner, U. (eds.) 2007
Konservieren oder Restaurieren: Die Restaurierung griechischer Vasen von der Antike bis heute, Beihefte zum Corpus Vasorum Antiquorum III. München.

Bergamini, M. 2007 (ed.)
Scoppietto I: Il territorio e I materiali (lucerne, opus doliare, metalli. Borgo S. Lorenzo.

Bergquist, B. 1996
The archaic Greek temenos. A study of structure and function. Lund.

Bernal, D., Sáez, A.M., Montero, R., Díaz, J.J., Sáez, A., Moreno, D. & Toboso. E. 2005
Instalaciones fluvio-marítimas de drenaje con ánforas romanas: a propósito del embarcadero Flavio del caño Sancti Petri (San Fernando, Cádiz), *SPAL Revista de Prehistoria y Arqueologia* 14, 179-230.

Bernard, A. 1972
Le Paneion d'El Kanais: les inscriptions grecques. Leiden.

Berry, J. 1997a
Household Artefacts: Towards a Re-interpretation of Roman Domestic Space, in: Laurence, R. & Wallace-Hadrill, A. (eds.), *Domestic Space in the Roman World: Pompeii and Beyond,* JRA Supplementary Series 22. Portsmouth, 183-195.

Berry, J. 1997b
The Conditions of Domestic Life in Pompeii in A.D. 79: a Case Study of Houses 11 and 12, Insula 9, Regio I, *BSR* 65, 102-125.

Bes, P. 2008
New perspectives on Roman pottery, *EurJA* 11, 267-270.

Бильде, П.Г, Аттема, П., Ланцов, С.Б., Смекалова, Т.Н., Столба, В.Ф., де Хаас, Т., Хандберг, С. & Винтер Якобсен, К. 2007
Джарылгачский исследовательский проект. Результаты сезона 2007 г. [The Džarylgač Survey Project. Results of the 2007 season], in: Гульдагер Бильде, П., Вахтина, М.Ю., Зуев, В.Ю., кашаев, С.В., Соколова, О.Ю. & Хршановский, В.А. (eds.). *Боспорский феномен: Сакральый Стысл Региона, Памятников, Находок* 2007 no. 2. [The Phenomenon of the Bosporan Kingdom: Sacred Meaning of Region, Sites and Objects 2007 no. 2]. Санкт-Петербург, 107-118.

Bilde, P.G., Bøgh, B., Handberg, S., Højte, J.M., Nieling, J., Smekalova, T. & Stolba, V. 2008
Archaeology in the Black Sea Region in Classical Antiquity 1993-2007, *ARepLond* 2007-2008, 115-173.

Bilde, P.G., Højte, J.M. & Stolba, V.F. (eds.) 2003
The Cauldron of Ariantas. Studies presented to A.N. Ščeglov on the Occasion of his 70th Birthday, Black Sea Studies 1. Aarhus.

Binford, L. 1983
In Pursuit of the Past: Decoding the Archaeological Record. New York.

Bingen, J. 1992
Les *architektones* du Mons Claudianus (15-47), in: Bingen *et al.*, 39-55.

Bingen, J. 1997
Lettres privées (279-303), in: Bingen *et al.*, 113-140.

Bingen, J., Bülow Jacobsen, A., Cockle, W.E.H., Cuvigny, H., Kayser, F. & Van Rengen, W. 1997
Mons Claudianus. Ostraca Graeca et Latina 2 (O.Claud. 191 à 416), Documents de fouilles de l'Institut français d'archéologie orientale 32. Cairo.

Bingen, J., Bülow Jacobsen, A., Cockle, W.E.H., Cuvigny, H., Rubinstein, L. & Van Rengen, W. 1992
Mons Claudianus. Ostraca Graeca et Latina 1 (O.Claud. 1 à 190), Documents de fouilles de l'Institut français d'archéologie orientale 29. Cairo.

Bizzarri, M. 1962
La necropoli di Crocifisso del Tufo in Orvieto, *StEtr* 30, 1-154.

Blanchard-Lemée, M., Ennaïfer, M., Slim, H. & Slim, L. 1996
Mosaics of Roman Africa: Floor Mosaics from Tunisia. London.

Blázquez Martínez, J.Ma, García-Gelabert Pérez, Ma P. & López Monteagudo, G. 1991
El transporte marino de ánforas en los mosaicos romanos, in: *Alimenta. Estudios en homenaje al Dr. Michel Ponsich*, Gerión. Anejos 3. Madrid, 323-328.

Blázquez Martínez, J.M. & Remesal Rodríguez, J. (eds.) 1999 *Estudios sobre el Monte Testaccio (Roma)* I, Col·lecció Instrumenta 6. Barcelona.

Blázquez Martínez, J.M. & Remesal Rodríguez, J. (eds.) 2001 *Estudios sobre el Monte Testaccio (Roma)* II, Col·lecció Instrumenta 10. Barcelona.

Blitzer, H. 1984
Traditional Pottery Production in Kentri, Crete: Workshops, Materials, Techniques and Trade, in: Betancourt, P.B. (ed.), East Cretan *White-on-Dark Ware: Studies on a Handmade Pottery of the Early to Middle Minoan Periods*. Philadelphia, 143-157.

Blitzer, H. 1990
ΚΟΡΩΝΕΙΚΑ. Storage-Jar Production and Trade in the Traditional Aegean, *Hesperia* 59, 675-711.

Blue, L. & Da Silva, R. in press
The context and construction of Roman amphora jetties, in: Tzalas, H.E. (ed.), *Tropis 10, 10th international symposium on ship construction in antiquity, Hydra* 2008. Athens.

Boardman, J. 2001
The History of Greek Vases: Potters, Painters, and Pictures. London.

Börker, C. 1978
Der rhodische Kalender, *ZPE* 31, 193-218.

Börker, C. 1998
Teil I. Der Pergamon-komplex, in: Burow, J. & Börker, C., *Die hellenistischen Amphorenstempel aus Pergamon*, Pergamenische Forschungen 11. Berlin, 3-69.

Böttger, B. 1992
Die kaiserzeitlichen und spätantiken Amphoren aus dem Kerameikos, *AM* 107, 315-381.

Boetto, G. 2001
Les navires de Fiumincino, in: Descæudres (ed.), 121-130.

Boggess, E.M. 1970
A Hellenistic Pithos from Corinth, *Hesperia* 39, 73-78.

Bonifay, M. 2004
La Production des Céramiques Sigillées Africaines. Etudes sur la Céramique Romaine Tardive d'Afrique, BAR International Series 1301. Oxford.

Bonifay, M., Mukai, T., Pieri, D. & Treglia, J.-C. 2004
Observations préliminaires sur la céramique de la nécropole de Pupput, in : Ben Abed, A. & Griesheimer, M. (eds.), *La nécropole romaine de Pupput*, Collection de l'École française de Rome 323. Rome, 21-57.

Boulter, C. 1953
Pottery of the Mid-Fifth Century from a Well in the Athenian Agora, *Hesperia* 22, 59-115.

Bounegru, O. 2005-2006
Naves actuariae – Seeschiffe für den Amphorentransport in römischer Zeit? Eine ikonographische und historische Untersuchung, *Skyllis* 7, 136-139.

Bragantini, I. & de Vos, M. 1982
Museo Nazionale Romano. Le Pitture II,1: Le decorazioni della villa romana della Farnesina. Roma.
Brann, E.T.H. 1962
The Athenian Agora VIII: Late Geometric and Protoattic Pottery, Mid 8th to Late 7th Centuries B.C. Princeton.

Breccia, E. 1930
Monuments de l'Égypte gréco-romaine publiés par la Société royale d'archéologie d'Alexandrie sous les auspices de Sa Majesté Fouad Premier Roi d'Égypte II 1: Terrecotte figurate greche e greco-egizie del Museo di Alessandria. Bergame.

Bresson, A. 1986
Remarques sur la dispersion des amphores rhodiennes, in: Empereur & Garlan (eds.), 81-86.

Briant, P. & Descat, R. 1998
Un register douanier de la satrapue d'Égypte à l'époque achéménide, in: Grimal, N. & Menu, B. (eds.), *Le commerce en Égypte ancienne.* Le Caire, 59-104.

Bricault, L., Versluys, M.J. & Meyboom, P.G.P. (eds.) 2007
Nile into Tiber. Egypt in the Roman World. Proceedings of the IIIrd International Conference of Isis studies, Faculty of Archaeology, Leiden University, May 11-14 2005. Leiden & Boston.

Brijder, H.A.G. 1983
Siana Cups I and Komast Cups. Amsterdam.

Broneer, O. 1954
Corinth I, 4: The South Stoa and its Roman Successors. Princeton, N.J.

Bülow-Jacobsen, A. 1992
The private letters (137-171), in: Bingen *et al.*, 123-157.

Bussière, J. 2000
Lampes antiques d'Algérie, Monographies instrumentum 16. Montignac.

Cahill, N. 2002
Household and City Organization at Olynthus. New Haven & London.

Calament, F. 2007
La représentation des amphores dans la petite plastique à l'époque romaine, in: Marchand, S. & Marangou, A. (eds.), *Amphores d'Égypte de la Basse Époque à l'époque arabe*, Cahiers de la céramique égyptienne 8. Le Caire, 737-750.

Camodeca, G. 2006.
Graffito con Conto di Infornata di Sigillata Tardo-Italica da Isola di Migliarino (Pisa), in: Menchelli, S. & Pasquinucci, M. (eds.), *Territorio e Produzioni Ceramiche: Paesaggi, Economica e Società in Età Romana. Atti del Convegno Internazionale Pisa 20-22 Ottobre 2005.* Pisa, 207- 216.

Camp II, J.McK. 1977
The Water Supply of Ancient Athens from 3000-86 B.C., Ph.D. Dissertation, Princeton University.

Camp II, J.McK. 1996
Excavations in the Athenian agora, 1994 and 1995, *Hesperia* 66, 231-261.

Cankardeş Şenol, G. 2001
Metropolis'den hellenistik döneme ait bir grup amphora mühürü, *Olba* 4, 101-115.

Cankardeş Şenol, G., Şenol, A.K. & Doğer, E. 2004
Amphora Production in the Rhodian Peraia in the Hellenistic Period, in: Eiring & Lund (eds.), 353-359.

Carandini, A. & Saguì, L. 1981
Ceramica Africana, Terra sigillata: Vasi. Produzione C, in: *Enciclopedia dell'arte antica classica e orientale, Atlante delle forme ceramiche I: Ceramica fine romana nel bacino mediterraneo (medio e tardo impero)*. Roma, 58-78.

Carandini, A. & Tortorella, S. 1981
Ceramica Africana, Terra sigillata: Vasi. Produzione D, in: *Enciclopedia dell'arte antica classica e orientale, Atlante delle forme ceramiche I: Ceramica fine romana nel bacino mediterraneo (medio e tardo impero)*. Roma, 78-117.

Carlson, D.N. 2003
The Classical Greek Shipwreck at Tektaş Burnu, Turkey, *AJA* 107, 581-600.

Carter, J.C. 2006
Discovering the Greek Countryside at Metaponto. Ann Arbor.

Cerdá, D. 1987
Las anforas de la nave de el Sec, in: Arribas, A., Trias, G., Cerdá, D. & de la Hoz, J., *El Barco de el Sec (Calvià, Mallorca). Estudio de los materials*. Mallorca, 401-499.

Charleston, R.J. 1955
Roman Pottery. London.

Chiaramonte Treré, C., Romanazzi, L. & Volonté, A. M. 1986
Nuovi contribute sulle fortificazioni pompeiane, Quaderne di Acme 6. Milano.

Clarke, J.R. 1998
Looking at Lovemaking: Constructions of Sexuality in Roman Art, 100 B.C.-A.D. 250. Berkeley.

Clarke, J.R. 2003
Art in the Lives of Ordinary Romans. Visual Representation and Non-Elite Viewers in Italy, 100 B.C.-A.D. 315. Berkeley, Los Angeles & London.

Clarke, J.R. 2007
Three Uses of the Pygmy and the Aethiops at Pompeii: Decorating, "Othering", and Warding off Demons, in: Bricault *et al*. (eds.), 155-169.

Cockle, H. 1981
Pottery Manufacture in Roman Egypt: a New Papyrus, *JRS* 71, 87-97.

Cohen, B. 2006
The Colors of Clay: Special Techniques in Athenian Vases. Los Angeles.

Combès, J.L. & Louis, A. 1967
Les potiers de Djerba. Publication du Centre des Arts et Traditions Populaires 1. Tunis.

Connor, P.J. 1996
A leaper, a rivet, and graffiti on a bilingual eye-cup of the early red-figure period, *AA*, 363-370.

Conspectus = Ettlinger, *et al*. 1990.

Cook, R.M. 1997
Greek Painted Pottery, 3rd ed. London & New York.

Corbett, P.E. 1949
Attic Pottery of the Later Fifth Century from the Athenian Agora, *Hesperia* 18, 298-351.

Costaki, L. 2006
The intra muros road system of Ancient Athens, Ph.D. Dissertation, University of Toronto.

Costin, C.L. 2000
The Use of Ethnoarchaeology for the Archaeological Study of Ceramic Production, *Journal of Archaeological Method and Theory* 7, 377-403.

Costin, C. 2008
Thinking About Production: Phenomenological Classification and Lexical Semantics, in: Hruby & Flad (eds.), 143-162.

Crown, P.L. 2001
Learning to Make Pottery in the Prehispanic American Southwest, *Journal of Anthropological Research* 57, 451-469.

Cuomo di Caprio, N. 1971/1972
Proposta di classificazione di fornaci per ceramica e laterizi nell' area italiana, *Sibrium* 11, 371-414.

Cuomo di Caprio, N. 1984
Pottery Kilns on Pinakes from Corinth, in: Brijder, H.A.G. (ed.), *Ancient Greek and Related Pottery: Proceedings of the International Vase Symposium Amsterdam 12-15 April 1984*. Amsterdam, 72-82.

Cuomo di Caprio, N. 1993
Morgantina Studies III: Fornaci e Officine da Vasaio Tardo-Ellenistiche. Princeton, New Jersey.

Cuomo di Caprio, N. 2007
Ceramica in archeologia. Antiche tecniche di lavorazione e moderni metodi di indagine, 2, Nuova edizione ampliata. Roma.

Curtis, R.I. 1991
Garum and Salsamenta. Production and Commerce in Materia Medica. Leiden.

Cuvigny, H. 2005
L'organigramme du personnel d'une carrière impériale d'après un ostracon du Mons Claudianus, *Chiron* 35, 309-353.

Damyanov, M. 2003
On the Local Population around the Greek Colonies in the Black Sea Area (5th-3rd centuries BC), *AncWestEast* 2, 253-264.

D'Andria, F. 1975
Scavi nella zona del Kerameikos (1973), in: Adamesteanu, D., Mertens, D. & D'Andria, F., *Metaponto I, NSc* suppl. Roma, 355-452.

Dark, K.R. 1990
Proto-Industrialisation and the End of the Roman Economy, in: Dark, K.R. (ed.), *External Contacts and the Economy of Late Roman and Post-Roman Britain*. Woodbridge, 1-22.

Dasen, V. 1994
S.v. Pygmaioi, *LIMC* VII. Zürich & München, 594-601.

Daszewski, W.A. 2005
Egypt, Birds and Mosaics, in: Moulier, H., Bailly, C., Janneteau, D. & Tahri, M. (eds.), *La mosaïque gréco-romaine* 9, Collection de l'École française de Rome 252. Rome, 1143-1152.

David, N. & Kramer, C. 2001
Ethnoarchaeology in Action. Cambridge.

Dawdy, S.L. 2006
The Taphonomy of Disaster and the (Re)Formation of New Orleans, *American Anthropologist* 108, 719-730.

Deal, M. 1985
Household pottery disposal in the Maya highlands: An ethnoarchaeological interpretation, *Journal of Anthropological Archaeology* 4, 243-291.

Deal, M. 2008
Abandonment Patterning at Archaeological Sites, in: Sullivan III, A.P. (ed.), *Archaeological Concepts for the Study of the Cultural Past*. Salt Lake City, 141-157.

De Caro, S. 1994
La villa rustica in località Villa Regina a Boscoreale, Pubblicazioni Scientifiche del Centro di Studi della Magna Grecia dell'Università degli Studi di Napoli Federico. Roma.

Degryse, P. & Poblome, J. 2008.
Clays for mass production of table and common wares, amphorae and architectural ceramics at Sagalassos, in: Degryse, P. & Waelkens, M. (eds.), *Sagalassos VI. Geo- and Bioarchaeology at Sagalassos and in its territory.* Leuven, 231-254.

Deneauve, J. 1969.
Lampes de Carthage. Paris.

Denon, V. 1803
Travels in Upper and Lower Egypt I-II. New York.

Desbat, A. & Batigne-Vallet, C. & Bertrand, E. & Bonnet, C. & Gayte, P. & Lenoble, M. 2006
L'atelier de Potiers Antique de la Rue du Chapeau Rouge à Vaise (Lyon 9e). Lyon.

Descædres, J.-P. (ed.) 2001
Ostia: port et porte de la Rome antique. Genéve.

Диатроптов, П.Д. 2006
Керамические клейма [Ceramic Stamps], in: Айбабин, А.И. et al. (eds.), Древнейший теменос Ольвии Понтийской, МАИЭТ Supplement 2 [The Ancient Temenos of Olbia Pontike, MAIET Supplement 2]. Симферополь, 137-146

Dittenberger, W. & Purgold, K. 1896
Olympia. Die Ergebnisse der von dem Deutschen Reich veranstalteten Ausgrabung V. Die Inschriften von Olympia. Berlin.

Dobres, M.A. 2000
Technology and Social Agency: Outlining a Practical Framework for Archaeology. Oxford.

Doğer, E. 1986
Premier remarques sur les amphores de Clazomènes, in: Empereur and Garlan (eds.), 461-471.

Doğer, E. 1991
Les produits agricoles aux environs de Clazomènes dans les sources antiques, in: Malay, H. (ed.), *Erol Atalay Memorial*. Izmir, 47-50.

Doğer, E. 1994
Rodoslu çömlekçi Hieroteles, *Arkeoloji Dergisi* 2, 195-218.

Doğer, E. & Şenol, A.K. 1996
Rhodos peraiası'nda iki yeni amphora atölyesi, *Arkeoloji Dergisi* 4, 59-73.

Dooijes, R. & Nieuwenhuyse, O.P. 2007
Ancient repairs: techniques and social meaning, in Bentz & Kästner (eds.), 15-20.

Doulgéri-Intzessiloglou, A. & Garlan, Y. 1990
Vin et amphores de Péparéthos et d'Ikos, *BCH* 114, 361-389.

Dufaÿ, B., Barat, Y., & Raux, S. 1997
Fabriquer de la vaisselle à l'époque romaine. Yvelines.

Dunand, F. 1979
Religion populaire en Égypte romaine. Les terres cuites isiaques du Musée du Caire, EPRO 67. Leiden.

Dunbabin, K.M.D. 1978
The Mosaics of Roman North Africa. Studies in Iconography and Patronage. Oxford.

Dunbabin, K.M.D. 2003a
The Roman Banquet. Images of Conviviality. Cambridge.

Dunbabin, K.M.D. 2003b
The Waiting Servant in Later Roman Art, *AJPh* 124, 443-467.

Dunbabin, K.M.D. 2004
Problems in the iconography of Roman mime, in: Hugoniot, C., Hurlet, F. & Milanezi, S. (eds.), *Le statut de l'acteur dans l'antiquité grecque et romaine. Actes du colloque qui s'est tenu à Tours les 3 e 4 Mai 2002,* Perspectives historiques 9. Tours, 161-181.

Dupré Raventós, X. & Remolà, J.A. (eds.) 2000
Sordes urbis: la eliminación de residuos en la ciudad romana, Biblioteca Italica 24. Roma.

Dzierzbicka, D. 2005
Wineries and their elements in Graeco-Roman Egypt, *Journal of Juristic Papyri* 35, 9-91.

Eilmann, R. 1944
Die Badeanlage am Kladeos. Die Zeitbestimmung, in: Kunze & Schleif (eds.), 70-104.

Eiring, J. & Lund, J. (eds.) 2004
Transport Amphorae and Trade in the Eastern Mediterranean, Acts of the International Colloquium at the Danish Institute at Athens, September 26-29, 2002, Monographs of the Danish Institute at Athens 5. Athens.

Eiseman, C.J. & Ridgway, B.S. 1987
The Porticello Shipwreck: A Mediterranean Merchant Vessel of 415-385 B.C. College Station.

El-Ashmawi, F. 1998
Pottery Kiln and Wine-factory at Burg el-Arab, in: Empereur, J.-Y. (ed.), *Commerce et artisanat dans l'Alexandrie hellénistique et romaine: Actes du Colloque d'Athènes 11-12 décembre 1988,* BCH Supplement 33. Athènes & Paris, 55-64.

Ellis, S.J.R. 2005
The Pompeian Bar and the City: Defining Food and Drink Outlets and Identifying their Place in an Urban Environment, Ph.D. Dissertation, The University of Sydney.

Elston, M. 1990
Ancient Repairs of Greek Vases in the J. Paul Getty Museum, *GettyMusJ* 18, 53-68.

Empereur, J.-Y. 1988.
Producteurs d'amphores dans les ateliers de Reşadiye (péninsule de Datça), *Araştırma Sonuçları Toplantısı* 6, 159-163.

Empereur, J.-Y. & Garlan, Y. (eds.) 1986
Recherches sur les amphores grecques, Actes du colloque international organisé par le centre national de la recherche scientifique, l'Université de Rennes II et l'École française d'Athènes (Athènes, 10-12 Septembre 1984), BCH Supplément 13. Athènes & Paris.

Empereur, J.-Y., Hesse, A. & Tuna, N. 1999
Les ateliers d'amphores de Datça, péninsule de Cnide, in: Garlan, Y. (ed.), *Production et commerce des amphores anciennes en Mer Noire. Colloque international organisé à Istanbul, 25-28 mai 1994.* Aix-en-Provence, 105-115.

Empereur, J.-Y. & Picon, M. 1986a
Des ateliers d'amphores à Paros et à Naxos, *BCH* 110, 495-510.

Empereur, J.-Y. & Picon, M. 1986b
À la recherche des fours d'amphores, in: Empereur & Garlan (eds.), 103-126.

Empereur, J.Y. & Picon, M. 1992
La reconnaissance des productions des ateliers céramiques: l'exemple de la Maréotide, *Cahiers de la céramique égyptienne* 3, 145-152.

Empereur, J.-Y. & Tuna, N. 1988
Zenon et l'epave de Serçe Limanı, BCH 112, 341-357.

Ennaïfer, M. 1976
La cité d'Althiburos et l'édifice des Asclepieia. Tunis.

Ersoy, Y. 2003
Pottery production and mechanism of workshops in Archaic Clazomenae, in: Schmalz, B. & Söldner, M. (eds.), *Griechische Keramik in kulturellen Kontext*. Münster, 254-257.

Ettlinger, E., Hedinger, B., Hoffmann, B., Kenrick, Ph.M., Pucci, G., Roth-Rubi, K. Schneider, G., von Schnurbein, S., Wells, C.M. & Zabehlicky-Scheffenegger, S. 1990
Conspectus formarum terrae sigillatae italico modo confectae, Materialen zur Römisch-Germanischen Keramik 10. Bonn.

Evely, D. 1988
Minoan Craftsmen: Problems of Recognition and Definition, in: French & Wardle (eds.), 397-415.

Φιλήμονος-Τσοποτού, Μ. 2004
Ρόδος Ι: Η ελληνιστική οχύρωση της Ρόδου. Αθήνα.

Finkielsztejn, G. 2001
Chronologie détaillée et révisée des eponyms amphoriques rhodiens, de 270 à 108 av. J.-C. environ: Premier bilan, BAR International Series 990. Oxford.

Finkielsztejn, G. 2002
Du bon usage des Amphorae hellénistiques en contextes archéologiques, in: Blondé, F., Ballet, P. & Salles, J.-F. (eds.) *Céramiques hellénistiques et romaines. Productions et diffusion en Méditerranée orientale (Chypre, Égypte et côte syro-palestinienne)*, Travaux de la Maison de l'Orient Méditerranéen 35. Lyon, 227-233.

Finkielsztejn, G. 2006
Production et commerce des amphores hellénistiques: recipients, timbrage et métrologie, in: Descat, R. (ed.), *Approches de l'économie hellénistique*, Entretiens d'archéologie et d'histoire 7. Saint-Bertrand-de-Comminges, 17-34.

Fischer, J. 1994
Griechisch-römische Terrakotten aus Ägypten. Die Sammlungen Sieglin und Schreiber. Dresden, Leipzig, Stuttgart, Tübingen, Tübingen Studien zur Archäologie und Kunstgeschichte 14. Tübingen.

Fjeldhagen, M. 1995
Graeco-Roman Terracottas from Egypt. Copenhagen.

Floriani Squarciapino, M. 1956-1958 [1959]
Piccolo corpus dei mattoni scolpiti ostiensi, *BullCom* 76, 183-204.

Fokaefs, A. & Papadopoulos, G. 2004
Tsunamis in the area of Cyprus and the Levantine Sea, European Geosciences Union 6.

Francis, E.D. & Vickers, M. 1988
The Agora Revisited: Athenian Chronology c. 500-450 B.C., *BSA* 83, 143-167.

Frankel, D. & Webb, J.M. 2001
Population, Households, and Ceramic Consumption in a Prehistoric Cypriot Village, *JFieldA* 28, 115-129.

Fraser, P.M. & E. Matthews (eds.) 1997
A Lexicon of Greek Personal Names IIIA: The Peloponnese, Western Greece, Sicily and Magna Graecia. Oxford.

Freed, J. 2008
Review of Peña 2007, *AJA* 112, 368-369.

Frel, J. 1973
Panathenäische Preisamphoren. Berlin.

French, E.B. & Wardle, K.A. (eds.) 1988
Problems in Greek Prehistory. Papers Presented at the Centenary Conference of the British School of Archaeology at Athens, Manchester April 1986. Bristol.

Frey, D. 1982
Shipwrecks, Surveys, and Turkish Sponge Divers, *INA Quarterly 9(1)*, 1-5.

Friedman, Z. 2005-2006
Sea-Trade as Reflected in Mosaics, *Skyllis* 7, 126-134.

Fröhlich, T. 1991
Lararien- und Fassadenbilder in den Vesuvstädten. Untersuchungen zur volkstümlichen pompejanischen Malerei, Mitteilungen des Deutschen Archäologischen Instituts. Römische Abteilung. Ergänzungshefte. Mainz am Rhein.

Fülle, G. 1997
The Internal Organization of the Arretine Terra Sigillata Industry: Problems of Evidence and Interpretation, *JRS* 87, 111-155.

Fulford, M. & Peacock, D.P.S. 1984
Excavations at Carthage: the British Mission, vol. I.2: The Avenue du Président Habib Bourguiba, Salammbô: the Pottery and Other Ceramic Objects from the Site. Sheffield.

Furtwängler, A. & Reichhold, K. 1904
Griechische Vasenmalerei 1. München.

Galli, G., 1993
Ponza, il relitto della "Secca dei mattoni", *ASubacq* 1, 117-129.

Gallimore, S. forthcoming
Amphora production in the Roman world: a view from the papyri.

Garlan, Y. 1999
Les timbres amphoriques de Thasos. 1 Timbres protothasiens et thasiens anciens, Études thasiennes 18. Athènes & Paris.

Garlan, Y. 2000
Amphores et timbres amphoriques grecs. Entre erudition et idéologie. Paris.

Garlan, Y. 2004
Les timbres ceramiques sinopeens sur amphores et sur tuiles trouves a Sinope. Presentation et catalogue. Istanbul.

Garlan, Y. 2004[2006]a
Η ανάγνωση των σφαγίσματων αμφορέων 'με τρόχο' απο την Άκανθο, *AErgoMak* 18, 181-190.

Garlan, Y. 2004[2006]b
Η προέλευση της 'ομάδας Παρμενίσκου' από τη Μένδη, *AErgoMak* 18, 141-148.

Garlan, Y. 2004-2005
En visitant et revisitant les ateliers amphoriques de Thasos, *BCH* 128-129, 269-329.

Garlan, Y. 2006
Interprétation des timbres amphoriques 'à la roue' d'Akanthos, *BCH* 130, 263-291.

Garlan, Y. & Empereur, J.-Y. 1992
Bulletin Archéologique: amphores et timbres amphoriques (1987-1991), *REG* 105, 176-220.

Gibbins, D. 2001
Shipwrecks and Hellenistic trade, in Archibald *et al.* (eds.), 273-312.

Gibson, D. & Lucas, G. 2002
Pre-Flavian Kilns at Greenhouse Farm and the Social Context of Early Roman Pottery Production in Cambridgeshire, *Britannia* 33, 95-127.

Gosden, C. & Marshall, Y. 1999
The cultural biography of objects, *WorldA* 31(2), 169-179.

Gould, R.A. & Watson, P.J. 1982
A Dialogue on the Meaning and Use of Analogy in Ethnoarchaeological Reasoning, *Journal of Anthropological Archaeology* 1, 355-381.

Grace, V.R. 1953
Wine Jars, in: Boulter, C., Pottery from the Mid-Fifth Century From a Well in the Athenian Agora, *Hesperia* 22, 101-110.

Grace, V.R. 1971
Samian Amphorae, *Hesperia* 40, 52-95.

Grace, V.R. 1979
Amphorae and the Ancient Wine Trade, Agora Picture Book 6, rev. ed. Princeton.

Grace, V.R. 1985
The Middle Stoa Dated by Amphora Stamps, *Hesperia* 54, 1-54.

Grahame, M. 1997
Public and Private in the Roman House: The Social Order of the Casa del Fauno, in: Laurence, R. & Wallace-Hadrill, A. (eds.), *Domestic Space in the Roman World: Pompeii and Beyond*, JRA Supplementary Series 22. Portsmouth, RI, 137-164.

Grandjean, Y. 1992.
Contribution à l'etablisement d'une typologie des amphores thasiennes, le material amphorique du quartier de la porte du Silene, *BCH* 116, 541-584.

Greene, K. 2008
Learning to consume: consumption and consumerism in the Roman Empire, *JRA* 21, 64-82.

Griffiths, J.G. 1975
Apuleius of Madauros. The Isis-Book (Metamorphoses, Book XI), EPRO 39. Leiden.

Guidobaldi, F., Pavolini, C. & Pergola, P. (eds.) 1998
I materiali residui nello scavo archeologico. Teste preliminari e Atti della Tavola rotunda organizzate dall'École française de Rome e dalla Sezione romana "Nino Lamboglia" dell'Istituto internazionale di studi liguri, in collaborazione con la Soprintendenza archeologica di Roma e la Escuela española de historia y arquelogia (Roma, 16 marzo 1996), Collection de l'École Française de Rome 249. Roma.

Gumerman, G. 1997
Food and Complex Societies, *Journal of Archaeological Method and Theory* 4, 105-139.

Hampe, R., & Winter, A. 1962
Bei Töpfern und Töpferinnen in Kreta, Messenien und Zypern. Mainz.

Hampe, R. & Winter, A. 1965
Bei Töpfern und Zieglern in Süditalien, Sizilien und Griechenland. Mainz.

Hannestad 2005
'How much came from where':
the proportion of local, regional
and 'long-distance' pottery from
rural settlement in the Crimea, in:
Archibald *et al.* (eds.), 165-187.

Hannestad, L., Stolba, V.F. & Ščeglov,
A.N. (eds.) 2002
*Panskoye I. Vol. 1. The Monumental
Building U6.* Aarhus.

Hansson, M. & Foley, B. 2008
Ancient DNA Fragments inside
Classical Greek Amphorae Reveal
Cargo of 2400-year-old Shipwreck,
JASc 35, 1169-1176.

Harrell, J. & Lewan, M.D. 2002
Sources of Mummy Bitumen in
Ancient Egypt and Palestine,
Archaeometry 44, 285-293.

Hasaki, E. 2002
*Ceramic Kilns in Ancient Greece:
Pyrotechnology and Organization of
Ceramic Workshops,* Ph.D. Dissertation,
University of Cincinnati.

Hasaki, E. 2004
*Replication of an Ancient Kiln Tucson
AIA Chapter. University of Arizona
Department of Classics Website,* http://
www.classics.web.arizona.edu/hasaki,
accessed 11 June 2009.

Hasaki, E. 2005
The Ethnoarchaeological Project of
the Potters' Quarter at Moknine,
Tunisia. Seasons 2000, 2002, in:
Kallala, N. (ed.), *Africa, Nouvelle Série
des Séances Scientifiques* III. Tunis,
137–180.

Hasaki, E. 2006
Ancient Greek Ceramic Kilns and
their Contribution to the Technology
and Organization of the Potters'
Workshops, in: Tasios, P. (ed.),
*Proceedings of the Second International
Conference on the Ancient Greek
Technology.* Athens, 221-227.

Hasaki, E. 2010
A Stratigraphy of Meanings:
Integrating Antiquities into Daily Life
at Paroikia, Paros, in: Stroulia, A. &
Sutton, S.B. (eds.), *Archaeology in Situ:
Sites, Archaeology, and Communities.*
Lexington, 373-396.

Hasaki, E. in preparation
Crafting Pottery Workshop Spaces at
Moknine, Tunisia, *Leiden Journal of
Pottery Studies.*

Hasaki, E. forthcoming
*The Penteskouphia Plaques from
Ancient Corinth and their Imagery of
Potters at Work,* Hesperia Supplement.
Princeton, New Jersey.

Hasaki, E. & Nell, E. 2004
Ethnoarchaeology and Spatial
Analysis of a Potters' Quarter at
Moknine, Tunisia, *Archaeological
Computing Newsletter* 61, 7–15.

Χατζηδημητρίου, Α. 2005
*Παραστάσεις εργαστηρίων και
εμπορίου στην εικονογραφία των
κλασικών χρόνων.* Αθήνα.

Hayden, B. & Cannon, A. 1983
Where the Garbage Goes: Refuse
Disposal in the Maya Highlands,
Journal of Anthropological Archaeology
2, 117-163.

Hayes, J.W. 1973
Roman Pottery from the South Stoa at
Corinth, *Hesperia* 42, 416-470.

Hayes, J.W. 1983
The Villa Dionysos Excavations,
Knossos: The Pottery, *BSA* 78, 97-169.

Hayes, J.W. 1985
Sigillate orientali, in: *Enciclopedia
dell'arte antica classica e orientale,
Atlante della forme ceramiche II:
Ceramica fine romana nel bacino
mediterraneo (tardo ellenismo e primo
impero).* Roma, 1-96.

Hayes, J.W. 2008
*The Athenian Agora XXXII: Roman
Pottery: Fine-Ware Imports.* Princeton,
New Jersey.

Hemelrijk, J.M. 1991
A Closer Look at the Potter, in:
Rasmussen & Spivey (eds.), 233-256.

Helbig Fürer = Helbig, W. 1963-1972
Fürer durch die öffentlichen
Sammlungen klassischer Altertümer
in Rom, l-lV. Tübingen.

Henrickson, R.C. 2005
The Local Potter's Craft at Phrygian
Gordion, in: Kealhofer, L. (ed.), *The
Archaeology of Midas and the Phrygians.
Recent Work at Gordion.* Philadelphia,
124-135.

Hildebrand, J.A. & Hagstrum, M.B.
1999
New Approaches to Ceramic Use
and Discard: Cooking Pottery
from the Peruvian Andes in
Ethnoarchaeological Perspective, *Latin
American Antiquity* 10, 25-46.

Hilton, M.R. 2003
Quantifying Postdepositional Redistribution of the Archaeological Record Produced by Freeze-Thaw and Other Mechanisms: An Experimental Approach, *Journal of Archaeological Method and Theory* 10, 165-202.

Höckmann, O. 1994
Bemerkungen zur caudicaria/codicaria, *AKorrBl* 24, 425-439.

Hope, C. 1977
Excavations at Malkata and the Birket Habu, 1971-1974. Jar sealings and amphorae of the 18th dynasty: a technological study, Egyptology Today 2.5. Warminster.

Horden, P. & Purcell, N. 2000
The Corrupting Sea: A Study of Mediterranean History. Oxford.

Hornig, K. 2005-2006
Zu Amphoren aus Unterwasser-Fundkontexten – Entwurf einen Funddatenblattes, *Skyllis* 7, 116-123.

Hruby, Z.X. & Flad, R.K. (eds.) 2008
Rethinking Craft Specialization in Complex Societies: Archaeological Analyses of the Social Meaning of Production, Papers of the American Anthropological Association. Berkeley.

Humphrey, J.H. (ed.) 2009
Studies on Roman Pottery of the Provinces of Africa Proconsularis and Byzacena (Tunisia): homage à Michael Bonifay, JRA Supplementary Series 76. Portsmouth.

Hurwit, J.M. 1989
The Kritios Boy: Discovery, Reconstruction and Date, *AJA* 93, 41-80.

Hurwit, J.M. 1999
The Athenian Acropolis. History, Mythology, and Archaeology from the Neolithic Era to the Present. Cambridge.

Hutson, S.R. & Stanton, T.W. 2007
Cultural Logic and Practical Reason: the Structure of Discard in Ancient Maya Households, *CambrAJ* 17, 123-144.

Ibrahim, L., Scranton, R. & Brill, R. 1976
Kenchreai, Eastern Port of Corinth 2: The Panels of Opus Sectile in Glass. Leiden.

Immerwahr, S.A. 1971
The Athenian Agora XIII: The Neolithic and Bronze Ages. Princeton, New Jersey.

Ionas, I. 2000
Traditional Pottery and Potters in Cyprus. The Disappearance of an Ancient Craft Industry in the 19th and 20th Centuries, Birmingham Byzantine and Ottoman Monographs 6. Aldershot, Burlington USA, Singapore & Sydney.

Jackson, M. & Greene, K. 2008
Review of Peña 2007, *Antiquity* 82, 517-518.

Januševič, Z.V. & Ščeglov, A.N. 2002
Palaeoethnobotanical Material, in: Hannestad et al. (eds.), 327-331.

Jöhrens, G. 2004
Amphorenstempel aus Didyma, in: Wintermeyer, U., *Didyma III.2: Die hellenistische und frühkaiserzeitliche Gebrauchskeramik.* Mainz am Rhein, 153-169.

Johnston, A.W. 1985
A Greek Graffito from Arezzo, *OxfJA* 4, 119-124.

Καλτσάς, Ν. 1998
Άκανθος I: Η ανασκαφή στο νεκροταφείο κατά το 1979. Αθήνα.

Kamp, K. 1991
Waste disposal in a Syrian village, in: Staski, E. & Sutro, L. (eds.), *The Ethnoarchaeology of Refuse Disposal,* Arizona State University Anthropological Research Papers 42. Tempe, 23-31.

Kampen, N. 1981
Image and Status: Roman Working Women in Ostia. Berlin.

Καντζιά, Χ. 1994
Ένα κεραμικό εργαστήριο αμφορέων του πρώτου μισού του 4ου αι. π.Χ., in: *Γ' Επιστημονική συνάντηση για την ελληνιστική κεραμική 1991.* Αθήνα, 323-354.

Kardulias P.N. 2000
The 'Traditional' Craftsman as Entrepreneur: A Potter in Ermioni, in: Sutton, S.B. (ed.), *Contingent Countryside: Settlement, Economy, and Land Use in the Southern Argolid since 1700.* Stanford, 275-289.

Kassab Tezgör, D. 1996
Fouilles des ateliers d'amphores à Demirci près de Sinop en 1994 et 1995, *AnatAnt* 4, 335-354.

Kassab Tezgör, D. & Tatlıcan, I. 1998
Fouilles des ateliers d'amphores à Demirci près de Sinop en 1996 et 1997, *AnatAnt* 6, 423-442.

Katzev, S.W. 2005
Resurrecting an Ancient Greek Ship: Kyrenia, Cyprus, in: Bass, G.F. (ed.), *Beneath the Seven Seas: Adventures with the Institute of Nautical Archaeology.* London, 72-79.

Kehrberg, I. 1992
Flaked Glass and Pottery Sherd Tools of the Late Roman and Byzantine Periods from the Hippodrome at Jerash, *Syria* 69, 451-464.

Kent, S. 1984
Analyzing Activity Areas: An Ethnoarchaeological Study of the Use of Space. Albuquerque.

Kent, S. 1999
The Archaeological Visibility of Storage: Delineating Storage from Trash Areas, *American Antiquity* 64, 79-94.

Knigge, U. 1976
Kerameikos. Ergebnisse der Ausgrabungen 9: Der Südhügel. Berlin.

Knigge, U. 1991
The Athenian Kerameikos: History – Monuments – Excavations. Athens.

Koehler, C. 1986
Handling of Greek Transport Amphorae, in: Empereur & Garlan (eds.), 49-67.

Kolb, C. 2007
Archaeological Ceramics, *Society for Archaeological Sciences Bulletin* 30.3, 15-16.

Κουράγιος, Γ. & Λετοράτου, Σ. 2002
Πάρος. Νέα σημαντικά ευρήματα, *Corpus* 43, 66-79.

Кравченко, Е.А. 2005
Поселения Кизил-Кобинской культуры Гераклейского полуострова VI–IV вв. До н. э. [Settlements of the Kizil-Koba Culture on the Herakleian Peninsula in the 6th-4th c. BC.], in: Зубарь, В.М. et al. (eds.), *Херсонес Таврический в третьей четверти VI – середине I вв. До. Н. Э. Очерки истории и културы. [Tauric Chersonesos in the 3rd quarter of the 6th c. BC – Early 1st c. BC. Essays, Histories and Cultures].* Киев, 547-553.

Kramer, C. 1997
Pottery in Rajasthan: Ethnoarchaeology in Two Indian Cities. Washington, D.C. & London.

Kroll, E.M. & Price, T.D. 1991 (eds.)
The Interpretation of Archaeological Spatial Patterning. New York.

Kruit, N. 1992
The Meaning of Various Words Related to Wine, *ZPE* 90, 265-276.

Kruit, N. & Worp, K.A. 2000
Geographical Jar Names. Towards a Multi-Disciplinary Approach, *ArchPF* 46, 65-146.

Kunze, E. & Schleif, H. 1941
Die Südhalle, in: Kunze, E. & Schleif, H. (eds.), *III. Bericht über die Ausgrabungen in Olympia. Winter 1938/39.* Berlin, 30-37.

Kunze, E. & Schleif, H. (eds.) 1944
IV. Bericht über die Ausgrabungen in Olympia. 1940 und 1941. Berlin.

Κυριαζόπουλος, Β. 1984
Ελληνικά παραδοσιακά κεραμικά. Αθήνα.

Kyrieleis, H. 1994
Die Ausgrabungen 1962 bis 1966, in: Kunze, E., Kunze-Götte, E. & Mallwitz, A. (eds.), *IX. Bericht über die Ausgrabungen in Olympia.* Berlin-New York, 1-26.

Кутайсов, В.А. 2004
Керкинитида в античную эпоху [Kerkinitis in the Ancient period]. Киев.

LaMotta, V.M. & Schiffer, M.B. 1999
Formation Processes of House Floor Assemblages, in: Allison (ed.), 19-29.

Lang, F. 2002
Housing and Settlement in Archaic Greece, *Pallas* 58, 13-32.

Langner, M. 2002
Szenen aus Handwerk und Handel auf gallo-römischen Grabmälern, *JdI* 116, 299-356.

Laurence R. 1995
The organization of space in Pompeii, in: Cornell, T.J. & Lomas, K. (eds), *Urban Society in Roman Italy.* London, 63-78.

Lawall, M.L. 1995
Transport Amphorae and trademarks: Imports to Athens and economic diversity in the 5th c. BC, Ph.D. Dissertation University of Michigan, Ann Arbor.

Lawall, M.L. 1999
Studies in Hellenistic Ilion: The Lower City. The Transport Amphorae, *StTroica* 9, 187-224.

Lawall, M.L. 2002
Early Excavations at Pergamon and the Chronology of Rhodian Amphora Stamps, *Hesperia* 71, 294-324.

Lawall, M.L. 2002[2003]
Ilion before Alexander: Amphorae and Economic Archaeology, *StTroica* 12, 197-243.

Lawall, M.L. 2004a
Archaeological Context and Aegean Amphora Chronologies: A Case Study of Hellenistic Ephesos, in: Eiring & Lund (eds.), 171-188.

Lawall, M.L. 2004b
Amphorae Without Stamps: Chronologies and Typologies from the Athenian Agora, in: *ΣΤ' Επιστημονική συνάντηση για την ελληνιστική κεραμική*. Αθήνα, 445-454.

Lawall, M.L. 2005
Amphorae and Hellenistic Economies: Addressing the (Over)Emphasis on Stamped Amphora Handles, in: Archibald *et al.* (eds.), 188-232.

Lawall, M.L. 2006
Amphorae and Economic History, in: Scherrer, P., Trinkl, E., Fabrizii-Reuer, S. et al., *Die Tetragonos Agora in Ephesos*, Forschungen in Ephesos XIII.2. Wien, 253-255.

Lawall, M.L. in press a
Socio-Economic Conditions and the Contents of Amphorae, *Paper delivered at the Second International Roundtable: Production and Trade of Amphorae in the Black Sea, Bulgaria, Sept. 26-Oct. 1 2007.*

Lawall, M.L. in press b
Early Hellenistic Amphorae from two closed contexts: Kerynia shipwreck and Ephesos well LB, in: *Z' Επιστημονική συνάντηση για την ελληνιστική κεραμική, Αίγιο.* Αθήνα.

Lawall, M.L. (with a contribution by Jawando, A.) 2002
Notes from the Tins 2: Research in the Stoa of Attalos, Summer 2000: Amphorae as Paint Pots?, *Hesperia* 71, 416-419.

Lawall, M.L., Lejpunskaja, N.A., Diatroptov, P. & Samojlova, T.L. 2010
Transport amphoras, in: Lejpunskaja, N.A., Bilde, P.G., Højte, J.M. Krapivina, V.V. & Kryžickij, S.D. (eds.), The Lower City of Olbia (Sector NGS) in the 6th century BC to the 4th century AD, Black Sea Studies 13. Aarhus, 355-405.

Lazarides, D. 1971
Thasos and its peraia, Ancient Greek Cities 5. Athens.

Леви, Е.И. 1964
Керамический комплекс III-II вв. до н.э. из раскопок ольвийской агоры [A Pottery Complex of the 3rd-2nd Centuries BC from Excavations of the Agora of Olbia], in : Гайдукевич, В.Ф. (ed.), *Ольвия. Теменос и Агора [Olbia. Temenos and Agora].*Москва-Ленинград, 225-280.

Leeuw, S.E. van der, 1976
Studies in the Technology of Ancient Pottery, Ph.D. Dissertation, Universiteit van Amsterdam.

Leeuw, S.E. van der 1977
Towards a Study of the Economics of Pottery Making, in: Beek, B.L. van, Brandt, R.W. & Groenman-van Waateringe, W. (eds.), *Ex Horreo: IPP 1951-1976.* Amsterdam, 68-76.

Lemonnier, P. (ed.) 1993
Technological Choices: Transformation in Material Cultures since the Neolithic. London.

Le Ny, F. 1988
Les fours de tuiliers gallo-romains. Méthodologie. Etude technologique, typologique et statistique. Chronologie, Documents d'archéologie française 12. Paris.

Lindenlauf, A. 1997
Der Perserschutt der Athener Akropolis, in: Hoepfner, W. (ed.), *Kult und Kultbauten auf der Akropolis.* Berlin, 46-115.

Lichocka, B. & Meyza, H. 2001
Seismic Events and the Evidence of Coins and Pottery. The Case of Destruction of the House of Aion in Paphos, *EtTrav* 19, 145-208.

Λιλιμβάκη, M. & Ακαμάτης, N. [2008] in press
Ένα νέο εργαστήριο κεραμικής στην Πέλλα, *AErgoMak 22.*

Lisse, P., & Louis, A. 1956
Les potiers de Nabeul: étude de sociologie tunisienne. Tunis.

Loebert, H.W. 1984
Types of Potter's Wheels and the Spread of the Spindle Wheel in Germany, in: van der Leeuw, S.E. & Pritchard, A.C. (eds.), *The Many Dimensions of Pottery: Ceramics in Archaeology and Anthropology.* Amsterdam, 203-230.

London, G., Egoumenidou, F. & Karageorghis, V. 1990
Traditional Pottery in Cyprus. Mainz.

London, G. 2000
Continuity and Change in Cypriot Pottery Production, *Near Eastern Archaeology* 63, 102-110.

López Monteagudo, G. 2001-2002
¿Ánforas hispánicas en un mosaico de Herculano? *AnMurcia* 16-17, 375-382.

López Varela, S.L., McAnany, P.A. & Berry, K.A. 2001
Ceramics Technology at Late Classic K'axob, Belize, *JFieldA* 28, 177-191.

López Varela, S.L., van Gijn, A. & Jacobs, L. 2002
De-mystifying Pottery Production in the Maya Lowlands: Detection of Traces of Use-Wear on Pottery Sherds through Microscopic Analysis and Experimental Replication, *JASc* 29, 1133–1147.

Lund, J. 1999
Rhodian amphorae in Rhodes and Alexandria as Evidence of Trade, in: Gabrielsen, V., Bilde, P., Engberg-Pedersen, T., Hannestad, L. & Zahle, J. (eds.), *Hellenistic Rhodes: Politics, Culture, and Society,* Studies in Hellenistic Civilization 9. Aarhus, 187-204.

Lund, J. 2007
Transport amphorae as a possible source for the land use and economic history of the Akamas Peninsula, Western Cyprus. In: Bonifay, M. & Tréglia, J.-C. (eds.), *LRCW 2: Late Roman Coarse Wares, Cooking Wares and Amphorae in the Mediterranean. Archaeology and Archaeometry,* BAR International Series 1662 (II). Oxford, 781-789.

Lund, J. in press a
Rhodian transport amphorae as a source for economic (ebbs and) flows in the Eastern Mediterranean in the 2nd century BC, in: Archibald, Z.H., Davies, J.K. & Gabrielsen, V. (eds.), *The Economies of Hellenistic Societies, Third to First Centuries BC.* Oxford.

Lund, J. in press b
North African lamps showing a woman with a transport amphora.

Lynch, K.M. 1999
Pottery from an Athenian House in Context, Ph.D. Dissertation, University of Virginia.

Lynch, K.M. forthcoming
The Symposium in Context: Pottery from a Late Archaic House Near the Athenian Agora, Hesperia Supplement 46. Princeton, New Jersey.

Mackensen, M. (with a contribution by Storz, S.) 1993
Die Spätantiken Sigillata- und Lampentöpfereien von El Mahrine (Nordtunesien): Studien zur nordafrikanischen Feinkeramik des 4. Bis 7. Jahrhunderts, Münchner Beiträge zur Vor- und Frühgeschichte 50. München.

Mackensen, M. & Schneider, G. 2002
Production centers of African red slip ware (3rd-7th c.) in northern and central Tunisia: archaeological provenance and reference groups based on chemical analysis, *JRA* 15, 121-158.

Maiuri, A. 1924
Una fabbrica di anfore Rodie, *ASAtene* 4–5, 1921–1922 [1924], 249–269.

Maiuri, A. 2002
L'ultima fase edilizia di Pompei, Reprint. Napoli.

Malfitana, D., Poblome, J. & Lund, J. (eds.) 2006
Old Pottery in a New Century. Innovating perspectives in Roman pottery studies, Monografie dell'Istituto per I Beni Archeologici e Monumentali-CNR 1. Catania.

Mallwitz, A. 1958
Das Gebiet südlich der Bäder am Kladeos. Der Baubefund, in: Kunze, E. (ed.), *VI. Bericht über die Ausgrabungen in Olympia. Winter 1953/1954 und 1954/1955.* Berlin, 12-41.

Marchand, S. & Marangou, A. (eds.) 2007
Amphores d' Égypte de la Basse Époque à l'époque arabe, Cahiers de la céramique égyptienne 8. Le Caire.

Marichal, R. 1988
Les Graffites de la Graufesenque. Paris.

Marlière, É. 2002
L'outre et le tonneau dans l'Occident romain, Monographies instrumentum 22. Montegnac.

Marsh, G. 1981
London's Samian Supply and its Relationship to the Development of the Gallic Samian Industry, in: Anderson, A.C. & Anderson, A.S. (eds.), *Roman Pottery Research in Britain and North-West Europe: Papers Presented to Graham Webster,* BAR International Series 123. Oxford, 173-238.

Martin, A. 2000
Amphorae at Olympia, *ReiCretActa* 36, 427-433.

Martin-Kilcher, S. (with a contribution from Schaub, M.) 1994
Die römischen Amphoren aus Augst und Kaiseraugst. Ein Beitrag zur römischen Handels- und Kulturgeschichte 2: Die Amphoren für Wein, Fischsauce, Südfrüchte (Gruppen 2-24) und Gesamtauswertung, Forschungen in Augst 7. Augst.

Марченко, И.Д. 1967
Местная расписная керамика Пантикапея VI-V вв. до н. э. (Local Painted Pottery of Pantikapaion in the 6th – 5th Century BC), *SovA* 1967.2, 146-154.

Mathieu, J. (ed.) 2002
Experimental Archaeology: Replicating Past Objects, Behaviors, and Processes, BAR International Series 1035. Oxford.

Matson, F.R. 1972
Ceramic Studies, in: McDonald, W.A. & Rapp, Jr., G.R. (eds.), *The Minnesota Messenia Expedition: Reconstructing a Bronze Age Regional Environment.* Minneapolis, 200-224.

Maxfield, V.A. & Bingen, J. 2001
The southern sebakh, in: Maxfield & Peacock 2001a, 89-125.

Maxfield, V.A. & Peacock, D.P.S. 2001a
Survey and excavations Mons Claudianus 1987-1993 II: Excavations Part 1, Institut français d'archéologie orientale, Fouilles de l'IFAO 43. Le Caire.

Maxfield, V.A. & Peacock, D.P.S. 2001b
The Roman Imperial quarries. Survey and excavation at Mons Porphyrites 1994–1998. 1: topography and quarries, Egyptian Exploration Society Sixty-Seventh Excavation Memoir. London.

Maxfield, V.A. & Peacock, D.P.S. (eds.) 2006
Survey and Excavation Mons Claudianus 1987–1993 III: Ceramic Vessels & Related Objects, Institut français d'archéologie orientale, Fouilles de l'IFAO 54. Le Caire.

Mayerson, P. 1997
A Note on κούφα 'Empties', *Bulletin of the American Society of Papyrologists* 34, 47-52.

Mayerson, P. 2000a
A Note on P. Col. X 280.14: κενώματα μέτρῳ οἰνικῷ κοτυλῶν δεκαεννέα, *ZPE* 132, 255-256.

Mayerson, P. 2000b
The Meaning and Function of ΛΗΝΟϹ and Related Features in the Production of Wine, *ZPE* 131, 161-165.

Mayerson, P. 2003
ἀμπελουργός: More than a 'Vine Dresser', *Bulletin of the American Society of Papyrologists* 40, 187-190.

McCormick, M. 2001
Origins of the European Economy: Communications and Commerce, A.D. 300-900. Cambridge.

Mees, A.W. 2002
Organisationsformen römischer Töpfer-Manufakturen am Beispiel von Arezzo und Rheinzabern unter Berücksichtigung von Papyri, Inschriften und Rechtsquellen, Monographien Römisch-Germanisches Zentralmuseum 52. Mainz.

Meiggs, R. 1973
Roman Ostia, 2nd edition. Oxford.

Мелюкова, А.И. 1975
Поцеление и могильник скифского времени у села Николаевка [The settlement and burial ground of Scythian time at the village of Nikolaevka]. Москва.

Meyboom, P.G.P. & Versluys, M.J. 2007
The Meaning of Dwarfs in Nilotic Scenes, in: Bricault *et al.* (eds.), 170-208.

Michaelidis, P. 1993
Potters' Workshops in Minoan Crete, *SMEA* 32, 7-39.

Michaud, S. & Michaud, R. 1973
Bold Horsemen of the Steppes, *National Geographic* 144, 634-669.

Mielsch, H. 1975
Römische Stuckreliefs, Mitteilungen des Deutschen Archäologischen Instituts. Römische Abteilung. Ergänzungshefte 21. Heidelberg.

Mielsch, H. 2001
Römische Wandmalerei. Darmstadt.

Miller, S.G. 1974
Menon's Cistern, *Hesperia* 43, 194-245.

Mitchell, S. & Waelkens, M. 1987
Cremna and Sagalassus, *AnatSt* 37, 37-45.

Mitford, T.B. 1971
The Inscriptions of Kourion. Philadelphia.

Modée, J. 2007
Outline of a new theory of artifacts, *Facta. A Journal of Roman Material Culture Studies* 1, 31-49.

Monaco, M.C. 2000
Ergasteria: impianti artigianali ceramici ad Atene ed in Attica dal protogeometrico alle soglie dell'ellenismo. Roma.

Moore, M.B. 1997
The Athenian Agora XXX: Attic Red-Figured and White-Ground Pottery. Princeton.

Moore, M.B. & Bothmer, D. von 1972
A neck-amphora in the collection of Walter Bareiss, *AJA* 76, 1-11.

Moore, M.B. & Philippides, M.Z.P. 1986
The Athenian Agora XXIII: Attic Black-Figured Pottery. Princeton, New Jersey.

Morel, J.-P. 1981
Céramique campanienne: les formes, BEFAR 244. Rome.

Murray, P. 1980
Discard Location: The Ethnographic Data, *American Antiquity* 45, 490-502.

Μυλωνάς, Γ.Ε. 1957
Ὁ πρωτοαττικός ἀμφορεύς τῆς Ἐλευσίνος. Αθήνα.

Mylonas, G.E. 1959
Aghios Kosmas: An Early Bronze Age Settlement and Cemetery in Attica. Princeton, New Jersey.

Μυλωνάς, Γ.Ε. 1975
Τὸ δυτικόν νεκροταφείον τῆς Ελευσίνος. Αθήνα.

Nadalini, G. 2003
Considerazioni e confronti sui restauri antichi presenti sulle ceramiche scoperte a Gela, in: Panvini, R. & Giudice, F. (eds.), *Ta Attica: veder Greco a Gela. Ceramiche attiche figurate dall'antica colonia.* Roma, 197-205.

Nadalini, G. 2007
Restauri antichi su ceramiche greche: differenziazione dei metodi, in: Bentz & Kästner (eds.), 29-34.

Needham, S. & Spence, T. 1997
Refuse and the formation of middens, *Antiquity* 71, 77-90.

Nenna, M.-D. 2008
Un bol en verre peint du Ier siècle après J.-C. à représentation nilotique, *JGS* 50, 15-29.

Nielsen, E. 1987
Some preliminary thoughts on new and old terracottas, *OpRom* 16, 91-119.

Nieto, X. 1997
Le commerce de cabotage et de redistribution, in: Pomey (ed.), 146-159.

Nijboer, A.J. 1998
From household production to workshops; archaeological evidence for economic transformations, pre-monetary exchange and urbanisation in central Italy from 800 to 400 BC. Groningen.

Nikolaenko, G.M. 2006
The Chora of Tauric Chersonesos and the Cadastre of the 4th-2nd Century BC, in: Bilde, P.G. & Stolba, V.F. (eds.), *Surveying the Greek Chora: The Black Sea Region in Comparative Perspective.* Black Sea Studies 4. Aarhus 151-174.

No author 1990
Euphronios, peintre à Athènes au VIe siècle avant J.-C. Paris.

Noble, J.V. 1988
The Techniques of Painted Attic Pottery, rev. ed. London.

Nogara, B. 1951
Un frammento di Douris nel Museo Gregoriano-Etrusco, *JHS* 71, 129-132.

OC = Oxé, A. & Comfort, H. 1968

OCK = Oxé, A., Comfort, H. & Kenrick, P. 2000

Orton, C., Tyres, P. & Vince, A. 1993
Pottery in archaeology. Cambridge.

O. Claud 1 = Bingen, J., Bülow Jacobsen, A., Cockle, W.E.H., Cuvigny, H., Rubinstein, L. & Van Rengen, W. 1992

O. Claud 2 = Bingen, J., Bülow Jacobsen, A., Cockle, W.E.H., Cuvigny, H., Kayser, F. & Van Rengen, W. 1997

Opaiţ, A. 2007
A Weighty Matter: Pontic Fish Amphorae, in: Gabrielsen, V. & Lund, J. (eds.), *The Black Sea in Antiquity: Regional and Interregional Economic Exchanges,* Black Sea Studies 6. Aarhus, 101-121.

Orton, C. 1989
An introduction to the quantification of assemblages of pottery, *JRomPotSt* 2, 94-97.

Osborne, R. 2004a
Greek Archaeology: A Survey of Recent Work, *AJA* 108, 87-102.

Osborne, R. 2004b
Workshops and the Iconography and Distribution of Athenian Red-Figure Pottery: A Case Study, in: Keay, S. & Moser, S. (eds.), *Greek Art in View: Essays in Honour of Brian Sparkes.* Oxford, 78–94.

Ottenburgs, R. & Viaene, W. & Jorissen, C. 1993
Mineralogy and firing properties of clays at and near the archaeological site of Sagalassos, in: Waelkens, M. & Poblome, J. (eds.), *Sagalassos II. Report on the third excavation campaign of 1992,* Acta Archaeologica Lovaniensia Monographiae 6. Leuven, 209-219.

Outschar, U. 1993
Produkte aus Ephesos in alle Welt, in: Beyll, D., Outschar, U. & Soykal, F., Terra sigillata aus der Marienkirche in Ephesos. Erste Zwischenbilanz. Produkte aus Ephesos in alle Welt? Eine spätklassische Terrakottastatuette der Kybele aus Ephesos, *BerMatÖAI* 5, 47-52.

Outschar, U. 1998
Amphoren Peacock Class 47, in: Zabehlicky-Scheffenegger, S. (ed.), *RCRFragmenta. Beiträge zur Keramik in Ephesos Herausgegeben anläßlich des XXI. Internationalen RCRF-Kongresses in Ephesos und Pergamon 1998.* Wien & Selçuk, 20-21.

Owens, E.J. 1983
The Koprologoi at Athens in the Fifth and Fourth Centuries B.C. *ClQ* 33, 44-50.

Oxé, A. & Comfort, H. 1968
Corpus vasorum arretinorum, Antiquitas 3, 4. Bonn.

Oxé, A., Comfort, H. & Kenrick, P. 2000
Corpus Vasorum Arretinorum. A Catalogue of the Signatures, Shapes and Chronology of Italian Sigillata, 2nd edition, Antiquitas 3, 41. Bonn.

Pallecchi, S. 2007
Le fornaci da anfore di Giancola (Brindisi) in età repubblicana. Un caso di studio, in: Vitali, D. (ed.), *Albinia 1: Le fornaci e le anfore di Albinia. Primi dati su produzioni e scambi dalla costa tirrenica al mondo gallico. Atti del seminario internazionale. Ravenna, 6-7 maggio 2006.* Bologna, 181-188.

Pallecchi, S. 2008
Le fornaci romane di Albinia: identificazione delle unità funzionali e ricostruzione delle linee di produzione, in: Acconcia, V. & Rizzitelli, C. (eds.), *Materiali per Populonia 7.* Pisa, 323-338.

Panas, C. & Pontes, H. 1998
Stamped Amphora and Lagynos Handles from the 1989-1995 Seasons, *StTroica* 8, 223-262.

Papadopoulos, J. 2003
Ceramicus Redivivus: The Early Iron Age Potters' Field in the Area of the Classical Athenian Agora, Hesperia Supplement 31. Princeton, N.J.

Papadopoulos, S. 1995
L'organisation de l'espace dans deux ateliers de potiers traditionnels de Thasos, *BCH* 119, 591-606.

Παπαδόπουλος, S. 1999
Παραδοσιακά αγγειοπλαστεία της Θάσου. Αθήνα.

Παπαθωμά, Ε. 2001
Κεραμεικών εμπόριο: Λεύκωμα. Αθήνα.

Pauketat, T.R. 1989
Monitoring Mississipian Homestead Occupation Span and Economy Using Ceramic Refuse, *American Antiquity* 54, 288-310.

Peacock, D.P.S. 1982
Pottery in the Roman World: an Ethnoarchaeological Approach. London & New York.

Peacock, D.P.S. 1996
A Note on the Distribution of Porphyry and Other Rocks on Roman Sites in the Eastern Desert, in: Bailey, D.M. (ed.), *Archaeological Research in Roman Egypt,* JRA Supplementary Series 19. Ann Arbor, 20-22.

Peacock, D.P.S. 2007
Excavation at the Fort in Wadi Abu Ma'amel, in: Peacock & Maxfield, 9-23.

Peacock, D.P.S., Béjaoui, F. & Belazreg, N. 1989
Roman Amphora Production in the Sahel Region of Tunisia, in: *Amphores romaines et histoire économique: dix ans de recherche. Actes du colloque de Sienne, 24-26 mai 1986,* Collection de l'Ecole française de Rome 114. Paris & Rome, 179-202.

Peacock, D.P.S. & Blue, L. (eds.) 2006
Myos Hormos – Quseir al-Qadim.
Roman and Islamic Ports on the Red Sea.
Survey and Excavations 1999 – 2003.
Oxford.

Peacock, D.P.S. & Maxfield, V. *et al.*
1997
Survey and excavations Mons
Claudianus 1987-1993 I: Topography
and Quarries, Fouilles de l'Institut
français d'archéologie orientale du
Caire 37. Le Caire.

Peacock, D.P.S. & Maxfield, V.A. 2007
The Roman Imperial Quarries. Survey
and Excavation at Mons Porphyrites
1994-1998 II: Excavations and Finds,
Egyptian Exploration Society Eighty-
Second Excavation, London.

Peacock, D.P.S. & Williams, D.F. 1986
Amphorae and the Roman economy: an
introductory guide. London & New York.
Peacock, D.P.S., Williams-Thorpe, O.,
Thorpe, R.S. & Tindle, A.G. 1994
Mons Claudianus and the problem of
the 'granito del foro': a geological and
geochemical approach, *Antiquity* 68,
209–230.

Pearson, M.P. & Richards, C. 1994
Architecture and Order: Approaches to
Social Space. London.

Pékary, I. 1999
Repertorium der hellenistischen und
römischen Schiffsdarstellungen, Boreas
Beiheft 8. Münster.

Peña, J.T. 1999
The Urban Economy during the Early
Dominate. Pottery evidence from the
Palatine Hill, BAR International Series
784. Oxford.

Peña, J.T. 2007
Roman Pottery in the Archaeological
Record. Cambridge.

Peña, J.T. 2009
A new journal of Roman material
culture studies, *JRA* 22, 495-498.

Peña, J.T. & McCallum, M. 2009
The Production and Distribution of
Pottery at Pompeii: A Review of the
Evidence; Part 1, Production, *AJA* 113,
57-79.

Pesavento Mattioli, S. (ed.) 1998
Bonifiche e drenaggi con anfore in epoca
romana: aspetti tecnici e topografici.
Atti del seminario di studi Padova 19-20
ottobre 1995. Modena.

Peterson, B. & Winbladh, M.-L. 1976
A Selection of Some Recent
Acquisitions, *MedelhavsMusB* 11, 65-
73.

Pfisterer-Haas, S. 2002
Antike Reparaturen, in: Bentz,
M. (ed.), *Vasenforschung und*
Corpus Vasorum Antiquorum:
Standortbestimmung und Perspektiven,
Beihefte zum Corpus Vasorum
Antiquorum I. München, 51-57.

Picon, M. & Garlan, Y. 1986
Recherches sur l'implantation des
ateliers amphoriques a Thasos at
analyse de la pate des amphores
thasiennes, in: Empereur & Garlan
(eds.), 287-309.

Pippidi, D.M. 1975
Scythica Minora. Recherches sur les
colonies grecques du littoral roumain de
la mer Noire. Bucarest.

Pisani Sartorio, G. 1994
Mezzi di trasporto e traffico, Vita e
costume dei romani antichi 6, 2nd
edition. Roma.

Platon, L. 1993
Ateliers palatiaux minoens: une
nouvelle image, *BCH* 117, 103-122.

Poblome, J. 1996
The Ecology of Sagalassos Red Slip
Ware, in: Lodewijckx, M. (ed.)
Archaeological and Historical Aspects
of West-European Societies. Album
Amicorum André Van Doorselaer,
Acta Archaeologica Lovaniensia
Monographiae 8. Leuven, 499-512.

Poblome, J. 1999
Sagalassos Red Slip Ware Typology
and Chronology, Studies in Eastern
Mediterranean Archaeology 2.
Leuven.

Poblome, J. 2004
Italian sigillata in the eastern
Mediterranean, in: Poblome, J. &
Talloen, P. & Brulet, R. & Waelkens,
M. (eds.), *Early Italian sigillata. The*
chronological framework and trade
patterns. First international ROCT
conference, BABesch Supplement 10.
Leuven, 17-30.

Poblome, J. 2006a
Made in Sagalassos. Modelling
regional potential and constraints,
in: Menchelli, S. & Paquinucci, M.
(eds.), *Territorio e produzioni ceramiche:*
paesaggi, economia e società in età
romana, Instrumenta 2. Pisa, 355-421.

Poblome, J. 2006b
Mixed feelings on Greece and Asia
Minor in the third century AD, in:
Malfitana *et al.* (eds.), 189-212.

Poblome, J. forthcoming
The Eastern Slope of the Potters' Quarter of Sagalassos. Craft Production in the Roman East, in: Waelkens *et al.* (eds.), *Sagalassos* VII. Leuven.

Poblome, J., Bounegru, O., Degryse, P., Viaene, W., Waelkens, M. & Erdemgil, S. 2001
The Sigillata Manufactories of Pergamon and Sagalassos, *JRA* 14, 143-165.

Poblome, J., Degryse, P., Librecht I. & Waelkens, M. 1998
Sagalassos Red Slip Ware. The Organization of a Manufactory, *MünstBeitr* 17, 52-64.

Poblome, J., Degryse, P., Viaene, W. & Waelkens, M. 2002
An Augustan Pottery Workshop at Sagalassos, in: Kilikoglou, V., Hein, A. & Maniatis, Y. (eds.), *Modern Trends in Scientific Studies on Ancient Ceramics*, BAR International Series 1011. Oxford, 335-341.

Poblome, J. & Malfitana, D. & Lund, J. 2006
A concluding dilemma – Sisyphos versus Daidalos, in: Malfitana *et al.* (eds.), 557-579.

Poblome, J. & Malfitana, D. & Lund, J. 2007
Tempus fugit, "FACTA" manent. Editorial statement, *Facta. A Journal of Roman Material Culture Studies* 1, 13-20.

Poblome, J. & Waelkens, M. 1998
Recent Excavations in the Potters' Quarter of Roman Sagalassos, *Near Eastern Archaeology* 61, 129.

Pomey, P. (ed.) 1997
La Navigation dans l'Antiquité. Aix-en-Provence.

Preka-Alexandri, K. 1992.
A Ceramic Workshop in Figareto, Corfu, in: Blondé, F. & Perrault, J.Y. (eds.), *Les ateliers de potiers dans le monde grec aux époques géometrique, archaïque et classique. Actes de la Table Ronde organisée à l'École française d'Athènes (2 et 3 octobre 1987)*, BCH Supplément 23. Athènes & Paris, 41-52.

Prunier, G. 2005
Darfur: The ambigrous Genocide. Ithaca, NY.

Pryor, S. & Slane, K. 2008
Review of Peña 2007, *BrMaClR* 2008 no. 05, *http://ccat.sas.upenn.edu/bmcr/2008.*

Psaropoulou, B. 1986
The Last Potters of the East Aegean. Nafplion.

Ψαροπούλου, Μπ. 1990
Η κεραμεική του χθές στα Κύθηρα και στην Κύθνο. Αθήνα.

Ψαροπούλου, Μπ. 2005
Η κεραμεική του χθές στη Νάξο. Ρέθυμνο.

Ψαροπούλου, Μπ. & Σημαντηράκης, Ν. 2007
Θραψανό: Χωριό των αγγειοπλαστών. Αθήνα.

Pulak, C. & Townsend, R.F. (with an appendix by Koehler, C.G. & Wallace, M.B.) 1987
The Hellenistic shipwreck at Serçe Limanı, Turkey: Preliminary report, *AJA* 91, 31-57.

Rabold, B. 1995
Das Bad Kreuznacher Oceanusmosaik. Neue Aspekte zu Handel und Verkehr im Mainzer Grossraum, *AKorrBl* 25, 221-232.

Randsborg, K. 1994
A Greek Episode. The Early Hellenistic Settlement on the Western Crimea, *ActaArch* 65, 171-196.

Rashed, D. 2002
Dumping the *zabaleen*, in: Al-Ahram 594 (11-17 July 2002) *http://weekly. ahram.org.eg/2002/594/eg7.htm* accessed June 2008

Rasmussen, T. & Spivey, N. (eds.) 1991
Looking at Greek Vases. Cambridge.

Ray, N. 2009
Household consumption in ancient economies: Pompeii and the wider Roman world, Ph.D. Dissertation, University of Leicester.

Reger, G. 1994
Regionalism and Change in the Economy of Independent Delos, 314-167 B.C., Hellenistic Culture and Society 14. Berkeley/Los Angeles/Oxford.

Reichhold, K. 1919
Skizzenbuch griechischer Meister. München.

Reynolds, P. 1995
Trade in the Western Mediterranean, AD 400-700, BAR International Series 604. Oxford.

Rice, P.M. 1987
Pottery Analysis: A Sourcebook. Chicago & London.

Richter, G. M. A. 1923
The Craft of Athenian Pottery: an Investigation of the Technique of Black-Figured and Red-Figured Athenian Vases. New Haven.

Richter, G.M.A. 1946
Attic Red-Figured Vases: a Survey. New Haven.

Richter, G.M.A. & F.L. Hall 1936
Red-Figured Athenian Vases in the Metropolitan Museum of Art. New Haven.

Riley, J.A. 1979
The Coarse Pottery from Berenice, in: Lloyd, J.A. (ed.), *Excavations at Sidi Khrebish Benghazi (Berenice)* II, Libya Antiqua Supplement V. Tripoli, 91-467.

Roberts, S.R. 1986
The Stoa Gutter Well, a Late Archaic Deposit in the Athenian Agora, *Hesperia* 55, 1-74.

Robinson, D.M. 1950
Olynthus XIII: Vases Found in 1934 and 1938. Baltimore.

Robinson, H.S. 1959
The Athenian Agora V: Pottery of the Roman Period: Chronology. Princeton, NJ.

Robinson, H.S. 1962
Excavations at Corinth, 1960, *Hesperia* 31, 95-133.

Robinson, H.S. 1969
A Sanctuary and Cemetery in Western Corinth, *Hesperia* 38, 1-35.

Robinson, O. 1993
Ancient Rome: City Planning and Administration. London & New York.

Rodríguez-Almeida, E. 1984
Il Monte Testaccio. Roma.

Рогов, Е.Я. 2002
Херсонес и варвары юго-западного Крыма в IV. До *н.э.* [Chersonesos and Barbarians in North-Western Crimea in the 4th *c. BC.*], *Античный мир и археология 11*, 2002. Саратов. 140-152.

Rose, C.B. 1998
The 1997 Post-Bronze Age Excavations at Troia, *StTroica* 8, 71-113.

Rotroff, S.I. 1982
The Athenian Agora XXII: Hellenistic pottery: Athenian and Imported Moldmade Bowls. Princeton, NJ.

Rotroff, S.I. 1994
The satyr cistern in the Athenian agora, in: *Γ' Επιστημονική συνάντηση γιά τήν ελληνιστική κεραμική: Χρονολογημένα συνολα εργαστήρια, 24-27 Σεπτεμβρίου 1991 Θεσσαλονίκη.* Αθήνα, 17-22.

Rotroff, S.I. 1996
The Missing Krater and the Hellenistic Symposium: Drinking in the Age of Alexander the Great, Broadhead Classical Lecture 7. Christchurch.

Rotroff, S.I. 1997
The Athenian Agora XXIX: Hellenistic Pottery: Athenian and Imported Wheelmade Table Ware and Related Material. Princeton, New Jersey.

Rotroff, S.I. 2000
A Sullan Deposit at the Athenian Agora, in: *Ε' Επιστημονική Συνάντηση για την ελληνιστική κεραμική: Πρακτικά.* Αθήνα, 375-380.

Rotroff, S.I. 2006a
The Athenian Agora XXXIII: Hellenistic Pottery: The Plain Wares. Princeton, New Jersey.

Rotroff, S.I. 2006b
The Introduction of the Moldmade Bowl Revisited: Tracking a Hellenistic Innovation, *Hesperia* 75, 357-378.

Roux, V. & Corbetta, D. 1989
The Potter's Wheel: Craft Specialization and Technical Competence. Oxford & New Delhi.

Rudolph, W.W. & Sheehan, M.C. 1979
Excavations at Porto Cheli and Vicinity Preliminary Report V: The Early Byzantine Remains, *Hesperia* 48, 294-324.

Rye, O. 1981
Pottery Technology: Principles and Reconstruction. Washington D.C.

Rye, O. S. & Evans, C. 1976
Traditional Pottery Techniques of Pakistan: Field and Laboratory Studies. Washington D.C.

Samson, R. (ed.) 1990
The Social Archaeology of Houses. Edinburgh.

Sanidas, G.M. n.d.
Espace mental et espace concret en Grèce ancienne: à propos de la production artisanale dans l' espace urbain de la cite.

Saprykin, S.Y. 1998
The foundation of Tauric Chersonesus, in: Tsetskhladze, G.R. (ed.), *The Greek Colonisation of the Black Sea Area,* Historia Einzelschriften 121. Stuttgart, 227-248.

Savarese, N. (ed.) 2007
In scaena: Il teatro di Roma antica. The Theater in Ancient Rome, Mostra Roma 3 ottobre 2007-17 febbraio 2008. Milano.

Schauer, C. 1991
Μήτρες λύχνων πρωτοχριστιανικής εποχής από την Ολυμπία, in: Ριζάκης, Α.Δ. (ed.), *Αρχαία Αχαΐα και Ηλεία. Ανακοινώσεις κατά το Πρώτο Διεθνές Συμπόσιο, Αθήνα 19/21 Μαΐου 1989.* Αθήνα, 373-378.

Schauer, C. 2002
Εργαστήριο Κεραμικής του 5ου μ.Χ. αιώνα στην Ολυμπία, in: Θέμελης, Π.Γ. & Κόντη, Β. (eds.), *Πρωτοβυζαντινή Μεσσήνη και Ολυμπία. Αστικός και αγροτικός χώρος στη Δυτική Πελοπόννησο. Πρακτικά του Διεθνούς Συμποσίου Αθήνα 29/30 Μαΐου 1998.* Αθήνα, 208-218.

Schauer, C. 2010
Early Byzantine Workshops in Olympia, *ReiCretActa* 41 269-235.

Scheibler, I. 1986
Formen der Zusammenarbeit in attischen Töpfereien des 6. und 5. Jahrunderts v. Chr., in: Kalcyk, H., Gullath, B. & Graeber, A. (eds.), *Studien zur Alten Geschichte. Siegfried Lauffer zum 70. Geburtstag am 4. August 1981.* Roma, 785-804.

Schiffer, M.B. 1972
Archaeological Context and Systemic Context, *American Antiquity* 37, 156-165.

Schiffer, M.B. 1983
Toward the Identification of Formation Processes, *American Antiquity* 48, 675-706.

Schiffer, M.B. 1996
Formation Processes of the Archaeological Record, 2nd edition. Salt Lake City.

Schleif, H. 1944
Die Badeanlage am Kladeos. Baubeschreibung, in: Kunze & Schleif (eds.), 32-69.

Schleif, H. & Eilmann, R. 1944
Die Palästra, in: Kunze & Schleif (eds.), 8-31.

Schmölder, A. 2001
Le ravitaillement en eau, in: Descœudres (ed.), 100-107.

Schöne-Denkinger, A. 2007
Reparaturen, antik oder nicht antik? Beobachtungen an rotfigurigen Krateren der Berliner Antikensammlung und Anmerkungen zur Verwendung geflickter Gefässe in der Antike, in Bentz & Kästner (eds.), 21-28.

Schreiber, T. 1999
Athenian Vase Construction: A Potter's Analysis. Malibu.

Schuchhardt, C. 1895
Amphorenstempel, in: Fränkel, M. (ed.), *Die Inschriften von Pergamon. Römischer Zeit – Inschriften auf Thon,* AvP VIII.2. Berlin, 423-498.

Sciallano, M. & Sibella, P. 1991
Amphores. Comment les identifier? Aix-en-Provence.

Scobie, A. 1986
Slums, Sanitation, and Mortality in the Roman World, *Klio* 68, 399-433.

Scognamiglio, E. 1993
Il relitto romano di Bacoli, *ASubacq* 1, 153-158.

Seipel, W. (ed.) 2006
Masterpieces in the Collection of Greek and Roman Antiquities, A Brief Guide to the Kunsthistorisches Museum Wien 4. Wien.

Sekerskaya, N.M. 2001
Nikonion, in: Tsetskhladze, G.R. (ed.), *North Pontic Archaeology: Recent Discoveries and Studies,* Colloquia Pontica 6. Leiden, Boston & Köln, 67-90.

Senior, L.M. 1995
The Estimation of Prehistoric Values: Cracked Pot Ideas in Archaeology, in: Skibo, J.M., Walker, W.H. & Nielsen, A.E. (eds.), *Expanding Archaeology.* Salt Lake City, 92-110.

Sethom, H. 1964
Les artisans-potiers de Moknine, *Revue Tunisienne des Sciences Sociales* 1, 53-70.

Shear, Jr., T.L. 1984
The Athenian Agora: Excavations of 1980-1982, *Hesperia* 53, 1-57.

Shear, Jr., T.L. 1993
The Persian Destruction of Athens: Evidence from Agora Deposits, *Hesperia* 62, 383-482.

Sheriff, B.L., Court, P., Johnston, S. & Stirling, L. 2002
The Source of Raw Materials for Roman Pottery from Leptiminus, Tunisia, *Geoarchaeology* 17, 835-861.

Shott, M.J. 1996
Mortal Pots: On Use Life and Vessel Size in the Formation of Ceramic Assemblages, *American Antiquity* 61, 463-482.

Shott, M.J. 1998
Status and Role of Formation Theory in Contemporary Archaeological Practice, *Journal of Archaeological Research* 6, 299-329.

Shott, M.J. & Sillitoe, P. 2001
The Mortality of Things: Correlates of Use Life in Wola Material Culture Using Age-at-Census Data, *Journal of Archaeological Method and Theory* 8, 269-302.

Shott, M.J. & Sillitoe, P. 2004
Modeling Use-Life Distributions in Archaeology Using New Guinea Wola Ethnographic Data, *American Antiquity* 69, 339-355.

Sidebotham, S.E., Barnard, H. & Pyke, G. 2002
Five Enigmatic Late Roman Settlements in the Eastern Desert, *JEA* 88, 187-225.

Siddall, R. 2006
Hydraulic Mortars in Antiquity. Analyses from Fountains in Ancient Corinth, in: Matttusch, C. (ed.), *Common Ground. Archaeology, art, science, and humanities. Proceedings of the XVIth International Congress of Classical Archaeology, Boston, August 23-26, 2003.* Oxford, 208-211.

Siddall, R. forthcoming
From kitchen to bathhouse: the use of waste ceramics as pozzolanic additives in Roman mortars, in: *Building Roma Aeterna* to be published by the Finnish Institute at Rome.

Sinn, U., Ladstätter, G., Martin, A. & Völling, T. 1994
Bericht über das Forschungsprojekt „Olympia während der römischen Kaiserzeit und der Spätantike" III. Die Arbeiten im Jahr 1994, *Nikephoros* 7, 229-250.

Slane, K.W. 1986
Two Deposits from the Early Roman Cellar Building, Corinth, *Hesperia* 55, 271-318.

Slane, K.W. 1997
The fine wares, in: Herbert, S.C. (ed.), *Tel Anafa II, I: The Hellenistic and Roman Pottery*, JRA Supplementary Series 10, part II, i. Ann Arbor, 247-406.

Slane, K.W. 2003
Corinth's Roman Pottery: Quantification and Meaning, in: ed. Williams II, C.K. and Bookidis, N. (eds.), *Corinth XX: The Centennary 1896-1996*. Princeton, 321-335.

Slane, K.W. 2004a
Amphorae – Used and Reused – at Corinth, in: Eiring & Lund (eds.), 361-369.

Slane, K.W. 2004b
Corinth: Italian sigillata and other Italian imports to the early colony, in: Poblome, J., Talloen, P., Brulet, R. & Waelkens, M. (eds.), *Early Italian sigillata. The chronological framework and trade patterns. Proceedings of the First International ROCT-Congress Leuven, May 7 and 8, 1999*, BABesch Supplement 10. Leuven, Paris & Dudley, Ma., 31-42.

Slane, K.W. in preparation
Corinth: Tombs along the North Terrace of Corinth.

Small, A., Roe, B., Hayes, J., Simpson, C., Guzzetta, G., MacKinnon, M. & Monckton, S. 1994
A Pit Group of c. 80-70 B.C. from Gravina di Puglia, *BSR* 62, 197-260.

Смекалова, Т.Н. 2007
Русские топографические карты XVIII-XX Веков как источник по изучению археологических памятников Западного и Восточного Крыма. [Russian topographic maps of the 18th-20th centuries as a source of studying archaeological resources of the western and eastern Crimea], *Боспорские Исследивания [Bosporan Studies]* 17. 78-111.

Smekalova, T.N. 2008
Kimmerian Bosporos, in: Bilde *et al.*, (eds.), 142-147.

Smoláriková, K. 2007
Egyptian and Aegean Amphorae from the Saite Shaft Tombs at Abusir, in: Marchand & Marangou (eds.), 189-197.

Snow, C.E. 1986
The Affecter Amphora: a Case Study in the History of Greek Vase Restoration, *JWaltersArtGall* 44, 2-7.

Соловьев, С. Л. & Шепко, Л. Г. 2004
Археологические памятники сельской окрыги Акры. Поселение Заветное 5. Итоги работ Античной комплексной археологической зкспедиции 2002 г. Часть I. [Archaeological monuments in the rural district of Akra. Results of the archaeological expedition of the ancient complex in the year 2002, vol. I]. Санкт-Петербург.

Soren, D. & Davis, T. 1985
Seismic Archaeology at Kourion: the
1984 Campaign, *RDAC*, 293-306.

Soren, D. & James, J. 1988
*Kourion: the Search for a lost Roman
City.* New York.

Soren, D., Leonard, J.R. & Molinari, P.
1988
University of Arizona excavations at
Kourion 1984-1987, *RDAC*, 171-178.

Sparkes, B.A. 1991
Greek Pottery: An Introduction.
Manchester.

Sparkes, B.A. & Talcott, L. 1970
*The Athenian Agora XII: Black and
Plain Pottery of the 6th, 5th, and 4th
Centuries B.C.* Princeton, New Jersey.

Spivey, N. 1991
Greek vases in Etruria, in: Rasmussen
& Spivey (eds.), 130-150.

Stähler, K. 1983
*Eine Sammlung griechisher Vasen:
Die Sammlung D. J. in Ostwestfalen.*
Münster.

Staski, E. & Sutro, L.D. (eds.) 1991
*The Ethnoarchaeology of Refuse
Disposal,* Anthropological Research
Papers No. 42, Department of
Anthropology, Arizona State
University. Tempe, AZ.

Stehmeier, S.R. 2006
Picknick auf pompeianische Art, *AW*
37.3, 41-47.

Stewart, A. 2008
The Persian and Carthaginian
Invasions of 480 B.C.E. and the
Beginning of the Classical Style, 1.
The Stratigraphy, Chronology, and
Significance of the Acropolis Deposits,
AJA 112, 377-412.

Stillwell, A.N. 1948
Corinth XV.1: The Potters' Quarter.
Princeton, New Jersey.

Stirling, L. 2006
Aspects of Punic and Roman Kiln
Design in North Africa, in: Akerraz,
A., Ruggeri, P., Siraj, A. & Vismara,
C. (eds.), *L'Africa romana 16. Mobilità
delle persone e dei popoli, dinamiche
migratorie, emigrazioni ed immigrazioni
nelle province occidentali dell'Impero
romano (Atti del XVI convegno di studio,
Rabat, 15-19 dicembre 2004).* Roma,
2405-2416.

Stirling, L.M. & Ben Lazreg, N. 2001
A Roman kiln complex (Site 290):
preliminary results of excavation, in:
Stirling, L.M., Mattingly, D.J. & Ben
Lazreg, N. (eds.), *Leptiminus (Lamta):
a Roman port city in Tunisia, report
no. 2: the East Baths, cemeteries, kilns,
Venus mosaic, site Museum, and other
studies, JRA* Supplementary Series 42.
Portsmouth, RI, 219-235

Stoian, I. 1987
*Inscripţiile din Scythia Minor Greceşti
şi Latine II. Tomis şi Teritoriul Său,
Inscripţiile Antice din Dacia şi Scythia
Minor.* Bucureşti.

Stolba, V.F. 2002
Handmade pottery, in: Hannestad *et
al.* (eds.), 180-200.

Stolba, V.F. 2005a
The Oath of Chersonesos and the
Chersonesean Economy in the Early
Hellenistic Period, in: Archibald *et al.*
(eds.), 298-321.

Stolba, V.F. 2005b
Hellenistic Chersonesos: Towards
Establishing a Local Chronology, in:
Stolba, V.F. & Hannestad, L. (eds.),
*Chronologies of the Black Sea Area in
the Period c. 400-100 B.C.,* Black Sea
Studies 3. Aarhus, 153-177.

Stolba, V.F. 2008
Western and central Crimea, in: Bilde,
P.G. *et al.* (eds.), 132-140.

Stolba, V.F. & Rogov, E.Ya.
forthcoming
Panskoye I. Vol. II. The Necropolis.
Aarhus.

Stoyanov, T., Mihaylova, Z., Nikov, K.,
Nikolaeva, M. & Stoyanova. D. 2006
*The Getic Capital in Sboryanovo. 20
years of investigations.* Sofia.

Styrenius, C.-G.1998
*Asine. En svensk utgrävningsplats i
Grekland/A Swedish excavation site in
Greece,* Medelhavsmuseets skrifter 22.
Stockholm.

Sullivan, A.P. 1989
The Technology of Ceramic
Reuse: Formation Processes and
Archaeological Evidence, *WorldA* 21,
101-114.

Sullivan, A.P. 2008
An Archaeological View of the
Archaeological Record, in: Sullivan III,
A.P. (ed.), *Archaeological Concepts for
the Study of the Cultural Past.* Salt Lake
City, 7-23.

Swan, V.G. 1984
The Pottery Kilns of Roman Britain, Royal Commission on Historical Monuments Supplementary Series 5. London.

Tamm, J. 2005
Argentum Potorium and the Campanian Wall-Painter. The Priscus service revisited, *BABesch* 80, 73-89.

Tani, M. & Longacre, W.A. 1999
On Methods of Measuring Ceramic Uselife: A Revision of the Uselife Estimates of Cooking Vessels among the Kalinga, Philippines, *American Antiquity* 64, 299-308.

Tchernia, A. 1997
Le commerce maritime dans la Méditerranée romaine, in: Pomey (ed.), 116-145.

Thomas, R. & Masser, P. 2006
Trench 8, in: Peacock & Blue, 127-140.

Thomas, R. with Tomber, R. 2006
Vessel stoppers, in: Maxfield & Peacock, 239-258.

Thompson, H. A. 1934
Two Centuries of Hellenistic Pottery, *Hesperia* 3, 311-480.

Thompson, H.A. 1940
The Tholos of Athens and its Predecessors, Hesperia Supplement 4. Princeton, New Jersey.

Thompson, H.A. 1959
Activities in the Athenian Agora: 1958, *Hesperia* 28, 91-108.

Thornton, J. 1998
A Brief History and Review of the Early Practice and Materials of Gap-Filling in the West, *Journal of the American Institute for Conservation* 37, 3-22.

Török, L. 1995
Hellenistic and Roman Terracottas from Egypt, Bibliotheca archaeologica 15. Roma.

Tomber, R. 1988
Multivariate Statistics and Assemblage Comparison, in: Ruggles, C.L.N. & Rahtz, S.P.Q. (eds.), *Computer and Quantitative Methods in Archaeology*, BAR International Series 393. Oxford, 29–38.

Tomber, R. 1993
Quantitative Approaches to the Investigation of Long-Distance Exchange, *JRA* 6, 142–166.

Tomber, R. 2001
Pottery, in: Maxfield & Peacock 2001b, 242-303.

Tomber, R. 2005
Living in the desert: mess kits from Mons Porphyrites, in: Crummy, N. (ed.), *Image, craft and the classical world. Essays in honour of Donald Bailey and Catherine Johns*, Monographies Instrumentum 29. Montagnac, 55-60.

Tomber, R. 2006a
Ceramic Objects, in: Maxfield & Peacock (eds.), 289-305.

Tomber, R. 2006b
The Pottery, in: Maxfield & Peacock (eds.), 1-236.

Tomber, R. 2007
Early Roman Egyptian Amphorae from the Eastern Desert of Egypt: a Chronological Sequence, in: Marchand & Marangou (eds.), 525-536.

Tomber, R. 2008
Using and re-using Roman pottery: identification and implications, *JRA* 21, 498-501.

Tomber, R. & Williams, D. 2000
Egyptian Amphorae in Britain and the Western Provinces, *Britannia* 31, 41-54.

Tosto, V. 1999
The Black-figure Pottery Signed ΝΙΚΟΣΘΕΝΗΣΕΠΟΙΕΣΕΝ, Allard Pierson Series 11. Amsterdam.

Tournavitou, I. 1988
Towards an Identification of a Workshop Space, in: French & Wardle (eds.), 447-468.

Τρακοσοπούλου-Σαλακίδου, Ε. 2004 [2006]a
Κεραμικοί κλίβανοι Ακάνθου, *AErgoMak* 18, 167-179.

Τρακοσοπούλου-Σαλακίδου, Ε. 2004 [2006]b
Άκανθος. Το ανασκαφικό έργο της χρόνιας του 2004, *AErgoMak* 18, 157-166.

Trotter, W. 1991
A Frozen Hell: The Russo-Finnish Winter War of 1939-1940. Chapel Hill, NC.

Τσατσοπούλου, Π. 1996
Μεσημβρία – Ζώνη 1987-1997, *AErgoMak* 10, 917-926.

Tuna, N., Empereur, J.-Y., Doğer, E. & Desbat, A. 1991
Rapport sur la première campagne de la fouille franco-turque de Reşadiye (péninsule de Cnide) – juillet 1988, *AnatAnt* 1, 38-49.

Vaag, L., Nørskov, V. & Lund, J. 2002
The Maussolleion at Halikarnassos. Reports of the Danish Archaeological Expedition to Bodrum 7: The Pottery. Ceramic Material and Other Finds from Selected Contexts. Aarhus.

Valavanis, P. 1986
Les amphores panathénaïques et le commerce athénien de l'huile', in: Empereur & Garlan (eds.), 453-460.

Βαλαβάνης, Π. 1990
Ένα εργαστήριο στην εποχή μας, *Αρχαιολογία* 36, 31-41.

Vanderpool, E. 1938
The Rectangular Rock-cut Shaft and Its Lower Fill, *Hesperia* 7, 363-411.

Vanderpool, E. 1946
The Rectangular Rock-cut Shaft: The Upper Fill, *Hesperia* 15, 265-336.

Van der Veen, M. 1998
Gardens in the Desert, in: Kaper, O.E. (ed.), *Life on the Fringe. Living in the Southern Egyptian Deserts During the Roman and Early-Byzantine Periods.* Leiden, 221-242.

Van Rengen, W. 2007
The Written Evidence – Inscriptions and Ostraca, in: Peacock & Maxfield, 397-411.

Varien, M.D. & Potter, J.M. 1997
Unpacking the Discard Equation: Simulating the Accumulation of Artifacts in the Archaeological Record, *American Antiquity* 62, 194-213.

Varien, M. D. & Ortman, S.G. 2005
Accumulations Research in the Southwest United States: Middle-Range Theory for Big-Picture Problems, *WorldA* 37, 132-155.

Versluys, M.J. 2002
Aegyptiaca Romana. Nilotic Scenes and the Roman Views of Egypt, Religions in the Graeco-Roman World 144. Leiden.

Viaene, W. & Ottenburgs, R. & Kucha, H. & Poblome, J. & Waelkens, M. 1995
Firing temperature of Sagalassos red slip ware, in: Waelkens, M. & Poblome, J. (eds.), *Sagalasos III. Report on the fourth excavation campaign of 1993,* Acta Archaeologica Lovaniensia Monographiae 7. Leuven, 235-243.

Vidale, M. 2002
L'idea di un lavoro lieve. Il lavoro artigianale nelle immagini della ceramica greca tra VI e IV secolo a.C., Saltuarie dal laboratorio del Piovego. Padova.

Viitanen, E.-M. 2008
Review of Peña 2007, *Arctos* 42, 341-342.

Vitelli, K.D. 1993
Excavations at Franchthi Cave, Greece 8: Franchthi Neolithic Pottery I: Classification and Ceramic Phases 1 and 2. Bloomington.

Vnukov, S.Y. 2001
The North-Western Crimea: An Historical-Archaeological Essay, in: Tsetskladze, G.R. (ed.), *North Pontic Archaeology. Recent Discoveries and Studies,* Colloquia Pontica 6. Leiden, Boston & Köln, 149-175.

Völling, T. 1995
Ein frühbyzantinischer Hortfund aus Olympia, *AM* 110, 425-459.

Volpi, E. 1997
Community organization and development among the *zabbalin* of Muqattam, in: *The zabbalin community of Muqattam,* Cairo Papers in Social Science 19(4). Cairo, 8-58.

Von Bredow, I. 1994
Der Begriff der Mixhellenes, in: Funck, B. (ed.). *Beiträge zur Erforschung von Akkulturation und politischer Ordnung in den Staaten des hellenistischen Zeitalters. Akten des Internationalen Hellenismus-Kolloquiums 9.-14. März 1994 in Berlin.* Berlin, 467-474.

Vos, M.F. 1981
Some Notes on Panathenaic Amphorae, *OudhMeded* 62, 33-46.

Vossen, R. 1984
Towards Building Models of Traditional trade in Ceramics: Case Studies from Spain and Morocco, in: Leeuw, S.E. van der & Pritchard, A.D. (eds.), *The Many Dimensions of Pottery: Ceramics in Archaeology and Anthropology.* Amsterdam, 339-406.

Voyatzoglou, M. 1972
The Jars at the Village of Thrapsano, Crete. The Technique and the Guilds of the Jarmakers, Aristotle University of Thessaloniki, Research Paper 19. Thessaloniki.

Voyatzoglou, M. 1973
The Potters of Thrapsano, *Ceramic Review* 24, 13-16.

Voyatzoglou, M. 1974
The Jar Makers of Thrapsano in Crete, *Expedition* 16, 18-24.

Voyatzoglou, M. 1984
Thrapsano. Village of Jar Makers, in: Betancourt, P.P. (ed.), *East Cretan White-on Dark Ware. Studies on a Handmade Pottery of the Early to Middle Minoan Periods,* University Museum Monograph 51. Philadelphia, 130-142.

Wagner, F.C. 2001
Potters' Settlements on the Island of Siphnos. An Example of Anonymous Architecture Reflecting the Natural Environment, Lifestyle, Economics, and Settlement Forms. Athens

Wallace-Hadrill, A. 1988
The Social Structure of the Roman House, *BSR* 56, 43-97.

Walter, H. 1958
Das Gebiet südlich der Bäder am Kladeos. Der archäologische Befund, in: Künze, E.(ed.), *VI. Bericht über die Ausgrabungen in Olympia. Winter 1953/1954 und 1954/1955.* Berlin, 41-73.

Wamser, L., Flügel, C. & Ziegaus B.(eds.) 2000
Die Römer zwischen Alpen und Nordmeer. Zivilisatorisches Erbe einer europäischen Militärmacht. Katalog-Handbuch zur Landesausstellung des Freistaates Bayern Rosenheim 2000. Mainz.

Ward, M. 1993
A summary of the Samian Ware from Excavations at Piercebridge, *JRomPotSt* 6, 15-22.

Wendrich, W.Z., Tomber, R., Sidebotham, S.E., Harrell, J.A., Cappers, R.T.S. & Bagnall, R.S. 2003
Berenike crossroads: the integration of information, *JESHO* 46(1), 46-87.

Whitbread, I.K. 1995
Greek Transport Amphorae, a Petrological and Archaeological Study, British School at Athens Fitch Laboratory Occasional Paper 4. Athens.

Whittaker, C.R. 2002
Proto-Industrialization in Roman Gaul, in: Ascani, K., Gabrielsen, V., Kvist, K., Rasmussen, A.H. (eds.), *Ancient History Matters: Studies Presented to Jens Erik Skydsgaard on His Seventieth Birthday.* Roma, 11-22.

Will, E.L. 1997
Shipping Amphorae as Indicators of Economic Romanization in Athens, in: Hoff, M.C. & Rotroff, S.I. (eds.), *The Romanization of Athens: Proceedings of an International Conference held at Lincoln, Nebraska (April 1996).* Oxford, 117-133.

Williams, C.K. II, in preparation
Corinth XIX: East of the Theater: Architecture.

Williams, C.K. II, & Fisher, J.E. 1976
Corinth, 1975: Forum Southwest, *Hesperia* 45, 127-135.

Williams, C.K. II, & Zervos, O.H. 1983
Corinth, 1982: East of the Theater, *Hesperia* 52, 1-47.

Williams, C.K. II, & Zervos, O.H. 1986
Corinth 1985: East of the Theater, *Hesperia* 55, 129-175.

Williams, C.K. II, & Zervos, O.H. 1987
Corinth, 1986: Temple E and East of the Theater, *Hesperia* 56, 1-46.

Williams, D. 1996
Refiguring Attic Red-Figure: a Review Article, *RA*, 227-252.

Willmott, H. 2001
A Group of 17th-Century Glass Goblets with Restored Stems: Considering the Archaeology of Repair, *Post-Medieval Archaeology* 35, 96-105.

Wiseman, J. 1967
Excavations at Corinth, the Gymnasium Area, 1965, *Hesperia* 36, 13-41.

Wolff, S.R. 2004
Punic Amphorae in the Eastern Mediterranean, in: Eiring & Lund (eds.), 451-457.

Wood, W.R. & Johnson, D.L. 1978
A Survey of Disturbance Processes in Archaeological Site Formation, *Advances in Archaeological Method and Theory* 1, 315-381.

Wright, K.S. 1980
A Tiberian Pottery Deposit from Corinth, *Hesperia* 49, 135-177.

Yiannouli E. & Mithen, S.J. 1986
The Real and Random Architecture of
Siphnos: Analyzing House Plans Using
Simulation, in: Boast, R. & Yiannouli,
E. (eds.), *Archaeological Review from
Cambridge* 5.2, 167-180.

Yardeni, A. 1994
Maritime Trade and Royal
Accountancy in an Erased Customs
Account from 475 B.C.E. on the
Ahiqar Scroll from Elephantine,
BASOR 293: 67-78.

Young, R.S. 1951
An Industrial District in Ancient
Athens, *Hesperia* 20, 135-288.

Zabehlicky-Scheffenegger, S., Sauer, R.
& Schneider, G. 1996
Graue Platten aus Ephesos und von
Magdalensberg, in: Herfort-Koch,
M., Mandel, U. & Schädler, U. (eds.),
*Hellenistische und kaiserzeitliche
Keramik des östlichen Mittelmeergebietes.
Kolloquium Frankfurt 24.-25. April
1995.* Frankfurt a.M., 41-59.

Ζαχαριάδου, Ο. & Κυριακού, Δ. 1988
Πλατεία Κοτζιά, *ADelt* 43, 22-29.

Zemer, A. 1977
Storage Jars in Ancient Sea Trade. Haifa.

Zimmer, G. 1982a
Römische Berufsdarstellungen,
Archäologische Forschungen 12.
Berlin.

Zimmer, G. 1982b
Antike Werkstattbilder, Bilderhefte der
Staatlichen Museen Berlin. Stiftung
Preussischer Kulturbesitz 43. Berlin.

Zimmer, G. 1999
Technik und Arbeitsweise rhodischer
Bronzegießer, in: *Ρόδος 2.400 χρόνια.
Η πόλη της Ρόδου από την ίδρυσή
της μέχρι την κατάληψη από τους
Τούρκους (1523). Πρακτικά Διεθνούς
Επιστημονικού Συνεδρίου, Ρόδος 24-
29 Οκτωβρίου 1993.* Αθήνα, 253-258.

Zubar', V.M. & Kravčenko, E.A. 2003
Interpretation of a Group of
Archaeological Sites in the Vicinity
of Tauric Chersonesos, in: Bilde *et al.*
(eds.), 185-195.

Щеглов А.Н. 1967
Исследование сельской округи
Калос Лимена [Investigations of the
Rural District of Kalos Limen], *SovA* 3,
234-256.

List of Authors

List of Authors

Benjamin Costello IV
Department of Classics
Monmouth College
700 East Broadway
Monmouth, Illinois 61462-1998
USA
bcostello@monm.edu

Søren Handberg
Department of Classical Archaeology
Institute of Anthropology,
Archaeology & Linguistics
University of Aarhus
DK-8000 Aarhus C
Denmark
klash@hum.au.dk

Eleni Hasaki
School of Anthropology
and Classics Department
University of Arizona
Emil W. Haury Building
P.O. Box 210030
Tucson, AZ 85721-0030
USA
hasakie@email.arizona.edu

Mark L. Lawall
Department of Classics
University of Manitoba
220 Dysart Rd
Winnipeg, MB R3T 2M8
Canada
lawall@cc.umanitoba.ca

John Lund
Collection of Classical and
Near Eastern Antiquities
The National Museum of Denmark
Frederiksholms Kanal 12
1220 Copenhagen K
Denmark
John.Lund@natmus.dk

Kathleen Lynch
Department of Classics
University of Cincinnati
410 Blegen Library
P.O. Box 210226
Cincinnati, OH 45221
USA
kathleen.lynch@uc.edu

Archer Martin
The America Academy in Rome
Via Angelo Masina 5
00153 Rome
Italy
archer.martin@alice.it

Elizabeth Murphy
Joukowsky Institute for Archaeology
& the Ancient World
Brown University
P.O. Box 1837/60 George Street
Providence, RI 02912
USA
elizabeth_murphy@brown.edu

J. Theodore Peña
Department of Classics
University of California
7308 Dwinelle Hall # 2520
Berkeley, CA 94720-2520
USA
tpena@berkeley.edu

Jeroen Poblome
Sagalassos Archaeological
Research Project
Katholieke Universiteit Leuven
Blijde Inkomststraat 21-box 3314
BE-3000 Leuven
Belgium
Jeroen.Poblome@arts.kuleuven.be

Susan I. Rotroff
Department of Classics
Campus Box 1050
Washington University
St. Louis, MO 63130
USA
srotroff@artsci.wustl.edu

Kathleen Warner Slane
Department of Art History
and Archaeology
University of Missouri-Columbia
109 Pickard Hall
Columbia, MO 65211
USA
slanek@missouri.edu

Roberta Tomber
Department of Conservation
and Scientific Research
The British Museum
Great Russell St
London WC1B 3DG UK
Great Britain
rtomber@thebritishmuseum.ac.uk